America's Strategic Blunders

Willard C. Matthias

AMERICA'S STRATEGIC BLUNDERS

Intelligence Analysis and National Security Policy, 1936–1991

The Pennsylvania State University Press
University Park, Pennsylvania

Library of Congress Cataloging-in-Publication Data

Matthias, Willard C.
America's Strategic Blunders : intelligence analysis and national security policy,
1936–1991 / Willard C. Matthias.
p.   cm.
Includes bibliographical references and index.
ISBN 0-271-02066-0 (cloth : alk. paper)
1. Intelligence service—United States—History—20th century.
2. United States—Foreign relations—20th century. 3. Cold War. I. Title.
JK468.I6 M42 2001
327.1273'009'045—dc21
00-022029

It is the policy of The Pennsylvania State University Press to use acid-free paper
for the first printing of all clothbound books. Publications on uncoated stock satisfy
the minimum requirements of American National Standard for Information
Sciences—Permanence of Paper for Printed Library Materials, ANSI Z39.48—1992.

Contents

Introduction

This book is a survey of more than fifty years of national security policy and of the role long-term analytic intelligence played — or should have played — in its formulation. Critical questions are at the heart of strategic analysis. Before 1941, U.S. foreign and military policymakers should have been asking such questions as, Japan's What are Japanese long-range plans for Asia? How do the Japanese think about American military capabilities in the Pacific? What are the implications of the Rome-Berlin-Tokyo Axis for U.S. interests in the Pacific? Had U.S. policymakers been well enough informed to have asked such questions, still there was no central analytic body to provide answers. The Japanese provided an answer on December 7, 1941, in the form of a surprise attack on an unprepared nation.

When war came, military planners were interested only in tactical intelligence, that is, the acquisition of information about enemy planes, forces, weaponry, and dispositions, in order to guide Allied military operations. They did not regard long-term strategic intelligence as their concern. In 1943, when Allied political and military leaders were considering war aims, they apparently settled for "unconditional surrender" without having made a careful study of the consequences within enemy countries. We now know that the tough language prolonged the war. Moreover, in 1943–44, Allied leaders, because of their preoccupation with tactical matters, failed to take into consideration the existence of an active anti-Hitler plot, which the OSS team in Berne had been reporting in detail. Even though Hitler had survived the attack, the Allied forces failed to exploit the great confusion provoked within the German army. Indeed, General Eisenhower thought the plot might have been faked.

After World War II ended, U.S. leaders set about to construct a peacetime intelligence system around the concept of a centralized, civilian intelligence agency whose primary function would be current intelligence reporting. In

1950, with the Korean War in progress, a strategic intelligence function was clearly recognized and assigned to a newly created Board and Office of National Estimates. The board was charged with supervising the production of National Intelligence Estimates and coordinating them with the intelligence staffs of other executive departments. In the pursuit of their mission, the new CIA strategic analysts soon encountered a military ethos and manner of thinking quite different from their own. This writer concluded that the military's approach to strategic questions could be explained by examining how U.S. military leaders conceived and pursued their World War II mission.

It now seems clear that the leaders developed and carried out their war plans on the assumption that their task was exclusively military—the destruction of the enemy forces and the governments that controlled them and, on achieving total victory, the establishment of military governments. Not only were they uninterested in political and psychological developments in enemy countries, their ethos of warfare did not include negotiating with the enemy or with dissident groups in enemy territory. This book shows that if the Allied commanders had paid greater attention to what was happening behind enemy lines, the wars in both Europe and the Far East could have ended much earlier, and at a much reduced cost in human life.

The state of mind that dominated the conduct of World War II carried over into the postwar years. The trauma created by Pearl Harbor convinced military leaders to be alert to possible surprise attacks by a militarily strong foreign power. That state of mind led to a quick identification of the USSR as the future enemy and plans to build a military force that could fight a general war against the Soviet Union. In making those decisions of the late 1940s and early 1950s, military and political leaders demonstrated a grievous failure to understand the Soviet leaders and Communist doctrine. It is true that the Soviets were truculent on the matter of a peace treaty and made a determined effort to establish pliant Communist regimes in Eastern Europe; they launched violent propaganda attacks upon the United States and stirred up political unrest in Western Europe. But the behavior of the Soviet leaders in critical situations and the character of their thinking as disclosed in Soviet archival material now available make it quite clear that the Soviets were fearful of a U.S. nuclear attack and were unwilling to undertake any actions that risked war with the United States. They were ambitious to create a Communist world, but they hoped to achieve it through nonmilitary means.

The National Intelligence Estimates, estimative memoranda, and other materials produced in the Office of National Estimates and its predecessors from 1946 onward show quite clearly that the CIG/CIA analysts were consistently correct in challenging the military view and in advancing their own analyses of Soviet thinking and behavior. The CIA analysts also pointed out that the Marxist conception of history, which Communism espoused, posited the eventual emergence of a Communist world without wars of Communist military conquest.

From these diverse views there developed a four-decade-long debate between the civilian and military intelligence agencies over Soviet intentions. We in the Office of National Estimates observed that when the United States took a firm position on historically strong grounds, the Soviet leaders would moderate their stand. We believed that we should keep Soviet policies under continuing review and not take refuge in any fixed theories about Soviet intentions. The military, on the other hand, saw military power as the prime determinant of the behavior of states. Hence, so long as the Soviets carried out programs that enhanced their military power, the U.S. military saw the USSR as committed to the pursuit of a Communist world, even at the cost of a nuclear war. This book is a partial history of that civilian-military debate. Now that the Cold War has ended, it is imperative that its history be brought into the public record. This book is a contribution to that enterprise. It has been made possible by the declassification and release of many CIA documents, beginning in the late 1980s, and by a partial opening of Soviet, East European, and Communist Party archives.

Selection of the particular cases for inclusion in this narrative has been strongly influenced by my personal experience. I was one of the principal CIA analysts during the period covered, and it has seemed to me imperative to exploit my experience by undertaking an effort to juxtapose important U.S. intelligence estimates with studies based on Communist archives covering the same events. During my years of service in the Office of National Estimates, I wrote or supervised the preparation of estimates on all parts of the world. I also wrote a periodic "Estimate of the World Situation."

Those world estimates were intended to identify trends in all parts of the world, but especially in Communist-controlled areas. In one such estimate published as early as 1958, we observed that liberalizing changes were taking place in the USSR, and we also saw a widening gap between Soviet and Chinese attitudes toward revolutionary action in the rest of the world. We reaffirmed our observations about the USSR in 1968, adding that liberalization had probably become irreversible and that the most important changes were occurring within the Soviet Communist Party itself. But after 1968, our rational and balanced approach to making judgments about the Soviets came under increasing attack.

When disorders and a series of revolutionary changes occurred in Africa and Southwest Asia during the late 1970s, anti-Communist hard-liners in and outside the government blamed State Department détentists and CIA analysts for what they saw as a decline in the U.S. world position. Hard-liners gained control of the directorship of the CIA in 1973, when Richard Helms was dismissed for refusing to allow the Agency to be used as a cover for the Watergate break-in. Abolition of the Board of National Estimates followed soon after, and by the end of the 1970s the interagency national estimating system was in a state of virtual collapse. In short, those who had disagreed with the judgments in the CIA estimates over the years since 1946 no longer needed to confine themselves to verbal dissent; they set out to destroy the CIA's commitment to the pursuit of a rational and nonpartisan estimating process, and they succeeded.

Those of us who had worked within the system since 1950 had built up a fine record and a high regard for both the content and the style of our product. We had made errors in judgment, some because we tried to accommodate our military colleagues and some because of an occasional intrusion of politics into the system. But outright politicization of the Agency came with the appointment of two Republican politicians to the directorship after Helms's dismissal. One of them, William Casey, attempted to use his position to advance his personal foreign-policy agenda.

So the post–World War II blunders that had begun with Korea and Vietnam intensified. No longer constrained by the views of CIA and State Department analysts, the U.S. military services persuaded their political chiefs and their supporters in Congress to undertake new and massive arms programs designed to secure a decisive military superiority over the USSR. Soviet military planners viewed the new programs with alarm and followed suit. By 1983, those programs had reached the point where each side had acquired a first-strike capability more conducive to the initiation than to the deterrence of a catastrophic nuclear exchange. With apocalypse staring them in the face, statesmen in both countries (George Shultz and Mikhail Gorbachev) moved to end the arms race and seek nuclear-arms reduction.

Not all the blame for the blunders from the nonuse of intelligence can be laid at the feet of elected and appointed policymakers. Sometimes subordinates with their own policy agendas withheld intelligence estimates from their superiors. Sometimes domestic politics and powerful bureaucracies intruded upon policy decisions. Some of the blunders were caused not so much by people failures as by inadequacies in the system. In any event, it seems clear that considerable repair work needs to be done before the intellectual integrity of the intelligence system can be restored.

Moreover, some blunders need to be taken to heart. Most important of all, the tragic waste of lives and treasure that accompanied the blunders of the past century—underestimating Japanese power and aggressiveness, ignoring the anti-Hitler plot, failing to recognize the German preparations for a pre-Christmas attack in the Ardennes, misjudging Soviet intentions after World War II, waging unnecessary wars in Korea and Vietnam, and conducting an enormously dangerous nuclear arms race—must never happen again. Ways must be found to supervene the power of the military-industrial complex and the proclivity of our society to elect leaders who are unschooled in the many historical, cultural, ideological, scientific, and economic movements that in the future will require a higher level of knowledge and wisdom than in the past.

Intelligence Triumphs and Failures in World War II

Why War Came

War was inevitable after the signing of the Nazi-Soviet pact on August 24, 1939. But those of us of military age who followed world politics had been apprehensive about the outbreak of a second world war for several years. As a senior in college during the early months of 1936, I was shocked when a group of radical Japanese military officers, in an attempted coup d'état, assassinated several high government officials and moderate military officers. They were seeking to overthrow the new Diet, which had a large number of members who opposed Japan's aggressive military policies in East Asia.

A few months after that, the Spanish general Francisco Franco along with a group of rightist military colleagues set about to overthrow a Socialist-led Popular Front coalition in Madrid, thus precipitating a bloody three-year civil war. The 1930s had already witnessed the Japanese seizure of Manchuria in 1931 and the Italian invasion of Ethiopia in 1935. But the events in Japan and Spain raised new questions. Was there a new wave of domestic political tensions developing in which right-wing groups under military leadership were moving against democratically elected governments under Socialist or moderate leadership? Were the fascist and nationalist doctrines of Mussolini and Hitler spreading around the world? Would there be a lining up of nations on opposing sides—one militarist and fascist and the other democratic and socialist?

As the 1930s progressed and the effects of the Great Depression deepened, internal politics in most of the advanced countries of Europe become more class-oriented. In Germany, junkers and other right-wing groups threw their political support to Adolf Hitler in January 1933 in the hope that he would help them to rid the country of Socialists, Communists, Jews, liberal intellectuals, and outré artists of one stripe or another. In Austria in 1934, there was a brief civil conflict as conservative political leaders set out to destroy Socialist neighborhoods by force. In Italy, Spain, and Greece the right-wing dictators sought to eliminate all sources of political opposition. The firing squad and the concentration camp became devices for cleansing central and southern Europe of those who—in the arts, universities, and factories—wished to change an economic and social system that for centuries had benefited the privileged. But the conservatives in Germany who sought to use Hitler's National Socialism for their own ends soon became his victims, as did conservatives elsewhere in Europe who followed his model or sought his help.

The Spanish Civil War became a focal point of the sociopolitical conflict as German and Italian military forces came in to assist the Francoists. The democratic governments of Britain and France did little or nothing to help Republican Spain. The French Popular Front coalition debated and dithered. The British Labour Party had lost its fighting spirit after failure of the general strike in 1926, and its leadership was later co-opted by the Tories during the Great Depression. Some Tories even saw the right-wing movements of Europe as a possible route toward destruction of the British left. So the Soviet Communists became the lone standard-bearers of democracy in Spain and thus sealed its doom.

With France divided and paralyzed and with Britain neutralized by the blindness of its doddering leadership, Hitler was able to play a trump card. Frightened Soviet leaders, weakened by their own purges and ideological contradictions, made a nonaggression pact with the Nazis in August 1939. By thus protecting his eastern flank, Hitler could turn his attention to France and Britain. His blitzkrieg quickly destroyed Poland and then France, and the Battle of Britain followed in the autumn of 1940.

Meanwhile, President Roosevelt, who was nearing the end of his second term in the White House, had become increasingly concerned with the turn of events, not only in Europe but in East Asia as well. Although the attempted coup of 1936 in Tokyo had failed, the military caste was still pressing for an activist expansionist policy in Asia. A minor firefight on July 6, 1937, between Japanese and Chinese troops at a railway bridge north of Beijing near the Manchurian border set off a Japanese attempt to conquer China proper.

Three years later, in July 1940, the moderates in Japan suffered a defeat when a new cabinet was installed that brought to power such strong advocates of expansionism as General Tojo at the Ministry of War. Shortly thereafter, when France fell to the Nazis, Japan joined the Rome-Berlin Axis.

Neutralist sentiment in the United States remained strong throughout the 1930s, and several neutrality acts were passed between 1935 and 1939 forbidding the sale or transport of arms to any belligerent, extension of private loans to belligerents, or the entry of U.S. ships into war zones.

Nevertheless, before his term ended, President Roosevelt took the lead in bringing about actions to protect the United States from future dangers. A naval expansion program was initiated, a National Defense Research Committee was set up, conscription was voted, and fifty mothballed U.S. destroyers were traded to Britain in return for U.S. naval and air bases in the West Indies, Newfoundland, and Bermuda, all during the summer and autumn of 1940.

Reelected in November to an unprecedented third term, President Roosevelt moved quickly after his inauguration in January 1941 to strengthen U.S. defenses and to assist the enemies of the Axis powers. With passage of the Lend-Lease Act in March 1941, the United States became, in popular parlance, the "Arsenal of Democracy." The pretense of neutrality was abandoned as the United States provided its new friends in Europe with some $50 billion in arms, food, and services.[1]

When the Lend-Lease bill was still before Congress in February 1941, I was asked to speak at a current affairs meeting of the Oxford (Ohio) Professional Women's Club. I was then a newly appointed member of the Government Department faculty at Miami University and fresh from a year on the staff of the Brookings Institution in Washington. In answer to a question about lend-lease, I expressed doubt that the proposed legislation would have much effect upon Hitler's expansionist plans, although it would help Britain defend itself against the expected German assault. I thought in any case that the most useful U.S. response to the Nazi threat would be for the United States to ally itself openly with the USSR, since we were the only two nonbelligerents potentially powerful enough to give Hitler pause. If our objective was to prevent the war from spreading, that was the route to take.

Though I was not aware of it at the time, Winston Churchill, David Lloyd-George, and leading members of the Labour Party made a similar argument

---

1. For a more detailed treatment of Roosevelt's response to the war in Europe, see Samuel Morison, *The Oxford History of the American People* (New York: Oxford, 1965), 996–99.

in the House of Commons in the spring of 1939. It was their position that it was folly for the British government to extend territorial guarantees to Poland unless there were a British-Soviet alliance of some sort. Negotiations between Britain and the USSR did take place during the summer of 1939, but the Soviets apparently concluded that Britain was trying to get the USSR into a war with Germany without Britain itself being committed to fight.[2] When negotiations broke down, the Soviets got at least some temporary protection against Nazi expansionism by accepting the nonaggression pact offered by the Germans and announced on August 24. The Nazis outbid the British by promising to divide Poland with the USSR, an offer that made a German attack on Poland inevitable.

Hitler, of course, broke his agreement with the USSR two years later after having occupied France and southeast Europe in 1940. With the German invasion of the USSR in June 1941, Britain did become an ally of the Soviet Union. Six months after that the Japanese attacked Pearl Harbor. The United States then also became an ally of the USSR when Germany declared war against the United States. I have often wondered since then what would have happened if we had openly allied ourselves with the USSR before Hitler had committed himself to the conquest of the Soviet Union.

Before the end of 1941, however, Hitler had already begun to lose momentum. He did not win the air battle over Britain, nor did Britain fall apart from internal social and political tensions, as he had hoped. The USSR did not collapse before the onslaught of Hitler's legions. In America, there arose a widening concern over the future of Western civilization. Defense programs were intensified, the draft was extended, and active U.S. diplomacy to halt Axis military aggression was initiated. The Pacific Basin was not yet an area of active military combat except in China, where Japan found itself unable to win a military triumph or to get a negotiated settlement on favorable terms. The Japanese then decided to seize control of Southeast Asia. The Western European colonial powers, they assumed, would be too weak to oppose such a Japanese move. Success there, they further assumed, would cut China off from the outside world and thus in time bring China to heel.

Taking advantage of its membership in the Rome-Berlin Axis, the Japanese then proceeded to utilize their association with Germany to apply pressure upon the defeated French regime at Vichy to allow Japan to establish air and

---

2. For a more detailed account of British-Polish and British-Soviet relationship at the time, see A.J.P. Taylor, *The Origins of the Second World War* (Greenwich, Conn.: Fawcett, 1966), 218–23.

naval bases in Indochina, allegedly to contain China. The Japanese then applied further pressure on Vichy to resolve an old Cambodian-Thai border dispute in Thailand's favor. In return they extorted from the Thai leaders permission to establish bases there. It was President Roosevelt's diplomatic maneuvers to slow down and if possible reverse those moves that caused the Japanese to advance their expansionist timetable in Southeast Asia. They then used their newly acquired bases in Thailand and Indochina to attack Malaya, Burma, Indonesia, and the Philippines, and—in a move primarily designed to hobble any U.S. effort to come to Southeast Asia's assistance—Pearl Harbor.

The Catastrophe at Pearl Harbor

The Japanese attack on Pearl Harbor on Sunday December 7, 1941, changed America's thinking about its role in the world. Domestic politics in the United States did not cease, but there developed a genuine bipartisan effort to build up the war-making capacity of the country as quickly as possible and to assist in the defense of the territories of our new allies in Europe and Asia. One of the major military steps undertaken in the United States was to strengthen the intelligence-gathering and intelligence-analysis capability of the military services. Before Pearl Harbor, the Army and Navy each had small detachments in their respective communications services who intercepted and decoded the diplomatic communications of certain foreign governments. Most intelligence services did this, some more aggressively than others, and U.S. cryptanalysts had succeeded in intercepting and reading hundreds of Japanese diplomatic messages in the months before Pearl Harbor. It is generally believed that if those messages had been properly understood and passed promptly to the responsible civilian and military commanders, the catastrophe at Pearl Harbor could have been averted.[3] Was there in fact an intelligence failure?

The question has been studied and restudied since the end of the war. In addition to a congressional investigation, historians both professional and amateur have worked over the data from the "ultra" intercepts along with excerpts from the diaries of the principals and from their memoirs. Much of the discussion has focused on assigning blame and identifying scapegoats. Admiral Kimmel and General Short, the two commanders at Pearl Harbor,

---

3. The texts of all the messages sent between July 1 and December 8, 1941, were declassified and made available to the Joint Congressional Committee on the Investigation of the Pearl Harbor Attack. They are available as a Joint Committee Print of the 79th Congress, 1st session.

were blamed for failing to take adequate precautions after receiving warning messages from Washington. General MacArthur was not blamed for allowing his bomber fleet in the Philippines to be destroyed on the ground even though he had had nine hours warning from the attack on Pearl Harbor.[4] Kimmel and Short were dismissed from the service; MacArthur went on to become the supreme commander in the Pacific and chief of the Allied occupation of Japan in 1945.

The intelligence "failure," if there was such, lay in the question of warning: how soon was it given, to whom, with what degree of alarm, and from what level of command. In the intelligence business we draw a distinction between "strategic warning" and "tactical warning." Strategic warning is based upon the historical context of an international dispute and especially upon the diplomatic state of play; it also takes careful account of military capabilities and force dispositions. Tactical warning is limited and definitive; it concerns the approximate time and place at which military or other compulsive actions are likely to occur.

The events of 1940 and 1941 which I have described above constituted a strategic warning, to wit: Japanese membership in the Rome-Berlin Axis, pressures upon Indochina and Thailand, the Japanese acquisition of bases in Southeast Asia, the U.S. attempts to slow down and if possible to reverse Japanese aggressive moves in East Asia. Finally, in August and September 1941 the moderates in Japan, making one last effort to avoid war with the United States, began pressing for a summit with President Roosevelt to seek an understanding on the future of East Asia. But the terms which U.S. negotiators advanced for holding such a meeting amounted to a demand that Japan reverse its East Asian policies. It was clear at that point that the United States and its European associates (Britain, France, and Holland) were on a collision course with Japan. Consequently, on the fifth of November, the Joint Army-Navy Board recognized the virtual inevitability of war and advised the President that a Japanese attack upon American, British, and Dutch territory would have to be met by "military action against Japan."[5]

The United States then entered a period when its political leadership and military commands *should* have been looking throughout the Pacific area for indications of a forthcoming Japanese military attack. Military commanders and staff officers at all levels should have been instructed to be alert to Japanese

---

4. See B. H. Liddell Hart, *History of the Second World War* (New York: Putnam's, 1971), 221.
5. Cited by Robert Devine, *The Reluctant Belligerent: American Entry into World War II* (Huntington, N.Y.: Krieger, 1965), 149.

military moves in order to provide the necessary warning to those forces and bases in exposed positions. There were a significant number of Japanese diplomatic messages that, if properly analyzed, would have provided clear warning. One intercepted message of November 22 even said that after November 29 "things are automatically going to happen" so that any modus vivendi with the United States would have to be completed by that date. On November 25 the U.S. Army and Navy chiefs, General George Marshall and Admiral Ernest King, sent war-warning messages to their commanders in the Pacific, and during the next ten days there was considerable diplomatic activity in Washington and consultations with the British and Dutch governments. Reports were received of troop movements in Indochina and of Japanese fleet and convoy movements into the Gulf of Siam on December 6. President Roosevelt then drafted a plea for peace to be sent to the Japanese emperor.

There was, finally, an intercept of several sections of a long telegram on December 6 from Tokyo to the Japanese embassy in Washington with an indication that the last section would not arrive until December 7. The last section did arrive as scheduled and announced that Japan was severing diplomatic relations with the United States. General Marshall, when he saw the intercept, prepared a second war-warning message to the Pacific commanders. But it was too late. The Japanese fleet had left the Kurile Islands south of Kamchatka on November 25 and passed undetected through the North Pacific, and its aircraft were already attacking Pearl Harbor. It had been clear for two weeks that war was imminent, but no effective warning was sent to the Pacific commanders. Authorities in Washington knew that war was coming, but they did not think that Hawaii was in danger, and they even doubted that there would be an attack on the Philippine Islands.

Those were only the principal elements of the events leading up to Pearl Harbor. They tell us little about the actual handling of intelligence materials in the weeks and months before the attack. Henry Clausen, an army officer who had been a lawyer in civilian life, was directed by Secretary of War Henry L. Stimson to investigate the whole Pearl Harbor affair. One of the most striking parts of his report is his description of how Japanese messages were disseminated to the President and the State Department. "The entire system was a shambles," he wrote in his book, *Pearl Harbor: Final Judgment*, published in 1992. "The Army and Navy signal people competed with and duplicated each other, each couldn't wait to run off" to the White House when it had an interesting message in hand. They finally agreed to share everything, and by January 1941 also agreed to service the White House on alternate months. But in May the Army decided that the office of the President's military aide was not secure, and it stopped all deliveries to the White House, while continuing deliveries to the State Department. The hiatus in deliveries to the White House continued until September, when Roosevelt succeeded in getting ultra materials from his naval aide.

Clausen remarks that while the services had people with the "genius" to read the encrypted Japanese traffic, no one seemed to "have the brains to know what to do with it." There was, he wrote, "no comprehensive method for either disseminating or evaluating the material." He concluded that if the military had created a more efficient system for analyzing and disseminating intercept intelligence, the Pearl Harbor disaster "could have been avoided," and the forces involved "would have been ready to repel the attackers instead of being asleep at the crucial moment."[6]

It also appears that the field commanders had not been privy to the intercepted intelligence, nor had they been provided with up-to-date reports on U.S.-Japanese negotiations. There apparently was no coordinating group in Washington systematically pooling information and discussing the implications of what was going on. Moreover, there appear to have been few if any formal policy meetings among the Washington principals. The authorities in Washington appear not to have known of the powerful role increasingly being played by radical military leaders in Japan or to have understood the full implications of the Greater East Asia concept already being played out in Japanese policy and action.

Careful strategic thinking about the role of U.S. forces in the Pacific does not seem to have taken place at all. Indeed, U.S. forces and bases should have been recognized, as they were by Japanese strategists, as major obstacles to Japanese control of the Western Pacific. It should have been obvious to U.S. strategists—if there were any—that U.S. forces and bases would have been an early target of Japanese attack in any outbreak of military hostilities in the Western Pacific.

There was an intelligence failure; the available intelligence was not communicated to the commanders who needed it, and they failed to take prudent action on the basis of the limited warnings they did receive. But the principal fault lay at the command level in Washington. Marshall and King failed to see that their field commanders were kept informed, they failed to appreciate the state of mind in Tokyo, they lacked an understanding of the strategic situation in the Pacific, and they had an inadequate appreciation of the capabilities of the Japanese naval and air forces.

6. Henry Clausen, *Pearl Harbor: Final Judgment* (New York: Crown, 1992), 45–47.

The Use of Ultra in the Pacific War and in Southeast Asia

Once they had recovered from the shock of Pearl Harbor and had begun to make plans for the future, the Secretaries of War and the Navy set about to improve and expand the use of communications intelligence. They especially sought to improve the analytic capability of their intelligence services and to revise the system for disseminating communications not only to the highest levels in Washington but also to the commanders in the field. They were, of course, mindful of the need to retain very limited access to communications intelligence methods and reports; the source itself would have dried up had our enemies learned that the United States was successfully intercepting and reading their communications. A Special Branch was established in the Military Intelligence Service (G-2) to do the analytic job and to guide and assist the Signal Corps in the interception and decryption effort. The Special Branch was the particular concern of Secretary Stimson, who put in charge of tje branch a hard-hitting New York lawyer named Alfred McCormack.

The Navy Department also strengthened its signal interception and decryption effort. Under the leadership of Commander Joseph Rochefort, the communications intelligence unit at Pearl Harbor concentrated upon the operations of Japanese naval forces in the entire Pacific Ocean area. That unit was able to estimate, by March 1942, that the Japanese were planning to exploit their December 7, 1941, victories by moving against both New Guinea and Hawaii. Careful analysis of Japanese communications prompted Admiral Nimitz to redeploy his forces to head off the New Guinea assault. The Japanese suffered severe losses at the ensuing Battle of the Coral Sea in May 1942, and they were obliged to recall their invasion.

Also, by mid-May, Japanese dispatches led Admiral Nimitz to conclude that Midway Island was the main object of Japanese naval forces in the central Pacific, while it appeared that a threat to the Aleutian Islands was being posed by a diversionary force. Nimitz did not allow himself to be diverted and concentrated his fleet strength for the defense of Midway. Ultra disclosed that the Japanese Midway operation was to begin on June 2, 1942. The battle of aircraft from the two carrier forces raged from June 3 to June 7. The outcome has been described as the "Miracle at Midway" and was characterized by one writer in these words: "Thanks to Ultra intelligence and superior tactics, the Americans inflicted a severe defeat on the Japanese which shifted the balance of sea power in the Pacific in their favor."[7]

---

7. Cited in the *Oxford Companion to World War II* (Oxford: Oxford, 1995), 749. See also the report on Ultra in the *Oxford Companion*, 1165–74.

Meanwhile, the Army's G-2 Special Branch was being expanded, and I was one of the junior officers transferred to it. The Economic Branch, to which I was assigned, did both economic and political reporting. Its principal source of information was the intercepted diplomatic traffic into, from, and among embassies and foreign ministries in Asia. Another source was the intercepted traffic between the Japanese merchant marine and their controlling offices in Japan and around the Pacific. I was not an expert on East Asia, but I soon had the history and geography in my sights and learned the cast of characters.

My section, the Southeast Asia Desk, was carefully watching the degree to which the Vichy French regime in Indochina and the royal regime in Thailand were complying with the directives of the Japanese military authorities. By the autumn of 1944, it became quite clear that the regimes in Saigon and Bangkok were becoming less and less compliant. For example, we saw that the Vichy French diplomats in Tokyo, Shanghai, Hanoi, and Saigon, stranded in the Far East by the German elimination of the Vichy regime early in 1944 and aware of Allied military successes in Europe, were trying to figure out some way to make contact with the Free French (Gaullist) Committee. Their aim was doubtless to save their careers but also to save for France at least a foothold in the Far East. This effort was quite evident among the French in Hanoi, who were able to make occasional contacts with Allied officers by traveling to Kunming in Southwest China, which was still under Chinese Nationalist control.

A much more interesting development of early 1945 was disclosed in a series of Japanese messages about a revolutionary guerrilla movement operating in the area north and west of Hanoi. One of the messages mentioned a leader named Nguyen Ai Quac and an organization whose name was difficult to decipher. As I was puzzling over the text, I recalled an Office of Strategic Services (OSS) report that mentioned an Ai Quac. I dug it out and learned that Ai Quac was an important figure in the nationalist movement among the Annamese people of Indochina who had become known to OSS operatives in the China theater as Ho Chih Minh. Documents about OSS activity in Indochina during the war and months immediately following were redacted and released to the Senate Foreign Relations Committee in 1972. They were made public in February 1973 as part of a committee print of its study, *The Causes, Origins, and Lessons of the Vietnam War*. From those documents it appears that Ai Quac had engaged in a variety of political activities against French rule in Indochina beginning in 1919. He was the author of a memorandum sent to the U.S. President and Secretary of State in June

1919 asking that the U.S. delegation "honor" the appeal of Annamese people for "national self-determination." The appeal listed a number of political freedoms which the Paris "Group of Annamite Patriots" desired to obtain, and they expressed a desire to have an elected delegation in the French parliament. Similar memoranda were addressed to Premier Georges Clemenceau and Prime Minister David Lloyd-George.

After receiving no response, Ai Quac apparently became more radical in his activities. He went to Moscow from Paris in 1923 as the Indochinese representative to an International Congress of Peasants. There he met Michael Borodin, who, as a functionary in the Soviet Communist Party's effort at the time to cooperate with socialist and moderate parties, had been sent to China to work with the Kuomintang. Ai Quac worked with Borodin in Canton from 1925 to 1927, but when Chiang Kai-shek got control of the Kuomintang, Ai Quac fled China with Borodin. He went back to China in 1929, where he organized the Indochinese Communist Party, was arrested in Hong Kong at the request of the French Sûreté, and sentenced to prison in Hong Kong. Released two years later, he became Ho Chih Minh and worked his way back to Indochina, where he went underground. In 1943 he made contact in Kunming with General Chennault of the Flying Tigers and then began to work with OSS operatives in setting up a network in Tonkin (northern Vietnam) to help downed American pilots. In July 1945, two OSS groups parachuted into his headquarters, and together with his troops, carried out commando operations. He set up a provisional government in August in collaboration with other nationalist groups, and after the Japanese surrender became president of the "Provisional Government of the Republic of Vietnam."[8]

I have reviewed the activities of Ho Chih Minh and his relationship with the OSS because it will be helpful, in the review of the Vietnam estimates which appear later in this book, to recall that American personnel once worked with him and his associates to defeat the Japanese, and to recognize that his personal history and Communist affiliations were well known and accepted at the time.

The spreading insurrection in North Vietnam and the French inability or unwillingness to cope with it led to a Japanese decision to set aside the French administration in Indochina and to establish a full military government there. We were able to follow their planning and to tell the Pacific commanders

---

8. Drawn from an OSS Report of October 17, 1945, which was included in Senate Foreign Relations Committee, *Hearings on the Causes, Origins, and Lessons of the Vietnam War*, 92d Cong., 2d. sess., May 9, 10, and 11, 1972, 312–17.

exactly when the Japanese move would occur and what it would entail. It took place on March 15, 1945. As the war drew to a close, we finally did learn directly from the OSS that their operatives had been in touch with Ho Chih Minh and provided him with arms and supplies. The messages we were reading clearly indicated that Ho and his guerrillas were having considerable success cutting Japanese supply lines.

The Japanese faced additional problems during the early months of 1945. They were suffering severe shipping losses as a consequence of the U.S. submarine campaign in the Western Pacific and South China Sea. The naval war and island invasion campaigns had given the Navy's submarine fleet greater access to the Japanese shipping lanes. Communications intelligence told us in many cases exactly where individual ships would be at particular times. Our submarines were thus able to reduce very substantially the volume of shipping going to and from the home islands. As a consequence, the Japanese messages were telling about shortages occurring in the south and about plans to return civilians in Southeast Asia to Japan.

Ultra on Japan and the U.S. Decision on the Bomb

After the end of the war in Europe in May 1945, and with the increasing toll being taken of the Japanese merchant marine by U.S. naval operations, we began to see signs of a change of mood in Tokyo. A civilian who was associated with the Far Eastern section, fluent in Japanese, and responsible for following Japanese radio news and commentary dropped by one day to say that he thought the Japanese were getting ready to quit. Their broadcasts had changed; it was hard to pinpoint exactly, he said, but they were different in tone and there were slight changes of wording in the usual comments and reports. We listened with great interest; he had not seen any of the diplomatic ultra going in and out of Tokyo at about the same time. One such was a message from the minister of the Portuguese legation to Tokyo reporting that the American bombing raids were "disastrous" and that people were trying to flee the capital. Each day, he wrote, "the progress of the war becomes more alarming." Nevertheless, the military intended to continue the war at all costs, because they had "everything to lose with the end of hostilities."[9]

Japanese civilian leaders were apparently starting to see the chances for victory slipping away and beginning to realize that their only hope and greatest danger lay in the role which the USSR was about to play in the new sit-

9. Cited by Bruce Lee, *Marching Orders* (New York: Crown, 1995), 475.

uation. On May 9 Ambassador Sato in Moscow wrote that the Soviets had gained an opportunity to settle accounts with Japan and might well enter the war or seek to mediate a peace which would be very close to unconditional surrender.[10] Later that month Sato was instructed to find out what Soviet intentions were and whether some understanding with the USSR could be reached. Sato replied to Tokyo that it would be "useless" to try to seek an understanding with the Soviets. He wrote that they did not want to improve relations with Japan, and he concluded with an extremely pessimistic assessment of Japan's military prospects: Japan was already in much the same position as Germany had been from Allied air attacks; the fall of Okinawa was certain; Manchuria would soon come under air attack; and if the USSR entered the war, there would be no hope at all of saving the empire.[11]

Sato's words must have had some effect. A message sent to him over a month later, on July 12, 1945, clearly indicated an interest in ending the war. The message is especially noteworthy because it indicates for the first time the involvement of the emperor. David McCullough, in his biography of President Truman, describes the Tokyo-Moscow exchange as follows:

> On July 12, the Japanese Minister of Foreign Affairs, Shiginori Togo, sent a "Very Secret, Urgent" radio message to Ambassador Sato stating that the Emperor was "greatly concerned over the daily increasing calamities and sacrifices faced by the citizens of the belligerent countries" and that it was "His Majesty's heart's desire to see the swift termination of the war." His Majesty wished to send Prince Konoye as a special envoy to talk.
>
> Sato responded that it was pointless talking about peace with the Soviets. Such proposed negotiations were entirely unrealistic, he stressed. Molotov was not interested. "In the final analysis," Sato bluntly told Togo, "If our country truly desires to terminate the war, we have no alternative but to accept unconditional surrender or something very close to it."

In his private journal, Truman bluntly characterized the message as the "telegram from the Jap Emperor asking for peace."[12]

Three days later the A-bomb test took place at Alamogordo, and a few days after that—on July 16, 1945—the Potsdam Conference began. During their

10. Ibid., 461.
11. Ibid., 478.
12. David McCullough, *Truman* (New York: Simon & Schuster, 1992), 413.

first private meeting, Stalin told Truman of the Japanese feeler and said he planned to "lull the Japanese to sleep" by telling them that the proposal for the Konoye visit was too vague to accept. In a private luncheon conversation between Truman and General Eisenhower, when the atomic weapon's use was discussed, Eisenhower told the President that he opposed the use of the bomb because Japan was already defeated.[13]

As the second week of the conference began on July 23, discussions took place within the U.S. delegation on the question of unconditional surrender. McCullough reports the following as having taken place: "Stimson thought it unwise at this point to insist on unconditional surrender, a term the Japanese would take to mean they could not keep their Emperor. . . . [Secretary of State James F.] Byrnes vehemently opposed any change. . . . Politically it would be disastrous. . . . Hirohito was the villainous symbol of Japan's fanatical military clique. . . . If Hirohito were to remain in place, then the war had been pointless."[14]

While all that was going on at Potsdam, Soviet Vice Foreign Minister Lozovsky told Ambassador Sato in Moscow on July 19 that because the Konoye mission was "in no way clear," the Soviets could not give a definite reply to the proposal. After reporting that to Tokyo, Sato sent a long message on July 20 pleading for surrender, with the sole reservation that Japan's "national structure" be preserved. Supporting his plea Sato made some extraordinary statements which were published in full in the Diplomatic Summary[15] with the following excerpts highlighted:

a. Since the Manchurian incident, Japan has followed a policy of expediency. When it came to the East Asia war, we finally plunged into a great world war which was beyond our strength.
b. Even since the conclusion of the Anti-Comintern Pact [in 1936] our foreign policy has been a complete failure.

---

13. Ibid., 428.
14. Ibid., 436.
15. The Diplomatic Summary (sometimes known as the "Magic Summary") was published daily during World War II and afterwards. It contained the texts (or excerpts) of selected ultra intercepts. It was compiled and published by Special Branch analysts in the Intelligence Division of the War Department General Staff. It had a severely limited distribution in Washington. Intelligence Division Special Security Officers were authorized to convey information passed to them from Washington to the supreme commander of the theater to which they were assigned. The opening paragraph of the next section of this chapter contains further information on ultra and its use in the European theater.

c. While it is a good thing to be loyal to the obligations of honor up to the very end of the Greater East Asia war, it is meaningless to prove one's devotion by wrecking the state.

d. I think we have the inescapable and fundamental obligation to resolve as quickly as possible to lay down our arms and save the State and its people.

e. Our people will have to pant for a long time under a heavy yoke of the enemy . . . but after some decades we shall be able to flourish as before.

f. Immediately after the war ends, we must carry out thoroughgoing reforms everywhere within our country. By placing our government on a more democratic basis and by destroying the despotic bureaucracy, we must try to raise up the real unity between the Emperor and the people.[16]

On July 28, Truman released the Potsdam Declaration. It promised that once political rights were in place and a responsible "peacefully inclined" government was elected, occupation forces would be withdrawn. The term "unconditional surrender" appeared only once, in the last paragraph, and applied only to the armed forces and not to the Japanese nation. The fate of the emperor remained ambiguous.[17]

The bombs were dropped on August 6 and 9, Tokyo time. On the evening of August 9 Hirohito decided to surrender, with the understanding that he would remain on the throne. Truman finally overruled Byrnes on the morning of August 10. The Japanese could keep their emperor. The word went back to Tokyo that the emperor would remain, "subject to the Supreme Commander of the Allied Powers." On August 14 the Swiss chargé d'affaires delivered the text of the Japanese surrender to Secretary Byrnes.

I have described in some detail the diplomatic messages concerning the end of the war, together with relevant information about events and discussions in Washington and Potsdam. I have done this because I have wanted to make clear that the diplomatic intelligence reporting was timely and carefully explained. We in the Economic Branch had also been following the results of U.S. attacks on Japanese shipping and of the air raids on the home islands. I personally had been following the deterioration of the Japanese position in Southeast Asia. The U.S. government and its military commands in the Pacific area were the best informed in modern history. There was no intelligence failure.

16. Lee, *Marching Orders*, 585–90.
17. McCullough, *Truman*, 447.

What was learned from intelligence, before the atomic bombs were used against two Japanese cities, is quite clear: There was, at least among Japanese civilians and some governmental authorities, a strong and growing belief that the war should be brought to an end. The report of the U.S. Strategic Bombing Survey concluded that the bomb drops in themselves did nothing to persuade the Japanese to accept unconditional surrender; they had already made up their minds. The report of the survey, "based upon the testimony of the enemy leaders who ended the war," states:

> The Emperor, the Lord Privy Seal, the Prime Minister, the Foreign Minister, and the Navy Minister had decided as early as May of 1945 that the war should be ended even if it meant acceptance of defeat on allied terms. The War Minister and the two chiefs of staff opposed unconditional surrender. The impact of the Hiroshima attack was to bring further urgency and lubrication to the machinery of achieving peace, primarily by contributing to a situation which permitted the Prime Minister to bring the Emperor overtly and directly into a position where his decision for immediate acceptance of the Potsdam Declaration could be used to override the remaining objections.[18]

While this conclusion of the Bombing Survey was admittedly based upon testimony of the defeated leaders, it is fully consistent with the intelligence available.

President Truman's decision to drop the bombs was not done without considerable prior consultation in Washington, and much has been written about the committees and consultants involved. His advisers and the scientists who developed the bomb were divided among themselves about the military advantages and moral disadvantages of using the bomb in populated areas and even about using it for military purposes at all. But some of those consulted were not privy to the ultra intelligence bearing upon Japanese thinking and logistic difficulties. Moreover, most of the consultations about use of the bomb took place before the July 1945 test at Alamogordo, and thus before there was clear definitive knowledge available about the immediate physical effects of an atomic blast. The Scientific Advisory Committee, which was composed of Compton, Fermi, Lawrence, and Oppenheimer, was not informed about the military situation in the Western Pacific and the planned invasion of the mainland. The Committee itself acknowledged that—while it was among

---

18. Cited in *The Truman Administration: A Documentary History*, ed. Barton Bernstein and Allen Matusow (New York: Harper & Row, 1968), 43–44.

the few citizens who had "had occasion to give thoughtful consideration" to the questions involved, its members had "no claim to special competence in solving the political, social, and military problems which are presented by the advent of atomic power."[19]

President Truman was in Potsdam when the Alamogordo test took place, and the advisers with him were the military leaders and political chiefs whose duty it was to achieve the established war aims. And those aims were still unconditional surrender, not merely a change of heart in Tokyo. The Alamogordo test was, of course, very much on the President's mind throughout the conference, and it surely affected his decisions and behavior. Indeed, it was during the conference, on July 24, that Secretary Stimson transmitted an order to the commander of the Army Strategic Air Forces directing that the first bomb should be dropped after August 3. That order was sent two days after Stimson and Prime Minister Churchill were discussing the report which President Truman had received about the Alamogordo test. Stimson recorded Churchill's reaction as follows:

> [Churchill] told me that he had noticed at the meeting of the Three yesterday that Truman was much fortified by something that had happened and that he stood up to the Russians in a most emphatic manner. . . . "[Truman] told the Russians just where they got on and off, and generally bossed the whole meeting."[20]

Truman's biographer reports that Truman was indeed "fortified by the news," and that he and Byrnes "felt their hand might be thus strengthened at the bargaining table with the Russians in time to come."[21]

In thinking about nuclear weapons as a major factor in future U.S.-Soviet relations, President Truman was certainly correct. In some ways it has no doubt proven to be an asset. But was a presumed future diplomatic edge over the Soviets an acceptable reason for using two of them against an already defeated enemy who was simply trying to find a way to save his civilization? If President Truman and his advisers had taken on board the intelligence available to them, they should have realized that it would not be necessary to drop an atomic bomb on a populated area, much less two bombs on two such areas, to bring about a capitulation already in progress.

19. Ibid., 15.
20. Ibid., 24–25.
21. McCullough, *Truman*, 432.

The Use of Ultra in the European War

By 1944, the collection and processing of enemy communications had become a worldwide affair and included more than diplomatic traffic. The entire range of communications were intercepted, decrypted, and analyzed. These included naval ship-to-shore and ship-to-ship messages, communications among army headquarters, ground-to-air exchanges, intelligence-agent networks, and—most important of all—messages between the German High Command and theater commands. The more valuable that communications intelligence became, the greater became the need to maintain close control over its dissemination and use. To this end, Special Security officers (SSOs) were established at all major commands, and the SSO chief was accredited only to the theater commander in chief and his immediate subordinates. U.S. and British resources were pooled, and there was a working arrangement that provided that most of the collection and dissemination in the European theater would be handled through British Special Liaison Units (SLUs), and in the Asia-Pacific theater by U.S. SSOs.

Not all of the ultra disseminated at high Allied headquarters appeared in the Diplomatic Summary published in Washington. Moreover, in many of the headquarters outside the home countries (United States, Britain, Australia), ultra materials were destroyed immediately after the recipient commander had read them. For that reason, there is less information available to historians about the uses and value of ultra in the European theater than about its use in the Pacific, the Pacific materials having been sent from Washington to the theater commander and copies retained in the national archives.

Neither General Eisenhower in his memoir, *Crusade in Europe,* nor Prime Minister Winston Churchill, in his *Memoirs of the Second World War,* mention the use of ultra. Nor did B. H. Liddell Hart in his definitive *History of the Second World War,* published in 1970. The first writer to deal directly with the use of ultra was Group Captain F. W. Winterbotham of the Royal Air Force, who was in charge of the security and dissemination of ultra for the British government. His book, *The Ultra Secret,* was published in 1974, and its introduction contains a copy of a letter of July 1945 from General Eisenhower to the chief of the British Secret Intelligence Service. In it, he thanked those who were engaged in the ultra effort. Ultra intelligence, he wrote, "simplified my task as a commander enormously" and "saved thousands of British and American lives."[22] A much more detailed study of the

---

22. F. W. Winterbotham, *The Ultra Secret* (New York: Harper & Row, 1974), 3.

uses of ultra in the European theater is contained in Ronald Lewin's *Ultra Goes to War*, published in 1978. His book tells the ultra story in the European theater in great detail from the inception of the communications intelligence effort to the final German defeat in 1945.

Exactly how much the victory over the Germans was in fact dependent upon ultra is still being debated. Henry Clausen (who had written the study of the role of ultra in the Pearl Harbor fiasco for Secretary Stimson) told Bruce Lee in 1992 that "everyone in Washington knew that Ike was being handed priceless information on a daily basis, [but] he never acknowledged it."[23] Lee, in his book *Marching Orders* (1995), suggests that Eisenhower did not want to acknowledge his reliance on ultra because he did not want to be second-guessed later. Others have thought that he did not want to acknowledge it because it would show that his successes were due to good intelligence rather than his own generalship. William Friedman, the U.S. cryptanalyst who was largely responsible for breaking the Japanese codes, has said that when Allied forces didn't have ultra information on particular times and places, "our troops took a beating."[24]

One place where U.S. troops took a beating was in the Ardennes in December 1944. After the Allied break-out from the Normandy peninsula at the end of July in 1944, the subsequent destruction of German forces in the Falaise pocket, the capture of Paris on August 24, and the British campaign to secure Antwerp early in September, Allied armies did not press on, but stopped at the German border. But the German situation was more parlous than General Eisenhower and his commanders realized. General Westphal, who was the German Chief of Staff on the Western Front, later described the German situation as follows:

> The over-all situation in the West was serious in the extreme. A heavy defeat anywhere along the Front, which was so full of gaps that it did not deserve this name, might lead to a catastrophe, if the enemy were to exploit his opportunity skillfully. A particular source of danger was that not a single bridge over the Rhine had been prepared for demolition, an omission which took weeks to repair. . . .
>
> Until the middle of October the enemy could have broken through at any point he liked, and then have been able to cross the Rhine and thrust deep into Germany almost unhindered.[25]

23. Lee, *Marching Orders*, 16.
24. Ibid., 17.
25. Cited by Liddell Hart, *History of the Second World War*, 556.

According to Liddell Hart, the Allied intelligence staff also recognized the German weakness and told General Eisenhower that the Germans could not possibly produce sufficient forces to hold the frontier line. But Eisenhower revealed his own failure to grasp the opportunity when he wrote to General Montgomery on September 15, "We shall soon have captured the Ruhr and the Saar and the Frankfurt area, and I would like your views as to what we should do next."[26] General Patton had seen the opportunity even earlier, having proposed on August 23 that his army should move north into Germany instead of west toward Alsace. But Allied Headquarters cut off his petroleum supplies. He was then a hundred miles closer to the Rhine and its bridges than the British were. It looks very much as if jealousy and indecision had replaced resourceful generalship. Liddell Hart summarizes the situation as follows: "None of the top planners had foreseen such a complete collapse of the enemy as occurred in August. They were not prepared, mentally or materially, to exploit it by a rapid long-range thrust."[27]

While the Allied commanders argued and debated about what to do next, the Germans—driven by a Hitler who had almost miraculously survived an assassination attempt in July—were busy refitting their panzer divisions and organizing new infantry divisions. By early December those divisions were on the frontier in the Ardennes. Various signs of a concentration of power were turning up in the headquarters of the U.S. First Army's G-2, Colonel Monk Dickson. These included POW statements, captured documents, reconnaissance photographs, and low-level logistics ultra. These were put together by Dickson, who on December 10 issued his "Estimate Number 37" to which he wrote the following conclusion: "It is apparent that Von Rundstedt . . . has skillfully defended and husbanded his forces and is preparing for his part in the all-out application of every weapon at the focal point and correct time to achieve defense of the Reich west of the Rhine by inflicting as great a defeat on the Allies as possible. Indications to date point to the location of this focal point as being between Roermond and Schleiden."[28]

Six days later, on the morning of December 16, the German forces attacked at precisely the focal point which Dickson had identified, and the Battle of the Bulge began.

British Group Captain Winterbotham was not in Europe at the time but in Washington on his way back to London from Australia and Honolulu.

---

26. Ibid., 567.
27. Ibid.
28. Winterbotham, *The Ultra Secret,* 179.

When he returned, he made it his business to find out "the real story" behind the Bulge. In his review of the intelligence data, he pointed out that, contrary to the case during the previous two and a half years, there had been a complete absence of "high-grade ultra" during December.[29] He commented that having had "the enemy's intentions handed to them on a plate" in the past, the high command had "come to rely on ultra to such an extent that when it gave no positive indication of a coming counter attack, all other indications were not taken seriously enough."[30] Why weren't they?

One reason was a Headquarters failure to think about the possible causes for the absence of high-level ultra. Always alert to the danger of having their signals intercepted and read, the German High Command apparently had decided to rely, for their high-level exchanges, on land lines rather than radio transmissions. This option had only become available to them after the retreat of their forces back into Germany and the subsequent rebuilding of their army command and communication structure. Winterbotham quickly concluded that such a shift had occurred and that the absence of high-level ultra in itself should have aroused suspicions. A second reason was that Dickson's warning was given less attention than it should have received because of dissension among the various G-2s within Army Group Command, including a belief that Dickson was an "alarmist."[31] General Omar Bradley, when discussing Dickson's estimate in his own memoirs, alleged that Dickson was not thinking in terms of "a major strategic counterattack."[32] It looks very much, however, that "a major strategic counterattack" was exactly what Dickson was thinking in terms of when he wrote that the purpose of the coming German offensive was "to achieve defense of the Reich west of the Rhine by inflicting as great a defeat on the Allies as possible."

Liddell Hart thought that the fault lay primarily in the mind-set of the Allied generals themselves. They counted on the orthodoxy of the German generals; the Allied generals thought that their German opponents knew they had taken a beating and knew they did not have the capability to hit back effectively.[33] What the Allied generals did not realize was that Hitler was still very much in charge and still capable of concocting daring military moves. They should have known of the brutal revenge wreaked by Hitler upon everyone he suspected of not faithfully carrying out his orders. They should have

29. Ibid.
30. Ibid.
31. Liddell Hart, *History of the Second World War*, 643.
32. Omar Bradley, *A General's Life* (New York: Simon & Schuster, 1983), 351.
33. Liddell Hart, *History of the Second World War*, 643.

recognized therefore that Hitler's generals would bend every effort to satisfy Hitler of their loyalty regardless of the military recklessness of his orders. Instead of confronting the intelligence data and discussing the possibilities implicit in the analysis—even though it did not have an ultra stamp on it—they relied upon their own professional assumptions, and those assumptions were wrong.

An intelligence failure did occur when the intelligence officers on the line failed to impress upon their superiors what was happening across the German border. A command failure occurred when the Allied generals, apparently hoping for a Christmas "pause," did not take seriously the intelligence provided them when it was not touted as the latest news from the German High Command. The result was a campaign in the Ardennes that cost about 80,000 casualties, the vast majority of which were American.

A bit further back in time, however, was a longer "pause," which developed after the capture of Paris on August 24. Instead of following Patton's request of August 23 that he exploit the German collapse in the West by moving north into Germany, Allied Headquarters cut off his access to the necessary logistics. General Montgomery was still in command in the West and would be until September 1, and he wanted to take control of all the supplies available in order to prepare for a thrust northward from Antwerp. His plan called for an airborne attack north of the Waal Rhine bridge at Nijmegen (in east-central Holland), along with a ground movement in a narrow corridor north from Antwerp. Most of the American generals opposed the idea. General Patton wrote in his diary at the time that "Monty does about what he pleases, and Ike says 'yes, sir.' Monty wants all supplies sent to him."[34]

General Kenneth Strong, the British officer serving as Eisenhower's G-2, had grave reservations about the Nijmegen operation because he did not know where one of the German panzer corps was located and feared that it might be available to counter the Montgomery attack.[35] Despite successes in the airborne assault at the outset, within a few days the operation became a thorough disaster. There was indeed a panzer corps in the area. Thirty-four years later, in 1978, there was a conference in England attended by commanders, operations officers, and intelligence officers who played a major role in the Nijmegen-Arnhem operation; they arrived at a consensus that their superiors were overconfident and that they had "not evaluated or even

---

34. David Eisenhower, *Eisenhower at War: 1943–1945* (New York: Random House, 1986), 469.
35. Ibid., 470.

accepted ultra indications along with more conventional sources available to them."[36]

Montgomery's defeat in Holland was the result of several factors: Montgomery's failure to understand the depth of the earlier German defeat, his failure to keep track of major German military units, his choice of a highly dubious strategy over a more promising one urged by Patton, and his insubordinate refusal to accept guidance from Eisenhower and his staff. The Nijmegen fiasco, though not much publicized or really understood by the British and American chiefs of staff, led to a loss of momentum and of confidence and to a mental block against the exploration of other ways to bring an early conclusion to the war.

Thus the autumn months of 1944 were a period of regrouping and rearming on both sides of the Rhine, which in turn led to the Battle of the Bulge. But the casualties of the Bulge itself were only a small part of those which occurred after Nijmegen. Liddell Hart has calculated that two-thirds of Allied casualties occurred after September and that millions more had died in concentration camps and from military action in Germany during the following eight months.[37]

The Anti-Hitler Plot: Allied Command Failures

The Nijmegen defeat, the Battle of the Bulge, and the heavy casualties which occurred after September 1944 would not have happened if Adolf Hitler's opponents—inside and outside the military establishment—had succeeded in their attempt to assassinate him and to establish a new German regime committed to making peace with the Allied powers. Anti-Hitler plotting had been going on for years. Western intelligence had been aware of it through occasional German approaches to representatives of the Western Allies.

This plotting was rapidly stepped up after the successful Allied landings in Normandy. During the six weeks from June 6 to July 20, the plotters were actively preparing a specific assassination attempt and lining up additional supporters. During the same period, the Allies were breaking out of the Normandy peninsula and inflicting the first of a series of defeats on the German forces in France, Allied forces in Italy were marching on Rome, and the Russians launched a summer offensive which by mid-July had driven the Germans out of White Russia and into northeastern Poland. The Germans

---

36. Ronald Lewin, *Ultra Goes to War* (New York: McGraw-Hill, 1978), 346–51.

37. Liddell Hart, *History of the Second World War*, 561.

were in retreat nearly everywhere. The plotters believed, therefore, that a successful assassination would precipitate a vast amount of confusion within the German military forces and lead to a rapid termination of the war.

The anti-Hitler plotting was monitored by Allen Dulles, then the chief of OSS for Europe, from his post in Switzerland. He arrived there in November 1942, with the mission of finding out what was going on in Germany. As he developed contacts with German exiles and disaffected German officials, he not only found out much about what was going on in Germany but also became a conduit to the West for the plotters in their search for encouragement and, if possible, cooperation from the Allied powers. They got very little. After the war, Dulles wrote an account of the plot in his book, *Germany's Underground*. In the foreword, he explained his purpose in writing it:

> There *was* an anti-Nazi underground working in Germany, despite the general impression to the contrary. It developed out of heterogeneous groups that finally achieved a working unity and reached into the vitals of the army and government services. Professional men, church and labor leaders, and high commanding officers on various (military) fronts participated. Even Field Marshals Rommel and von Kluge finally had a share, but this was late in the day, when they saw that military victory had eluded them. But there were others of a very different moral fiber, both civilian and military, who were not opportunists and who had fought Hitlerism for many years. The story of these anti-Nazi Germans who risked their lives deserves to be told.[38]

Plotting had begun in the autumn of 1938, when Colonel-General Ludwig Beck, Chief of Staff of the German Army, resigned over his objections to Hitler's policy toward Czechoslovakia. Over time he recruited many important figures, including Carl Friedrich Goerdeler (former mayor of Leipzig), Admiral Canaris (head of the German intelligence service), Pastors Niemöller and Bonhoeffer, and Counts Helmut von Moltke and Klaus von Stauffenberg, among others. One of the plotters' first efforts to get in touch with the Allied governments occurred in the spring of 1942, when contact was made in Stockholm with a high British churchman, the bishop of Chichester. These conspirators promised a new German government that would pledge—among other things—repeal of the Nuremberg Laws, withdrawal of the German armies from occupied and invaded countries, abandonment of the Japanese

---

38. Allen W. Dulles, *Germany's Underground* (New York: Macmillan, 1947), xii–xiii.

alliance, and cooperation with the Allies in rebuilding areas damaged by the war. They would also undertake the "strongest possible guarantee against militarism" and would renounce "annexationist designs" on the Soviet Union, where they already controlled a line a thousand miles long inside Soviet territory.

The bishop called upon Foreign Secretary Anthony Eden on June 30, 1942, and handed over a memorandum incorporating the conspirators' plans and promises. Eden told the bishop that his story confirmed reports which the Foreign Office already had, but that he did not wish to "appear to be entering into negotiation independently of Washington and Moscow." He sent a letter to the bishop three weeks later saying that the British government had decided that "no action should be taken" in response to the conspirators.[39]

By the end of 1942, the plot had widened by the inclusion of officers on the Eastern Front. Disaffection within the military had become aggravated by the terrible slaughter taking place in Russia and especially at Stalingrad, by the British victory at El Alamein, and by the American invasion of northwest Africa. But so had the discouragement of the plotters. Hans Gisevius, one of Dulles's principal sources and a renegade Gestapo official, complained to Dulles in January 1943 about the refusal of the Allied powers to give the conspirators any encouragement. "The answer is always given," he said, "that Germany must suffer a military defeat." What the Western powers did not seem to understand, he went on, is that "the Germans themselves are an oppressed people who live in an occupied country."[40]

Discouragement among the plotters was further intensified by the announcement in Casablanca on January 24, 1943, that President Roosevelt and Prime Minister Churchill would demand the "unconditional surrender" of their Axis enemies. The Casablanca conference had been dealing with such pressing matters as the upcoming invasion of France, to say nothing of touchy political negotiations with General de Gaulle. Surrender terms at that point in the war were—or should have been—a comparatively minor matter. According to Churchill's account, there had been some discussion about excluding Italy from the reach of the declaration, but the subject was excluded from the official communiqué on the conference. Churchill was "surprised" when the President spoke of imposing unconditional terms upon all the Axis

---

39. See J. W. Wheeler-Bennett, *The Nemesis of Power: The German Army in Politics, 1918–1945* (New York: Macmillan, 1956), 554–57.
40. Dulles, *Germany's Underground*, 131–32.

powers. Roosevelt later told Harry Hopkins that he and Churchill had not "prepared" for the press conference and left Hopkins with the impression that his remarks were "off-hand."[41] For a declaration of such import to have been issued after so little deliberation strains one's credulity, and it certainly caused enormous problems later.

During 1943 the Nazi propaganda machine made good use of the Casablanca declaration. Goebbels quickly twisted it into a formula for total slavery. The Russians, not bound by the declaration, made use of it to organize a "Free Germany Committee," which carried on a vigorous campaign promising freedoms in Germany and friendship with Russia in return for the elimination of Hitler. This led some of the German conspirators frustrated by the Casablanca statement to be drawn toward an "eastern solution." Dulles meanwhile continued his contacts among the plotters and tried to explain as best he could that the Allies had to be dealt with together and not separately.

In late November 1943, when Roosevelt and Churchill met with Stalin at Teheran to discuss strategy for 1944, Stalin himself raised the question of unconditional surrender with Roosevelt. According to a telegram from Foreign Secretary Eden to the Foreign Office on November 30, "Last night Marshal Stalin spoke to the President about unconditional surrender. Marshal Stalin said he considered this bad tactics vis-a-vis Germany, and his suggestion was that we should work out terms and let them be known generally to the people of Germany."[42]

A month later Roosevelt had no recollection of the conversation with Stalin but authorized the U.S. ambassador in London to take it up with Churchill. He himself made a public announcement on December 24, 1943, stating that the Allies had "no intention to enslave the German people." He went on: "We wish them to have a normal chance to develop in peace as useful and respectable members of the European family. But we most certainly emphasize the word 'respectable,' for we intend to rid them once and for all of Nazism and Prussian militarism and the fantastic and disastrous notion that they constitute the 'master race.'"

In transmitting his statement to the Prime Minister, the President added that he thought it best to rest their understanding of unconditional surrender upon those words. He thought that to list any specific conditions might omit or leave open some other conditions that might assume equal impor-

<hr>

41. Winston Churchill, *Memoirs of the Second World War* (New York: Houghton Mifflin), 670–73, passim.

42. Cited by Francis Loewenheim, Harold Langley, and Manfred Jonas, in their *Roosevelt and Churchill, Their Secret Wartime Correspondence* (New York: E. P. Dutton, 1975), 411.

tance later. Roosevelt then added the following: "We really do not know enough about opinions within Germany itself to go on any fishing expedition there at this time."[43] That statement is puzzling in the light of the Dulles reports from Berne and Eden's acknowledgment a year and a half earlier that the Foreign Office had reports along the lines of the plan presented to him by the bishop of Chichester.

There is no record of Churchill's response to the President, but he made a similar statement about unconditional surrender in the House of Commons on February 22, 1944. It did not mean, he said, "that the German people will be enslaved or destroyed." Nor did it mean, Churchill went on, that the victors are entitled to behave in a barbarous manner. The victors were not "bound to the Germans as a result of a bargain struck," but rather by their "own consciences to civilization."[44]

These declarations seem to have encouraged the conspirators to think that they could get some kind of favorable response from the Western Allies as they refined their organization and plans. Indeed, Allen Dulles during the spring months continued to report to Washington the plans, names, and character of the anti-Hitler conspirators. In April, *two months before the Normandy landings*, he sent the following assessment to Washington:

> The German situation is rapidly approaching a climax. The end of the war in Europe is definitely in sight. In this crisis the resistance group in Germany, headed by Goerdeler and General Beck, state that they are now willing and ready to endeavor to initiate action for the removal of Hitler and the overthrow of the Nazis. This group is the only one in Germany which commands sufficient authority in the Army and among certain active military leaders to make overthrow possible. It is also the only one which has personal access to the Nazi leaders, including Hitler, and sufficient arms available to carry through the action.

Dulles further reported that once the Nazis were overthrown, the German generals on the Western Front "would be prepared to give up resistance and to facilitate the landing of Allied troops" and "to open the way for American-British occupation of Germany while holding the Russians in the East."[45]

43. Ibid., 412.
44. Cited in Churchill, *Memoirs of the Second World War*, 670.
45. Dulles, *Germany's Underground*, 135–36.

Shortly before the Normandy invasion began, Dulles reported to Washington that Gisevius had sent word back to Germany that it would be useless to hope that the British and Americans would break faith with their Russian ally.[46] That word must have been taken to heart by the plotters, since Dulles wrote that he had learned later that the conspirators agreed, just before the attempt on Hitler's life, that they would surrender unconditionally to the Russians as well as to the Americans and the British as soon as Hitler was killed.[47]

Early in July—a month after the landings in Normandy—Dulles received a trusted messenger from the conspirators with details of the plot, which he reported to Washington on July 12 and 13. The attempt was made on July 20. The briefcase holding the bomb was carried into Hitler's staff meeting by Count von Stauffenberg—a leading conspirator and trusted Hitler aide— but was pushed under the conference table by another officer after Stauffenberg had left the room. The heavy table shielded Hitler from the main impact of the explosion; he survived with injuries and burns. Considering his survival "miraculous"—to use his own word—he was more certain than ever of his "great destiny."[48] The army fell into turmoil as the Gestapo sought out real and imagined conspirators. Over the next eight months hundreds of the finest people in Germany were hunted down and executed, or committed suicide.

The obvious question that emerges from the Dulles account is this: Who received his reports and what was done with them? The OSS records have been transferred to the National Archives and at this writing are still being declassified and indexed. But a limited comprehension of the impact in Europe of the Dulles reports can be gleaned from biographical materials which have been published. I have already noted above that at the end of 1943 Roosevelt had stated in a message to Churchill that "we really do not know enough about opinions within Germany itself to go on any fishing expeditions there." That confession might have resulted from one or more of several possibilities—that he had been orally briefed by General Bill Donovan (chief of OSS) but had forgotten, or that he had received written reports that he had not read or taken on board, or that Admiral W. D. Leahy (his Chief of Staff) had received reports but not passed them to the President or told him about them.

What was known or done by President Roosevelt, Admiral Leahy, or General Marshall in Washington was less important than what was known or done by

---

46. Ibid., 136.
47. Ibid., 140.
48. Wheeler-Bennett, *Nemesis of Power*, 644.

General Eisenhower and his staff and by the Allied commanders in France, both before and after the events of July 20, 1944. They were the ones who would have to take the actions necessary to capitalize on the assassination attempt if and when it occurred. But the record available to date is unclear about what was known or decided in Washington or in the military head-quarters in Britain and France.

Dulles in his account demonstrates that the plotters had made "a serious effort" to "get in touch with the Allies," but had received no encouragement from them. He did take note in his book that Clement Attlee had made an innocuous statement in the House of Commons about the necessity for the Germans to take the first steps to rid themselves of a criminal government, but that nothing similar had been said by the U.S. government.[49] David Eisenhower wrote in his account of the attempt to assassinate Hitler that the British War Cabinet had been "informed by the OSS that an attempt on Hitler's life would occur on the fifteenth or twentieth of July."[50] If that is cor-rect, it appears that the British might have heard directly from the OSS London station and that they had given the report more credence than had the author-ities in Washington or Eisenhower and his staff.

When the attempt was made public by the German radio, General Bradley described the news as "astonishing."[51] According to David Eisenhower, how-ever, reactions at SHAEF Headquarters (still in England) were "subdued," and General Eisenhower barely paid the news any attention. It is true that on July 20 the Allied armies were just beginning to break out of the Normandy peninsula; when one of his staff officers showed some excitement about the possibilities opened up, Eisenhower sharply reminded him that there were still eleven German divisions on the line in Normandy.[52] Eisenhower appar-ently had heard nothing of the Dulles reports about the readiness of the German generals in the West to give up resistance or even to surrender uncon-ditionally in the event Hitler was killed. He apparently felt fully engaged with his immediate battle in Normandy, and he was apparently supported in that view by General Strong (his British G-2).

According to David Eisenhower, "Both Strong and Eisenhower were sus-picious of the whole affair. It was conceivable that Hitler had trumped up the incident to gain a pretext to shake up the General Staff."[53] Did not

49. Dulles, *Germany's Underground*, 140–41.
50. Eisenhower, *Eisenhower at War*, 351.
51. Bradley, *A General's Life*, 277.
52. Eisenhower, *Eisenhower at War*, 371.
53. Ibid.

Eisenhower and Strong maintain regular communications contact with the War Cabinet? David Eisenhower has reported that four days after the assassination attempt the Prime Minister had telephoned General Eisenhower and spoken with him at length. The Prime Minister expressed "enthusiasm over the sign of German disarray," and he seemed, wrote David, "to be reproaching Eisenhower for remarks in recent days that indicated insensitivity to the fact that patriotic Germans had acted."[54]

Air Chief Marshal Arthur Tedder, Eisenhower's deputy at SHAEF, reacted quite differently from his chief. When he heard the news, he went at once to Eisenhower, to complain about inaction not by Eisenhower but by his compatriot, General Montgomery. Montgomery was in command of a large-scale air-supported tank-and-infantry movement out of Caen that would have forced either a general German retreat or a disastrous German disintegration. Code-named Goodwood, it began on July 18; two days later, in bad weather, Montgomery called it off. According to General Bradley, Tedder believed that "the news indicated a widespread revolt in the highest echelons of the German army, and that had Montgomery pressed Goodwood to the utmost it might have found a demoralized and confused enemy and overwhelmed him."[55] In Tedder's view Montgomery's failure had lost the opportunity offered by the attempt on Hitler's life. There can be little doubt but that the Goodwood affair was a major factor in what appears to have been SHAEF's failure to grasp the significance of the assassination attempt. Bradley described his view of the situation within the Allied high command at that time as follows:

> Monty's failure in Goodwood had infuriated both British and American airmen who had diverted so much of their air power to make it successful. Ike and Monty maintained a barely civil relationship. Monty knew that Ike was running him down at every opportunity and would relieve him if he had the authority. At the same time, Alan Brooke [Churchill's military adviser] was unstintingly defending Monty. His low opinion of Eisenhower had not changed. In a letter to Monty at this time Alan Brooke wrote that it was "clear that Ike has the very vaguest conception of war." For the moment, coalition warfare seemed not to be working; everybody was at each other's throat.[56]

54. Ibid., 377.
55. See Bradley, A General's Life, 272–77.
56. Ibid., 278.

It seems quite clear, from the above recollections of the persons involved, not only that there was a great deal of tension within the Western high command but also that any diversion from immediate war plans was virtually unthinkable, even if it was true that the German military establishment was in turmoil.

Eisenhower had troubles enough from the American side. At the same time that the Normandy invasion and breakout were under way, U.S. Secretary of the Treasury Henry Morgenthau came to London to discuss terms to be imposed upon the defeated Germans. According to Forrest Pogue, General Marshall's biographer, Morgenthau—who was a close friend of Roosevelt and one of several U.S. political and military figures concerning themselves with surrender terms—was "extremely upset" to discover that "a handbook then being developed at Supreme Headquarters for use by occupation officials in Germany came down on the side of softness." Further, according to Pogue, "Morgenthau returned to Washington to warn Roosevelt against permitting Eisenhower's staff to let down its guard. . . . Roosevelt at once directed the War Department to stop circulation of the handbook."[57]

It would not appear from his own account of the war that Eisenhower needed very much instruction on the principle of treating the German leaders and the German people harshly. In his book *Crusade in Europe* Eisenhower wrote of his German opponents during the fighting in North Africa:

> Daily as [the war] progressed, there grew within me the conviction that as never before in war between many nations the forces that stood for human good and men's rights were this time confronted by a completely evil conspiracy with which no compromise could be tolerated. Because only by the utter destruction of the Axis was a decent world possible, the war became for me a crusade in the traditional sense of that often misused word.[58]

If, indeed, General Eisenhower as early as the North African campaign had come to think of his mission in such moralistic terms, it is not surprising that he was unenthusiastic about the effort of a broad coalition of anti-Hitler Germans to oust the Nazi regime. Such a German effort was simply not consistent with Eisenhower's conviction that the Western Allies were facing "a completely evil conspiracy." One cannot help questioning the moral

57. Forrest Pogue, *George Marshall: Organizer of Victory* (New York: Viking, 1973), 466.
58. Dwight Eisenhower, *Crusade in Europe* (Garden City, N.Y.: Doubleday, 1948), 157.

and military judgment of a commander who persisted in his course—at great human and material costs to both sides—when the moral and military justification for doing so had been challenged by events.

It is especially ironic that the principal German commanders in the West at the time of the assassination attempt were Field Marshals Rommel and von Kluge, who were both associated with—though were latecomers to—the assassination plot. Their opponents on the Western side—Eisenhower, Bradley, Montgomery, Tedder, Strong, and Patton—were regrettably either unaware of the plot or had failed to appreciate its implications. Since the American generals in France were not privy to OSS communications about the plot, they presumably were also unaware that their German opponents were part of it. Thus they simply carried out their daily orders and instructions from their superiors, that is, from Eisenhower at Supreme Headquarters and Montgomery on the Continent. And their superiors appear to have been quite uninterested in the fact that the assassination attempt, though it had failed, had nevertheless fundamentally weakened the unity and greatly diminished the spirit of the German officer corps. H. R. Trevor-Roper, in his *Last Days of Hitler*, describes the situation in Germany at the time in these words: "Two months after the Normandy landings occurred the most spectacular political event [in Germany] since 1934; the Generals' plot of [the] 20th of July 1944, which showed that the leaders of the German Army regarded the war as lost and were at last prepared to break their alliance with the [Nazi] party."[59]

At the time of the Normandy landings, Rundstedt was in overall command in the West, with Rommel in command of the channel-front forces. But when Rundstedt suggested, after his failure to repulse the invasion forces, that Hitler should end the war, Rundstedt was replaced by Kluge (who had served on the Eastern Front and just recovered from injuries received in an auto accident). Then Rommel was nearly killed by a strafing attack on his auto on July 17, three days before the coup attempt. Thus Kluge became the focal point for collusion with the Western commanders if any contact was to be made.

On August 16, the Combined Chiefs of Staff (a combination of high British and American military officers who issued guidance to SHAEF and to the various air and naval forces in the European theater) finally did take cognizance of the dissension in the German forces. They issued an instruction to Eisenhower to accept any local capitulations of forces surrendering through their commanders. Such surrenders were to encompass all forces under the surrendering general, who was to obey "all orders issued by the United Nations [*sic*] commander."[60] But by then it was too late for the Allied commanders in France to react to a possible gesture which had occurred a day earlier, on August 15.

Kluge had taken over command in the West in late June, and his Chief of Staff described the new commander then as "cheerful and confident." But within a few days he became "sober and quiet," apparently because Hitler did not like the changing tone of his reports. After the assassination attempt on July 20, the Gestapo found his name on some of the conspirators' papers. Kluge came under suspicion, but remained in command. His Chief of Staff wrote the following account of what happened a few weeks later, on August 15:

> Shortly after General Patton's break-out from Normandy, while the decisive battle at Avranche was in progress, Field Marshal von Kluge was out of touch with his headquarters for more than twelve hours. The reason given was that he had gone up to the front and been trapped in a heavy artillery bombardment. Hitler suspected that the Field Marshal's purpose in going right up to the front was to get in touch with the Allies to negotiate surrender. The Field Marshal's eventual return did not calm Hitler.[61]

Ronald Lewin has also written an account of what happened that day, but has not disclosed the source of his information. If it was from ultra materials, it appears to have been unusually specific about Hitler's state of mind. Lewin wrote:

> What caused Hitler the greatest anguish was the knowledge that his suspect commander-in-chief in the West was missing. Surely he was negotiating a surrender with the Allies. "The measures taken by the Army Group," the Führer asserted, "cannot be explained except in the light of this assumption." The suspicion was false. On the 15th von Kluge was caught in an air attack while driving to the front from his headquarters at La Roche Guyon; his radio was destroyed, and for half a day he was out of touch. Montgomery, Eisenhower, and their chief intelligence officers have confirmed that no approaches were made to them by von Kluge.[62]

60. Cited in Eisenhower, *Eisenhower at War*, 908 n. 407.
61. Cited by Liddell Hart, *History of the Second World War*, 551.
62. Lewin, *Ultra Goes to War*, 341–42.

I do not believe that any definitive judgment about Kluge's intention can be drawn from Lewin's affirmation that no approaches were made to Eisenhower and the others. How could an approach have been made to commanders who apparently had no knowledge of the plotter's plans and who had no instructions about how to treat with any German commander who might offer to surrender? David Eisenhower's version of the Kluge escapade might be much closer to the truth:

> There is an undocumented account that on August 15 von Kluge drove away from his forward headquarters for twelve hours in an attempt to rendezvous with emissaries from Patton's Third Army. Von Kluge's plan, according to this account, was to discuss the unconditional surrender of his whole front, provided the Allies agreed to move through it quickly into Germany. Allegedly, however, von Kluge's motor caravan was side-tracked by an American fighter-bomber attack, and in order to avoid suspicion, the German commander was forced to return to his headquarters before making contact.[63]

It is possible, of course, that Kluge was vacillating; he had after all come lately to the plot. But he almost certainly knew that he was in trouble with Hitler by August 15. A more likely explanation for his actions is that he hoped Patton and the other commanders would have known of the plot and would seek him out, or at least call off the bombardment, as he approached the front. After that it was too late for Kluge to try again. He was dismissed on August 17, and he committed suicide on his way back to Germany on August 19.

The German military leaders who were left after Hitler's purge fought on under Hitler's relentless pressure. They did succeed in defeating Montgomery's attempt to cross the Rhine at Nijmegen in September, and they did throw a scare into the Western commanders in their pre-Christmas offensive in the Ardennes. But after that their hearts were no longer in it. Liddell Hart has reported that by February 1945, almost all of the German leaders were "empty of hope and will." They persisted in the struggle only because they "feared the punishment which the Allies ominously threatened to deal out after victory."[64] When the Allies finally crossed the Rhine in force in March 1945, they met with only token resistance. German troops were surrendering even to the Allied prisoners of war whom they were guarding.

63. Eisenhower, *Eisenhower at War*, 407.
64. Liddell Hart, *History of the Second World War*, 681.

After the middle of April, even Hitler's most loyal lieutenants began to desert him. Hitler finally killed himself in his Berlin bunker on April 30. On May 4 all German forces in northwest Europe formally surrendered, and three days later a formal surrender of all German forces took place at Rheims in the presence of American, British, French, and Soviet representatives.

Could the war have been ended earlier if the Allied political leadership and Allied military commanders had actively seized the opportunity provided by the anti-Hitler plotting? Even though the assassination attempt failed, should they have altered their plans in order to take advantage of the disarray of the German army during July and August 1944—a disarray occasioned by the confluence of military defeats on the Western Front, the assassination attempt and the subsequent confusion, and the possibilities opened up for further disintegration through rapid Allied military movements and attempts at direct contact with disaffected German generals? In short, were there things which could have been or should have been done during July and August in order to have ended most of the fighting at that time?

No answer can, of course, be definitive. But a number of structural anomalies and states of mind on the Allied side deterred, and perhaps prohibited, such steps from being taken:

1. The public commitment to unconditional surrender as the British-American war aim. This inhibited some German officers from joining the plot, fearing that they would still become victims of Allied retribution for the sins of the Nazis.
2. The Allied command structure, which was not unified on the ground (at the time Montgomery commanded in Europe and Eisenhower advised from Britain), and which took guidance from the Combined Chiefs of Staff in Washington and from occasional summit meetings of heads of government.
3. The absence of any clear functioning lines of communications between the OSS and the military commands on the Western Front. As a consequence, those commands did not seem to have been receiving high-level intelligence from the OSS (i.e., from Dulles in Berne) on a regular working basis.
4. A "tactical intelligence" state of mind which was encouraged by ultra and became over dependent upon it. Thus, the Allied commanders ignored solid intelligence indications of the pre-Christmas Nazi offensive in the Ardennes, and they lost the battle at Nijmegen when they did not have ultra intelligence identifying all the German forces in the area arrayed against them.

5. A commitment to established plans and an unwillingness to be flexible or consider different and perhaps riskier alternatives (such as Patton's proposal to move rapidly into the Reich in August 1944, and various possible responses to the anti-Hitler plotting and to the turmoil in the German army after the assassination attempt).

6. A moral self-righteousness and political naïveté that blinded the Allied political and military leaders to the efforts of moderates in Germany, who had for years and at great personal risk plotted to unseat the Nazi regime.

7. A concept of warfare that had shifted away from the Clausewitzian doctrine (continuation of diplomacy by other means) to one emphasizing societal destruction, punishment, and total "victory" regardless of human cost.

If there is any one clear lesson to be learned from the final months of the European and Pacific wars, it is that a better doctrine for the conduct of war needs to be formulated. It is not good enough simply to think about "winning" or "punishing." If there can be an acceptable doctrine for the conduct of war, it must be to change the policies and/or the leaders of one's enemy and in that process to minimize human casualties and to maximize the potential for change within the enemy nation. To accomplish that, our government must better explore the longer-range implications of its national security policies and must pay more serious attention than it has in the past to trends within enemy societies. The remainder of this book recounts how the postwar intelligence system coped with that responsibility.

How the Cold War Began

The final unconditional surrender of the Axis armies reordered the structure of world power. The United States was now unmistakably at the summit. American forces dominated the Pacific Basin, and they occupied Japan, South Korea, the Philippines, and a number of Pacific islands. U.S. military power had been the predominant force in the reconquest of Western Europe, and the United States was widely regarded as the strongest and most benevolent of the victorious Allies.

There were, of course, situations that the war had either created or left unresolved. There were still two Chinas: the Kuomintang China of Chiang Kai-shek, who had not stopped trying to reassert control over China after having been driven back into southwest China during the fifteen years of Japanese aggression, and the Communist China of Mao Zedong, who was still operating from his stronghold in northwest China. In Eastern Europe, the Soviet Union was clearly the dominant military and political force. Having driven the Germans out of most of the nations there, the Soviets felt free to establish Communist-dominated governments in them. And around the fringes of the principal war arenas in Europe and Asia were colonial peoples who believed the time had come to assert independence from their discredited European masters.

The Axis powers, who had believed that they could and should intervene in the affairs of other countries and bend them to their will because they thought themselves superior, had been destroyed. What would the victors do?

Would the occupiers simply become the new interventionists? Would they subject the occupied nations to a new kind of cultural and political imperialism? Or would they allow the former German, Italian, and Japanese satellites to become free and independent states? And would they allow the old colonies in Africa and Asia to become nations and to forge their own futures?

Those were some of the questions which the new intelligence system was designed to answer. During the first few months after the war ended, many of us who were still in G-2 were asking ourselves, "What do the Russians really want?" I, for one, went back to the history books to take a new look at the Russian Revolution. I carefully watched the postwar world unfold from my privileged position as editor of the daily (Ultra) Diplomatic Summary. It was distressing to see the successful wartime alliance disintegrate into wrangling and distrust.

Early Postwar Judgments on the Soviet Threat

There were those who quickly concluded that the Soviets were bound and determined to move aggressively toward a world dominated by the USSR and to do it by force if necessary. One of them was Brigadier General Carter Clarke, the deputy chief of G-2. He had been a colonel during the war and the regular army officer working with Alfred McCormack in building up G-2's capacity for utilizing ultra intelligence, and it was he who supervised the Diplomatic Summary operation for the War Department after McCormack's departure for the State Department. Thus I had occasional conferences with him, and one day he told me that he had sent to General Lauris Norstad (then Army Chief of Staff) a proposal for a "preventive war" against the USSR.

There were others in the military establishment who thought the same way and who said so publicly. It was their position that we had the bomb and the Soviets did not. We needed to force them by military action to change their leaders and their policies—before they could recover from the war, build up their military establishment, and develop their own atomic weapons capabilities. Otherwise they would chip away at the non-Communist world, build up a new Communist empire, and in the course of time become strong enough to dominate world politics. Their actions in Eastern Europe, the Chinese Communist seizure of large areas of China, and the energetic actions of the Communist parties in Western Europe were all considered proof that the USSR intended world domination.

Very few thoughtful Americans, in or out of government, agreed with the exponents of preventive war, but the question of Soviet intentions had clearly become a matter for intelligence study and analysis. On July 23, 1946, six months after the Central Intelligence Group was created by President Truman, its Office of Research and Evaluation produced its first estimate, ORE 1, entitled "Soviet Foreign and Military Policy." It reflected, I believe, the thinking of most Soviet specialists at the time. Its summary reads as follows:

1. The Soviet Government anticipates an inevitable conflict with the capitalist world. It therefore seeks to increase its relative power by building up its own strength and undermining that of its assumed antagonists.
2. At the same time the Soviet Union needs to avoid such a conflict for an indefinite period. It must therefore avoid provoking a strong reaction by a combination of major powers.
3. In any matter deemed essential to its security, Soviet policy will remain adamant. In other matters it will prove grasping and opportunistic, but flexible in proportion to the degree and nature of the resistance encountered.
4. The Soviet Union will insist on exclusive domination of Europe east of the general line Stettin-Trieste.
5. The Soviet Union will endeavor to extend its predominant influence to include all of Germany and Austria.
6. In the remainder of Europe the Soviet Union will seek to prevent the formation of regional blocs from which it is excluded and to influence national policy through the political activities of local Communists.
7. The Soviet Union desires to include Greece, Turkey, and Iran in its security zone through the establishment of "friendly" governments in those countries. Local factors are favorable toward its designs, but the danger of provoking Great Britain and the United States in combination is a deterrent to overt action.
8. The basic Soviet objective in the Far East is to prevent the use of China, Korea, or Japan as bases of attack on the Soviet Far East by gaining in each of those countries an influence at least equal to that of the United States.
9. The basic Soviet military policy is to maintain armed forces capable of assuring its security and supporting its foreign policy against any possible hostile combination. On the completion of planned demobilization these forces will still number 4,500,000 men.
10. For the time being the Soviets will continue to rely primarily on large masses of ground troops. They have been impressed by Anglo-American strategic air power however, and will seek to develop fighter defense and long-range bomber forces.
11. The Soviets will make a serious effort to develop as quickly as possible such special weapons as guided missiles and the atomic bomb.

The text of the estimate contains a section entitled "The Basis of Soviet Foreign Policy," a carefully crafted discussion of the role of Communist doctrine in the formulation of Soviet foreign policy. It notes in particular the belief in the inevitability of a Communist world arising from the "self-destructive tendencies of capitalism," which it is the Communists' responsibility to "accelerate." Until the inevitable collapse of capitalism occurs, the USSR is imperiled by the encircling ring of antagonistic capitalist states. The Soviet Union must therefore build up the power of the Soviet state and at the same time seize every opportunity to expand the "area of direct and indirect Soviet control" in order to provide "additional" protection to the vital areas of the Soviet Union. While the general outline of Soviet policy is based upon the conviction of a "latent and inevitable conflict" with the capitalist world, "it is manifestly in the Soviet interest to avoid an overt test of strength at least until the Soviet Union has become more powerful than any possible combination of opponents." It was therefore necessary for the Soviet Union to "seek to avoid a major open conflict for an indefinite period."

The writers of the estimate mentioned the Soviet withdrawal from Iran earlier in 1946 as a case in which the Soviets had yielded to strong diplomatic pressure from their wartime allies. They did not mention certain other events which had also demonstrated a Soviet desire to avoid antagonizing the Western powers, for example, Soviet troop withdrawals from northern Norway, the Danish island of Bornholm off the Polish coast, and the Republic of Czechoslovakia. The estimators thought the Soviets felt that interference in Czechoslovakia was unnecessary, since the Communists and related parties constituted a majority, and the non-Communist leaders were "friendly" to the USSR. The same judgment applied to Finland, where the leaders had become convinced that a "friendly" attitude toward the USSR was essential to Finland's national survival.

There was nothing in ORE 1 to suggest that the estimators regarded the USSR as preparing to initiate aggressive warfare against the capitalist states. On the contrary, the Soviets believed that they were the ones in peril and that they needed to acquire and maintain forces capable of ensuring Soviet security against any possible combination of foreign powers.

Joseph Stalin, if he had read the estimate, would have probably regarded it as essentially correct. Anatoly Dobrynin (who became Soviet ambassador to the United States fifteen years later and served throughout the remaining twenty-five years of the Cold War) wrote this about Stalin's views in his own recent autobiography:

Stalin saw U.S. plans and actions as preparations for an all-out war of aggression against the Soviet Union. As his successor Nikita Khrushchev later recalled, the Soviet leadership then believed that the United States, with its superiority in nuclear weapons, would ultimately go to war with the Soviet Union. Soviet diplomacy was heavily influenced by this Stalinist dogma about the inevitability of war, and this of course affected our relations with the United States at that time. But the dogma itself was also strengthened by the permanent post-war hostility of the United States and its own intransigence toward the Soviet Union.[1]

I myself did not read the estimate, or even learn of its existence at the time. (I was still in G-2 editing the Diplomatic Summary.) ORE 1 was classified Top Secret, and I do not know how widely it was distributed within the government. Implementation of the central intelligence concept was still in its infancy in July 1946, and intelligence reporting was primarily regarded as a daily or weekly affair rather than the preparation of longer-term analyses. In any event, ORE 1 did not bear the imprimatur of a politically powerful Director of Central Intelligence (DCI), as was the case for the estimates produced after 1950.

ORE 1 was nevertheless a good pioneering estimate on the USSR, and in the light of the history of the subsequent decades it has proven remarkably prescient. It laid out in calm language the principal factors underlying contemporary Soviet behavior; it accurately described their view of the world around them; it correctly identified what were to become the main geographic areas of major-power contention. It characterized the Soviet leaders as desiring a Communist world but in no hurry to achieve it or to get into a war with the United States. It did not say that the Soviets would not misbehave or miscalculate. It did not say that they would not propagandize against the United States or that they would not try to subvert Western nations. It did not sound the tocsin so much as try to tell readers how to think about the USSR.

Rethinking Soviet Intentions

It did not take long after the publication of ORE 1 for the critics of the USSR to begin to challenge the estimate's judgments. Only a month later, on August

1. Anatoly Dobrynin, *In Confidence* (New York: Random House, 1995), 26.

24, 1946, Hoyt Vandenberg (who had been sworn in as DCI on June 10) sent a Top Secret memorandum to President Truman reporting that "during the past two weeks there has been a series of developments which suggest that some consideration should be given to the possibility of near-term Soviet military action."

What had happened was a spate of Soviet propaganda attacks on "reactionary monopolistic cliques" and "military adventurers" who were directing U.S. policy toward "world domination" and "atomic diplomacy." Marshal Tito of Yugoslavia, still a member of the Soviet bloc, had spoken about a worldwide struggle against reactionaries, and the Soviets had reopened the Straits issue with a diplomatic note to Ankara demanding joint control of the Bosporus and the Hellespont by the Black Sea powers. These were treated in the memorandum as suggesting the possibility of aggressive Soviet intentions. Vandenberg went on to state, however, that there were no indications of any unusual troop movements or concentrations, no information of any change in the Soviet demobilization program, no indication of any warning to Soviet shipping, and no reason from the purely economic point of view to alter the previous estimate that the Soviets had a "vital need for a long period of peace before embarking upon a major war." In short, the memorandum engaged in a back-and-forth review of considerations bearing upon the question of Soviet military aggression.

In this back-and-forth argumentation, the memorandum included the incredible assessment that Soviet forces in Europe and northern Asia could in a sudden offensive "secure those areas without much difficulty." It also brought into the argument for near-term military action the bizarre suggestion that a "combination of militaristic marshals and ideologists might establish ascendancy over Stalin and the Politburo and decide upon a war of conquest." In its contest between arousing broad fears and calming immediate concerns, the memorandum finally concluded that "the recent disturbing developments" could be interpreted as "constituting no more than an intensive war of nerves," but that, nevertheless, "the possibility of direct Soviet military action or irresponsible action by Soviet satellites cannot be disregarded."

This episode in effect was the opening volley in what became a decades-long contest within the intelligence and the national-security-policy communities. One side characteristically advanced worst-case judgments that would require increased U.S. armament and strengthened military readiness, while the other side characteristically avoided making sweeping judgments about Soviet intentions and advocated careful and continuing analysis of Soviet policies and behavior.

After the Vandenberg memorandum had surfaced, analysts in the CIG Office of Research and Evaluation had little option but to take account of what had been regarded as a worsening of U.S.-Soviet relations. The Soviet charge of "atomic diplomacy," highlighted in the memorandum, was almost certainly a response to the first postwar atomic tests at the Bikini Atoll, which had taken place in June. While those tests were going on, Secretary of State Byrnes was discussing the future of Germany with Soviet Foreign Minister Vyacheslav Molotov in Paris. In an apparent response to this coincidence, the Moscow press published a photograph of a test, with its mushroom cloud, and accused the United States of seeking "world domination."

The tests had been decided upon by the Pentagon early in 1946 and had been discussed at a Cabinet meeting early in March. Byrnes took a dim view of the tests; he thought that they were "ill-advised" and would have a detrimental effect upon relations with the USSR. As a result of the discussion in the Cabinet, the tests were not canceled but postponed until summer—when they coincided with the Byrnes-Molotov talks.[2] Those talks did not seem to be going anywhere anyhow, but the big show the Pentagon staged before the whole world looked very much as if the U.S. military were trying to send the Soviets a message. Along with mutterings of "preventive war" by high military officials, the tests seem to have compounded Soviet fears of a Western attack. The Soviet propaganda blast should not in those circumstances have surprised the drafters of the Vandenberg memorandum.

The Soviet ambassador in Washington during 1946, Nikolai Novikov, was one of those in the Soviet Foreign Ministry who identified U.S. policy as the basic cause of the falling-out between Moscow and Washington during his tenure. Gar Alperovitz and Kai Bird have reported, in a recent article in *Foreign Policy*, that newly released documents on Novikov's writings had "painted a deeply disturbing picture of American intentions toward the Soviet Union in 1946." Novikov, they wrote, had cited in particular the U.S. "establishment of a system of air and naval bases stretching far beyond the boundaries of the United States" and the "creation of ever newer types of weapons."[3]

Stalin apparently did not share Novikov's views. He spoke positively in public during 1946 about the possibilities of future Anglo-Soviet-American cooperation. Also during 1946, Stalin encouraged the Western Communist

2. McCullough, *Truman*, 491.
3. See Gar Alperovitz and Kai Bird, "The Centrality of the Bomb," *Foreign Policy*, no. 94 (Spring 1994). See also "A Diplomat Reports," a review of the Novikov memoirs by Scott Parrish in the *Bulletin of the Cold War International History Project* (Woodrow Wilson Center for Scholars), no. 1 (Spring 1992): 16.

parties to join in coalitions with the bourgeois parties and continued to allow coalitions led by non-Communists to continue to govern Hungary and Czechoslovakia.[4] Stalin also withdrew Soviet troops from Manchuria in May 1946 and later that year warned Maurice Thorez, leader of the French Communist Party, not to attempt to seize power in France by force.[5] It was not until late in 1946 that Bulgaria and Rumania swung clearly into the Communist column; Poland followed suit in January 1947; Hungary followed in May 1947, and the Cominform was formally established in October.

It would appear that at least some of the writers of the Vandenberg memorandum in August 1946 were looking very hard for signs of Soviet aggressiveness without looking very hard for any counterindications in Soviet behavior. The released document does not indicate who the drafters were, whether they were CIG analysts or employees of one of the other executive departments, or whether there was any coordination within the intelligence community. In any event, it was clearly incumbent upon the CIG Office of Reports and Estimates to undertake a reexamination of the July estimate and to study all the evidence. On January 6, 1947, it published a revised estimate, ORE 1/1, "Revised Soviet Tactics in International Affairs."

This new estimate did not specifically refer to the Vandenberg memorandum, though it was clearly an answer to it. By implication it recognized that the Soviets knew that they had been misbehaving and had therefore begun to revise their stance toward the outside world. The first sentence of the revised estimate reads, "The USSR has apparently decided that for the time being more subtle tactics should be employed in implementing its basic foreign and military policy," as described in ORE 1. The new Soviet policy was marked by, inter alia, concessions on the Trieste issue, acceptance of the principle of free navigation on the Danube, agreement in principle to the international inspection of armaments, reductions in Soviet occupation forces, and agreement to have the deputy foreign ministers meet to draw up a draft treaty for Austria and Germany.

As to the future, the revised estimate stated the following: "Soviet leaders must have decided upon a temporary breathing space for the purpose of economic and ideological rehabilitation at home and the consolidation of positions abroad. We believe, however, that the Kremlin has not abandoned any of the long-range objectives described in ORE 1, but these objectives will be

4. Parrish, "A Diplomat Reports," 21.
5. Alperovitz and Bird, "Centrality of the Bomb," 12.

pursued where expedient by methods more subtle than those of recent months."
This meant, the estimate concluded, that the "USSR did not intend and was
not in a position to engage in immediate military conquests."

The authors of the estimate did not leave it there, however; they added
finally that the "new tactics of compromise and conciliation have been adopted
merely as a matter of expediency." The Kremlin's tactics were based upon
"the interplay of two apparently conflicting courses, international collaboration and unilateral aggression, and on its ability suddenly to shift from one
to another." This strategy was designed "to prevent the development [in the
West] of any long-range counter-strategy."

Thus as the year 1947 began, the intelligence community was still trying
to have it both ways: it was taking a calmer attitude toward Soviet policies,
but it was also warning that the USSR was a future military aggressor. The
Pearl Harbor syndrome was still alive and well. Those intelligence services
who had failed to provide warning of Japanese enmity and of the surprise
attacks of December 7 did not want to be caught napping again.

A Counterstrategy in the Making

Not long after the publication of ORE 1/1, the situation in Europe began
to worsen. In response, the U.S. government began to inch toward a counter-
strategy, but it was not one prompted by intelligence estimates. It developed instead from incremental changes in the political atmosphere of the
country, the Congress, and the foreign affairs bureaucracy. Winston
Churchill had earlier set the stage for a new strategy when he spoke at
Westminster College in Fulton, Missouri, in March 1946, with President
Truman in the audience. Out of power in London and thus possessing a
license to speak a bit carelessly about political geography, Churchill ignored
Czechoslovakia and Austria and created a mythological "Iron Curtain" that
had "descended across Europe" from Stettin on the Baltic to Trieste on the
Adriatic.

Also setting the intellectual and psychological stage in the United States
were the various writings and utterances of George Kennan. At about the
time Churchill was preaching to President Truman, Kennan sent a ser-
mon to the State Department from his post in Moscow advising the State
Department and the U.S. government on how to treat with the Soviet government. It contained such commandments as "Don't act chummy. . . .
Don't make fatuous gestures of good will. . . . Do not encourage high-level
exchanges with the Russians unless the initiative comes at least 50 percent

from their side. . . . Do not be afraid of unpleasantness and public airing of differences."[6]

That telegram got rather wide reading in Washington, and it resulted in his being recalled to Washington and assigned to the faculty of the National War College. His views, amplified and extended in talks at various forums, tended to encourage a hysterical anti-Communism which was already gaining currency because of the actions and pronouncements of certain congressional leaders and committees. That led Kennan to respond by telling one university audience that our nation needed "greater coolness, greater sophistication, greater maturity and self-confidence in our approach to this whole problem of Russia and Communism."[7] On another occasion, he told a similar audience that the Soviets did not wish to have a showdown with the United States, that we still had the preponderance of world opinion with us, and that with the edge that gave us we should be able, "if our policies are wise and non-provocative, to *contain them both militarily and politically, for a long time*" (emphasis added).[8]

So, by the beginning of 1947 the country had become increasingly divided over the Soviet question. Many editorialists and politicians had complained about the Churchill speech as poisoning the atmosphere of U.S.-Soviet relations. On the other hand, there were many who seized upon the Kennan telegram and its advocacy of firmness toward the Soviets as the proper approach for the administration to follow. The November 1946 congressional elections had resulted in a Republican Congress which had Richard Nixon and Joseph McCarthy among its new members. With anti-Communism on the rise and his own political position slipping, President Truman on January 7, 1947, accepted Jimmy Byrnes's resignation and appointed General George Marshall as Secretary of State. The appointment pleased both the Republican leadership and the country and created an improved atmosphere in Washington.

But in Europe uncertainty and disquiet were increasing. The second postwar winter was one of the worst on record. Hardships from the weather were compounded by economic near-collapse almost everywhere. The first major problem faced by Secretary Marshall and President Truman in 1947 was a crisis in Greece. What had happened there was a significant worsening of the domestic turmoil that had followed upon the departure of the Nazis in the spring of 1945. While World War II was still in progress, Communist and

---

6. George F. Kennan, *Memoirs, 1925–1950* (Boston: Little, Brown, 1967), 291–92.
7. Ibid., 301.
8. Ibid., 304.

non-Communist guerrillas fought against the Germans and to some extent against each other. When the Germans left, the Communists tried to seize Athens, but after bitter fighting signed a truce under British prodding. A rightist government installed after elections in March 1946 could not cope with both a miserable economy and continuing Communist guerrilla activities. Finally in February 1947 the British, who had been holding the Greek government and economy together, informed the State Department in Washington that it could no longer carry the burden.

Secretary Marshall and his deputy, Dean Acheson, urged the President to act immediately. On February 27, the President summoned his advisers and the congressional leaders to his office for a decision-making session. According to Truman's biographer, David McCullough, Marshall spoke "in measured tones," telling the others that the Greek crisis was "the first crisis of a series which might extend Soviet domination to Europe, the Middle East, and Asia." Acheson, by his own account, spoke more forcefully than Marshall and was supported by Senator Martin Vandenberg (chairman of the Senate Foreign Relations committee and uncle of the DCI). The latter conveyed the "clear implication" that aid to Greece and Turkey could be had "only if Truman shocked Congress into action."[9] The upshot was that the President went before a joint session of Congress on March 12, 1947, to ask its approval for a plan to provide economic and military assistance to Greece and Turkey. It was indeed a momentous speech, and it set the United States upon a new course in its postwar policy.

Still at the War College, Kennan was not a participant in the formulation of the "Truman Doctrine" or in the drafting of the program itself. The Greek crisis and Truman's response were nevertheless catalytic events in Kennan's thinking about Soviet Communism and the evolving Soviet role in the postwar world. He was called to the State Department and shown a copy of the final draft of the Truman speech before it was sent to the White House. The draft had been prepared largely by the State-War-Navy Coordinating Committee, an interdepartmental group set up to consider possible U.S. assistance to Greece. Kennan was "unhappy" at what he saw, and his reactions to the speech are spelled out at some length in his memoirs. What was "supposed to be primarily a political and economic program for Greece" had attached to it an aid program for Turkey. He thought that the problems of Turkey did not provide a "rationale" for a special aid program, and he suspected that this was a Pentagon effort to exploit a favorable opportunity "to infiltrate" a military

9. McCullough, *Truman*, 541–42.

aid program for Turkey into what was a needed program for Greece. He thought "the Soviet threat should be recognized for what it was—primarily a political one and not a threat of military attack."[10]

Kennan did support the idea of aid to Greece because it was needed to "stiffen the backs" of the non-Communists; otherwise the Communists would soon succeed in seizing power. If that happened, the consequences would be "most unfortunate," with repercussions in neighboring areas. He was not worried about the Muslim world because he did not believe the Russians could come to dominate it. A Communist success in Greece, however, could create an impression in Western Europe that the spread of Communism was inevitable, and that in itself would weaken the effort to prevent its spread.

What Kennan considered exceptionable, however, was the sweeping language of the President's message. "I believe," Truman had said, "it must be the policy of the United States to support free peoples who are resisting subjugation by armed minorities or outside pressures." It was that passage to which Kennan took strong exception because it placed the aid to Greece in a "framework of a universal policy rather than that of a specific decision addressed to a specific set of circumstances."[11] The interpretation given to the President's message—it became a doctrine in the same genre as President Monroe's famous declaration 125 years earlier—led America down a path where any nation in trouble could try to demonstrate the existence of a Communist threat and thus qualify for American aid.

What Kennan had run up against on the Greek-Turkish aid question was not unlike that which the CIG estimators had encountered with the War and Navy departments when formulating ORE 1 and ORE 1/1, namely, the Pentagon's penchant for interpreting all Soviet actions and policies as directed toward an eventual war of conquest against the West. Civilian intelligence officers in the CIG/CIA and the State Department, on the other hand, were disposed to make less sweeping judgments about Soviet intentions and to judge Soviet actions as driven more by the availability of targets and a pathological fear of the West than by a fixed Soviet long-term strategy. Unfortunately, this dichotomous approach continued to trouble the intelligence community throughout the next forty years of intelligence estimating.

---

10. Kennan, *Memoirs, 1925–1950*, 315–17.
11. Ibid., 318–20.

Origins of Containment

The Greek-Turkish aid program keynoted the counterstrategy which developed from 1947 through 1949. While the President had proclaimed the program as a doctrine applicable everywhere without time limit, in actual practice it was regarded during the late 1940s as applicable only to Europe and as essentially economic in character. It had become clear that the nations of southern and western Europe, and Germany in particular, had become a political battleground between the Soviet Union and the United States. The economic situation looked hopeless to many citizens of Europe, and the Soviet leaders—true to their doctrine of the historical inevitability of Communism—believed it their role, as instruments of history, to advance the spread of Communism in ways least threatening to the USSR as the "socialist homeland." That is what explains Stalin's policies in 1946, when he advocated Communist participation in coalition governments led by non-Communists and advised local Communists—except in Greece—to shun the use of force to attain power. It seemed to U.S. leaders in the State Department and White House, therefore, that the United States needed to shore up the economies of western and southern Europe in order to provide greater hope to populations who were hungry, unemployed, and tired of military and civil strife. The answer was the Marshall Plan.

Secretary Marshall's speech at the Harvard commencement of June 1947 was followed by legislation that stipulated that U.S. aid would be in the form of grants and that enjoined the Europeans to move toward economic integration, both as a step toward recovery and as a prerequisite for the granting of aid. Soon after the Marshall speech, the CIA released its first intelligence estimate after its formal creation under the National Security Act. It was CIA 1, dated September 26, 1947, and entitled "Review of the World Situation as It Relates to the Security of the United States." Its conclusions were the same as those which underlay the Marshall proposal:

1. Among foreign powers, only the USSR is capable of threatening the security of the United States.
2. The USSR is presently incapable of military aggression outside of Europe and Asia, but is capable of overrunning most of continental Europe, the Near East, northern China, and Korea.
3. The USSR is unlikely to resort to open military aggression in present circumstances. Its policy is to avoid war, to build up its war potential,

and to extend its influence and control by political, economic, and psychological warfare against the United States.

4. The greatest danger to the security of the United States is the possibility of economic collapse in Western Europe and the consequent accession to power of Communist elements.

5. Stabilization and recovery in Europe and Asia would tend to redress the balance of power and thereby restrain the USSR.

The estimate added a listing of the priority of world areas from the point of view of restraining the USSR. It placed Western Europe first, thus supporting the basic assumption underlying the Marshall Plan.

I do not know whether the estimate played any significant role in subsequent development of the Plan. Probably it did not. At the time of publication, the CIA had just gained statutory status and had as its new director a military officer, Admiral Roscoe Hillenkoetter, with no political clout and little experience at the policymaking level. It would take another three years before its estimates received high-level recognition or exercised significant influence upon foreign and military policy.

But during the summer of 1947 there occurred another event which had a profound effect upon national strategy. This was the "X-Article," which was published in June by *Foreign Affairs* magazine, the author of which was soon identified as George Kennan. The article soon set off, as Kennan later wrote, a "veritable whirlpool of publicity." He wrote further: "The term 'containment' was picked up and elevated, by common agreement of the press, to the status of a 'doctrine,' which was then identified with the foreign policy of the administration. In this way there was established—before our eyes, so to speak—one of those indestructible myths that are the bane of the historian."[12]

In his memoirs, Kennan has written that the article had serious deficiencies, which he later came to recognize, and that probably the "most serious" of them was his "failure to make clear" that when he mentioned "containment of Soviet power" it was "not the containment by military means of a military threat, but the political containment of a political threat."[13] He explained his views at considerable length in those memoirs, which were written some twenty years later, and I think it would be helpful to quote a fairly long passage without any interpolations on my part:

12. Ibid., 356.
13. Ibid., 358.

In writing the X-Article, I had in mind a long series of what seemed to be concessions that we had made, during the course of the war and just after it, to Russian expansionist tendencies—concessions made in the hope and belief that they would promote collaboration between our government and the Soviet government in the postwar period. I had also in mind the fact that many people, seeing that these concessions had been unsuccessful and that we had been unable to agree with the Soviet leaders on the postwar order of Europe and Asia, were falling into despair and jumping to the panicky conclusion that this spelled the inevitability of an eventual war between the Soviet Union and the United States.

It was this last conclusion that I was attempting, in the X-Article, to dispute. I thought I knew as much as anyone in the United States about the ugliness of the problem that Stalin's Russia presented to us. I had no need to accept instruction on this point from anybody. But I saw no necessity of a Soviet-American war, nor anything to be gained by one, then or at any time. There was, I thought, another way of handling this problem—a way that offered reasonable prospects of success, at least in the sense of avoiding a new world disaster and leaving the Western community of nations no worse off than it then was. This was simply to cease at that point making fatuous unilateral concessions to the Kremlin, to do what we could to inspire and support resistance elsewhere to its efforts to expand the area of its dominant political influence, and to wait for the internal weaknesses of Soviet power, combined with frustration in the external field, to moderate Soviet ambitions and behavior. The Soviet leaders, formidable as they were, were not supermen. Like all leaders of great countries, they had their internal contradictions and dilemmas to deal with. Stand up to them, I urged, manfully but not aggressively, and give the hand of time a chance to work.[14]

Mr. Kennan did in fact forecast with a great deal of accuracy what did happen in the USSR before and during the Gorbachev period. The "hand of time" did its work, and its impact upon Soviet society and policies were reported in national intelligence estimates beginning as early as 1958 (see Chapter 5. But the X-Article was also ambiguous, as Kennan himself later admitted, in its implications for the role of military force in the U.S.-Soviet

14. Ibid., 364.

relationship. His reference to containing the Soviets with "the adroit and vigilant application of counterforce at a series of constantly shifting geographical and political points"[15] was hardly a clarion call for Western rearmament, but neither was it a clear denial that the USSR's application of force was a preferred or even acceptable avenue for the construction of a Communist political bloc. Nevertheless, the Pentagon found the word "containment" highly compatible with what it considered its new "defense" mission. The U.S. military establishment and its political allies were easily persuaded to use the new "containment" doctrine to advocate inclusion within the U.S. defense perimeter any nation or area in the world where a conservative government was weak or where Communist or even Socialist leaders were striving for political power.

By persuading the White House to identify Turkey as a threatened area, even when no home-grown Communist threat existed, the Pentagon laid the groundwork for casting "containment" in a military mold and for the militarization of aid programs generally. The question of how great and what kind of military threat was actually posed by the USSR troubled national estimating from its beginning, as the passages cited above from ORE 1, ORE 1/1, and CIA 1 confirm. And as we shall observe as we proceed through this analysis, the problem not only was troublesome but also has had an enormous impact upon U.S. diplomacy and defense budgets.

Containment Through Political Action

By stiffening the backbones of non-Communist political leaders in the West and stimulating their economies, the Marshall Plan set Europe moving in a new direction. It also produced pessimism in the East. While the Soviets rejected participation in the Plan on the ground that its terms constituted an interference with national sovereignty, the overriding reason almost certainly was a recognition that it would lead to a setback in Soviet hopes for the early emergence of "friendly" governments in the West. Moreover, the Soviet leaders must also have been concerned lest participation in a scheme involving the market economies of the West would stimulate challenges to the underlying economic assumptions of the Soviet system itself.

U.S. policymakers did not, however, place their sole reliance upon improving economic conditions in southern and western Europe. They also established and implemented political and psychological action programs designed

15. Ibid., 359.

to counteract Soviet propaganda and to undermine the activities of the Soviet Union's political allies in the West. The CIA became the principal arm of the government for carrying out the covert aspects of those programs. In December 1947, the National Security Council issued a directive to the DCI specifically authorizing him to undertake "covert psychological operations." By that date, some of the structure needed to perform such operations had already been manned. The CIA had set up an Office of Special Operations (OSO) in July 1946 to carry on espionage and counterespionage operations. OSS field personnel, who had been transferred to War Department control at the end of World War II, were transferred to the OSO in October 1946, and the remaining headquarters personnel were brought into the OSO in April 1947.

The NSC directive was issued two months after the Communist Information Bureau (Cominform) held its first meeting in October 1947. This successor to the Communist International (Comintern) was ostensibly created as a Communist consultative group rather than as a conspiratorial arm of the Soviet government. But earlier in the year the Soviets had tightened Communist control over the Polish and Hungarian governments, so that the Cominform clearly appeared to be, not a debating society fostering the values of Communism, but rather a propaganda cover for Soviet actions designed to dominate the political and economic life of the Eastern European nations. That Soviet objective became even more evident when, in June 1948, Yugoslavia (the only nation in Eastern Europe which had established a Communist regime without the benefit of Soviet assistance) was thrown out of the Cominform for its resistance to the Stalinization of its party and governmental structure.

By the end of 1948, therefore, Europe had become a playing field contested by the propaganda and covert action organizations of East and West. CIA personnel and CIA money went to work to shore up the democratic regimes of France and Italy, to stabilize the anti-Communist government of Greece, and to promote the emergence of democratic parties in West Germany. The new Office of Policy Coordination proceeded to establish posts and to recruit assets around the world. A big expansion of personnel took place, a lot of enthusiasm was generated, and a good bit of money was spent. The existence of U.S. covert operations became widely known abroad, and CIA activities—real or imagined—often stimulated political gossip and press stories portraying the Agency in a bad light.

Unfavorable reporting finally prompted Walter Bedell Smith, who had been appointed to the directorship of the CIA in October 1950, to remind his senior staff directors in October two years later that the Agency's "primary mission" was "intelligence" and that he would approve "nothing which militated against accomplishing" that objective. According to the minutes of the staff conference, General Smith blamed "improperly trained or inferior personnel" for mistakes which had been made, and he directed the operations chiefs to limit the number of operations to what they "could do well" and not to attempt "to cover a broad field with poor performance."

The operations directorate went on for another forty years and no doubt carried out operations that contributed to U.S. national interests. Some of its operations, however, were clearly improper, some were poorly designed and executed, and some were assigned to the Agency by the White House for domestic political reasons. Evaluating the CIA's operational performance is not a part of the task I have assigned myself here. I leave that to professional historians. But some CIA operations have played an important role in the Cold War, and where they have done so I will refer to them.

The Road to NATO

The approach to U.S.-Soviet relations outlined by George Kennan, the proposals of Secretary Marshall for a European recovery program, and initiation of covert-action activities by the CIA were all part of a broad political strategy evolved during 1946 and 1947 to contain Soviet control within those areas which it had occupied during the final days of the war. During most of that time the Soviet leaders evidently believed they had a good chance of spreading their brand of Communism into southern and western Europe. But toward the end of the period, U.S. aid to Greece, the prospect for economic recovery in western Europe, and signs of growing anti-Communism in the United States and Britain led the Soviet leaders to a reassessment, the results of which became apparent during late 1947 and the first half of 1948.

One of the first signs of that reassessment was a harsh attack upon U.S. policy delivered by Soviet Foreign Minister Andrei Vishinsky at the UN General Assembly on September 18, 1947. He said, among other things: "A number of newspapers and magazines, mostly American, cry every day and in every way about a new war, systematically promoting this baneful psychological coaxing of public opinion of their countries. The warmongers indulge in propaganda under a smokescreen of cries about strengthening of national defense and the necessity to fight against a war danger, which allegedly comes from other countries."[16]

16. "Vishinsky's Attack on U.S. Policy," in Bernstein and Matusow, *Truman Administration*, 261.

Vishinsky went on to assert that the Soviet Union was "not threatening in any way an attack on any country." He also asserted that the USSR was devoting all its energy to the rehabilitation of war-damaged areas and to the development of its national economy. His reference to "warmongers" was no doubt triggered by the advocacy of a "preventive war" against the USSR by some high U.S. military officers. But he also seized the occasion to restate what was basic Soviet policy, namely, to avoid war and to build up the Soviet economy. The Vishinsky speech did betray two major concerns which the Soviets were almost certainly feeling in the autumn of 1947. Both had to do with Germany: the first was the prospect of economic recovery in Western Europe and a consequent reduced opportunity for revolutionary change; the second was the longer-term fear that Germany could become a jumping-off point for the Western Allies to involve the USSR in a new war before it could improve its own military capabilities and develop its own nuclear weaponry.

Shortly thereafter George Kennan, from his vantage point as chief of the State Department's Policy Planning Staff, took a new and careful look at the situation in Europe. He sent a memorandum to Secretary Marshall saying that he thought the Communist advance had been halted in the south and the west and that the Soviets had responded by moving to consolidate their position in Eastern Europe. He thought further that the Soviets "would soon find themselves obliged to clamp down entirely on Czechoslovakia" because Czechoslovakia "could too easily become a path of entry for truly democratic forces into Eastern Europe generally."[17] At a Cabinet meeting about the same time, Marshall predicted that because of U.S. actions in Germany, "the Soviets would have 'to clamp down completely' on Czechoslovakia and, when they did, it would be a 'purely defensive move.'"[18]

The Czech crisis erupted three months later, in late February 1948. The Czech Communist Party was the strongest in the country, and it could easily call out large numbers of demonstrators to demand a change of government. Suppression was out of the question, partly because of the large number of demonstrators and partly because the presence of Soviet military forces to the north and east posed the possibility of Soviet intervention in the event of domestic blood-letting. The government simply gave up and turned power over to the Communist leadership. Two weeks later, when the pro-Western Foreign Minister Jan Masaryk fell—or was pushed—out of a window to his death, the U.S. government, press, and public were shocked.

17. Kennan, *Memoirs, 1925–1950*, 378.
18. Cited by Alperovitz and Bird, "Centrality of the Bomb," 10.

The government at least should not have been, given Marshall's warning three months earlier.

Shortly after the Czech coup, on March 5, General Lucius Clay, the American military governor in Berlin, sent a telegram to Washington which exacerbated the alarm occasioned by the coup. It said:

> For many months, based on logical analysis, I have felt and held that war was unlikely for at least ten years. Within the last few weeks, I have felt a subtle change in Soviet attitude which I cannot define but which now gives me a feeling that it may come with dramatic suddenness. I cannot support this change in my own thinking with any data or outward evidence in relationships other than to describe it as a new tenseness in every Soviet individual with whom we have official relations. I am unable to submit any official report in the absence of supporting data but my feeling is real. You may advise the Chief of Staff of this for whatever it may be worth to you if you feel it advisable.[19]

The Clay telegram was addressed "Eyes Only" to the chief of Army intelligence, but he quickly passed it on to his new boss as Chief of Staff, General Omar Bradley. Bradley has written in his own memoirs that when he saw Clay's "lugubrious assessment" he was "lifted right out of [his] chair."[20] Kennan reported in his memoirs that the combination of the Czech coup with the Clay telegram had caused "a real war scare" in Washington, where "the military and the intelligence fraternity" had "overreacted in the most deplorable way."[21] Indeed the Joint Chiefs of Staff reacted a week later by deciding to request a supplemental military appropriation to bring the strength of the armed force "up to the point where it more nearly met the realities of the world situation" and by recommending "immediate reenactment of the draft law."[22]

General Clay had not seen, nor had any of the intelligence units operating out of Berlin, any of the sort of preparations in the surrounding Soviet occupation zone which one would expect to see in the event of a planned military operation. What he had probably noticed was disgruntlement among

19. From Bernstein and Matusow, *Truman Administration*, 269.
20. Bradley, *A General's Life*, 477.
21. Kennan, *Memoirs, 1925–1950*, 400.
22. *The Forrestal Diaries*, ed. Walter Millis (New York: Viking, 1951), 393.

Soviet personnel who were aware of the reassessment of Soviet policy under way and also aware of the American nervousness over the coup in Czechoslovakia. In fact, it was only a short time afterward when the Soviets instituted limited restrictions upon the Western position in Berlin which curtailed certain Western propaganda and intelligence activities. A full blockade came later, on June 24, three weeks after the Western occupation authorities announced their plans to establish political institutions in West Germany.

Kennan has written that the two major events of the spring of 1948 in Europe, the coup in Czechoslovakia and the attempt to force the West to give up Berlin were "defensive reactions" to the initial success of the Marshall Plan and to the preparations then being undertaken on the Western side to set up a separate German government in West Germany.[23] Thus, despite Kennan's effort to put Soviet actions in the perspective of a long-term political struggle, and despite the effort of the CIA intelligence estimators to explain that Soviet policy was to avoid armed conflict while pursuing political and psychological warfare against the West, the myth had already become well established in the Washington foreign policy and military establishments that the USSR posed a military as well as a political challenge to the West.

There can be no doubt that in 1948 the USSR had the military capability to overrun West Germany and most of its neighbors, had the Soviet leaders chosen to do so; in that sense the Western occupation forces in West Germany were indeed vulnerable to sudden attack. The Czech affair had also caused fright in Western Europe; perhaps it could be repeated elsewhere. If, for example, Communist-led trade unions in France or Italy initiated revolutionary actions which were accompanied by bellicose rhetoric from Moscow and threatening military movements in Soviet-occupied countries, their already unstable governments might find it difficult to hang on. In any event, most West Europeans at that point had had their fill of war and did not want their countries to become battlegrounds for civil war.

Fears such as those caused the Benelux governments to sign a defense pact with France and Britain in March 1948. Because it was an alliance without significant military power, the U.S. State Department began to advance the idea of an American endorsement of European collective defense. Desirous that any new U.S. commitment to Europe have bipartisan political support, the State Department entered into discussions with Senator Vandenberg, who had been helpful in bringing bipartisan support to the Greek-Turkish Aid and Marshall Plan programs. Those talks led to the so-called Vandenberg

23. Kennan, *Memoirs, 1925–1950*, 401.

Resolution, which was approved by the Senate in June 1948. The resolution advised the President to pursue a policy of "progressive development of regional and other collective arrangements for individual and collective self-defense in accordance with the purpose, principles, and provisions of the [United Nations] Charter." Using that rather vague resolution as an authorization, the State Department proceeded to the negotiation of the North Atlantic Treaty. It was signed in March 1949 and was ratified by the Senate in July 1949.

Shortly before the signing of the North Atlantic Treaty, the CIA's Office of Reports and Estimates completed a study of the changing U.S.-Soviet relationship implied by the treaty and its accompanying military aid program. This was ORE 41-49, "Effects of a U.S. Foreign Military Aid Program." It contained two significant paragraphs on the Soviet reaction:

> It is estimated that, in present circumstances, the Kremlin is content to pursue its ends by normal Communist techniques and is unlikely to resort to open military aggression. It has at present no compelling reason to resort to war. It has reason to avoid war in the still vastly superior war making potential of the non-Communist world and in U.S. possession of the atomic bomb. The consideration most likely to cause the Kremlin deliberately to resort to war would be a conviction that an attack on the USSR was actually in preparation and impossible to prevent by other means. . . .
>
> Except as attack may appear imminent and unavoidable, the Kremlin has no reason to abandon a strategy successful hitherto, and conceived to be scientifically certain of success, to accept the doubtful arbitrament of war.

This estimate stated quite clearly yet one more time that it was Soviet policy to avoid war and to rely upon the forces of history to bring about the ultimate Communist victory. It also introduced an important new expression about the doctrine under which the USSR might elect to go to war, namely, if an attack upon the USSR appeared "imminent and unavoidable." So, the Soviet Union would opt for a defensive political strategy; it would intensify its "peace offensive," attack the United States as an "imperialistic warmonger," and further consolidate its control in Eastern Europe, "including possible announcement of a corresponding defense pact."

The Western occupation authorities meanwhile moved openly to create a West German government. In September 1949 the first West German parliament convened, and U.S. military government was terminated. A month after that the USSR responded by creating the German Democratic Republic. The division of Europe was complete. The "iron curtain" of which Winston Churchill had spoken three years earlier had finally "descended" over Europe.

The Structure of World Power at the End of 1949

By the end of 1949, four years and a few months after the end of World War II, a new structure of world power had emerged. The Soviets had become the new interventionists in Eastern Europe; they had utilized their occupation prerogatives and their local Communist allies to establish regimes that were responsive to Soviet directives. The exception was Yugoslavia, which — though still Communist — had rejected Soviet domination. In Western Europe, West Germany had gained a goodly measure of self-government, though still host to the occupation forces of the victorious Western Allies. The United States had undertaken to stimulate economic reconstruction in Western Europe and had agreed to be its guarantor against military attack from outside the NATO area. The European Recovery program had given hope to inhabitants of war-torn countries still struggling to achieve a minimum level of economic well-being and still beset by internal political turmoil. Communism no longer looked inevitable, and fear of revolutionary violence began to fade. The division of Europe, however, and the division of Germany in particular, still lingered as fertile ground for a new war.

In Asia, the disintegration of the Nationalist regime of Chiang Kai-shek was followed in September 1949 by the proclamation in Beijing of the People's Republic of China under the leadership of Mao Zedong. Remnants of the Nationalist army then established themselves on Taiwan. Korea, having been divided into Soviet and American occupation zones at the thirty-eighth parallel, remained divided between a Communist regime in the north founded in May 1948 and a republican government in the south also proclaimed in May 1948. Vietnam, having been divided into Chinese Nationalist and British occupation zones at the sixteenth parallel, soon became the scene of an unresolved conflict between the followers of Ho Chih Minh and French forces trying to reestablish colonial control.

Elsewhere, there was the emergence of new nations in former colonial areas. The British had partitioned India in August 1947, leaving behind, when they withdrew, two new states, the Republic of India and the Islamic Republic of Pakistan; partition caused much violence and prompted some 12 million refugees to cross borders in an effort to join their ethnic communities. Britain departed Palestine in 1948 after turning the Palestine problem over to the United Nations. The UN voted to partition the country, but Palestine's Arab neighbors rejected that solution. Israel then declared itself a national state in May 1948 and fought off destruction by the invading Arab armies. Nearly everywhere in Southwest Asia, Southeast Asia, and Africa, anticolonialist movements were spreading, creating political instability and economic disorganization.

The most important single event contributing to the restructuring of world power was the successful testing of an atomic device in the Soviet Union in late August 1949. Western intelligence services had already become aware of Soviet efforts to develop heavy bombers and surface-to-surface missiles, so that it seemed likely that an atomic-weapons delivery capability would follow in due course. This likelihood, together with the implementation of U.S. military aid programs, clearly foreshadowed a fundamental change in the military and political relationship between the United States and the Soviet Union.

The CIA estimators had reacted to the prospective collapse of the Nationalist regime in China with ORE 29-49, "Prospects for Soviet Control of a Communist China," which was published in April 1949, some five months before the proclamation in September of the People's Republic. The writers were obviously handicapped by a paucity of intelligence regarding the Chinese Communist Party and its relations with the Soviet leaders at the time of writing. They concluded, for example, that "the strong influence exerted by the Soviet Union over the Chinese Party has been variously revealed and provides ample indication that the present leadership of the Chinese Communists identifies itself solidly with international Communism as promulgated by Moscow."

While the writers were wrong in concluding that Soviet influence over the Chinese party was "strong" and that the Chinese party identified itself with "international Communism as promulgated by Moscow," the writers did recognize that the Soviet-Chinese relationship would not be an easy one:

> It must be emphasized that the process of consolidation of Soviet control over China will unquestionably encounter considerable difficulty, in view of the many potential points of conflict between the USSR and the Chinese Communists, e.g., the issues of U.S. aid, control of peripheral areas, control of assistance to Communists movements in other Far Eastern areas, and the subservience which Moscow will

undoubtedly demand of the CCP. While some opposition to Moscow control probably exists in the CCP, for such opposition to be effective the dissident groups must wrest the control apparatus from the pro-Moscow leadership, or that leadership itself must change its policy toward Moscow. Until evidence is available that an effective opposition is developing, it is concluded that the CCP will remain loyal to Moscow.

It was twelve years later—in 1961—that the break between the two countries was openly acknowledged, and the precise steps in the break have only recently become reasonably clear. We did note in a world situation estimate written late in 1960 that the Chinese Communists were "presenting a major challenge to Moscow's position as the final authority in the Communist movement." But in 1949 it was generally accepted in Washington that the Communist victory in China contributed greatly to the strength of the Communist bloc and that this was a severe blow to the United States and its allies.

The Communist victory also had a profound effect upon U.S. internal politics. Fear of a stronger Communist bloc and an increasing sense of having been betrayed by our Soviet allies in matters affecting Eastern Europe generated an atmosphere of unease around the country, which was played upon by aspirants for political power. The Democratic leadership and the foreign affairs bureaucracy were attacked for having "lost China to the communists," even though an honest study of Chinese affairs from 1942 to 1949 would have shown that the United States had made strenuous efforts to prop up the Chiang Kai-shek government and to bring about a revival of the Nationalist-Communist coalition which had existed in the early 1920s. Despite very substantial military and economic aid provided by the United States, the Nationalist government failed to initiate and to carry out reforms in areas under its control. When the war ended, the Nationalists rapidly lost popular support to the Communist Party, and the Communist victory became virtually inevitable.

The fear of Communism which gripped some sectors of American opinion at the time also obliged U.S. policymakers to place all Communists in one basket, despite Tito's defection of a year earlier. There were some on the U.S. political scene who believed that the Tito affair was a Communist trick to mislead anti-Communists and to encourage them to let down their guard. That school of thought and the possibility that the Stalinists in Moscow and Belgrade might succeed in ousting Tito blocked U.S. policymakers from seriously examining the implications of the Tito affair. It also foreclosed acceptance of the warning in the CIA estimate that the Soviets would "unquestionably encounter considerable difficulty" in bringing the Chinese into line.

When the Soviet atomic test was announced a few weeks after the proclamation of the People's Republic, concerns about the growing momentum of Communist power were intensified. The intelligence community published an analysis of the atomic test entitled "The Effect of the Soviet Possession of Atomic Bombs on the Security of the United States." The analysis was not prepared by CIA analysts and coordinated with the other intelligence agencies, as was the usual practice, but by an appropriately named Ad Hoc Committee made up of representatives from the CIA, the intelligence office of the Department of State, and the intelligence agencies of the Army, Navy, and Air Force. There was considerable disagreement among the members of the Ad Hoc Committee, which delayed completion of the estimate. Finally a majority version was published early in June 1950 (ORE 32-50), which carried a dissent from the Navy. The two-sentence conclusion was frightening: "The Soviet possession of atomic weapons has increased the military and political subversive capabilities of the USSR and the possibility of war. Accordingly the security of the United States is in increasing jeopardy."

The reasons for this "increasing jeopardy" were an assemblage of long-term possibilities and dubious judgments. There would be "fear of a growing disparity between U.S. and Soviet military power, and a fear of atomic war in any case." This might "influence the present allies of the United States to refrain from joining this country in taking a more positive [sic] position against the USSR." The estimate also asserted that as the Soviet atomic stockpile developed, the U.S. "superiority in total numbers of atomic bombs will no longer in itself be a strong deterrent to war." Moreover, as the Soviet military potential progressed, the USSR would "doubtless be willing to take greater risks than before in pursuit of its aims." Finally, the estimate averred that "[if] U.S. defensive and retaliatory capabilities were to remain so limited as to permit a Soviet belief that the USSR could make a decisive attack on the United States with relative impunity, there will be grave danger of such an attack." The estimate's call for increased U.S. Air Force capabilities against the USSR could hardly be more clear.

The Navy dissent was a hard-hitting attack on the majority position. It made, inter alia, the following points:

> The reader is actually led to infer that the only factor under Soviet control which would influence a decision to attempt a surprise and crippling atomic attack on the U.S. is possession of what they estimate

to be a requisite number of atomic bombs to accomplish the task. It is inconceivable that the Soviets could arrive at such a decision without regard to political or economic factors and all the other military factors, offensive and defensive.

The security of the U.S. is affected by Soviet objectives and intentions as well as capabilities, since it is the combination of all those factors that produces the end product, probable courses of action. Soviet objectives and intentions stem principally from political, ideological and economic factors, historical experience and aspirations. Only when weighed together in the light of objectives and intentions will total capabilities—political, subversive, economic and military—combine to produce the probable courses of action which must be correctly estimated in order that proper steps may be taken to insure the security of the U.S. While many considerations affecting the Soviet objectives and intentions are "controversial," these considerations are, in this case, the vital issues in the problem. Their omission from the estimate is a fatal error.

[The Office of Naval Intelligence] believes that our bases for estimating Soviet objectives and intentions are at least as well founded as our bases for estimating their capabilities. They are, therefore, entitled to full consideration in the estimate, particularly in view of the uncertainty which must be expressed regarding quantities, dates of availability, and characteristics of Soviet atomic bombs.

The two diverse approaches toward estimating Soviet courses of action which are disclosed by the text and the dissent to this estimate troubled the intelligence community for many years. The question of how much weight should be given to military capabilities does not lend itself to quick and easy answers. Much of the Washington foreign-policy making community was obliged to reconsider that question when, on June 24, 1950, the news reached Washington that Communist North Korea had launched a military assault upon South Korea. For the school of thought which believed that the Soviets planned to expand the Communist world by military action carried out by Soviet forces or those of satellite countries, the North Korean attack was proof positive of their beliefs; Communist military capabilities were being built up to enlarge the Soviet empire.

The Korean War   A Pivotal Event

The Invasion from the North

When news of the North Korean attack reached Washington it was a Saturday evening. Secretary Acheson telephoned President Truman at his home in Independence, Missouri, to pass on the news. He informed the President that he had already asked the Secretary General of the United Nations to call an emergency meeting of the Security Council for the next day. The President left Independence for Washington early Sunday afternoon. That evening his daughter Margaret wrote in her diary for June 25, 1950: "Everything is extremely tense. . . . Northern or Communist Korea is marching in on Southern Korea and we are going to fight."[1] When the President arrived in Washington that evening, he was met at the airport by Acheson, Undersecretary of State James Webb, and Secretary of Defense Louis Johnson. He said to them on the drive in from the airport, "By God, I am going to hit them hard."[2]

There was a meeting that evening at Blair House (because the White House was being remodeled), and there were daily sessions over the next few days, as State and Defense Department officials met with the President to discuss the U.S. response. While the President was still in the air, the United Nations Security Council met—with the Soviet representative absent—and voted a

1. McCullough, *Truman*, 776.
2. Ernest R. May, *Lessons of the Past* (New York: Oxford, 1973), 70.

resolution calling upon North Korea to cease hostilities and to withdraw to the thirty-eighth parallel.

Omar Bradley, who attended the various Blair House sessions as Chairman of the Joint Chiefs of Staff, described the first session as permeated by "an intense sense of moral outrage." He later wrote: "Everyone present seemed to be of the opinion that the failure to take action to protect South Korea would be appeasement and History [sic] proves that one appeasement leads to another and this inevitably leads to war."[3]

Both the Sunday and Monday meetings, Bradley reported, "were dominated by Acheson." Acheson, by his own account, had concluded before the Sunday evening meeting that "it seemed close to certain that the attack had been mounted, supplied, and instigated by the Soviet Union and that it would not be stopped by anything short of force. If Korean force proved unequal to the job, as seemed probable, only American military intervention could do it."[4] Acheson made three recommendations to the Sunday evening group concerning the immediate military steps to be taken. He reported that his recommendations were supported by the group "with varying degrees of detail," and that the President accepted them as the meeting ended.[5]

At the second meeting and at the others which followed, the President made further military decisions and issued a statement on Wednesday June 27 which outlined the military undertakings that he had ordered, and he explained his views on the Korean affair in these words: "The attack on Korea makes it plain beyond all doubt that Communism has passed beyond the use of subversion to conquer independent nations and will now use armed invasion and war."[6]

Having made up their minds before the meetings on Sunday and Monday to respond to the invasion by military force, Truman and Acheson had no difficulty bringing the military leaders with them. Bradley apparently needed little convincing. When he wrote his account of the meetings, using such words as "appeasement" and "History proves," he signaled that in his mind the North Korean invasion of South Korea was in the same genre as the Nazi seizures of territory in Europe, beginning with Austria in the spring of 1938. Neither the President, nor Acheson, nor Bradley seem to have had much difficulty in overruling their own decision of a few months earlier to withdraw from South Korea because it was of little strategic value to the United States.

---

3. Bradley, A General's Life, 535–36.
4. Dean Acheson, Present at the Creation (New York: W. W. Norton, 1969), 405.
5. Ibid., 406.
6. Cited in Bernstein and Matusow, Truman Administration, 437–38.

Ernest May, in his book *Lessons of the Past*, has described how U.S. policy moved deliberately toward the exclusion of Korea from the U.S. defense perimeter in the Western Pacific and how the National Security Council then proceeded to direct a phased withdrawal of U.S. occupation forces, a withdrawal that was completed in June 1949. After his review of the events of late June 1950, May concluded that "it seems plain that the President made his basic choice during the first twenty-four hours" regardless of the NSC decisions he had participated in and signed off on. May acknowledges that while Truman took one action at a time and waited on events, Truman seemingly never doubted that the Soviets had planned the action, and he wondered only where they might strike next. Truman and his advisers, May pointed out, never really explored any alternatives to the actions which they took.[7]

So, without consultation with any Soviet specialist or intelligence officer, Secretary Acheson and President Truman concluded almost immediately that the North Korean actions were a Soviet-instigated and Soviet-directed operation. George Kennan was away during the weekend, but had returned on Sunday afternoon and gone to the State Department. He was available to attend the evening meeting on Sunday, but for reasons not entirely clear was excluded from that meeting and from participation in the policy decisions that followed. He had shortly before asked to go on leave from the State Department in order to join the Institute for Advanced Study at Princeton; one of the principal reasons for his request was what he described in his memoirs as increasing worry "over the growing evidence of difference in outlook between myself and my colleagues [in the State Department], including the Secretary of State."[8] It was perhaps that difference in outlook that led to his exclusion, even though he was not only the Department's leading Sovietologist but its third-ranking officer. On the other hand, there was no reason to expect the DCI to be brought into the high-level discussions, since the CIA was still regarded in Washington as a fledgling agency in the foreign affairs business and its director looked upon as a locum tenens until some more distinguished and active figure could be chosen for that position.

Nevertheless, there was relevant intelligence available bearing on the question of Soviet and North Korean intentions at the time. As noted in the previous chapter, CIA estimates had generally concluded that it was Soviet policy to avoid war and that the only situation which would cause them to resort to war would be the conviction that the USSR itself was about to be attacked.

---

7. May, *Lessons of the Past*, 70, passim.
8. George F. Kennan, *Memoirs, 1950–1963* (Boston: Little, Brown, 1967), 3.

The most recent estimate (ORE 41-49) had stated that the Soviets would see no reason to abandon a strategy they "conceived to be scientifically certain of success." With specific reference to Korea, the CIA produced on February 28, 1949, an estimate entitled "Consequences of U.S. Troop Withdrawal from Korea in Spring 1949" (ORE 3-49). The summary of ORE 3-49 reads:

> Withdrawal of U.S. forces from Korea in the spring of 1949 would probably in time be followed by an invasion, timed to coincide with Communist led South Korean revolts, by the North Korean Peoples Army possibly assisted by small battle-trained units from Communist Manchuria. Although it can be presumed that South Korean security forces will eventually develop sufficient strength to resist such an invasion, they will not have achieved that capability by the spring of 1949. It is unlikely that such strength will be achieved before January 1950. Assuming that Korean Communists would make aggressive use of the opportunity presented them, U.S. troop withdrawal would probably result in a collapse of the U.S.-supported Republic of Korea, an event which would seriously diminish U.S. prestige and adversely affect U.S. security interests in the Far East.
>
> In contrast, continued presence in Korea of a moderate U.S. force would not only discourage the threatened invasion but would assist in sustaining the will and ability of Koreans themselves to resist any future invasion once they had the military force to do so and, by sustaining the new Republic, maintain U.S. prestige in the Far East.

The withdrawal of U.S. occupation forces was completed in June 1949. The North Korean invasion took place a year later.

There obviously was a failure of U.S. policymaking before the invasion occurred; the NSC did not take full account of what it would be faced with if all U.S. occupation forces withdrew and South Korea were invaded, an event that should have been anticipated—even without an intelligence estimate at hand to predict it. Moreover, when the event did occur, the Truman-Acheson reaction was based more upon emotion and careless historical analogy than upon reasoned policymaking procedures. The significance and meaning of the invasion were not explored with the available Soviet experts in the State Department before irreversible decisions were made. Truman and Acheson rushed to judgment about Soviet intentions with a public declaration that the Soviets had shifted their strategy from subversion, propaganda, and political action to military invasion and war in order to expand the

Communist world. They rushed into a war that caused more than 100,000 U.S. casualties including almost 34,000 dead. What is more important is that they set in motion a U.S. rearmament effort and a U.S.-Soviet arms race that continued for the next forty years.

The Soviet View of the Invasion

A considerable amount of information shedding light upon how the North Korean invasion came about has been made available to U.S. scholars. One particularly useful document was a historical study on the war's origins prepared in 1966 by staff members of the Soviet Foreign Ministry. Studies and translations based upon that and other documents have been published in the *Bulletin* of the Cold War International History Project of the Woodrow Wilson Center for Scholars during the period from the autumn of 1993 to March 1998. One scholar who made an intensive study of those documents is Kathryn Weathersby of the Center's staff. She found the Foreign Ministry report especially useful, since it appeared to have been honest and well documented. She based that judgment partly upon the fact that it "baldly contradicted" Soviet public assertions on the subject.

Indeed, the Soviet Foreign Ministry report certainly did not describe a Soviet leadership eager and determined to approve and support a North Korea assault against the South. The report, she wrote, supported the revisionist argument that "the impetus for the war came from Pyongyang, not Moscow. This was Kim Il Sung's war; he gained Stalin's reluctant approval only after persistent appeals (48 telegrams!)."[9]

According to the Weathersby study, the question of a North Korean attack on the South had become the subject of a Politburo decision as early as September 1949, seven months after CIA estimators concluded that sometime after U.S. occupation forces withdrew there would probably be an invasion of the South. Following the Politburo meeting, instructions were sent to the Soviet ambassador in Pyongyang directing him to tell Kim Il Sung that in Moscow's opinion the Peoples Army was not prepared for such an attack and that there was danger it could turn into "a prolonged military operation." The Politburo further thought that an attack was "also not prepared for," because not enough had been done "to develop a partisan movement" in the South. Moreover, said the instruction, "if military actions begin at

9. Katherine Weathersby, "New Findings on the Korean War," *Bulletin of the Cold War International History Project*, no. 3 (Fall 1993): 14.

the initiative of the North and acquire a prolonged character, then this can give the Americans cause for any kind of interference in Korean affairs."[10]

Kim Il Sung did not limit himself to seeking Soviet approval and aid for an attack against the South. He also visited Mao Zedong. Another of the scholars at the Woodrow Wilson Center studying the Korean War was Evgeni Bajanov (director of the Institute for Contemporary International Problems at the Russian Foreign Ministry). His report sheds considerable light upon the Chinese role in the planning of the attack upon South Korea. The Bajanov report shows that Mao Zedong, as early as May 1949 (three months before the Soviet Politburo took up the Korean matter), promised to assist Kim "to liberate" the South. But Mao also warned Kim not to move "in the near future." Mao thought that the world situation at the time was "unfavorable," and he recommended that Kim postpone the war until China was united under Communist control. China was, Mao said, still, preoccupied with the civil war. Then, he added, when the war against the South did come and if it proved necessary, "we can throw in for you Chinese soldiers, all of us are black, Americans will not see the difference."[11] In March 1950, Mao was still speaking in an encouraging fashion to the North Koreans. He told the North Korean ambassador in Beijing that a "peaceful" unification of Korea was "impossible." He further said that the North Koreans should not be afraid of the Americans because the Americans "would not start a third world war over such a small territory."[12]

Also by then Stalin had taken a more favorable attitude toward the invasion idea. On January 30, 1950, he sent a telegram to the Soviet ambassador in Pyongyang saying that "[Kim Il Sung] must understand that such a large matter in regard to South Korea such as he wants to undertake needs large preparations. The matter must be organized so that there would not be too great a risk." But Stalin also instructed the ambassador to tell Kim that "I am ready to help him in this matter."[13]

Having agreed to help Kim, Stalin then set about pushing the responsibility off onto the Chinese. Kim went to Moscow in April 1950 at Stalin's behest in order to discuss war plans. According to Bajanov, Stalin's intent was to plan the war with Kim "without Chinese interference and objections

10. Katherine Weathersby, "To Attack or Not to Attack? Stalin, Kim Il Sung, and the Prelude to War," *Bulletin of the Cold War International History Project*, no. 5 (Spring 1995): 7–8.

11. Evgeni Bajanov, "Assessing the Politics of the Korean War, 1949–51," *Bulletin of the Cold War International History Project*, no. 6–7 (Winter 1995–96): 87.

12. Ibid.

13. Weathersby, "To Attack or Not to Attack?" 9.

and then present Beijing with a fait accompli, when Mao would have no choice but to agree with the invasion and assist it."[14] After this meeting and at Stalin's direction, Kim proceeded from Moscow to Beijing to obtain Chinese support. Stalin himself sent a message to Mao stating that "the final decision must be made jointly by Chinese and Korean comrades. If the Chinese comrades disagree, the decision must be postponed until a new discussion."[15]

In the light of the Politburo's reluctance to approve the project in the preceding September, why did Stalin have change of heart on January 30, 1950? There is strong circumstantial evidence that Stalin was greatly influenced by Secretary Acheson's foreign policy address at the National Press Club eighteen days earlier, on January 12. Acheson did not mention Korea, but he did discuss U.S. military security in the Pacific area, and he did identify the U.S. defense perimeter in the Pacific as running from the Aleutian Islands to Japan and the Ryukyus to the Philippines. Some of Acheson's critics believe that this part of his speech (which simply announced publicly NSC decisions taken as far back as 1947) was a virtual invitation to the North Koreans to invade South Korea.

In his own memoirs, Acheson wrote that he made the speech from a page or two of notes after having read drafts prepared for him by staff members. It probably was therefore more revealing of his thinking than State Department policy statements usually are. The purpose of the speech was to deal with China policy. But Acheson also discussed Communism, and in doing so betrayed his own failure to understand what Soviet motivations really were. "Communism," he said, "is the most subtle instrument of Soviet foreign policy that has ever been devised, and it is really the spearhead of Russian imperialism." Soviet interest in the Far East, he added, was in the Russian tradition of attempting "to dominate Asian peoples."[16] He said nothing about the historical pretensions of Marxism or its ideological commitment to the achievement of a Communist world; Soviet expansionism was straight Russian imperialism.

When Acheson did move on to discuss the U.S. defense perimeter, it became clear that the NSC decision to exclude Korea from the U.S. zone of national security was based essentially upon military grounds and military advice, exclusive of political considerations. He was, he said, following a line set down by General MacArthur a year earlier and approved by the Joint

14. Bajanov, "Assessing," 87–88.
15. Ibid.
16. See Acheson, *Present at the Creation*, 354–56; also Bernstein and Matusow, *Truman Administration*, 434–63.

Chiefs of Staff. What the U.S. military had been thinking about was not the future of Korea, but a defensible military position in the Pacific in the event of a general war with the USSR. The NSC decision, like Acheson's speech, did not demonstrate any real understanding of the USSR's ambitions and methods, or any comprehension of the political consequences of the military dispositions and strategic plans which its decisions had ordained.

The Joint Chiefs of Staff, whose representatives were active participants in drafting the NSC decision papers, had been moving for several years toward planning for a general war with the USSR. The Clay telegram, continued Soviet military occupation in Eastern Europe and the imposition there of loyal Communist regimes, relentless accusations by the Soviets of U.S. war-mongering, repeated displays of intransigence in U.S.-Soviet negotiations, the Greek civil war, and Soviet diplomatic pressure on Turkey, all these had led many in the Pentagon and State Department to conclude that the Soviets were preparing for a global military struggle. The Soviets were indeed trying to expand the Communist world, but what was more important to them at the time was the implementation of a series of defensive measures to deal with the growing U.S. atomic capability. They believed that they needed to make the air and ground defenses of the Soviet Union as strong as possible, and they believed that they needed to maintain a strong capability to seize Western Europe. From their viewpoint, they needed to accomplish those military objectives, along with continued political and diplomatic actions, in order to deter the United States from initiating the preventive war that some U.S. generals had advocated. They also wished to deter the United States from brandishing its atomic capability in an effort to make the USSR more pliant in bilateral negotiations. Instead of advocating political or political-military responses to Soviet probes and subversive actions, as the United States had done in Europe (e.g., military and economic aid to Greece, the Marshall Plan), the Pentagon was moving toward a response which was actually *militarized containment on a global scale.* In that context, Korea was expendable.

Those in Washington who believed the myth that the USSR was hell-bent to expand its dominion by military force took the invasion of South Korea as proof that the myth was true. They insisted that it was therefore necessary to fight off the North Koreans and accept general war if the Soviets came to their defense, for if the United States and the world did not respond, the Soviets would only grow stronger, other such wars even likelier, and the final victory of Communism even harder to prevent. Either way, the mythmakers created a Damoclesian sword to hang over the table at which they sat.

Just how and how far they were off the mark Henry Kissinger makes clear in his book *Diplomacy*:

> The belief that the Soviet leaders stood poised for general war revealed an extraordinary loss of touch with the real power relationships. Stalin was not looking for a pretext to start a general war; he was most eager to avoid it. Had he sought a confrontation, there were more than enough pretexts available in Europe or in the military actions already taking place in Korea. Not surprisingly, at no stage of the war did the Soviet Union threaten to intervene or to take military action. Nothing in Stalin's cautious and suspicious character suggested the reckless adventurer; he always preferred stealth and indirection to actual confrontation, and had been especially careful not to run a risk of war with the United States—with good reason. Given the disparity in the nuclear capabilities of the two sides, it was the Soviet Union which had everything to lose in a general war.[17]

The intelligence estimates prepared by the CIA (and its predecessor the CIG) from 1946 through 1950 had made that clear also. But nobody in the policy loop read them or took them seriously.

U.S. Policy Blunders of Autumn 1950

U.S. policymakers thus made two major blunders in Korea during 1949 and through June 1950. The first was to withdraw U.S. occupation forces completely in 1949 and then publicly announce in January 1950 that Korea was outside the U.S. defense perimeter. The second was to misjudge the attack on South Korea as a fundamental change in Soviet political strategy and to conclude that it was the opening blast in a new round of Soviet-planned military actions to enlarge the Communist empire. A third seems to have occurred in late September and early October, when intelligence judgments, NSC policy decisions, and General MacArthur's actions in the theater resulted in the entry of the Chinese Communists into the war.

Outmanned and outgunned, the South Korean forces and the hurriedly deployed U.S. reinforcements were soon driven into and contained within what became known as the Pusan perimeter on the southeast coast. Douglas MacArthur, who had been named commander of the UN/U.S. forces, by

---

17. Henry Kissinger, *Diplomacy* (New York: Simon & Schuster, 1994), 487.

early August had within that perimeter a force of nearly 100,000 men, half of them South Koreans. When the military situation became stabilized, he conceived the idea of winning the war by making an amphibious landing at Inchon on the west coast near Seoul. Some of the members of the Joint Chiefs of Staff in Washington thought it was a nutty idea, but the President approved the operation. It was a success. The North Koreans did not at first realize that they were about to be trapped. When they did, they fled northward in disarray and suffered substantial losses. The operation began on September 15. Twelve days later most of South Korea was under control of UN/U.S. troops.

Before the Inchon operation began, there had already developed a serious debate about what U.S. military and political objectives should be. As early as July 17, President Truman had, according to General Bradley, "queried the NSC about how to wind up the war."[18] George Kennan—who had asked earlier for a leave of absence because of the growing difference in outlook between himself and his State Department colleagues—was still in Washington during the summer months and was advocating extreme care when the forthcoming defeat of the North Koreans became obvious. If UN/U.S. forces crossed the thirty-eighth parallel, he warned, the Russians would not "sit by"; they might themselves reoccupy North Korea or introduce Chinese Communist forces. They would not "leave the field free for us to sweep up the peninsula and place ourselves forty or fifty miles from Vladivostock."[19]

Kennan's views were supported by Chip Bohlen, the other leading Soviet specialist in the State Department. The Policy Planning Staff in the State Department was at that time still under the influence of Kennan (who was not to leave for Princeton until September), and it produced a paper stating that as UN/U.S. forces approached the thirty-eighth parallel, "the danger of conflict with Chinese Communist and Soviet forces would be greatly increased." General Bradley comments in his memoirs (written some thirty years later) that the Planning Staff paper was "full of good sense" but did not get a wide enough reading, "because Dean Acheson and his chief Far Eastern advisers, Dean Rusk and John Allison, had adopted a hawkish stance on crossing the 38th parallel." Bradley added that the U.S. military establishment itself was "unanimous" in supporting the Acheson view that "the North Korean Army should be utterly destroyed."[20]

The military and the Acheson group in the State Department won the day. On September 27, twelve days after the Inchon landing, President Truman

18. Bradley, A General's Life, 558.
19. Kennan, Memoirs, 1950–1963, 14.
20. Bradley, A General's Life, 558–59.

signed a formal order for MacArthur to go beyond the thirty-eighth parallel with the mission of destroying the North Korean forces and occupying the entire country. The die was cast. The United States had completely altered its war aim. The U.S. objective was no longer a police action to save South Korea; it was the destruction of the North Korean regime and the political unification of the country.

But, as Kennan had predicted, the Soviets and Chinese got very nervous about U.N./U.S. military actions as the North Korean forces were thrown back toward the north-south boundary. Early on the morning of October 1, Stalin received a desperate plea for help from Kim Il Sung. He then wired Mao Zedong asking him to send five or six divisions toward the thirty-eighth parallel so that the North Koreans could regroup and form new troop units under the protection of the Chinese forces. He also sent to the Soviet UN delegation a draft resolution on the Korean question. The resolution called for an immediate cease-fire, withdrawal of foreign troops, and general elections in all of Korea under international supervision. But South Korean troops had already crossed the border a few hours earlier, and in view of the orders issued to MacArthur a few days before that, the Soviet UN maneuver was a fruitless effort.[21] So also was an attempt made by Chinese foreign minister Chou En-lai on October 2 to send a warning to the United States and the United Kingdom through the Indian ambassador in Beijing. Apparently unaware that South Korean forces had already crossed into the North, Chou told him, in a warning obviously intended to be passed on, that if U.S. troops crossed the parallel, China would enter the war. At the same time Chou himself was arguing in the Chinese Communist Central Committee against Chinese intervention.[22] Thus the Soviets and Chinese, like the principal Soviet specialists in the State Department, had come to realize that the status quo ante was the best way out of the war. But the rush to judgment by Truman, Acheson, and the Joint Chiefs of Staff kept the war going for a lot longer than anyone wanted.

It was at that time, Bradley later wrote, that "the JCS and everyone else committed one cardinal sin. We seriously misjudged Communist reaction to our plans to cross the thirty-eighth parallel."[23] Acheson said little about this in his memoirs, writing only that "Chou's words were a warning not to be

21. Alexandre Mansourov, "Stalin, Mao, Kim, and China's Decision to Enter the Korean War, September 16–October 15, 1950," *Bulletin of the Cold War International History Project*, no. 6-7 (Winter 1995–96): 99–100.

22. Ibid., 100.

23. Bradley, *A General's Life*, 561.

disregarded, but, on the other hand, not an authoritative statement of policy."[24] But Acheson obviously disregarded the warning.

Several weeks went by before Washington realized that Chinese intervention was actually taking place or about to occur. The question was still a live one at the CIA. On October 12, CIA Director Bedell Smith sent a long memorandum to the President discussing the possibility of Chinese and Soviet intervention in Korea and in other areas of the Far East. On Korea, the memorandum concluded: "While full-scale Chinese Communist intervention in Korea must be regarded as a continuing possibility, a consideration of all known factors leads to the conclusion that barring a Soviet decision for global war, such action is not probable in 1950. During this period, intervention will probably be confined to continued covert assistance to the North Koreans."

Underlying that judgment, of course, was the general belief in the West that the Chinese would act only in tandem with the Soviets. The CIA's judgment of Soviet intentions in the same estimate reads: "It is believed that the Soviet leaders will not consider that their prospective losses in Korea warrant direct military intervention and a consequent risk of war. They will intervene in Korea only if they have decided, not on the basis of the Korean situation alone, but on the basis of over-all considerations, that it is to their interest to precipitate a global war at this time."

The message the estimate was sending was one that had underlain most of the CIA estimates up to that time, namely, that the Soviets did not want to fight a global war against the United States. But because of the general belief in Washington and elsewhere that the Chinese would act only at Soviet bidding, estimators and Far Eastern specialists took the erroneous view that if the Soviets shunned intervention, the Chinese would do likewise.

In July, just after the invasion began, the DCI's Office of Reports and Estimates established a Special Staff to handle estimative questions concerning the Korean War. Consistent with the view that Soviet objectives were worldwide, it consisted of one staff member from each regional branch, all three members of the Global Survey Group, and myself from the communications intelligence group (although it was not known as such at that time). When we received the report of the conversation between Chou and the Indian ambassador, we like everyone else in Washington that day were wondering whether it was a genuine warning or only a bluff. The Far Eastern branch member of the Staff brought in his branch chief, who assured us with great self-confidence that it was a Chinese bluff.

24. Acheson, *Present at the Creation*, 452.

I was not by any means a specialist on China, but I had worked in the Far Eastern section at G-2 during the war, and for that reason probably had a somewhat better understanding of Chinese behavior than the others around the table. I also had been reading the diplomatic mail of other countries for some six years. I found myself taking the view that when a Foreign Minister—and especially one as serious and astute as Chou En-lai—called in an important ambassador to issue a private warning presumably for transmission to the Americans and the British, it should be taken seriously and not treated simply as a propaganda maneuver to scare off the United States. But I was only a new boy with a mysterious background, and I was paid no heed. (Some months later when the Office of National Estimates [O/NE] was formed, both the Far Eastern branch chief and his representative on the Special Staff were transferred to nonanalytic assignments, while most of the rest of us were assigned to the new Office.) None of us knew then what has recently been learned from Soviet archives about the indecision and near chaos in the Communist camp over the question of whether the Chinese should enter the war.

How the Chinese Entered the War

It was after the Inchon landing on September 15 that things began to look bad for the Communist side. On September 21, Chou En-lai told the Soviet ambassador in Beijing that some of the Chinese were complaining that the war "would drag on and require sacrifices on the part of the Chinese."[25] Ten days after that, on October 1, Stalin concluded that China's help was needed to save Kim from collapse, and he asked the Chinese to move five or six divisions into Korea north of the thirty-eighth parallel.[26] It was then that Chinese and Soviet relations began to get very rough.

Mao refused Stalin's request on the ground that Chinese troops were not strong enough and that a clash between China and the United States would ruin China's plans for peaceful reconstruction and could even drag the USSR into a war with the United States. He told Stalin that the North Koreans should simply admit defeat and resort to guerrilla tactics.[27] According to Bajanov, the Soviets were "stunned." Bajanov describes as follows what happened thereafter:

25. Bajanov, "Assessing," 89.
26. Ibid.
27. Ibid.

Stalin reminded the Chinese of their previous promise and urged them again to move into the conflict. The Soviet dictator tried to convince Beijing that the Americans would not dare to start a big war and would agree on a settlement on Korea favorable to the Communist camp. Under such a scenario China would also solve the Taiwan issue. He added that even if the USA provoked a big war, "Let it take place now rather than a few years later when Japanese militarism will be restored as an American ally, and when the United States and Japan will possess a military springboard on the continent in the form of Rhee's Korea."

Stalin informed Kim Il Sung about his attempts to persuade the Chinese and called upon the North Koreans "to hold firm to every piece of land." However, on 12 October 1950, eleven days later the Soviet leader told Kim that the Chinese leaders had refused again and that Korea had to be evacuated. On the next day, however, Stalin had better news: the Chinese after long deliberations and discussions, had agreed to extend military aid to North Korea. Moscow in exchange agreed to arm the Chinese troops and to provide them with air cover.[28]

Bajanov reported further that according to available sources whom he did not identify, the decision came after difficult discussions within the Chinese leadership. Those favoring Chinese intervention argued that "if all of Korea was occupied by the Americans, it would create a mortal danger for the Chinese revolution." Those on the other side complained about Soviet refusal to participate in the conflict, and some even suggested that "China should accept the American advance, even occupation by the USA of Manchuria—because in this case a war between Moscow and Washington would break out and China would stay away from trouble."[29]

Bajanov's report strongly suggests that the conversation between Chou En-lai and the Indian ambassador on October 3 was neither a bluff nor a policy statement. It almost certainly was an effort to encourage the Americans to pause long enough to allow those opposed to intervening—including Chou himself—a chance to work toward restoring the status quo ante and toward avoiding a war between China and the United States. But U.S. intelligence analysts and policymakers stumbled over the question of whether or not *on its surface* the statement was a bluff and failed to consider Chou's possible

28. Ibid.
29. Ibid.

reasons for making it. Was he trying to explore the possibility of a diplomatic way out? Was he suggesting that the war could be brought to an end if the United States would stop at the thirty-eighth parallel?

While this was happening on the Chinese side, Stalin was directing a diplomatic move of his own in the UN. As mentioned earlier, Soviet foreign minister Andrei Vyshinsky presented a resolution to the Political Committee of the UN General Assembly on October 2 calling for an immediate cease-fire, withdrawal of all foreign troops, and general elections in all Korea to be held under international supervision. But the authorities in Washington had already decided to go for all of Korea by military means, and the Soviet draft resolution was tabled.[30] Scenting victory, and apparently in any case unwilling to consider a change in military plans, the Truman administration simply charged on ahead. Although South Korean forces had crossed the border on October 1, they could have been easily recalled and held back with American forces, who did not cross into North Korea until October 7. Clearly there was no interest in Washington in even exploring the possibilities of a peaceful resolution of the conflict.

A detailed study, from the Soviet archives, of the relations among Stalin, Mao, and Kim during the month following the Inchon landing has been undertaken by Alexandre Mansourov of the Center for Korean Research at Columbia University. His study shows that there was a great deal of tension among the three Communist allies resulting from domestic politics and from bargaining within the alliance.[31] Mansourov observes that when Stalin was advised of Mao's refusal on October 12 to intervene in Korea, he directed Kim to abandon the defense of North Korea and to pull the remnants of the North Korean army into guerrilla camps in China and the Soviet Far East. As noted in Bajanov's account, Stalin quickly reversed himself when Mao changed his mind and agreed to bring China into the war. Mansourov draws the following conclusion from Stalin's original decision:

> [It] dramatically revealed the limits of the Soviet national security interest on the Korean peninsula. In Stalin's own words (as recalled by Khrushchev), he was willing to abandon North Korea and allow the United States to become the USSR's neighbor, with its troops deployed in Korea, if this was the price to pay for avoiding direct military confrontation with the U.S. at that time.[32]

30. Mansourov, "Stalin, Mao, Kim," 99–100.
31. Ibid., 105.
32. Ibid.

Mansourov places some of the responsibility for continuation of the war and for survival of the North Korean regime upon misconceptions and mistakes in U.S. diplomatic and military policy:

> Obviously, there was little political will and much less hope in Moscow, Beijing, and even Pyongyang to defend Korea to the last man when the military situation collapsed in mid-October 1950. Therefore, had the United States been less ambivalent, more consistent, and more persuasive on the diplomatic front in stating to Moscow and Beijing the goals of its Korean campaign—e.g., that it had no desire to attack mainland China or threaten the territory of the Soviet Far East—the Soviet and Chinese Governments could well have decided to let Kim Il Sung's regime go under and acquiesced to a UN-proposed Korean settlement. However, Gen. MacArthur's repeated unconditional surrender demands, coupled with barely veiled direct threats against the PRC and the USSR, coming out of Tokyo headquarters, literally pushed the insecure Chinese to the brink, compelling them almost against their will to intervene in Korea, thereby providing Stalin a legitimate reason to reconsider his own decision to evacuate Korea.[33]

So, in the end, after three years of warfare, the status quo ante was restored. Both the United States and the USSR suffered from the conflict and the outcome. Stalin was defeated through his own misjudgments and duplicity. The United States achieved a stalemate in a war that should not have occurred and that would have had no casus belli if U.S. leaders had read and believed the intelligence judgments of the CIA about the Korean matter. The United States would not have been panicked into a high-pressure rearmament program if its leaders had read and believed the CIA's explications of Soviet motivations and methods.

Stalin thought he was in the clear after Acheson pronounced that the United States would not fight for South Korea. But he took out insurance by maneuvering the Chinese into approving Kim Il Sung's adventure. Many Chinese no doubt felt duped, and some even wanted to play the "American card" as a maneuver to oblige the Soviets either to fight the Americans or to accept the loss of a strategic position in East Asia.

But the United States came to the Soviets' rescue. By refusing to take up the Soviet offer of a UN-sponsored electoral solution in Korea and by adher-

33. Ibid.

ing to a bellicose attitude toward all three of the Communist powers in East Asia, the United States lost the opportunity to encourage further differences among them. It also lost the chance to move toward a united Korea without the further shedding of American blood. What the United States unwittingly gained was an actual increase in Soviet-Chinese tensions, although most U.S. policymakers continued to believe for another decade that all Communists were cut from the same cloth.

Both the United States and the USSR in the long run were worse off— the United States by drawing the wrong lesson from the invasion and setting out on a forty-year militarization of U.S. foreign policy and an arms race, and the USSR by appearing to be the aggressive imperialist that those on the political right in America believed it to be.

The Impact of War: The Revival of NSC-68

The dark days that followed the Chinese intervention in Korea did lead to a facing of facts in Washington. On November 28, 1950, President Truman called a war council of the top leadership of the State and Defense departments, plus CIA Director Bedell Smith. Bradley has reported that they all felt, "as Acheson expressed it, that we had moved much closer to general war with the Soviets and that, above all, war had to be avoided." There was agreement that no action should be taken which would provoke Soviet intervention in Korea or a "big war elsewhere." General Marshall opposed sending more troops and advocated finding a way out "with honor." The most important consensus, Bradley reported, was agreement that the pending NSC-68 recommendations (sent to the NSC in April) for general rearmament should be implemented whatever the cost.[34]

The Joint Chiefs and the NSC then swung into action on the policy front. The Joint Chiefs declared in a policy paper: "The United States faces today one of the greatest dangers in its history. The Korean war could be the first phase of a global war between the United States and USSR. No areas of agreement which might lessen or end this global struggle are apparent, except those based upon appeasement of the Soviets." The Joint Chiefs followed that up with a "war warning" message to all theater commanders. The NSC resumed discussions on NSC-68 and asked the President to declare a state of emergency.[35] From blithely having directed MacArthur two months earlier

---

34. Bradley, *A General's Life*, 599.
35. Ibid., 609.

to seize all of Korea, U.S. political and military leaders had switched to pessimism and panic.

The panic that manifested itself in November and December 1950 actually had its intellectual and emotional beginnings in such earlier events as the Communist coup in Czechoslovakia, the Berlin Blockade, and the collapse of the Nationalist regime in China. Although the first two of those events were Soviet defensive reactions to U.S. moves in West Germany and the third the consequence of the manifest failures of the Chiang Kai-shek government, they were widely interpreted as indications of a Soviet intention to dominate the world and to do so by military force if necessary. Secretary of State Acheson, indeed the entire Democratic administration of Harry Truman, was accused by Republican politicians as having "lost China" to the Communists. Thus, when the Communists struck in Korea, Acheson and the President were strongly offended. But even before the invasion, Acheson had directed Paul Nitze, whom he had designated to replace George Kennan as chief of the State Department's Policy Planning Staff, to prepare a new NSC policy paper to deal with the Communist problem.

Nitze had been a highly successful New York investment banker who had come to Washington during World War II to join the Board of Economic Warfare. He served with the group that conducted the Strategic Bombing Survey of Japan in 1945–46, and then with the State Department Bureau of Economic Affairs. He joined the Policy Planning Staff shortly before Kennan's leave of absence began. He and Acheson shared a common patrician background and were both deeply concerned with Soviet postwar policies in Europe and Asia. Under Acheson's direction, Nitze became the principal drafter of the new policy paper (NSC-68), and Acheson himself became its principal sponsor and advocate. The Joint Chiefs of Staff made major contributions to the paper; the policy statement and "war warning" messages quoted above reflect judgments spelled out in the NSC paper. NSC-68 was delivered to President Truman on April 7, 1950, and according to McCullough "discussed with him for the first time" at a White House meeting on April 25.

Secretary Acheson wrote in his memoirs that the "primary purpose" of NSC-68 had been to "so bludgeon the mass mind of 'top government' that not only could the President make a decision but that it could be carried out." He also wrote that throughout 1950 he went about the country "preaching" the premise of NSC-68 that the Soviet rulers were giving priority to "world domination" in contrast to the American aim of creating "an environment in which free societies could exist and flourish." Acheson further explained that in a paper such as NSC-68 "qualification must give way to simplicity of statement, nicety and nuance to bluntness, almost brutality, in carrying home a point."[36]

According to David McCullough in his biography of Truman, the President "was not to be bludgeoned." Truman's response was to put NSC-68 "under lock and key"; the President wanted to "make no move until he knew more." On a tour of the country in May 1950, he made over fifty speeches and "never once sounded a call to arms." The Cold War, Truman said, "would be with us for a long time," and there was "no quick way, no easy way to end it."[37]

The language of NSC-68 was, as McCullough put it, "apocalyptic." On its opening page, it states that the Soviet Union was "animated by a new fanatic faith, antithetical to our own, and seeks to impose its absolute authority over the rest of the world." It goes on: "Any substantial extension of the area under the domination of the Kremlin would raise the possibility that no coalition adequate to confront the Kremlin with greater strength could be assembled. It is in this context that this Republic and its citizens in the ascendancy of their strength stand in their greatest peril. The issues that face us are momentous, involving the fulfillment or destruction not only of this Republic but of civilization itself."[38]

As Acheson admitted, the text of NSC-68 is profusely sprinkled with inflammatory rhetoric and distortions designed to picture the USSR in the worst possible light. In the first two pages of a discussion of this conflict of "ideas and values" between the United States and the Kremlin, the words "slavery" and "slave state" are used five times to define the USSR. Moreover, NSC-68 asserted that to the USSR any state, even "the most mild and inoffensive free society is an affront, a challenge and a subversive influence" which cannot be "tolerated"—even though the USSR was "tolerating" Finland and would continue to do so until its own fall in 1991. Indeed, the drafters of NSC-68 insisted that "the only apparent restraints" upon a Soviet resort to war were "calculations of practicality."[39]

These "considerations" and "calculations" were, of course, of great importance in making estimates of Soviet intentions, but the writers of NSC-68 saw no reason to take much account of them. They wrote, "So long as the Kremlin retains the initiative, so long as it can keep on the offensive unchallenged by clearly superior counterforce—spiritual as well as material—its

36. Acheson, *Present at the Creation*, 374–75.
37. McCullough, *Truman*, 772–73.
38. NSC-68, 4.
39. Ibid., 13.

vulnerabilities are largely inoperative and concealed by its successes."[40] Thus, they took no account of Kennan's belief in Sovietism's internal contradictions or of the notable and undeniable early successes of the Marshall Plan and other programs designed to stabilize the situation in Europe. Their call to arms and to a moral crusade was clear, loud, and untroubled by the facts or contrary judgments.

The authors of NSC-68 were clearly preoccupied with military power rather than careful analysis. They went on to state that the USSR was already well along in its development of a military capacity to support its design for world domination; it already possessed "armed forces far in excess of those necessary to defend its national territory"—thus completely ignoring the developing U.S. nuclear weapons delivery capability. Indeed, the policy paper went on to state that the Joint Chiefs of Staff "considered" that in the current year (1950) the USSR and its satellites were in "a sufficiently advanced state of preparation immediately to undertake and carry out campaigns:

a. To overrun Western Europe, with the possible exception of the Iberian and Scandinavian Peninsulas; to drive toward the oil bearing areas of the Near and Middle East;[41] and to consolidate Communist gains in the Far East.

b. To launch air attacks against the British Isles and air and sea attacks against the lines of communications of the Western Powers in the Atlantic and the Pacific.

c. To attack selected targets with atomic weapons, now including the likelihood of such attacks against targets in Alaska, Canada, and the United States. Alternatively, this capability, coupled with other actions open to the Soviet Union, might deny the United Kingdom as an effective base of operations for allied forces. It also should be possible for the Soviet Union to prevent any allied "Normandy" type amphibious operations to force a reentry into the continent of Europe.[42]

Then, after completing its initial campaigns and consolidating its position in Western Europe, the Soviets could, according to the Joint Chiefs, "simultaneously conduct":

40. Ibid., 16.
41. "Near East" refers to the region at the eastern end of the Mediterranean; "Middle East" to the countries from Iran to Burma.
42. NSC-68, 17–18.

a. Full-scale air and limited sea operations against the British Isles;
b. Invasions of the Iberian and Scandinavian Peninsulas;
c. Further operations in the Near and Middle East, continued air operations against the North American continent; and air and sea operations against Atlantic and Pacific lines of communication; and
d. Diversionary attacks in other areas.[43]

The attribution of such capabilities to the USSR and its European satellites at that time seems to us today to have been not just fanciful but deliberately misleading and downright dishonest. The fact is that the U.S. intelligence community at that time, still disparate and disorganized, was in no position to say anything about Soviet military capabilities that had any persuasive evidentiary base. It was several years later before the intelligence community developed the information acquisition and analytic capability to make such sweeping judgments as those which underlay the apocalyptic tone of NSC-68. As a consequence, much of which passed as serious analysis of the USSR in the national security community was actually based upon the doctrinal biases of those preparing the assessments and upon their political, bureaucratic, and professional interests.

It should be recalled that after the close of World War II, the prevailing public mood in the United States was a desire to bring the boys home and to allocate the growing economic and financial power of the country toward civilian requirements and demands. On the other hand, U.S. military leaders recognized that their predecessors had failed to perceive the danger to the United States posed by German Nazism and Japanese militarism, and they did not want such a failure to occur again. Those military leaders and the military-industrial complex associated with them quite naturally strove to keep an effective military establishment in existence. In any case, no military force was deemed likely to be effective without an identifiable future enemy—preferably one of a different culture or different political persuasion. In the new era of nuclear weaponry, whose terrifying and deadly character was still being discovered, it had become more necessary than ever that the chosen enemy be one intent upon our destruction and fundamentally evil in his objectives and methods.

Thus, NSC-68 provided the rationale for the U.S. military establishment's existence and for its expansion over the next forty years. It also embodied all of the doctrines necessary to justify the militarization of U.S. foreign policy,

43. Ibid., 18.

and it promulgated a definition of national security as the possession of an unchallengeable military superiority. It became the undeclared myth that underpinned U.S. rearmament programs during the entire Cold War era.

It is unfortunate that the authors and advocates of NSC-68 were political and military leaders with only a superficial knowledge of Russian history, Marxian doctrine, and political and economic conditions around the world. At the time, the CIA—whose intelligence analysts had quite accurately described and predicted Soviet motivations and conduct—was not in the policy circuit. Senior policymakers in 1950 generally thought of the intelligence function as the production of periodic reports from highly classified sources, rather than as an analytic arm of the policymaking process. The really difficult analytic judgments about the intentions and outlooks of Communist leaders in Europe and Asia were being made by amateurs—often with their own axes to grind—while those qualified to make them in the CIA were ignored and those qualified to do so in the State Department were mistrusted, or shunted aside.

The Impact of War: The Reform of the Intelligence Analysis System

Looking back on the years from the inception of the central intelligence system in January 1946 to the Chinese intervention in Korea in October 1950 indicates that the intelligence analysts in the CIA (and in its predecessor, the CIG) were essentially correct on the major questions facing U.S. policymakers. The first estimate on the USSR, completed in July 1946, stated that the Soviets would seek to avoid a military conflict with the capitalist world but would maintain armed forces capable of protecting themselves against any possible hostile combination. Despite alarms and crises in U.S.-Soviet relations from 1945 to 1950, CIA analysts stuck with their view that—while the Soviets were aggressively attempting by political means to expand the area of their influence and control—they would resort to war only if they were convinced that an attack upon themselves was imminent and unavoidable.

There was also a February 1949 estimate that clearly stated that the withdrawal of U.S. forces from South Korea would in time be followed by an invasion of the South. Yet the top policymakers in Washington, both military and civilian, were shocked by the invasion when it came, and thought that this action by the North Koreans was but a prelude to new Soviet moves around the world. The CIA estimates had obviously had no impact. The DCI was not consulted when major policy decisions were made; the principal source of intelligence information and judgment was the Joint Chiefs of Staff, and they in turn were dependent upon the separate intelligence organizations of three military services, each of which had an individual service bias. Clearly, the new CIA was not playing a significant role in the policymaking process. It lacked forceful leadership, respect within the national security apparatus, and political support in Congress.

Even before the invasion of South Korea shocked the President and the leaders of the State and Defense departments, however, some steps had been initiated to make the CIA an effective player in the national security machinery. Secretary of Defense James Forrestal, before his retirement, had asked a small group of New York lawyers, who had been wartime intelligence officers, to study the CIA and to report to the NSC their criticisms and recommendations. Their report—which became known as the Dulles-Jackson-Correa Report—went to the NSC in early 1949. On the analytic side, the report urged a stronger role for the DCI in coordinating intelligence, and it suggested the recruitment of a small staff to prepare National Intelligence Estimates; it also proposed that the preparation of estimates be separated from current intelligence reporting. The report languished in the CIA files for over a year, awaiting the appointment of a new and forceful director to carry out a reorganization of the Agency. Finally, just before the invasion, the President decided to appoint Walter Bedell Smith as director, but had to wait until Smith's health permitted him to come on board. He took over in October 1950.

One of Smith's first actions was to create the O/NE. He placed it under the temporary charge of Ludwell Montague, who was chief of the Global Survey Group in ORE and who had carried the main burden of preparing the estimates cited in this and the preceding chapter. The first chief of the O/NE and the first chairman of the Board of National Estimates was William L. Langer, professor of history at Harvard and dean of American diplomatic historians. He had also been chief of the Research and Analysis Branch of the OSS during the war.

By early 1951, the board and staff were largely in place. Also a historian, Sherman Kent came down from Yale to become vice chairman of the board. Kent had served in the Research and Analysis Branch of the OSS, and after his return to Yale had become a recognized academic theorist of intelligence. The initial board also included such distinguished figures as Clarence Huebner, a corps commander in Europe during World War II; Raymond Sontag, a diplomatic historian from Berkeley; and Calvin Hoover, a Duke University economist. It also included a Boston lawyer named Max Foster, who by his own account had been persuaded to come by a telephone call from Smith telling him that "the Republic was in danger" and that it was his duty to "serve," as he had on Smith's staff during the war. I was one of about twenty-five staff officers assigned to the new office from the old ORE.

A series of essays written by Kent on the production of national intelligence estimates, from both the theoretical and experiential points of view, is included in a small volume entitled "Sherman Kent and the Board of National Estimates" published by the CIA History Staff in 1994. I am not repeating here what has been well covered elsewhere, but for the purposes of this book I think it will be helpful to the reader to have a sketch of what we in the O/NE were trying to do and how we did it.

We were trying to prepare authoritative analyses of the world, or particular areas of it, or particular countries, or particular problems. We were not strictly speaking in the prediction business, but if the analysis could support clear predictions, we made them; if not, we tried to distinguish degrees of probability. The estimates were signed by the DCI; the O/NE was the director's instrument for their preparation. Requests for estimates came from the NSC or from the State and Defense departments; we initiated some ourselves. We normally solicited written contributions from the appropriate departments of the intelligence community and from CIA research offices. The O/NE staff drafted the estimates and submitted them to the board for review. While the board took corporate responsibility, one board member was assigned the "chairmanship" of each estimate, and three or four other members assumed special responsibility for following the paper through the process.

Once approved by the board, the paper was sent out for review by the various intelligence agencies; these were the State Department's Bureau of Intelligence and Research, the Defense Department's Joint Staff, the intelligence organizations of the Army, Navy, and Air Force, and the National Security Agency (NSA). Meetings were held to consider suggestions and amendments from the agencies. Usually agreement was reached; sometimes an agency would reserve its position. The paper then went to the agency chiefs, namely, the United States Intelligence Board (USIB), which met weekly to review and generally to approve the estimates and to conduct other business. Any one of them could dissent in whole or in part; this was infrequent. The estimate would then be printed and disseminated. The chairman of the Board of National Estimates and the board member who had directed and presided over the production of the estimate sat with the Intelligence Board during the approval process.

The Board of National Estimates and the process were designed to enhance the CIA role in the preparation of estimates. We had control of the process and the document. The board was intended to have the prestige to overwhelm petty departmental interests and to prevent special pleading from corrupting an honest intellectual approach. Success was not complete, but the process did force participants to base their arguments or objections, on the surface at least, on intellectual or factual grounds and not upon political, departmental, or ideological interests. By appointing to the original board a group of distinguished academics and retired military officers, Bedell Smith did achieve his purpose of gaining for the estimates a high degree of respect within the foreign policy and defense agencies as well as at the White House itself. Thus, when the year 1951 began, the CIA had in place the structure and personnel to play a more effective role in support of the National Security Council.

The 1950s Evolving U.S. Views of the Soviet Threat

1950: An Alarmist View from the Pentagon

The job of reassessing Soviet intentions after the outbreak of the Korean War began in 1951. The previous autumn, the board and staff of the O/NE had been recruited and the procedures for producing National Intelligence Estimates had been developed. The O/NE did prepare and issue several short estimates which dealt with specific questions about Korea and Germany, but no general review of Soviet intentions was undertaken until the beginning of 1951.

The O/NE was officially created on November 13, 1950, and two days later it issued an estimate entitled "Soviet Capabilities and Intentions." But that estimate—numbered NIE 3—was not actually its product; it was an annotated edition of a Pentagon Joint Staff paper, JIC 531/10, and it was so identified. The title page described NIE 3 as an "editorial adaptation" of the JIC paper, with "certain modifications and additions to bring it up to date." JIC 531/10 was quite obviously the one used in the elaboration of the Soviet military capabilities described in NSC-68.[S.G.3]

NIE 3 declared that the "ultimate objective" of the Soviet leaders was "to establish a Communist world controlled by themselves or their successors." Their "immediate objectives" included "the elimination of U.S. influence in Europe and Asia" and the establishment of "Soviet domination" in its place. While they could "suppose" that in favorable circumstances, they might eventually achieve those and their other aims "without use of Soviet forces," they nevertheless believed that their objectives could not "be fully attained without a general war with the Western powers." Thus, the JIC estimators concluded, the Soviet rulers might "deliberately provoke such a war at a time when, in their opinion, the relative strength of the USSR is at its maximum."

Such a period, the estimate went on to state, "will exist from now through 1954, with the peak of Soviet strength relative to the Western powers being reached about 1952." The year 1952 was selected as the peak period because that was the time when the USSR would have "made good certain deficiencies" in its atomic bomb stockpile and in certain types of aircraft. It would also be a time before the Western economy had been "fully geared for a war effort." While admitting that intelligence was "lacking" to permit a valid projection as to "whether or when the USSR would actually resort deliberately to a general war," the estimate concluded: "It must be recognized, however, that a grave danger of general war exists now, and will exist hereafter whenever the Soviet rulers may elect to take action which threatens the vital interests of the Western powers."

NIE 3 went on to state the following about Soviet intentions toward general war during the period just ahead:

> The commitment of Chinese Communist forces, with Soviet material aid, indicates that the USSR considers the Korean situation of sufficient importance to warrant the risk of general war. The probability is that the Soviet Union considers that the U.S. will not launch a general war over Chinese Communist intervention in North Korea and the reaction thereto. The principal risk of general war is through the exercise of Soviet initiative which the Kremlin continues to hold. The probability is that the Soviet Government has not yet made a decision directly to launch a general war over the Korean-Chinese situation. There is a good chance that they [sic] will not in the immediate future take any such decision. At what point they will [sic] take a decision to launch a general war is not now determinable by Intelligence.

The thinking that went into those conclusions was more important than the intelligence data, as the writers readily admitted; they added a footnote to the conclusions which stated, "The problem of whether and when the USSR may resort deliberately to general war is under continuing consideration and will be the subject of future reports as pertinent information is developed." Despite their acknowledged ignorance of specific factual information

regarding Soviet intentions, the JIC authors were quite prepared, nevertheless, to express the view that the Soviet rulers intended to dominate the world,
that they believed it would be necessary to fight a general war against the
West to attain their objective, and that there was grave danger that the Soviets
would indeed launch a general war at some date not then "determinable."

From what we now know about Stalin's thinking and actions the writers
of JIC 531/10 were clearly wrong in their interpretation of Soviet actions
regarding Korea. The information now available from the Soviet archives
supports the CIG-CIA estimates, which were that the Soviets would refrain
from actions which in their opinion would provoke a general war with the
United States and the Western powers. Archival information also shows that
Stalin did not agree to the North Korean assault until Secretary Acheson's
public statements indicated that the United States had written off South
Korea as a U.S. national security concern.

The JIC writers, of course, had no access to the data available today, but
they would have been better informed had they taken into account the fact
that the National Security Council and the Secretary of State had virtually
invited a North Korean effort to seize the southern half of the peninsula, and
had they troubled to look at the CIA/ORE estimate of February 1949, which
declared the probability of an invasion if U.S. troops were totally withdrawn
from the South. Nor did the writers indicate in any way that they knew of the
diplomatic move made by the Soviet foreign minister at the United Nations
on October 2—before Chinese intervention occurred—to bring about an
immediate cease-fire in Korea, to be followed by general elections under
international supervision. In short, the intelligence officers involved apparently came to some very important judgments without considering relevant
intelligence estimates, NSC papers, or the diplomatic state of play.

But the Pentagon intelligence analysts were not the only culpable players
in the Korean tragedy. The principals who had gathered at Blair House on
June 25 had reacted emotionally, and they seemed not to have thought about
exploring Soviet intentions through diplomatic channels. Then, at the end
of September, when President Truman signed an order directing General
MacArthur to seize all of North Korea, he again acted without having engaged
in any diplomatic exchanges with the USSR. Nor did the United States respond
when—a few days later—the Soviets made their move in the UN to bring an
end to the fighting. (A decade later, when the Soviets began placing short-
range missiles in Cuba, the Kennedy administration was careful to combine
military deployments with diplomatic actions, and was thus able to bring the
Cuban missile crisis to an end without a shot having been fired.)

One might well stop here and ponder why the Pentagon's intelligence analysts and their military superiors, in contrast to those in the CIG/CIA, were so strongly disposed to sound the tocsin at every Soviet and Communist gain during the early postwar years and at every propaganda blast against the capitalist West and the United States. One reason no doubt goes back to Pearl Harbor and the failure of the military chiefs in Washington to understand either the early signs of Japanese aggressiveness or the intercepted diplomatic communications which provided tactical warning. The postwar military wanted to be sure that it was alert to any threat. Another reason was the need for an identified future enemy, a factor I alluded to in the preceding chapter.

A third factor is a proclivity in military doctrine to define the threat posed by an enemy or adversary in terms of his military capabilities, to measure those capabilities in arithmetical and geographical terms, and in the absence of adequate data to the contrary to paint those capabilities in "worst-case" language. Military intelligence officers are normally constrained from playing an adversary's capabilities against those of their own forces; that is the prerogative and responsibility of the commander. Actually, in the JIC paper there are several references to existing U.S. capabilities and future plans in comparison with those of the USSR. Those references are, however, comparisons without war-gamed, net-capability estimates of the sort necessary for a realistic threat evaluation. The absence of a net evaluation and the presence of raw, worst-case figures thus led the JIC analysts into expressing an exaggerated threat with frightening implications. They did not, in effect, recognize the limitations on Soviet capabilities which the Soviets themselves had recognized and which had stayed their hand.

One particular arithmetical estimate was especially alarming; it was said in the body of the estimate that the Soviet army was composed of 175 line divisions, that it could rapidly mobilize about 145 more, and that it could subsequently increase that number as required. The fact is that the USSR was a terribly ravaged country short of manpower, logistics, and nearly everything else. Nobody in the Pentagon, West Germany, or the CIA had more than the flimsiest informational base for estimating the Soviet force size, equipment availability, transport capacity, or operational skills for carrying out the campaigns estimated, to say nothing of the damage that such forces would have suffered from U.S. and Western counteraction in an actual war situation.

Another very important factor in estimating the Soviet threat at that time was a determination of the USSR's developing atomic weapons capability.

The JIC paper estimated a Soviet atomic bomb stockpile of 22 in mid-1950, rising to 165 in mid-1953 and to 235 in mid-1954. But the Joint Ad Hoc Committee only a few months earlier had projected a figure of 10–20 for mid-1950 and a figure of 70–135 for mid-1953. Moreover, it had said then that even for 1953 there was a large amount of uncertainty and that no "well-founded estimate" could be made for the years after 1953. The Office of Naval Intelligence took serious exception to the Joint Ad Hoc Committee's estimate, which was designed primarily to discuss the consequence of Soviet possession of atomic weapons for U.S. security. Its dissent claimed that the Ad Hoc Committee was at fault for not adequately discussing Soviet intentions and objectives and that this lack was a "fatal error," particularly "in view of the uncertainty which must be expressed regarding quantities, dates of availability, and characteristics of Soviet atomic bombs." The JIC paper, which appeared a short time later, not only used much higher figures but also failed to deal with the question of bomb characteristics and reliability, or the availability of weapons delivery systems. U.S. nuclear weapons systems, including numbers available, were perhaps not even known to the estimators, but they needed to have been taken into account in some manner in order to arrive at a realistic estimate of the threat that the Soviet arsenal posed to the United States.

Thus, as the year 1951 began, the O/NE faced a daunting task. The nation was confronted by a worldwide political movement that posited a historical doctrine predicting the collapse of the capitalist system and its replacement through a world socialist-communist revolution. The leaders of the USSR believed that it was their historic mission to promote that revolution and to protect their socialist homeland from a capitalist counterrevolution. Their efforts, during the early postwar years, to expand the Communist world and simultaneously to develop the military capabilities they thought necessary to defend the revolution raised questions in the West about their intentions. In particular, questions were raised about whether the Soviets would use military force to expand the Communist world and especially about the degree to which they would risk general war to do so. The JIC paper strongly implied that the Soviets would accept high risks of general war and that they might at some early date actually deliberately choose to precipitate one.

It was the JIC view that greatly influenced the formulation of NSC-68, and the North Korean assault on South Korea was generally regarded in Washington as proof of Soviet plans to use military force—preferably through a satellite Communist country—to achieve its ends. We now know that the Korean affair was undertaken only after the risk of general war with the United

States appeared to have been greatly reduced by NSC actions and by Secretary Acheson's public statements. What we have learned from the Soviet archives emphasizes the point that none of the intelligence agencies had an adequate informational basis for dealing with the difficult questions which were then confronting U.S. policymakers. The USSR had only recently become a major U.S. intelligence target, and the intelligence agencies of the Defense Department and the CIA were only beginning to develop information-collection systems over and above the very limited open and official sources available. It was essential, until those assets began to bring in reliable information, to do the best possible job by looking at the open and official sources against the historical, doctrinal, geographic, scientific, and cultural background data on the Soviet Union to which everyone had access.

In such circumstances, a premium is put upon analytic methods and approaches. Unlike the intelligence organizations of the Defense and State departments, the O/NE had no departmental or bureaucratic interest to protect. The O/NE could and did expect that its own staff, and those staffs in the other intelligence agencies with whom it dealt, would follow the most stringent and careful practices in the use of evidence and in drawing judgments there from. The first major effort to do so was the preparation of NIE 25.

1951: A Turning Point in Estimating Soviet Intentions

In accordance with the procedures developed by William Langer and by Ray Cline, the O/NE's Chief of Estimates Staff, the task of preparing an estimate was normally assigned to a member of the General Group, one of six analysts recruited from the old ORE or from outside the Agency. In the case of the new Soviet intentions estimate, however, Cline chose to write it himself. Langer, as chairman of the board, chose to assume the chairmanship of all meetings on the new paper, as he had done even on the less critical estimates the O/NE had undertaken. Early in the year, Cline turned out a draft of NIE 25 for consideration by the board. I thought it was a splendid paper. I had always had high respect for Cline, who had a fine logical mind and who had the best academic training among my colleagues. He had known Langer at Harvard, and they got along well. But his draft estimate ran into serious trouble.

For days on end, the board wrangled and quarreled with Cline and among themselves. Though I was not a Soviet expert in the sense of reading the Russian language or having detailed knowledge about Soviet internal political and economic doings, I had been following Soviet policies carefully since the end of World War II. I attended the board meetings on the Cline draft and tried to understand all that was being said, both pro and con. Cline defended his draft, I thought very persuasively, but he won support only from Langer, Montague, and Van Slyck. Some members were strongly opposed, and two or three sat by rather passively. To my recollection, Cline at one point told the board that they would have found the paper more acceptable if he had used the words "them bastards" instead of the more polite "Soviet leaders" when referring to the men who ruled the USSR. In his recollection of those early months of 1951, Cline himself has written that he had been, he supposed, "pretty rude to the older men on the Board." They seemed to him to have been "interminably verbose, infatuated with their own prose, and likely to be carried away by ideas that could not be supported by the evidence."[1]

After days of rancorous meetings, Ludwell Montague, though a board member, offered to write a new draft himself. He was more courtly than Cline, and perhaps he could convey much the same message about Soviet intentions as Cline had done, but manage to get his board colleagues to go along. But he too failed; some board members attacked his draft as fiercely as they had Cline's.

The next step was that I was asked to try my hand. Since I was less experienced with Soviet affairs than Cline or Montague and was thought of as a scribe rather than an expert, it was apparently believed that I might be able to reflect the various views expressed around the table without advancing my own. I decided upon a short paper, which would reduce the number of debatable statements. I would try to avoid Communist ideology and references to Russian history and culture. I would try to rely as much as possible upon the overall Soviet-U.S. balance of military power, but in general terms rather than through the use of questionable specific figures about particular military forces or weapons systems.

It took time and many more days of dispute, but that approach worked. My draft was subjected to numerous revisions and shifts of nuance, but we finally had a paper that the board agreed upon and that went through the process of coordination with the other intelligence agencies without mishap. After it was finally approved on August 2, 1951, I and many of my colleagues heaved a huge sigh of relief. Although many others had participated in the writing process and contributed to the final language, I was congratulated by

---

1. Ray S. Cline, *Secrets, Spies, and Scholars* (Washington, D.C.: Acropolis Books, 1976), 123.

several board members in language that spoke meaningfully about the depth of the struggle we had gone through. General Huebner told me in his fatherly manner that I had shown a great deal of patience in the face of attacks from some of his board colleagues upon the judgments I had expressed. One of his colleagues, he reported, had even expressed a suspicion that I was a Communist because I had not been tough enough on the Russians.

A more interesting response to the completion of the estimate came from Max Foster, the Boston lawyer whom Bedell Smith had recruited to join the board some eight months earlier. Max had played his role as the outsider very well. He had been the board member most vociferous in challenging the Cline and Montague drafts for being too soft about Soviet intentions. A few days after the approval of the estimate, he asked me to join him at dinner one evening when he learned that Sally was out of town, and he told me that he was resigning from the board. When Bedell Smith had recruited him, Max said, Bedell had told him that "the Republic was in danger." Now that we had convinced him that such was not the case, he was going back to his family and his law practice in Boston.

The designated purpose of the exercise had been "to estimate probable Soviet courses of action to mid-1952 with particular reference to the probability of direct hostilities between the United States and the USSR." From the date when the estimate was initiated, that time period was about eighteen months in length; in those panicky times most estimates had a short "look-ahead" scope. In this case, the redrafting and coordination process took so long that the operative concluding date was slightly less than one year down the road. But the time span covered by the estimate was less important than the probing and explicating of the factors most likely to underlie Soviet courses of action, and we wrote no oversimplified statement of conclusions. The estimate contained only twenty-nine paragraphs, and it covered, as specifically as possible, the several main areas of policy concern in Washington at the time, namely, those related to the possibility of Soviet or Soviet-sponsored military action in Eurasia or against North America. The discussion was broken down into four categories: Soviet Objectives, Military Considerations Underlying Soviet Action, Possible Soviet Courses of Action Without Intent to Precipitate or Incur Serious Risk of General War, and Possibility of General War.

Under Soviet objectives, the estimate paid its respects to Soviet doctrinal concerns: the ultimate objective of a Communist world dominated by the USSR, and the inevitable eventuality of an armed conflict between the USSR and the United States. But it focused attention on more immediate and identifiable Soviet objectives: dividing the West, preventing German and Japanese rearmament, preventing implementation of the U.S. overseas base policy, maintenance of military readiness, offsetting increases in U.S. military capabilities, preventing the development of any threat to Soviet vital interests or to Soviet control of the Eastern European satellites, seeking geographical expansion of the Soviet orbit, seeking to undermine governments free of Soviet domination, and promoting neutrality in the East-West struggle among uncommitted nations.

Under the heading of military considerations, the estimate conceded that the armed forces of the USSR could overrun Continental Europe and adjacent areas of the Near East. It also conceded that the Soviet Air Force could provide tactical support to Soviet ground campaigns against Continental Europe and the Near East, and that it could "attempt" a strategic air offensive against Britain and North America. On the question of how the Soviets might regard the relative effectiveness of Soviet and U.S. atomic warfare capabilities, the estimate stated that it was impossible to judge what the Soviets might conclude. It was probable, however, that "uncertainty concerning relative atomic warfare capabilities and concerning the effectiveness of atomic weapons in determining the issue of a general war will be a major, though not necessarily a decisive, deterrent to the Kremlin in making a decision to initiate or deliberately provoke a general war with the U.S."

In the light of that deterrent, the estimate went on to state that "the Kremlin presumably prefers if possible to attain its objectives by courses of action short of resort to general war," and that it believed opportunities existed to make "limited progress" toward its immediate and long-term objectives "at least during the period" of the estimate "without provoking general war." To that end, it would employ various forms of political warfare such as a "peace campaign" exploiting fear of war and encouraging hopes for a settlement of outstanding issues.

The estimate then went on to catalog places where the Soviets might think that limited military operations could be conducted by Chinese Communist or European satellite forces to seize territories without precipitating general war. It ruled out attempts against Taiwan, Hong Kong, Macao, and Burma, but thought northern Indochina "a possibility." The estimate thought the Kremlin would rule out the use of European satellite forces against Yugoslavia because of the "impact on NATO interests." It also stated that satellite capabilities against Greece and Turkey were too limited to be effective and in any case would entail serious risk of U.S. or UN intervention.

As far as the direct commitment of Soviet forces was concerned, the estimate said that any open attempt to support or buttress Chinese or satellite forces would greatly increase the risk of general war and would be unlikely unless some area of "great importance" to the USSR became involved. Indeed, the estimate stated: "The Kremlin almost certainly estimates that overt and recognized commitment of Soviet forces against U.S. forces in any area would involve not only a local war with the United States, in which the U.S. might well use atomic weapons, but also the strong probability of general war with the United States, including a U.S. strategic atomic attack on the USSR."

That unambiguous statement did not, however, end the discussion about the possibility of a general war arising out of an aggressive use of Soviet military forces. There still needed to be considered the possibility that the Soviet leaders might decide to precipitate or accept general war without the stimulus of a local war, as in Korea, or of some other local situation involving important U.S. or Soviet interest. One factor which the board thought could cause the Soviets to consider such a step would be NATO, West German, or Japanese rearmament to a degree that threatened Soviet conventional force superiority, particularly in Europe. If, said the estimate, the Kremlin leaders thought that rearmament threatened their "vital interests" and if they thought they could "wage war successfully," they would indeed precipitate general war. If they did not think they could do so successfully, they would "modify" their policy and "attempt to relax international tension," at least temporarily. The estimators thought that the Kremlin was unlikely to conclude that U.S. and Western rearmament constituted an immediate threat to Soviet "vital interests."

Nevertheless, a war warning still needed to be sounded. The Kremlin might "at any time conclude that the Western rearmament program constitutes an eventual but already unacceptable threat to its interests," or it might "at any time misinterpret Western defensive measures as indicating an imminent attack upon the USSR. There was, moreover, a serious possibility of general war developing within the period of this estimate from an action or series of actions not intended to produce that result." While existing intelligence did not make a precise forecast possible, the USSR had "the capability to launch general war and may decide to precipitate general war." Moreover, the estimate concluded, "the international situation is so tense that at any time some issue might develop to a point beyond control."

I personally did not agree with the alarmist attitude expressed on the general war question, but I was merely the scribe. The board accepted, in my opinion, too much of what the Pentagon urged. But the military were not entirely of one view. The Director of Naval Intelligence dissented from the final paragraph, which he wished to have read as follows:

It is recognized that precise information on enemy intentions is rarely available and that enemy counteraction cannot be accurately predicted. However, all aspects of the Soviet problem considered, we believe it unlikely that the USSR will deliberately choose to precipitate or undergo the hazards of general war during the period covered by this estimate. Although the possibility of war by miscalculation cannot be discounted during periods of high international tension, we believe that in pursuing various courses of action short or war with the U.S., the USSR will seek to increase its power and damage the interests of the U.S. whenever and wherever feasible, but will at every turn attempt to exploit each course of action with such caution as to avoid direct military aggression against the vital interests of the United States.

In the light of subsequent events, it has become clear that the Naval Intelligence view was the correct one. Except for the outbreak of the Korean War in 1950 and the Cuban missile crisis of 1962, there have been no serious war scares. Indeed, from the end of World War II until the preparation of NIE 25, there had been a pattern of advance and retreat in Soviet political, propaganda, and diplomatic maneuvers, but retreats had predominated—especially when the United States and the Western powers had taken firm positions. The Soviets withdrew their military forces from Manchuria, Iran, northern Norway, and the Danish island of Bornholm; they retreated from their blockade of Berlin; they abandoned the local Communists in Greece; they instructed the French Communists not to try to seize power by force. (The Soviets did initiate a blockade of Berlin and execute a coup in Czechoslovakia, but both were protective measures prompted by the West's actions in its occupation zones.) The Navy's representative at the meetings on NIE 25 had discerned what those of us on the O/NE staff had also discerned, namely, that the guiding principle of Soviet behavior had been reliance upon political action rather than military aggression to expand the Communist world.

It is true, of course, that during the writing and coordinating of NIE 25 we still had no persuasive secret intelligence information upon which to make firm judgments. Our judgments were based very heavily upon the deterrents to Soviet military action. We looked at the forces that would be arrayed against any Soviet bloc military aggression and at the international complications for the Soviet bloc which military aggression would have entailed. We did consider U.S. atomic weapons capabilities and we did conclude that the Soviet and Chinese leaders were aware of the risks for their own survival which would have been involved in provoking or precipitating large-scale war with the United States and its allies. We admitted that the international climate was dangerous but we also believed that the Soviet leadership, though hardly trustworthy and not always consistent, would refrain from actions involving the threat of general war when it did not have the means to wage it successfully.

In our discussion of the possibility of general war, we came to few firm judgments, but we did explore the subject, and in doing so we were able at least to temper the alarms that had been set off by JIC 531/10 and NSC-68. In that sense, NIE 25 was a turning point. In the years that followed, we were able, because of better information and longer observation of Soviet behavior, to discuss the Soviet "threat" in more realistic ways and with more solidly based judgments.

1952: Will the Soviets Initiate General War?

NIE 25 did not put to rest the fears in Washington that the Soviet Union might yet deliberately initiate a full-scale general war against the United States at some early date. Our judgments were, after all, quite conditional and tentative on some important points. So, in late 1951, we geared up for a new attack on those questions, and a new estimate was completed on January 7, 1952, and became NIE 48. Although it covered some of the same ground as NIE 25, discussion and conclusions had moved sufficiently toward the position of Naval Intelligence that there was no Naval dissent. NIE 48 was the first estimate to spell out the factors that, in both theory and practice, would deter the Soviet leaders from deliberately initiating war against the United States and its allies or, contrarily, induce them to do so.

The conclusions were less tentative and conditional than the judgments in NIE 25:

> On balance we believe it unlikely that the Kremlin will deliberately initiate general war during 1952. We believe that the Kremlin prefers to pursue its objectives through methods short of deliberate resort to war with the U.S. and its allies, and moreover, probably estimates that possibilities for progress through such methods will continue to exist through 1952. We believe that in these circumstances the Kremlin is likely to be deterred from a deliberate resort to war with the U.S. and its allies in 1952, by the certainty of extensive destruction in the USSR as well as by the risk that the Soviet system might be destroyed.

We recognize, however, the continuing grave danger of a general war in 1952 resulting from a Kremlin action or series of actions not intended to have that result, or even from actions which, in the Kremlin's view, entailed that risk, but not the certainty thereof. We recognize also the danger that general war might arise from Soviet-initiated activities which the Kremlin intended to limit to a particular area.

In one of the paragraphs that discussed deterrents, the estimate assumed that in the case of a general war the Soviets might have initial successes, but that they would also have to recognize that

> At least a substantial portion of the power potential of the U.S. would remain, and probably would in time be brought to bear in a continuation of the struggle. In these circumstances the Kremlin would expect to be faced with operations of such magnitude as, at the least, to make the war long and costly to the USSR. The Kremlin would have to consider, in this situation, whether or not it could survive the political, economic, psychological and military strains of a prolonged war of attrition.

The Director of Naval Intelligence at that point in the discussion wished to attach an additional paragraph spelling out further the "grave dangers" which the Soviets would face in such a war, for example, "persistent and growing air attacks, including atomic attacks, possibly resulting in serious economic breakdowns and the disruption of Soviet administrative and police machinery." In areas which the Soviets might have overrun, the Navy wished to add, they would face logistical problems, the possibility of widespread guerrilla resistance supported and directed by the United States and its allies, ideological contamination of its occupation forces, and the probable existence of bridgeheads available to the allies for a counteroffensive.

These real-life calculations—which the Soviets would have had to make—stand in sharp contrast to the shrill language of JIC 531/10 and NSC-68. The estimate in effect cut down to size the "Russians-are-all-ten-feet-tall" syndrome that had until then tended to dominate Pentagon thinking about the Soviet "threat." But the estimate still had to deal with certain particular events that could lead to general war, such as, for example, an attack upon the USSR by the Western powers and especially the United States.

The estimate in its final section contained a cogent paragraph on that subject, and it was one recognizing a problem in U.S.-Soviet relations that persisted in one form or another for the next four decades:

> If . . . the Kremlin concluded that a Western attack on the USSR were imminent and unavoidable, and that Soviet chances of surviving such an attack would be improved by seizing the initiative and attacking first, it would almost certainly do so. We have no way of knowing what interpretation the Soviet leaders may be placing upon the informa-tion available to them concerning Western plans and preparations. But in view of apparent longstanding Kremlin concern over real or imagined threats to Soviet security, Marxist warnings over the ever-present danger of capitalist attack on the Communist world, of expressed Soviet suspicion of various recent Western military measures, and of various recent statements by Western public officials and of articles in the Western press, we believe that the Kremlin is probably disturbed over Western intentions.

Now that Soviet archival information for the time period of NIE 25 and NIE 48 is available it is possible to look at how Stalin might have viewed U.S. intentions. Two Russian writers, Vladislav Zubok and Constantine Pleshakov, both of whom were researchers at the Soviet Institute of U.S. and Canada Studies, devote two chapters to Stalin and his policies in their book, *Inside the Kremlin's Cold War* (published in 1996). They point out that Stalin did not seem to have acknowledged in any of his telegrams or in discussions with the Chinese that the Korean War had given a decisive impulse to West German rearmament, to the strengthening of NATO, or to the CIA's Cold War oper-ations. At one stage of the war (June 1951), Stalin had written to Mao that a protracted war in Korea was a good thing; it would "unsettle the Truman regime" and "interfere with U.S. preparations for a new world war." He dis-paraged American "land power" and claimed that all the U.S. strength was in "air raids and the atomic bomb." While thus pretending not to fear U.S. military power, Stalin nevertheless encouraged the Chinese to step up their own rearmament program. But in trying to appease Chinese fears of the United States, Stalin actually acknowledged indirectly that the United States was rearming and that the United States did have a significant atomic weapons capability.

Zubok and Pleshakov, citing Stalin's last published writings and the words of Nikita Khrushchev, concluded that Stalin was in fact worried and "bewil-dered" by the growth in U.S. economic and military power. According to

Khrushchev, Stalin began to fear U.S. superiority toward the end of his life (in 1953) and left "warnings about a future war ringing in Khrushchev's ears." In his own last published writings, Stalin himself charged that Churchill and his American allies were "mortal enemies" of the USSR. The two Russian writers described Stalin's foreign policy as "cautious expansionism in those areas that Stalin and his advisers defined as Soviet 'natural' spheres of influence." Stalin had no master plan, and his ambitions "had always been severely limited by the terrible devastation of the USSR during World War II and the existence of the American atomic monopoly."[2]

There was nowhere in Stalin's writings or secret correspondence any indication that Stalin would have liked to initiate any hostile action to destroy U.S. military power. The two Russian writers quoted favorably Robert Conquest's assessment that although Stalin was "occasionally erratic," his "sense of realism" was "still adequate enough" for him to avoid a headlong clash with the United States.[3] Thus it would appear that despite the alarms sounded in some U.S. circles and despite the lack of specific inside information at the time, the intelligence estimators were essentially correct in their assessment that the USSR would refrain from deliberately initiating general war or from actions likely to precipitate it.

1953: NSC Study of Soviet Nuclear Threat

Despite the reasoned analysis in NIE 48 of Soviet attitudes toward general war, there were still many in Washington who thought the Soviets were more aggressive and foolhardy than the estimators believed. They remained very nervous about Soviet intentions and about the USSR's growing nuclear capability. Thus it was on January 19, 1953, the day before General Eisenhower assumed the presidency, that the Truman NSC created a Special Evaluation Subcommittee to "prepare a summary evaluation of the net capability of the USSR to inflict direct injury on the United States during the period up to July 1, 1955."

The subcommittee consisted of Lt. Gen. Idwal Edwards (USAF, Retired) as chairman; Lt. Gen. Harold R. Bull (USA, Retired), representing the CIA; Maj. Gen. Robert M. Webster (USAF), representing the Joint Chiefs of Staff; and representatives of two interdepartmental internal security committees.

2. Vladislav Zubok and Constantine Pleshakov, *Inside the Kremlin's Cold War* (Cambridge: Harvard University Press, 1996), 70–76, passim.

3. Cited from Robert Conquest, *Stalin: Breaker of Nations* (London: Weidenfeld & Nicolson, 1991), 281; cited in Zubok and Pleshakov, *Inside the Kremlin's Cold War*, 74.

A navy captain, Henry Bruton, was named executive officer, and staff members were seconded from the three military services. I was chosen by General Bull, who was then a member of the Board of National Estimates (and who had been chief of plans at SHAEF Headquarters in World War II), to act as his staff assistant. We were given a very brief lead time; the report was due on May 15, 1953.

When we began our work, I for one was quite unaware of the debate apparently going on within the government over the military and diplomatic uses to which nuclear weapons should be put. We certainly did not know of the worry and bewilderment of Joseph Stalin (as reported by Zubok and Pleshakov in their book on the Cold War) over the growth of U.S. economic and military power during the early 1950s. We knew, of course, of the extension of U.S. conscription, of U.S. financial assistance to other members of NATO, and of U.S. plans to double the strength of all military forces. We assumed that U.S. atomic weaponry was also expanding, although the size and characteristics of the U.S. stockpile were known to only a few security policy insiders.

The NSC had accepted in its papers the general line of the intelligence estimates that the Soviets would not deliberately initiate or provoke a general war with the United States because of the marked U.S. atomic superiority.[4] What remained open for discussion in Washington was the question of using or threatening to use the atomic weapon as a means not only for deterring Communist military action but also for compelling Communist nations to act in consonance with U.S. policy objectives.

Indeed, the Truman NSC, in its final review of national security policy on the day before Eisenhower's inauguration, concluded that if the United States decided to build a thermonuclear weapon it would have an "enhanced deterrent to general war." But if the Soviets did likewise, the Council concluded, such a development "could tend to impose greater caution on our [own] Cold War policies to the extent that those policies involved a significant risk of war."[5] So, what we on the subcommittee were being asked to do was to study a not very likely possibility, namely, a Soviet deliberate initiation of general war in an atomic weapons environment, an environment which could in due course be superseded by a thermonuclear environment.

4. NSC 114/2 (October 1951); cited in John Lewis Gaddis, The Long Peace (New York: Oxford, 1987), 117.
5. NSC 141; cited in Gaddis, The Long Peace, 123.

The subcommittee and its staff were not, of course, aware of what the NSC members and staff had been thinking concerning the implications of going ahead with the thermonuclear weapon. We simply proceeded within the frame of reference we were given, that is, an analysis of the "net capability of the USSR to inflict direct injury on the United States" regardless of the diplomatic or military situation which might prompt an attack. Nevertheless, what we did report also applied in a general way to the thermonuclear environment about which Truman's National Security Council and Staff were so concerned at their final meeting on January 19, 1953.

One of the first steps in our study was to visit the relevant military commands for briefings about their capabilities and about the assumptions upon which they were proceeding. Our first stop was at the headquarters of the Strategic Air Command (SAC) near Omaha. It was SAC's view that the optimum date for the Soviets to attack the United States was in October 1954, some eighteen months hence. (Six years later I was back at SAC for a briefing on a subsequent net estimate of the Soviet threat. I was fascinated to learn then that the optimum time for the Soviets to attack the United States was still eighteen months hence!)

We next visited the headquarters of the North American Air Defense Command (NORAD) near Colorado Springs. At this underground headquarters we were impressed by the various systems in place for identifying, tracking, and intercepting hostile aircraft. At Edwards Air Force Base in California, we watched an exercise, planned especially for us, involving a scramble by interceptors and pilots on continuous alert. Finally, we went to the Atomic Weapons Facility at Sandia near Albuquerque, where I for one learned a great deal about atomic weapons, the effects of atomic explosions, and the varieties of atomic weapons in existence and under development. We also visited an underground site where atomic weapons were stored and armed. It was all thought-provoking.

On our flight back to Washington, I did think about what ought to be in our report. I scratched out a general outline, and General Edwards called a meeting of the group to discuss it. Our principals thought it looked good, and a few assignments were made. The outline was really a very simple listing of proposed chapter headings: Soviet Capabilities to Attack the United States, U.S. Defense Capabilities, U.S. Vulnerability to Atomic Attack, Soviet Concept of Operations and Plan of Attack, Estimate of Damage to the United States. I agreed to do the first chapter. General Edwards offered to do the second. The other chapters were assigned to other staff members.

Regarding Soviet capabilities, the report (NCS 140/1) credited the USSR with being able to have 120 atomic weapons with yields of eighty kilotons by mid-1953 and 300 by mid-1955. The number of weapons available could have varied upward or downward depending upon the Soviet capacity to make larger or smaller weapons using the amount of fissionable material estimated to be available to them; if larger weapons were made, there would be fewer of them; if smaller ones were made, there would be more. Delivery of these weapons to the United States would be effected by a fleet of TU-4 medium bombers (a copy of the U.S. B-29), which if stripped down and flown from peripheral bases with the use of range-extension techniques could reach any target in the United States on one-way missions. A heavy bomber with the capability of a round trip through the use of range-extension techniques would be available by 1955. Aside from any combat losses that might occur, we thought that about 30 percent of the bombers launched would abort or suffer operational failures. Another 10 percent, even if they reached their targets, would be rendered ineffective as a result of gross errors or weapons failures.

We considered other means of attack upon the U.S. mainland. In most cases they were of negligible importance, except possibly against Alaska, where a limited amphibious and/or airborne attack could be mounted. We also considered the possibility of sabotage by members of the U.S. Communist Party, but its small membership and the fact that it had been thoroughly penetrated by U.S. security agencies rendered it virtually useless to the USSR. We further considered the clandestine introduction of saboteurs and atomic weapons and their components, but believed that such methods would involve a high risk of detection and thus compromise any advantage such an attack could hope to gain through surprise. Concerning surprise, we made the following observation: "Surprise is the strongest weapon in the Soviet arsenal. Because of this, the USSR would not be able to engage in preparations to carry out certain naval, ground, amphibious, airborne, clandestine, and even air operations which might disclose a positive intent to deliver an attack upon the United States. A single instance of detection might alert the entire defense system of the Western world and the U.S. air atomic counteroffensive forces."

We thought that if the USSR chose to attack the United States—despite the risks involved and despite a shortage of atomic bombs and the lack of an effective and reliable delivery capability—it would do so with the aim of "inflicting maximum direct injury" upon the continental United States and upon those installations outside the United States which were important to the U.S. strategic offensive capability. Its first priority, therefore, would be continental U.S. bomber bases and selected air bases and air forces outside the United States; its second priority would be major population, industrial, and control complexes in the United States. Assuming that the USSR had approximately 300 eighty kiloton weapons in 1955, for example, we thought its military planners would allocate approximately 90 to the first priority targets (SAC), about 150 to the second priority targets (population, etc.), and hold back about 60 for other purposes.

When we came to gaming out the assumed Soviet attack, both U.S. air defense forces and the extent of available warning played decisive roles. For mid-1953, we calculated that because of the limited capability of the warning system, U.S. air defenses would kill only 7 percent of the attacking force before it reached the bomb-release line; by 1955, because of the extended warning net which would then be in place, we calculated that about 27 percent of the attacking aircraft would be destroyed. Also by mid-1955, the additional warning that would be operative would allow a greater dispersal of SAC's bombers away from their bases; a two-hour warning would permit a 65 percent dispersal, and a six-hour warning would permit an 85 percent dispersal. The effect of the likely mid-1955 warning time would thus enable SAC to carry out its planned counteroffensive. We therefore concluded that as of mid-1955 a Soviet atomic attack "could not reduce SAC's capability to a level that would inhibit heavy retaliatory attacks on the USSR."

As for damage to the U.S. economy, we concluded that the USSR did not possess "a sufficient stockpile of weapons or the necessary operational capabilities to insure elimination of a remunerative proportion of critical [US] industries." The Soviet attacking force in 1955 could seriously damage the U.S. economy, but the area bombing of which it was capable would be "unlikely" to destroy "a critical proportion of any important industry" or "seriously cripple any critical category of war industry." Because of facilities located in areas that would be free of atomic attack, U.S. industry would still be able to support large-scale and extensive military operations.

As for personnel casualties, the total number could go as high as 12,500,000 when computed on the basis of a minimum 30 minutes warning with an average of one hour for the populations attacked. Half of those casualties could be deaths. We thought actual casualties could be as low as half of the figure cited above because optimum aiming points and weapons placement would be unlikely in many cases. The most serious consequence of a Soviet atomic attack would be its psychological impact, and much would depend upon the "resolution and resourcefulness with which government and leadership dealt with the problems of waging the war." We concluded "that over-all damage to the U.S. would not be such as to prevent the delivery of a powerful initial retaliatory air atomic attack, the continuation of the air offensive, and the successful prosecution of the war."

I was not in a position to judge what effect this net evaluation had on thinking in Washington; I left for London soon after its delivery to the White House. The report was classified Top Secret, and the executive secretary of the NSC directed that "special security precautions" be observed in the handling of the report, that access to it should be "strictly limited and individually controlled," and that "no additional copies of the report or any part of it . . . be made." My only role after delivery was a visit to the NSC staff offices when one of the NSC staff members asked me to stop by for a general discussion of the problem of defense against air attack. As I recall, we agreed that no satisfactory air defense was likely to be developed within the limits of present concepts and that some new concept was necessary if the United States wished to prepare to defend itself from overhead attack.

The Net Evaluation Subcommittee's report must have had at least a modest calming effect upon those military planners who were having nightmares about a Soviet attack on the United States from the air. The Soviets could indeed kill a lot of people and do a lot of damage, but during the next few years such an attack could not bomb the United States into submission or destroy its ability to give back much greater than it received. It was probably that realization which had caused Stalin's worry and bewilderment during the final months of his life. (He died in March 1953, when our study was just getting under way. Stalin's successors proved to be more rational than he was, and in any case the deconcentration of power which followed his death made it even less likely that the Soviet leaders could agree to undertake such a risky venture as an unprovoked attack upon the United States.)

Yet those who wished the United States to continue its rearmament programs no doubt found support in our report, for example, in the expressed need to strengthen the warning network and to ensure the survival of SAC's strike forces. The defense planners could, and indeed for some years thereafter did, work toward a deterrent strategy. On the other hand, it also should have become clear that the United States needed to develop a stance, both in military posture and foreign policy, which would not cause the Soviet leaders to fear a U.S. first strike or force them to choose between an unacceptable diplomatic defeat and mutual destruction.

Perhaps the most valuable consequence of the exercise was that the NSC made an annual net-capability estimate a part of its established program. The Defense Department some years later took over the responsibility for the growing staff and for much of the research necessary to achieve greater accuracy and reliability in the product. The annual exercise filled an important gap in the data needed for both military and diplomatic policy planning. It made it respectable for Soviet intelligence analysts to utilize judgments of net capability in estimating Soviet policies and intentions. In effect, we became qualified to think about Soviet power in dynamic rather than arithmetic terms and to consider how Soviet forces and weaponry would weigh and function in actual combat against U.S. forces and strategies.

In the fall of 1954, when the NSC machinery geared up to prepare a new net estimate, the CIA again detailed General Bull to become a subcommittee member, and this time Ray Cline, our Soviet staff chief, was designated to perform the duties which I had assumed eighteen months earlier. This time, a longer lead-time was possible, and Cline succeeded in getting the war-gaming staff of the Joint Chiefs engaged for a much more comprehensive "netting out" of the Soviet attack and the U.S. response. I had written most of the previous report, except for General Edwards's chapter; the Subcommittee Staff members assigned to the other chapters had simply failed to come up with acceptable drafts, and I had taken over their materials and written new drafts in order to create a readable and unified report. Cline reported in his memoirs that his role was even more intensive than mine had been; he wrote "every word" of the new net estimate and of the oral briefing at the White House, which all the top Pentagon brass attended. Also in his memoirs, Cline made the following observation about the work of both the Office of National Estimates and the Net Evaluation Subcommittee in the early 1950s: "This Net Estimate and the NIE's of this 1950s era succeeded in reducing the Soviet military threat to the United States to reasonable proportions in the minds of war-planning staffs. The CIA never accomplished more of value to the nation than this quiet, little-remarked analytic feat."[6]

1954: First General Estimate of Soviet Intentions

Following the endorsement in NIE 3 of the Pentagon's estimate of "Soviet Capabilities and Intentions" in November 1950, the Office of National Estimates prepared no general paper on Soviet intentions and capabilities until 1954. NIE 25 (1951) and NIE 48 (1952) were substantial modifications of the views expressed in NIE 3 and superseded it. But NIE 25 was a short paper on probable Soviet courses of action over a brief time span, and NIE 48 was specifically concerned with the likelihood of a Soviet deliberate

6. Cline, *Secrets, Spies, and Scholars*, 143.

initiation of general war. There was a considerable number of other estimates prepared regarding the Soviet problem during the years from 1951 to 1954: to wit, special estimates or NIEs on Soviet economics, Soviet science, and Soviet politics; estimates on Soviet foreign policies in the Far East, the Middle East, and Europe; estimates on particular Soviet capabilities or on Soviet courses of action in particular situations. There was also an experiment with a two-part estimate covering Soviet capabilities in a document separate from probable Soviet courses of action (NIE 64, parts 1 and 2) completed late in 1952, and a similar effort in the summer of 1953 through the publication of two separately numbered estimates (NIEs 90 and 95). Finally, in the spring and summer of 1954, a comprehensive estimate was undertaken with a substantial time span. This was NIE 11-5-54, "Soviet Capabilities and Main Lines of Policy Through 1959."

As the chief of the O/NE's Soviet staff, Cline directed the preparation of this new estimate, and as one of its consumers in London, I was eagerly awaiting it. NIE 11-5-54 differed from NIE 25 primarily by bringing to bear upon its judgments "selected facts and significant figures," as Cline described it in his memoirs. Consequently, it was considerably longer than NIE 25, but this extra length made it both more useful and persuasive. It carried a seven-paragraph set of conclusions and an additional thirty-nine paragraphs of discussion and pertinent information. It had one dissenting paragraph (concerning China) from the chief of Air Force intelligence. The discussion covered Soviet objectives and beliefs, Soviet political stability, relations with China, Soviet economic growth, Soviet scientific resources, and Soviet military expenditures and military strength (with data on nuclear weapons, jet bombers, guided missiles, air defense, and submarines). Finally, there were paragraphs on the main lines of Soviet policy and likely Chinese Communist courses of action.

On Soviet objectives and beliefs, NIE 11-5-54 restated the observation made in earlier estimates that the Soviets envisaged an eventual Communist world, but that the Soviet leaders also recognized the possibility of a long struggle that would not necessarily involve general war. They saw the current period of "coexistence" as one that they needed in order to build up their strength while seeking to "divide and weaken" the non-Communist world. In Soviet domestic affairs, the post-Stalin period—with Beria also out of the way—had settled into a system of joint authority with a balance of power among leaders. Changes could occur within the ruling group and in the relative power positions of its individual members. It was possible that one man could gain absolute power, but for the next five years it seemed unlikely that conflicts within the ruling group would impair the stability of the regime or weaken its authority. It was possible, however, that for reasons of advancing their domestic agenda, the Soviet leaders would exercise their police powers "somewhat more moderately and less arbitrarily than in the past."

The estimate acknowledged the emerging complexities of the Sino-Soviet relationship. It noted that China was more an "ally" than a "satellite" of the USSR, possessed some capability for independent action, and was increasing its stature within the Sino-Soviet partnership. The "main outlines of Communist policy in Asia" were probably determined jointly by Moscow and Beijing, but the national interests of the USSR and Communist China in some cases were "conflicting," and this constituted "potential sources of friction between the two powers." Obviously, the students of Sino-Soviet relations within the intelligence community were unaware of the frictions and jockeying about, which had taken place four years earlier between Moscow and Beijing over Chinese entry into the Korean War, but even so it was already becoming clear that trouble lay ahead. It was in connection with Sino-Soviet relations that the Air Force dissented. The Air Force intelligence chief agreed that the two countries' leaders shared a common view about advancing Communist interests, but he was of the opinion that the "motives and judgment" of the Chinese leaders were such as to make Communist China "dangerously unpredictable under outside pressure of any appreciable magnitude." The analysts supporting that view were also unaware of what we know now about the cautiousness of the Chinese leaders and their resistance to Soviet pressures to intervene in Korea.

That part of the estimate (and of most of those published over the next thirty-five years) which was of most interest to military planners and budgeters was that dealing with military strength and weapons development. In general terms, NIE 11-5-54 pointed out that the Soviet armed forces had been maintained at high levels of strength and war-readiness and would continue quality improvement in weapons, equipment, and training. Soviet military policy over the upcoming five years appeared likely to emphasize an increase in the nuclear weapons stockpile, an improvement in delivery capability, improvements in weapons systems for air defense, and increases in the long-range submarine force.

The problem of estimating nuclear weapons proved a difficult one; the evidence was simply not available. The estimate listed several alternative assumptions about weapons sizes and about uses of the available fissionable materials in order to produce a variety of total yields; these assumptions led to total yield calculations running from 50 million to 206 million tons, with the total number of weapons running from about 1250 to somewhat over 2,000 for 1959. Those calculations did not include the possibility of thermonuclear weapons, which if successfully tested and produced could increase total energy yields by factors of five to twenty-five.

The estimators were also uncertain about the production of medium and heavy jet bombers (capable of striking the continental United States), but thought a substantial number of the latter could be in service by 1957. The estimators were also aware that the USSR was pressing hard to develop guided missiles, but had no evidence that any were operational. They thought there would be none capable of attacking the United States by 1959. Two long-range submarine types were under development, and some had been produced with an operational radius of 6700 miles. By 1959 the Soviets might have developed a nuclear-propulsion submarine.

In considering how the military balance would affect Soviet courses of action, the estimators judged that the Soviets themselves considered that there was a "rough strategic equilibrium between the Soviet bloc and the U.S.-NATO coalition." While the Soviet leaders "probably believe that they cannot be certain of winning a war," they gave no indication "of feeling that the balance of world power" was developing unfavorably to their basic interests. As for general war, the estimate stated:

> The Soviet leaders probably believe that general war would be a hazardous gamble for them, possibly involving the destruction of the Soviet system. On this basis, the Kremlin probably would conclude that the USSR should try during this period to avoid courses of action which in its judgment would clearly involve substantial risk of general war. The Kremlin will, however, probably continue to consider general war a possibility that cannot be excluded, and the USSR will almost certainly continue to build up its military and economic strength against this eventuality. We believe that the Kremlin would not be deterred by the risk of general war from taking counteraction against an action by the U.S. or its allies which the Kremlin considered an imminent threat to Soviet security.

The military section of the estimate concluded with some generalizations about trends emerging from the increased nuclear weapons development programs under way on both sides:

The progress being made by the USSR in the development of nuclear weapons, and the increasing Soviet capability to deliver these weapons, are changing the world power situation in important respects. As these Soviet capabilities increase, the U.S. is losing a great advantage which it has heretofore held in the struggle. Unless defensive capabilities develop beyond the degree now foreseen, both the U.S. and the USSR within the period of this estimate probably will have sufficient capabilities to cripple each other, though only at grave risk of receiving crippling blows in return.

The estimators thought that the Kremlin would follow its "present lines of policy throughout the period of this estimate," namely, through 1959. The Soviet leaders would believe, however, that because of the USSR's increasing nuclear capabilities, they would have "greater freedom of action" without running substantial risk of general war. They would be "increasingly ready to apply heavy pressure" on the non-Communist world when they observed any "signs of major dissension or weakness among the U.S. and its allies." They might attempt to gain some of their objectives by "local military actions," but the estimate made no mention of any world area where this might occur. In discussing Chinese Communist courses of action, the estimate thought the Chinese would be "reluctant" to undertake any action which they thought would involve substantial risk of provoking "unlimited war" with a major power.

The estimators believed that both the Soviet and Chinese leaders regarded Southeast Asia as the most favorable area for Communist expansion. Chinese pressure to gain control of Taiwan was not mentioned, nor was any area of the Near or Middle East mentioned as a likely Soviet target. The estimators had earlier in the estimate expressed the view that Soviet authority over the Communist satellite regimes in Eastern Europe would "remain intact" over the coming five years. In all the areas mentioned above, except Southeast Asia, the history of the next five years proved to be quite different from that which the estimate foresaw.

1953–1956: Post-Stalinist Changes in Europe

NIE 11-5-54 made an important contribution in its recognition that the world power situation was changing because of the increasing capability of the USSR to manufacture and deliver nuclear weapons. The implications of that judgment certainly became more and more evident as the 1950s progressed. As a consequence, the Soviet leaders became increasingly confident of their survival and of their eventual success in achieving a Communist world. They began to exploit emerging possibilities to expand their influence in under-developed areas. But they also had troubles of their own; the Korean War had changed American thinking about the USSR and had prompted a substantial U.S. rearmament effort; and the death of Stalin in 1953 led to new thinking in Eastern Europe and in the USSR itself. The major Western powers were also disagreeing among themselves over how to react to the changes in the Communist world and especially to changes in the former colonial areas of Africa and Asia.

Some important changes were clearly not foreseen in the intelligence estimates. For most intelligence officers, military and civilian alike, the safest course is to foresee military threats but not to engage in risky predictions about spontaneously emerging revolutionary movements. The influence of the military, whose business it is to foresee any threat to life as it is, clearly played an important role in conceptualizing NIE 11-5-54, most of which is concerned with military power and weaponry. The political world outside and beyond that of the main players in the Cold War appears to have been touched on only lightly.

In retrospect it is clearly evident that in the world of the mid-1950s what was happening in the Communist world was at least as important as the progressive buildup of nuclear capabilities by the United States and the USSR. Moreover, if it was Stalin's bad judgment that set off the Cold War, it was also the ill-informed response of the U.S. leaders that continued it and that militarized it beyond realistic requirements. Stalin's death should have been recognized as foreshadowing significant changes, but intelligence officers and political leaders alike thought that things in the Communist world were likely to go on as before. They did not.

The first major turning point after Stalin's death was the arrest and execution of the notorious Secret Police chief, Lavrenti Beria, in June 1953. A dramatic account of that event is laid out by Nikita Khrushchev in his memoir, *Khrushchev Remembers*. Strobe Talbott, who translated and edited the rather disorganized reminiscences of the former Soviet leader, has written that while Khrushchev was probably a leading spirit in Beria's removal, there were others inside and outside the Presidium (formerly the Politburo) who also wanted to be rid of him as soon as possible.[7] In an editorial comment, Talbott noted that Khrushchev assumed the vacant post of First Secretary of the Communist Party only three months later, and that "thenceforth, the fic-

---

7. Nikita S. Khrushchev, *Khrushchev Remembers* (Boston: Little, Brown, 1970), 321–22.

tion of collective leadership so assiduously maintained, began rapidly to dis-integrate."[8] Malenkov, who had assumed the twin offices of prime minister and first secretary upon Stalin's death, had been forced to give up the first secretaryship very soon thereafter, and then in February 1955—sixteen months after Khrushchev became first secretary—Malenkov was forced out as prime minister. NIE 11-5-54 had quite correctly pointed out that Khrushchev's star was rising, but thought that the then current modus operandi would persist for some time.

It did persist, and—despite Talbott's belief in its fictional character—it lasted for a good many years into the future. It is true that after Malenkov's dismissal in February 1955, Khrushchev set about concentrating power in his own hands. One step in his ascent, and a most important step in the history of the USSR and of international Communism itself, was Khrushchev's famous Secret Speech denouncing Stalin and his crimes, delivered at the Twentieth Congress of the Communist Party in February 1956. That speech did strengthen his leadership of the Soviet Communist Party; it also set off anti-Stalinist rebellions in the Communist Parties of Poland and Hungary. Those devel-opments, and certain other actions which Khrushchev had taken, prompted a group of old Stalinists in the Presidium to attempt in June 1957 to oust him. Led by Malenkov and Molotov, a majority voted against Khrushchev, but he appealed to the Party's Central Committee, which supported him and removed his principal opponents from the Presidium. Khrushchev named his opponents to posts outside Moscow, but made no effort to imprison or execute them. The post-Stalin political system thus passed an important test; from that point on, power struggles in the Soviet Union were no longer fatal for the losers..

The most dramatic consequences of the Secret Speech were the events that took place in Warsaw and Budapest in October 1956. Leaders of the so-called "fraternal" parties attended the Twentieth Party Congress, and copies of the speech were soon circulating within the Communist world and by mid-year in the Western press.

In Poland, Wladyslaw Gomulka, a long-time Communist who had run afoul of Stalin's secret police and was rehabilitated in 1955, resumed polit-ical activity in Warsaw after the denunciation of Stalin became known. When Stalin had purged the Polish Communist Party's refugee leadership in Moscow during the big purge of 1937 to 1939, Gomulka had escaped execution because he was in jail in Warsaw. When Poland was liberated, he again became a

8. Ibid., 341.

party activist, but in 1949 he was again arrested and accused of Titoism. When he resumed political activity in 1956 after the Secret Speech, one of his principal demands was the withdrawal of all Soviet officers and advisers from the Polish military and security apparatus. He held a series of meetings with the Polish Party's Politburo during October 1956, as a consequence of which he was restored to membership on the Politburo, and the pro-Soviet members—including the Soviet Marshal Rokossovski, who was defense minister and commander of the Polish army—were excluded. That upset the Soviet leadership in Moscow, which decided to send a delegation to Warsaw to discuss the situation in Poland.

The Soviet delegation was headed by Khrushchev and included Mikoyan, Molotov, Zhukov, Kaganovich, and Marshal Konev (the commander of the Warsaw Pact forces). The Soviet delegation arrived at the Warsaw airport at 7 A.M. on October 19, 1956, and an angry confrontation ensued. (What happened then in Warsaw and later in Budapest was described in some detail in a report that reached the Czechoslovak Communist Party's Politburo on October 25. The report was apparently written by an aide of Antonin Novotny, the Czech party leader, who attended a session of the Presidium of the Communist Party of the Soviet Union on October 24, at which Khrushchev briefed the Presidium and representatives of the "fraternal" parties on what had transpired in both capitals up to that time. (The report was translated and summarized by Mark Kramer in the Bulletin of the Cold War International History Project, no. 5.) Gomulka promptly demanded that Soviet officials pledge not to interfere in Poland's internal affairs and that Rokossovski and all other top Soviet officers in the Polish army be removed. While these exchanges were going on, Gomulka was informed by an aide that Soviet tank and infantry units were advancing on Warsaw. Gomulka demanded that they be pulled back, and Khrushchev, after some hesitation, complied and ordered Konev to halt all troop movements.[9]

But there was no meeting of minds, and the Soviet delegation returned to Moscow the next day. In Poland, pro-Gomulka rallies took place in all the major cities over the next several days, climaxing in a demonstration in Warsaw involving a half-million people. Polish officials began distributing firearms to "workers' militia" units, and Polish army and Interior Ministry troops were preparing to defend Warsaw against the entry of any Soviet forces. These cir-

9. This account is based upon "Hungary and Poland, 1956," a document from the Czechoslovak Communist Party archives, translated and annotated by Mark Kramer, in the Bulletin of the Cold War International History Project, no. 5 (Spring 1995): 50–51.

cumstances were so inauspicious for a military solution that Khrushchev soon thereafter moved to develop a modus vivendi with the new Polish leadership.

Meanwhile, the situation in Budapest was deteriorating. On October 23, three days after the Khrushchev delegation returned to Moscow, a huge demonstration was organized in downtown Budapest by students from the university expressing approval of what happened in Poland and demanding the same treatment for Hungary. The rally became violent late in the day, shooting occurred, and the Hungarian police and security forces were soon overwhelmed by the spreading uprising. When Khrushchev was apprised of the deteriorating situation, he ordered the two Soviet mechanized divisions stationed in Hungary to intervene and reinforced them with a division from Rumania and two from the Ukraine. Some 31,000 Soviet troops and over 1,000 tanks became engaged by the morning of October 24. But they were ineffective and even counterproductive; some elements of the Hungarian army, police, and even security forces joined the rebellion. Fierce fighting went on for another week, until a full-scale Soviet invasion force arrived on November 1 and completely suppressed the uprising.

What actually happened between October 24 and November 1 is still somewhat unclear. Charles Gati, in his *Hungary and the Soviet Bloc* (published in 1986), affirms that Imre Nagy, the newly named Communist Party leader, tried to calm the rebellion and save a relationship with Moscow by promising reforms. But the rebellion and fighting continued. Nagy concluded on October 28 that both the Hungarian party and the relationship with Moscow needed to be completely revamped. The Soviet ambassador, Yuri Andropov, and Presidium members Mikoyan and Suslov, who were in Budapest, apparently agreed with him. But when Soviet troops crossed the border on November 1, Nagy realized that he had been betrayed and that the Soviet leaders were no longer interested in a political solution.[10]

Why did Khrushchev and his colleagues in the Presidium think differently about Hungary than they had about Poland a few days earlier? One difference between the two cases was that Gomulka was better able to lead public opinion in Poland. It rallied to his side when he needed public support, and, when speaking at a mass rally in Warsaw on October 24—the same day that things got rough in Budapest—Gomulka took a conciliatory tone and referred to the need for political and military ties with the USSR.[11] In Budapest,

---

10. Summarized from a letter to the editor of the *Bulletin of the Cold War History Project*, no. 6-7 (Winter 1995/1996): 283, in which Gati quotes from his book *Hungary and the Soviet Bloc* (1986).

11. "Hungary and Poland, 1956," 51.

Nagy's efforts to continue ties with the USSR did not calm, but actually aggravated, the popular mood. When he played his final card by telling the public that Hungary would withdraw from the Warsaw Pact, it was too much and too late.

There obviously had been indecision in Moscow about military intervention. In his memoirs, Khrushchev gives an account which is at variance with the facts and highly defensive. He did consult the fraternal parties, including the Chinese (whose representative, Liu Shao-chi, said at one point that the Soviets should get out of Hungary), but Khrushchev claims he finally got the acquiescence of the Chinese, Poles, and even Tito, largely on the need to restore order. He went to great lengths in his memoirs to condemn Nagy as a counterrevolutionary, but the weight of evidence suggests that Nagy himself went to great lengths to try to save a role for the USSR and for socialism.

The most likely explanation for the Soviet harshness in Hungary is that because the revolution there came immediately upon concessions to the Poles, the Soviet leaders were fearful that if concessions were made to Hungary, they would be followed by an epidemic of similar events elsewhere, events that would have brought down, not only the Soviet empire in Eastern Europe, but socialism itself. In reporting on the debate with the Chinese on the question of military intervention, Khrushchev wrote that "someone warned of the danger that the working class might take a fancy to the counter-revolution."[12] That was the crux of the matter.

According to Zubok and Pleshakov, the events in Poland and Hungary had really "taken Khrushchev aback." He was frightened and especially fearful that the USSR's own intellectuals and artists who were challenging official forms of art "would develop a Hungarian-type of secret society and attempt to 'kill the politburo.'" His fear was intensified a few days after the suppression of the Hungarian revolt, when Soviet troops in East Germany were faced with furious crowds of protesters. Khrushchev didn't dally; he ordered the Soviet commander in East Germany to fire on the crowds if necessary.[13]

All of these events show that the situation in Eastern Europe was more fragile than the writers of NIE 11-5-54 had believed. Soviet authority over the satellite regimes did not "remain intact" during the second half of the 1950s, as the estimators had believed. Khrushchev blamed the revolts directly upon the "roll-back" policy of John Foster Dulles, Eisenhower's Secretary of

12. Khrushchev, *Khrushchev Remembers*, 418.
13. Zubok and Pleshakov, *Inside the Kremlin's Cold War*, 187.

State. Since John Foster's brother Allen was in charge of the operational arm of the CIA, it was thought in both the United States and abroad that the "roll-back" policy would involve more than mere propaganda. Indeed, one covert operation was attempted. It was against Albania, thought to be a rather soft spot and therefore the best place to get the ball rolling. It was to be a joint U.S.-British operation, and Albanian exiles and defectors were recruited and trained to be dropped into the country to stir up rebellion. The trouble was that each time a drop took place a reception committee was present to round up the interlopers for execution. A mole was suspected, and suspicion fell upon several of the U.S. planners. But it was not an American who betrayed the operation; it was Kim Philby, the head of the British intelligence mission in Washington. Like several other British moles, Philby fled some years later into the USSR, where he stayed for the rest of his life..

I do not know enough about CIA operations to confirm or deny Khrushchev's assertions about the role of the United States in the Hungarian and Polish revolutions. There was certainly enough unrest in both countries to stimu-late uprisings, but the trigger was Khrushchev's own Secret Speech. The anti-Stalinist message of the Secret Speech had trickled down to the party cadres throughout Eastern Europe. Whether they were party members by conven-ience or by belief, they set about to test the new atmosphere. But Khrushchev sent them a message in return. Fedor Burlatsky, a Khrushchev adviser, wrote in 1988:

> He [Khrushchev] executed Nagy as a lesson to all the other leaders in Socialist countries, thinking as he did so of Gomulka, Kadar [who took over in Budapest after the suppression], and also perhaps of Tito and Mao. In his eyes, political expediency was superior to morality.
> Perhaps without knowing it, Khrushchev was thereby firing on potential reformers in Budapest, in Prague, and in the Soviet Union. He set a bad example for his successors. Brezhnev was guided by it when he ordered troops into Czechoslovakia [in 1968] and "interna-tionalist aid" to Afghanistan [in late 1979].[14]

The fact is that even before the events of 1956 in Poland and Hungary, the United States had backed away from its policy of sponsoring revolts in Eastern Europe. According to a study, "New Findings on the 1956 Hungarian

---

14. Fedor Burlatsky, *Khrushchev and the First Russian Spring* (New York: Charles Scribner's Sons, 1988), 93.

Revolution" by Csaba Bekes, in the second issue of the *Bulletin of the Cold War International History Project* (Fall 1992), the U.S. National Security Council in July 1956 adopted a policy paper in which the U.S. government disavowed any political and military intervention in the satellite countries. Bekes also wrote, "The Western powers were caught by surprise with news of the revolt in Budapest, and thereafter pursued a policy of nonintervention to avoid antagonizing the Soviets."[15] Indeed, according to research by Janos Rainer of the Institute for the History and Documentation of the Hungarian Revolution in Budapest, the U.S. Department of State sent instructions to the U.S. embassy in Moscow on October 29—three days before the massive Soviet invasion occurred—which gave "clear signals of [U.S.] nonintervention."[16]

I was not aware at the time that the United States had reversed its position on stimulating revolution in Eastern Europe. I was upset, as many Americans were, over the mildness of the U.S. response to the Soviet reaction to the uprising. I remember well Radio Budapest's desperate call for help—as the Soviet forces were closing in—to save Hungary and, as they put it, to "save Europe." All they received was sympathy and an open Austrian border. Shortly thereafter, during a discussion of the Hungarian affair one afternoon in his office, Allen Dulles put the U.S. position quite bluntly: the question of assisting the Hungarian revolutionists was really a question of "whether we wanted to start World War III."

The Eisenhower administration acted wisely despite the discomfort its decision was causing. The decision was in line with the intelligence estimates; NIE 11-5-54 had explicitly stated that the USSR would not be deterred from taking counteraction to any action by the United States or its allies "which the Kremlin considered an imminent threat to Soviet security." But many of us thought that the "roll-back" ballyhoo had created a problem which should have been foreseen. The NSC's July 1956 action did recognize the mistake, but the genie could not be put back in the bottle.

As a consequence of the Hungarian uprising, de-Stalinization in the USSR suffered a setback. Georgi Arbatov has reported in his memoirs that as a result of Hungary "the brakes were applied at home" to the policy of reform, and Khrushchev began to encounter new difficulties in pursuing his anti-Stalinist policy. Indeed, the Hungarian affair was one of the events that stimulated the attempt of the old Stalinists to remove him in June 1957. On the other

---

15. See *Bulletin of the Cold War International History Project*, no. 2 (Fall 1992): 3.
16. *Bulletin of the Cold War International History Project*, no. 5 (Spring 1995): 26.

hand, the Secret Speech at the Twentieth Party Congress, which had triggered the Polish and Hungarian uprisings, also created a new atmosphere in the Soviet Union, an atmosphere that persisted and fundamentally altered the character of Soviet society. Arbatov put it this way:

> The Congress awakened the conscience of the people. Of course there were individual heroes who did not allow themselves to be intimidated or silenced—though tragically you can count on your fingers the ones who survived. For years we were obedient and fearful subjects of a totalitarian state. After the Congress, we started to become citizens and rebels. A new vitality of thought blossomed that was not quashed even during the frequent lapses into neo-Stalinism. I am convinced that this was one of the essential sources for perestroika and glasnost.[17]

1956: Khrushchev's Venture into the Arab World

If the Hungarian affair had caused Khrushchev to make critical decisions which later came to haunt him, he was still riding high as 1956 came to an end. The Presidium had decided in 1955 to take advantage of the growing nationalist movement in the Arab world, and the USSR made a deal to supply major military equipment to Egypt, including tanks and aircraft. The president of Egypt, Gamal Abdel Nasser, was aspiring to the leadership of the Arab world in an endeavor to throw off the remnants of colonialism and also to avenge the Arab defeat by the new Israeli state in 1949. He was also attempting to improve the Egyptian economy by building a dam at Aswan on the Upper Nile. The U.S. government had offered to help finance the dam, but withdrew the offer in July 1956 in retaliation for Nasser's growing ties with the Communist world, including the 1955 arms deal. Nasser responded to the withdrawal of the U.S. offer by nationalizing the Suez Canal in order to use its revenues to finance the building of the dam.

That step set off an Israeli-British-French invasion of Egypt on October 28, 1956, just as the Soviet Presidium was deciding what to do about Hungary and just before the U.S. election in which Eisenhower was campaigning for a second term of office. Neither Khrushchev nor Eisenhower knew how to respond, and both kept quiet for a few days. But when John Foster Dulles condemned the action of the Israelis, British, and French in a public statement at the UN, the United States—despite its disapproval of Nasser's actions—

---

17. Georgi Arbatov, *The System* (New York: Random House, 1992), 60.

saved Nasser. It chose to see the invasion of Egypt as "a golden opportunity to win Egyptian and Arab friendship."[18]

But Nikita Khrushchev also saw a golden opportunity in the U.S. response to the invasion. Zubok and Pleshakov described the Soviet leader's reaction to the new situation this way: "The Soviet leader quickly understood that the nuclear sword cut two ways: the Americans used it to contain Communism and, if possible, roll it back. Why shouldn't the Soviets similarly use it to contain American imperialism and, by providing an 'atomic umbrella' for anti-colonialist movements, accelerate the roll-back of capitalism?"[19]

Khrushchev persuaded the Presidium to send official letters to the three invaders, threatening them with Soviet military retaliation. Zubok and Pleshakov quote Khrushchev as having said the following (the brackets in the quotation below indicate inserts by the writers to clarify Khrushchev's remarks):

> The British and the French decided that the Russians had gotten stuck in Hungary. So, [they reasoned,] let us strike Egypt, [the Soviets] will not be able to come to its assistance, they cannot fight on two fronts. We will splash the Russians with mud, knock Egypt out, undermine the influence of the USSR in the Middle East. [But] we found resources both to keep troops in Hungary and to warn the imperialists that, if they would not stop the war in Egypt, we might use missile armaments. Everyone admits that with this we decided the fate of Egypt.[20]

It is very doubtful that Khrushchev's threats did in fact decide the fate of Egypt. The Eisenhower-Dulles position probably was the deciding factor. But both the USSR and Nasser claimed victory and received most of the credit in the Arab world.

In a more general sense, the Suez War and the roles played by the U.S. and Soviet governments in its termination led into a succession of events that had a profound effect upon future U.S.-Soviet relations. In Moscow in mid-1957 Khrushchev was chided by Molotov and his allies for accepting the idea of a "nuclear stalemate" and the related idea that nuclear bi-polarity could lead to "an agreement" between the United States and the USSR. Molotov, according to Zubok and Pleshakov, wanted instead to use the USSR's grow-

---

18. John Spanier, *American Foreign Policy Since World War II*, 7th ed. (New York: Praeger, 1977), 1.

19. Zubok and Pleshakov, *Inside the Kremlin's Cold War*, 190–91.

20. Ibid., 191–92.

ing nuclear capability to apply "pressure not only on America, but also on other states that distance themselves from [the United States] and are not firmly on the side of capitalism." Only in such a way, thought Molotov, would it be possible "to weaken America itself."[21] Molotov, as noted earlier, prevailed in the Presidium, but then lost out to Khrushchev in the Central Committee. With that victory achieved, Khrushchev went on to stun the United States and the rest of the world by placing Sputnik in orbit. He followed that up with a statement at a missile plant early in 1958 that if the missiles produced there were deployed, he "would guarantee that there would be no third world war."[22]

But while Khrushchev was trying to suggest that he would be satisfied with a U.S.-Soviet strategic military balance, his missile threat of October 1956 was seen in Washington as the sign of an upcoming Soviet plan to acquire allies and influence in the Near East. Accordingly, in the spring of 1957 the Eisenhower administration supported a Congressional Joint Resolution which declared that the United States would militarily support any Near Eastern nation "requesting assistance against armed aggression from any country controlled by international Communism." The underlying assumption of that so-called "Eisenhower doctrine" was its acceptance of Khrushchev's "nuclear sword" bluff as genuine. What U.S. leaders did not understand was that the root problem for the United States in the Arab world was Arab nationalism itself and not Nasser's flirtation with Moscow. Indeed, Nasser's political victory in the Suez War inspired nationalist activity all over the area.

The first political target of the newly flourishing Arab nationalism was Jordan's King Hussein. Despite riots and demonstrations during the spring months of 1957, Hussein survived through quick U.S. moral and financial support. U.S. action in Jordan also encouraged the moderate and conservative Arab governments in the region to resist nationalist activity. A year later, however, Egypt and Syria formed the United Arab Republic (UAR), and the Egyptians proceeded to encourage Nasserists in Iraq and Lebanon to rise against their regimes. That summer nationalist officers in Iraq did overthrow the government in Baghdad and execute its pro-British king and prime minister. About the same time Nasserists in Lebanon began to agitate for joining the UAR, and pro-Western Christians there began to fear an uprising that would destroy the political balance among religious communities. Eisenhower then sent 14,000 troops into Lebanon in an effort to stabilize the situation.

21. Ibid., 191.
22. Ibid., 192.

A few months later, when things appeared to have settled down, the U.S. forces were withdrawn.

There was no immediate response from Moscow, thus demonstrating that Khrushchev—while willing to use his strategic power to remind the Western leaders that the USSR could also play the big-power game—was not willing to challenge the United States on the ground. Nasser then began to lose power and followers. The Iraqi military leaders proved to be more Iraqi nationalist than Arab nationalist and proceeded to liquidate Nasserist elements. The Syrian military also proved to be neither pro-Nasserist nor pro-Iraqi and withdrew from the UAR. By stretching the Eisenhower Doctrine and using it to stabilize Jordan and Lebanon, the United States managed to hold back, at least temporarily, the radical Arab nationalist tide. Thus, the Near East began to settle into a number of separate radical nationalist states, a few moderate and conservative states, and the isolated Israelis. By the end of 1960, the Arab world was still unsettled, politically nervous, and disorderly, but not in any early likelihood of falling into the Communist camp.

Much of what is reported above was derived from study of Soviet archival and other declassified materials. Most of us in the intelligence analysis business at the time did not know more than a small fraction of the thinking and disputation which went on in Communist councils. We did, however, develop a sense of what was going on from what became public and from what we could infer from Soviet behavior in the world arena. It was my task, assigned during the winter of 1957–58, to describe what appeared to be a rapidly forming change in the structure of world power.

1958: The CIA's Portentous Review of the World Situation

When examining the structure of world power, it is necessary to consider factors other than the military capabilities of nations or blocs. The structure of world power, as I use the term in this book, also takes account of nations' historic policies and modern objectives; their alliances, hegemonic positions, and territorial ambitions; their levels of economic and cultural development; their domestic problems, governmental methods, and firmness of purpose; and even their religious and moral predilections. It is a daunting assignment. It demands intensive study of the current world political scene and a strong commitment to objectivity. Fortunately, I had at my disposal the entire reporting and analytic output of the intelligence community. I was steeped in data.

What was needed at the end of 1957 was not a recital of Soviet nuclear-weapons delivery systems, but an examination of the implications for world politics of the impending Soviet capability to bring North America under nuclear attack. After the dramatic events of October 1956, the times also called for a good look at the cohesiveness of the Western alliances and the Soviet bloc. Moreover, with the USSR showing a growing interest in the underdeveloped and uncommitted countries, it seemed appropriate to review what kind of problems those countries were facing and how they were dealing with them. In any event, since the Cold War had come to involve old and new countries alike, it seemed desirable to probe the psychological impact of the U.S. and Soviet postures upon the world at large. Finally, an estimate of such scope needed to review the likelihood of new wars, both local and general, and the long-term prospects opened up by the death of Stalin and the subsequent changes in the Communist world.

The draft estimate, completed in February 1958 (NIE 100-58), passed board scrutiny and survived the process of interagency coordination more or less intact. We made a few verbal concessions to the patriotic instincts of the Pentagon representatives, but the paper—on the whole—was improved by the process.

The overall tone of the estimate was not very cheerful. We concluded that there would continue to be an intensive and worldwide competition between the Soviet bloc and the United States. We thought that the Soviet bloc would "wage vigorous economic and political offensives against the U.S.," that it would "take advantage of trouble spots," and that it would exploit the "nationalist and revolutionary emotions" of people in the emerging countries. We thought that the USSR and China would achieve "some measure of success" in those efforts, and that this would "generate increasing nervousness in the West over real or imagined losses of position." Here follow paraphrased excerpts of major judgments in the estimate, which was issued on February 26, 1958.

Impact of the New Strategic Situation: Some nations under U.S. protection will come to fear that the United States will no longer be willing to threaten nuclear retaliation in order to deter Soviet pressure or Soviet action in matters of vital concern to them. We believe, nevertheless, that the Soviets will continue to respect U.S. nuclear power and will not pursue courses of action which in their judgment seriously risk general war. As the USSR enlarges its capability to inflict major devastation upon the United States, however, the Soviet leaders will judge that the United States will risk devastation only for the gravest reasons. The Soviets might therefore think that there is a somewhat wider range of actions which they can undertake without serious risk of general war. They might also "utilize war-by-proxy" in order to gain local advantage if they calculate that the United States or its allies are unlikely to use nuclear weapons to defend their position.

Psychological Impact of Soviet and U.S. Policies: During the past several years, the USSR has appealed more successfully than the United States to the emotional needs of many of the world's peoples. Our political beliefs and legal traditions are often regarded as unrealistic in countries where the struggle for existence and social traditions do not encourage such civilized attitudes. Moreover, even among educated classes almost everywhere, many resent the high level of American consumption and deplore what they see as a U.S. preoccupation with military security. Also: "Although not necessarily pro-Communist, and often opposed to Communism, they . . . look upon U.S. policy as too inflexible and moralistic, and too exclusively concerned with the struggle against Communism."

Cohesiveness of the Sino-Soviet Bloc: Since the death of Stalin, there has been a trend toward redefinition of relationships within the bloc. Moscow's leadership monopoly has been diminished by the growing power and influence of Communist China. These changing relationships have created problems for Moscow. We see little chance that during the next several years, short of major changes within the Soviet regime itself, any of the Communist states will alienate themselves from the USSR to an extent that would damage the Soviet world position.

Cohesiveness of the Western Alliance System: Soviet bloc military aggression has for some time appeared to most of the NATO partners to be much less imminent than when the alliance was formed. It is still valued as the chief counterbalance to bloc military power, but there is a declining confidence in the deterrent effect of U.S. military power. There is currently much soul-searching going on about the military and political adequacy of NATO. The United Kingdom and the major continental powers have asserted more independent positions within the alliance, and this tendency will likely continue. In particular, the United States may encounter problems in attempting to establish missile bases or further deployment of nuclear weapons overseas.

Problems in Underdeveloped and Uncommitted Nations: There are wide variations among the growing number of nations and peoples in the non-Communist and non-Western world. Most have two things in common; they want to modernize their countries, and they do not want to become engulfed in the U.S.-USSR power struggle. Many are unstable politically and socially, and some are falling under authoritarian leaders. The Soviets have made offers of economic aid to some of these countries without apparent strings attached, and some are becoming increasingly susceptible to Sino-Soviet influence. The United States, on the other hand, appears to many Asian and African countries as attempting to force them into the Western alliance system. In the Middle East, the Soviets have skillfully represented themselves as ideologically and emotionally on the side of the Arab nationalists, while the United States is identified in the popular mind with Israeli imperialism, support of the colonial powers, and exploitation of oil resources.

The United States has greater assets in Asia than in the Middle East. In some countries, U.S. aid has been recognized as essential to the establishment and maintenance of independence, but great problems remain because of the rubble of insurrection, subversion, ethnic differences, and political ineptitude. The existence of divided nations—Korea, Vietnam, China—is a constant source of apprehension over the future. In Latin America, antipathy to the United States is relatively limited, but in some countries unpopular ruling classes—often supported by U.S. citizens—have become popularly identified with "yankee imperialism."

Likelihood of General War: As the leaders of the United States and USSR jockey for position, calculating the risks involved in their actions—or their inactions—in particular situations will be difficult. If local wars break out, we believe the great powers will attempt to keep them limited, but we can conceive of a variety of ways in which they could expand, even when the initial intention of the parties involved was to keep the conflict limited. While we believe that the Soviets will not deliberately initiate general war during the next five years, we believe that the chances of keeping wars limited whenever major areas or causes could be affected are at best not very promising.

Evolution in the Communist World: Despite some current tightening of controls, we foresee a continuation of the trend toward greater flexibility in bloc relations and toward greater recognition of individual differences among the bloc members. But we think that prolonged development in this direction would be necessary before serious differences arise within the bloc on questions of relations with the Western powers; here the cement of common interests and a common ideology among the various regimes is exceedingly strong.

We went on:

> Because the USSR will remain the keystone of the bloc structure, the most important changes will be those which will occur within its own borders. More widespread and better education, the growth of a professional and managerial class, greater personal freedom, expectations

of higher living standards, and more contact with other countries are indications of significant changes within Soviet society. These changes might in the long run alter profoundly the content and structure of Soviet political life, possibly through a dissipation of the Communist Party's unchecked monopoly of power, more likely through a change in the political climate within the ruling Party. . . .

The liberalizing tendency within the USSR and in intra-bloc relations could not be reversed without considerable difficulty, but the Soviet leadership has been generally successful in controlling its pace and course. We do not believe that such tendencies will significantly weaken the bloc during the next five years.

Impact of the 1958 World Review

Few estimates produced during the 1950s had such a thorough study as the 1958 "Estimate of the World Situation." Staffs in the various intelligence agencies had taken the draft seriously and, as indicated above, had made suggestions which improved its quality. Our principal problem in getting the estimate formally approved came from our own director, Allen Dulles. Dulles was unhappy with the gloomy outlook in the estimate, and he particularly objected to those paragraphs which noted a decline in the U.S. world position and a rising respect being accorded the Soviet Union. Although he did not identify particular paragraphs by number, we guessed that those especially difficult for him to accept were those which dealt with the psychological impact of U.S. and Soviet policies. One of the paragraphs on that subject was described by our board chairman, Sherman Kent, in one of his more colorful phrases, as "the-John-Foster-Dulles-is-a-self-righteous-son-of-a-bitch-paragraph."

In order to deal with the Dulles problem, the board chairman for the estimate, Abbott Smith, decided to present the paper to our panel of consultants, who were meeting in Princeton in mid-February, and to invite Allen to come. Sherman Kent and one or two others from the O/NE also attended. The consultants were a distinguished group. One member was Hamilton Fish Armstrong, an old friend of Allen and editor of *Foreign Affairs*. Also present were Harold Linder, a former board member, economist, and later president of the Export-Import Bank; Joseph Strayer, also a former board member and professor of history at Princeton; Phil Mosely of Columbia; Robert Bowie, director of the Center for International Affairs at Harvard; and two more Princetonians, Klaus Knorr, professor of history, and Cyril Black, chief of the

Center for International Studies. At a dinner session in the Nassau Tavern, Allen began by expressing his reservations about the paper. He immediately received a torrent of criticism from the consultants.

Armstrong found the paper the most useful he had seen since the "X-Article" written by George Kennan in 1947. He offered to publish the paper in *Foreign Affairs* with the authorship attributed to "Mr. Y." (Since the paper had already been coordinated with the other intelligence agencies, it would have stirred up a hornet's nest had we attempted to get their approval for publication, and the idea was dropped.) Linder offered to pay for the printing of hundreds of copies and mailing them to opinion leaders in the United States. Bowie and Black were especially strong in their support of the paper as written. Dulles was shocked, and he agreed to go back home and think it over.

Allen did think about it. The following week he held two successive evening meetings with me and a half-dozen board members. Dulles asked each of them individually if he agreed with the draft. They all did. I recall, the second evening, seeing the Director rise out of his chair, stride across the room, and then turn to us to say that he would accept the estimate as written. It was not, he said, a question of his brother being Secretary of State; he simply had not believed that world support was turning away from what the United States was trying to do. We had convinced him.

The USIB took up the estimate a few days later and approved it without dissent. We had worried for a few days because the State Department member was a career foreign service officer who wanted to hear from us about Allen's position before signaling his own consent. His staff people, who had been very supportive of the estimate, were delighted when I was able to tell them that our director had come around to our view. After publication a few days later, it was sent to the NSC Planning Board for study.

The Planning Board discussed the estimate at a succession of weekly meetings, and I was invited to join them at their final session in mid-March. Robert Cutler, a cultivated lawyer from Boston and a special assistant to President Eisenhower for National Security Affairs, presided. After the meeting, he sent a memorandum to the President reporting that the Planning Board and its consultants had been studying "this remarkably informative and significant paper" for several weeks and thought it "a very superior piece of work." The Planning Board would develop, he reported, some points for discussion at the NSC meeting of March 20, at which Allen Dulles would present a short introductory summary of the paper. Finally, he hoped, the President would "look through" the entire paper. I did prepare a summary for Allen to take with him, and it was later reported back to me that he wanted me to know that he had read it to the NSC "word-for-word." I also learned that, according to his own account, he had gotten into "one hell of an argument" with his brother.

Much of the impact of the estimate flowed from the review process and from the contention over its message. It was taken on board by the intelligence agencies, by the NSC members and NSC staff, and by influential opinion leaders in the academic and foreign affairs communities. No one expected any alterations in foreign and defense policy would follow. Indeed, the estimate was designed to recount and explain happenings in the world and to provide signposts for policymakers in their thinking about future probabilities and possibilities. Policymakers at the NSC level are seldom able to undertake the luxury of looking behind and ahead of current policy questions. The estimate and the NSC machinery provided the vehicle and occasion to do so.

The estimate, as the excerpts indicate, did not provide a comforting or optimistic outlook. It said that the world was still a dangerous place. But it also took note of the changes in the USSR and in the Communist world, and it suggested that there was good chance of fundamental changes occurring within the Soviet system. It implied that the USSR as we then knew it would not be a permanent enemy. It predicted that the Soviet Union would pursue bolder policies than in the past as it exploited, under the cover of its growing strategic power, opportunities that would arise to spread its influence.

The estimate recognized that an emerging sense of U.S. vulnerability to Soviet attack was changing how U.S. power and leadership were perceived abroad. The estimate added a warning that it would not be possible to alter that trend simply by strengthening the free world militarily. But we also repeated our frequently expressed judgments that the Soviets fully appreciated the extraordinary destructiveness of nuclear weapons and would do nothing that they thought would involve serious risk of general war. Those judgments were a far cry from the estimates of the early 1950s, which had demonstrated an undignified sense of panic within the U.S. defense community.

While the estimate set forth quite clearly the longer-term prospects for the USSR as well as the newer problems inherent in the emerging world strategic situation, it did not foresee the revolutionary changes within the so-called Third World that became manifest during the five years which followed. Nor did it explore the dangers to strategic stability that could ensue from the development of new and more powerful weapons. In order to examine those matters and to explore other likely problems in the decade ahead, we undertook in the autumn of 1960 to prepare a new world estimate to have at hand when President Kennedy assumed office on January 21, 1961.

1958–1960   A New Communist-Bloc Activism?

In the 1958 world estimate, we had predicted that the Soviet bloc would "wage vigorous economic and political offensives against the U.S." and that it would "exploit the nationalist and revolutionary emotions" of peoples in the emerging world. Before the end of 1958, that prediction manifested itself in a Chinese Communist move against Taiwan, a new Soviet move against Berlin, a leftist revolution in Cuba embraced by the USSR, and the initiation of a new phase in the struggle over Vietnam. All of these posed, directly or indirectly, threats of major confrontations, major-power military actions, and risks of general war.

The Taiwan Crisis

The Taiwan crisis began quite suddenly in August 1958, when Chinese artillery on the mainland began a heavy bombardment of two offshore islands, Quemoy and Matsu, which were under the control of the Chiang Kai-shek (Kuomintang) regime on Taiwan. The two islands had not been put under U.S. protection in the Treaty of Mutual Defense signed with the Chiang government in 1954, but President Eisenhower later had assured Chiang that the United States would defend them as well. Also, the U.S. Congress in January 1955 authorized the use of American forces to protect Taiwan and related territories. While the bombardment was going on, the Eisenhower administration took steps to help the Taiwanese regime reinforce the islands and evacuate civilians. U.S. naval forces established and maintained effective U.S. control of the Formosa Strait, not only to deter any Chinese amphibious assault, but also to demonstrate a firm U.S. intention to prevent any forceful change in the status of Taiwan.

The Chinese halted the daily bombardment in October, having apparently concluded that military action would not be successful. But we now know that the Taiwan affair was much more complicated than the question of success or failure in a military operation. Apparently the Chinese had told the Soviet leaders that they were planning an operation against the Chiang regime and had asked the Soviets for air cover and long-range artillery. The initial Soviet response was favorable. Khrushchev claimed in his memoirs that the Soviets had provided what was requested and that "at the moment, we did not deter them but, on the contrary, considered such actions to be correct, leading to the reunification of China."[1] But Zubok and Pleshakov report that in August Mao told Khrushchev that Taiwan was their affair and that he wanted no interference from Khrushchev. According to the two Russian scholars, Mao also told an associate: "[Khrushchev] wants to improve relations with the United States? Good, we will congratulate him with our guns. . . . Let's get the United States involved, too. Maybe we can get the United States to drop an atomic bomb on Fujian [province]. . . . Let's see what Khrushchev says then."[2]

Zubok and Pleshakov believe that Mao had not really expected that an attack on the islands would mean "an all-out offensive against Taiwan" and that Mao had "no intention of ultimately capturing it." Instead, he wanted "a grand provocation meant to send a message to Khrushchev."[3] When Foreign Minister Andrei Gromyko came to Beijing in mid-September to discuss the Taiwan matter, Chou En-lai told him that the Chinese had considered the possibility of local war between China and the United States resulting from the Taiwan matter and they were "ready to take all the hard blows, including atomic bombs and the destruction of cities."[4] Mao himself spoke to Communist bloc diplomats in Beijing early in October expressing "satisfaction that he 'caught' John Foster Dulles in Taiwan" and lecturing them on the benefits of "prolonged brinkmanship."[5]

1. Zubok and Pleshakov, *Inside the Kremlin's Cold War*, 220.
2. Ibid., 221.
3. Ibid., 222.
4. Ibid., 225.
5. Ibid., 236.

That kind of jockeying and jostling went on for several more weeks. Then, on October 25 the crisis suddenly ended with a declaration by the Chinese minister of defense that he had been ordered to stop firing on even days. Later the Chinese declared that they had achieved their goal of increasing the "contradiction between Chiang Kai-shek and the United States." The quarrel over Taiwan and over the Chinese refusal to accept Soviet guidance on the Taiwan matter turned out to have been a major turning point in Soviet-Chinese relations. During the years that followed, even though we did not then know the depth of animus displayed in the archival data cited above, we were able to detect signs of the widening rift that finally became public four years later, in 1962.

The Berlin Ultimatum

On November 27, 1958, barely a month after the Chinese signaled the end of the Taiwan crisis by announcing that they were reducing their bombardment of Quemoy and Matsu, Nikita Khrushchev proposed a German peace treaty that recognized the existence of two Germanies and a "free city" of West Berlin. He further declared that if the Western powers refused to negotiate such a treaty, the Soviet Union would negotiate a separate peace with East Germany, and the Western powers would then have to negotiate with the East Germans concerning their rights and access to West Berlin. Zubok and Pleshakov have reported that a former Soviet ambassador to East Germany warned Khrushchev that he was embarking on a risky course. But the Soviet leader thundered back that the U.S. leaders were "not idiotic enough to start fighting over Berlin" and would not start a war "even if the Soviets kicked them out of the city by force."[6]

Khrushchev was not, however, anxious to follow through on that threat. He apparently planned from the very beginning to move with caution. The East German ambassador in Moscow wrote a report in early December 1958 on the Khrushchev initiative, and Hope Harrison of CWEHO Staff has prepared a commentary on that report. Her summary reads: "The document indicated several times that the Soviets were careful to proceed gradually and cautiously in implementing the threats contained in the ultimatum so as to gauge the Western reaction. This is typical of Khrushchev. His diplomacy of 1958–1962 showed that he liked to push the West 'to the brink,' but that just

6. Ibid., 198.

before the brink, he would wait to see what the West would do and would generally adjust his policy accordingly."[7]

What appears to have happened in this case was that Khrushchev's threats did have an effect in the West. British and American leaders had no stomach for a war that would begin over Berlin, and they started to show signs of wanting to talk. Finally, President Eisenhower invited Khrushchev to pay a formal visit to the United States in September 1959. Khrushchev came amidst great pomp, and he behaved in a statesmanlike manner. Pleased to have been treated with respect and pleased to have heard the President suggest that the Berlin matter should be discussed at a four-power summit in the spring of 1960, Khrushchev agreed to lift the ultimatum.[8] The crisis wasn't over, but the immediate threat disappeared.

Just before the summit conference was scheduled to open in Paris, an American U-2 aircraft, with photographic equipment on board and piloted by a CIA employee, was shot down over the Soviet Union. The White House, after first lying about the aircraft's mission, admitted that it had been gathering intelligence and advanced the claim that the United States had a right to fly over Soviet territory in order to get information about the USSR's capability to launch a surprise attack upon the United States. Khrushchev was furious and excoriated the President at the summit meeting. Eisenhower promised that there would be no more flights while he was President, but that did not satisfy Khrushchev, who then suggested that the conference be postponed until a new president was in office.[9] Thus it became clear that when John Kennedy assumed the presidency on January 21, 1961, one of his first problems would be to set up a summit meeting with Khrushchev and to face up to what could become a new and dangerous crisis over Berlin.

The Cuban Revolution

I was out of Washington during the months immediately preceding and following the Cuban revolution. I watched the telecast of Castro's triumphal march into Havana on January 1, 1959. I later learned that soon thereafter Castro had come to Washington in an attempt to establish a relationship with President Eisenhower, but that the President was unwilling to talk with the radical revolutionary upstart accused of being a Communist. Before I left

7. Hope M. Harrison, "New Evidence on Khrushchev's 1958 Berlin Ultimatum," *Bulletin of the Cold War International History Project*, no. 4 (Fall 1994): 36.

8. Zubok and Pleshakov, *Inside the Kremlin's Cold War*, 200–201.

9. Spanier, *American Foreign Policy Since World War II*, 145–46.

Washington in September 1958, I had not seen any persuasive evidence that the Soviet government had instigated the Cuban revolution or provided it with arms. When I returned in the autumn of 1959, I realized that U.S. policymakers were treating the Castro regime as if it were a Communist government. Lacking any substantiated evidence that Castro was indeed a Communist and working with the Soviets, the NSC applied strong pressure upon the CIA clandestine service to find evidence of Soviet involvement. One senior officer of the CIA Operations Directorate told me a dozen years later that one CIA station chief in a Latin American capital had in fact forged a Communist Party membership card with Castro's name on it. I cannot vouch for the accuracy of that report except to say that I have the highest respect for the integrity of the officer who gave me that information. The fact is, of course, that Castro was not then or later a servant of the Kremlin.

In their book, *The Kremlin's Cold War*, Zubok and Pleshakov report the following about Khrushchev and the Cuban revolution:

> The Soviet leader discovered and embraced the Cuban revolution. Initially, in 1959 and 1960, the Soviet leadership did not believe that there could be any chance for "proletarian" revolution on the semi-colonial island with a small monoculture economy. The survivors of the old Comintern network described Fidel Castro, Che Guevara, and other Cuban revolutionaries as anything but Marxists, and discounted their chances for success. Had Stalin been in the Kremlin, the Soviets would never have assisted the radical Cuban regime. At best, Stalin and Molotov would have tried to trade their role in Cuba for American concessions elsewhere. Khrushchev and his colleagues in the Presidium, however, saw the young Cubans as heroes who had revived the promise of the Russian Revolution and dared to do it under the very nose of the most powerful imperialist country on earth.[10]

Zubok and Pleshakov added that when Khrushchev saw—during the autumn of 1960—how Castro was in fact carrying out "socialist" measures in Cuba, the Soviet leader changed his attitude "from surprise to admiration." It was then that the USSR began to support Cuba economically.

This episode demonstrates an important aspect of Soviet thinking—at least that of Khrushchev and some of his Presidium associates. They were not thinking of war as the way to expand the Communist world. Instead they were

10. Zubok and Pleshakov, *Inside the Kremlin's Cold War*, 206–7.

exulting in the correctness of their doctrine that the peoples of the "Third World" would come into the Communist camp on their own initiative. It was only necessary for the Soviets to support them in their "sacred struggle" against the expected imperialist counterattack.[11]

As the Soviet reaction to the Cuban revolution proceeded from surprise to admiration to support during 1959 and 1960, the Washington reaction moved from angry tolerance to efforts to isolate and finally to an attempt to destroy. And as Fidel Castro moved steadily leftward in his domestic policy and as the Soviets moved toward economic support, Castro became increasingly a hero among Latin American anti-Yankee militants. By 1960, it no longer mattered whether Castro had embraced the USSR because of U.S. hostility or because of persuasion by radical leftists within the Cuban revolutionary movement. The Eisenhower administration came to fear the Cuban revolution, not only because of its socialist policies and spreading support in Latin America, but also because it seemed likely to become a Soviet-Communist outpost in the Western Hemisphere which eventually could pose a military threat to the United States. Moreover, the administration wanted to rid the hemisphere of Castroist influence, lest U.S. business interests suffer and U.S. security be endangered by popular revolutionaries who had identified the United States with their local oligarchies and thus become easy targets for Soviet blandishments.

So it was that in the spring of 1960, Tracy Barnes, who was the CIA's Assistant Deputy Director for Operations, came to pay a visit to the Board of National Estimates. Barnes was a charming fellow who had pulled off the overthrow of the Arbenz regime in Guatemala in 1954; he had been assigned by Dulles and Richard Bissell (the new Deputy Director for Operations) to do the same thing to the Castro regime.

Barnes's visit with the board did not help him very much. He probed and searched for some clue or judgment from us that Castro's position was weak, that the Cubans were disappointed in him, and that they would rise up and support an alternative force if one appeared on the scene. We were quite clear that whatever his politics, Castro was a popular figure, that he had rid the country of an alliance between U.S. criminals and a cruel Cuban regime, and that he had become a symbol of hope for a better life among the majority of the Cuban people. Barnes went away and never came back, nor did anyone in the CIA or in the U.S. government at any time ask any component of the CIA's Intelligence Directorate for a judgment on the prospects for success in any operation against Castro.

11. Ibid., 208.

The Eisenhower administration's problem with Castro and Cuba was exacerbated by the 1960 presidential election campaign. Vice President Richard Nixon, who was running for the presidency on the Republican ticket, had based much of his political career on anti-Communism; hence, the administration could not appear to be ignoring the threat the country believed was posed by the Cuban revolution. Moreover, Senator John Kennedy, the Democratic candidate, was strongly denouncing the Eisenhower administration for allowing a "Communist" regime to establish itself "only 90 miles" from the U.S. shores. There was also an alleged "missile gap" between U.S. and Soviet intercontinental nuclear attack capabilities, which Kennedy was exploiting to allege that the administration was lax in its stance against growing Soviet military power. There was, indeed, a "missile gap" but it was the other way around; U.S. capabilities for intercontinental attack substantially exceeded those of the USSR. The "missile gap" was a journalistic invention based upon false information leaked by certain sources in the Pentagon in order to gain increased appropriations for military hardware. In any event, at a time when the United States was already looking as if it were losing its grip on world power and leadership, strong psychological and political pressure had arisen in the country to eliminate the bearded upstart in "our own backyard."

Early in 1960, therefore, the CIA Operations Directorate, with Bissell and Barnes in the lead, began drafting plans to get rid of Fidel Castro. That was when Barnes paid his visit to the Board of National Estimates. What followed was surely one of the worst botches in the history of the CIA. That tale is told elsewhere; one of the latest versions is that of Evan Thomas in *The Very Best Men*. At one point the planners even made an effort to recruit someone in the U.S. criminal underworld to assassinate Castro.[12] The public evidence—which is all that I have addressed here—is not clear about what President Eisenhower knew of the operational plans or what he actually authorized the Agency operatives to do. In any event, during the eight months after the board told Barnes that it was most unlikely that any substantial number of the Cuban people would rise up against Castro, the CIA plotters had moved from sending in saboteurs and infiltrators to setting up a full-scale invasion.

Dulles and Bissell briefed Kennedy in mid-November, two weeks after the election. The President-elect was "impassive" and made no commitment, according to Bissell's account as reported by Evan Thomas. After the inauguration Kennedy was further briefed. In response to his questions and his suggestions that the U.S. role be reduced, plans were revised. But plans for

12. Evan Thomas, *The Very Best Men* (New York: Simon & Schuster, 1995), 226–28.

an invasion proceeded, with a Cuban exile brigade undergoing training in Central America and an air base established in Nicaragua. As preparations for the invasion proceeded, a lot of things went wrong.[13] When Kennedy finally told Bissell to go ahead on a weekend in mid-April, everything went wrong. That is when those of us in the Intelligence Directorate learned about the operation — we read about it in the newspapers.

President Kennedy assumed full responsibility for the fiasco, and it was quite proper that he should. He knew that the operation had a high chance of failure and that some of his closest advisers opposed it. But he also had to weigh that chance and that advice along with the political hazards of calling off the effort. After the noise he had made in the campaign about his predecessor's inadequate response to the arrival of a "Communist" regime so close to home, he needed at least to approve an invasion attempt. Then, in allowing it to fail by not intervening, Kennedy escaped widespread condemnation in Latin America and kept alive the hope that his "Alliance for Progress" program in Latin America could reduce the pressures for revolution there. Thus Cuba remained an embarrassing problem, with no obvious and simple solution, for the new administration to handle.

Cuba: A Crisis for Covert Operations

The Cuban episode presented to the new President yet another conceptual and political problem — what attitude to take toward covert operations designed to affect the course of events in foreign lands. During the 1950s, the United States had set up a clandestine service within the CIA designed to "contain" Communism by strengthening the economies of Western Europe, by stiffening the backbones of the non-Communist leaders, and by carrying out political action programs to counteract Soviet propaganda and to neutralize the USSR's political allies in the West. It was a sound policy, and it worked. It was needed in order to undermine the myth of the historical inevitability of a coming Communist age. But the policy of containment, by definition and in its original formulation, did not include a "rollback" of the Soviet position in Eastern Europe. That was a John Foster Dulles and Frank Wisner policy. The new CIA Office of Policy Coordination (OPC), under Wisner's leadership, became the clandestine action arm for carrying it out. "Rollback" became a moral crusade for the OPC chiefs, who collected ideologically committed Cold Warriors with a swashbuckling mentality and supplied them with a lot of money and free rein.

13. Ibid., 241–63, passim.

When their rollback policy foundered in the mountains of Albania and was reversed when Budapest exploded, they were devastated. They obviously had not read, thought about, or believed the estimates produced by the analytic side of the Agency. From CIA 1 (1947) through NIE 25 (1951) and beyond, the estimates had emphasized that the USSR was determined to hold onto its position in Eastern Europe. The estimates warned in effect that if the Western powers attempted to intervene militarily in support of political disturbances or uprisings in the satellite countries, such actions would provoke dangerous U.S.-Soviet confrontations.

After the U.S. Cold Warriors finally recognized the dangers and the futility of the rollback policy and deserted the Hungarian revolutionists, the clandestine action people shifted their major effort toward preventing the Soviets and Chinese Communists from gaining footholds in the so-called Third World. But the clandestine activists never really understood what the problems in the Third World actually were. We attempted to spell out those problems in NIE 100-58, where we wrote, for example, that "most of the peoples of the underdeveloped countries have one primary political and social aim: they want to modernize their countries. They are not greatly concerned with what we regard as the evils of Communism. What we regard as the advantages of democracy and capitalism are associated in their minds with the evils of colonialism."

In some of these countries there was clearly a strong susceptibility to revolutionary doctrines, but mostly their peoples were simply interested in a better life. Many of the leaders were new and floundering. In their search for solutions, they often moved quickly toward nationalization of business enterprises and land reform. In many cases, especially in Latin America, such actions damaged or threatened the financial stake of U.S. companies and the privileges of the local oligarchs associated with the U.S. owners and managers. That is what happened in Guatemala and Cuba and prompted U.S. efforts to remove the new leaders.

The major misconception underlying much U.S. clandestine action during the 1950s was a tendency to regard all revolutionary agitation and ferment as Soviet-inspired and susceptible to Soviet exploitation. That tendency, with its overtones of moral superiority, permeated much—though not all—of the covert action staff of the Agency. It underlay the thinking and planning pursued by Frank Wisner during the years in which he ran the action staff; it also underlay the thinking and writing of his good friend Paul Nitze, not only when Nitze was writing NSC-68, but also in the decades following, when Nitze continued to exercise a strong influence over U.S. foreign and military policy.

The Communist Challenge in Vietnam

The situation in Vietnam was relatively quiet during the latter years of the Eisenhower administration. The North Vietnamese were concentrating upon economic development and the execution of a "Three-Year Plan" for transforming the economy and the society. In the South, the Diem regime was concentrating upon building up its military and security forces.

Then, in the spring of 1959, the Vietnamese Communist Party ordained a return to revolutionary activity in the South. A year later, taking note of "disintegration" in the South, the Party called upon the North Vietnamese to support the South Vietnamese comrades in their guerrilla warfare against the Diem regime.[14] So, with a more activist Communist effort getting under way in the South, the Eisenhower administration was forced to choose between fighting a land war in Asia and permitting the Communists to make further gains. To understand the complexity of that choice, we need to review what happened in French-Vietnamese relations, in U.S.-Vietnamese relations, and in Vietnam itself after the Japanese surrender in September 1945.

Upon learning of the Japanese decision to surrender, Ho Chih Minh proclaimed himself president of the "Provisional Government of the Republic of Vietnam." Almost immediately thereafter, the situation throughout the country became chaotic and suffused with brutality. In Saigon, French paratroopers and Foreign Legionnaires newly released from Japanese POW camps, joined by some remaining French civilians, went on a rampage of beating, shooting, and destruction that the British occupation force was either unable or unwilling to bring under control. In the North (above the sixteenth parallel), the Chinese occupation force behaved in an even more brutal and rapacious fashion, stealing everything in sight from farm animals to doorknobs. In the North alone, some two million Vietnamese died of famine during the autumn and winter of 1945–46.[15]

The first phase of the Vietnam War began, in effect, within two months of the Japanese surrender. General Douglas Gracey, the commander of the British occupation forces, wanted to turn his authority over to the French as soon as possible, and did so when French forces dispatched by General de Gaulle arrived in late October. The French commander, General Jacques Leclerc, made it his prime objective to establish French authority in the countryside. To do so, he had to drive back the Vietminh forces in the South

---

14. Qiang Zhai, "Beijing and the Vietnam Conflict, 1964–65: New Chinese Evidence," *Bulletin of the Cold War International History Project*, no. 6–7 (Winter 1995–96): 234.
15. Stanley Karnow, *Vietnam* (New York: Penguin Books, 1984), 675–76.

who were loyal to Ho Chih Minh. He claimed to have succeeded in that effort by the spring of 1946, but French control was never more than widely scattered and tentative. In their desire to return to the North and at least to establish a presence there, the French then made a deal with the Chinese Nationalist government whereby the French would renounce their extraterritorial rights in China in return for Chinese withdrawal from North Vietnam. France then recognized Vietnam as a "free state" within the French Union, and Ho agreed that French troops could enter the North to replace the Chinese.[16]

In his history of Vietnam, Stanley Karnow remarks at this point in his narrative that Ho realized that he was "trapped." Karnow went on: "The United States, despite [Ho's] repeated pleas, had decided to support France. The Soviet Union had neither endorsed his regime nor, [Ho] remarked ruefully, even assigned an observer to Hanoi. Nor could he count on the French Communist Party, whose boss, Maurice Thorez, then vice president of General de Gaulle's government, later said that he 'did not want to liquidate the French position in Indo-China.'"[17]

The French forces who had moved into the North with Ho's reluctant consent soon began skirmishing with Vietnamese troops. Those skirmishes became particularly rough in the port of Haiphong and spread into Hanoi as well. By the end of December 1946, these skirmishes had become a real war. Ho's forces pulled out of the cities, maneuvered to avoid pitched battles, and used typical guerrilla tactics to harass and weaken the French.[18] With a variety of ups and downs, this went on until 1949. When the Chinese Communists arrived on the Vietnamese border late in 1949, they began providing Ho's forces with arms and military advice. By the end of the year 1949, therefore, the Vietnamese position was beginning to improve, and French forces were beginning to suffer setbacks.

The question of Ho's allegiance, and the prospects for Vietnam if the Vietnamese succeeded in establishing their independence, troubled the policy scene during most of the early postwar period. As early as February 1947, the State Department concluded that Ho Chih Minh had a "direct Communist connection" which would result in an independent Vietnam falling under Kremlin control.[19] But Ho Chih Minh went on for another two years fighting

16. Ibid., 150.
17. Ibid., 152.
18. Ibid., 157–58, passim.
19. Testimony of Abbot Low Moffat, in Senate Foreign Relations Committee, *Hearings on the Causes, Origins, and Lessons of the Vietnam War*, 170.

the French without any endorsement or assistance from the USSR or the French Communist Party. Finally in the spring of 1949, Ho made one more appeal for a compromise with France, and he openly promised that he would guarantee Vietnam's neutrality in the U.S.-Soviet Cold War then getting under way. The appeal evoked no response, and early in 1950 he gave up hope for a reconciliation with France and persuaded Moscow and Beijing to recognize his regime, then known as the Democratic Republic of Vietnam (DRV).[20]

That event—Soviet and Chinese Communist recognition of the DRV— ended the first phase of U.S. post–World War II policy on the Vietnam question. It was during that first phase that the United States passed up the opportunity to establish an influence in Vietnam that could have led to a quite different history of Southeast Asia. It is quite clear that Ho wanted U.S. help (he had indeed sought it as early as the Paris Peace Conference in 1919) to save Vietnam from both French and Chinese imperialism. But U.S. policymakers were so obsessed with a fear of Communism that they were unable to explore even the possibilities of a rapprochement with Ho. Karnow writes about that matter as follows:

> For a brief moment early in 1950, American experts suddenly won-dered whether Ho Chih Minh might not be a Soviet surrogate since he requested and obtained recognition of his regime from Marshal Tito of Yugoslavia, one of Moscow's principal enemies. But they never explored the mystery further—as they never had in the past. In June 1948, for example, CIA officials had rejected a proposal to contact Ho covertly because, "A white man would be very conspicuous. . . . In order to have an effective intelligence officer, he would have to have a little brown blood. Then, we wouldn't be able to trust him."[21]

Secretary Acheson reported occasionally in his memoirs about the Vietnam problem. He reported, for example, that in September 1949 he had discussed Indochina with French foreign minister Robert Schuman and had told Schuman that France could do more to prevent "Communist domination" in all three former colonies (Vietnam, Laos, and Cambodia) by "moving more quickly to satisfy nationalist aspirations."[22] He admitted later in retrospect

20. Karnow, *Vietnam*, 175.
21. Ibid., 176.
22. Acheson, *Present at the Creation*, 327.

that U.S. policy in Indochina was perhaps a "muddled hodgepodge," but declared that he could think of no better course to have followed in view of France's importance as a U.S. ally.[23] He did make an important speech on Asian policy at the National Press Club on January 12, 1950, in which he made some statements about U.S. policy in Asia, the significance of which he almost certainly did not fully appreciate at the time.

The speech was designed primarily to answer his critics and especially those Republicans who claimed that the Democratic administration had "lost" China to the Communists. In reference to U.S. security interests in Asia, Acheson had said—as I mentioned in Chapter 3—that the U.S. defense perimeter in the Western Pacific ran from the Ryukyu Islands to the Philippines, thus excluding mainland Asia. Without naming any country in particular, Acheson also stated that there were "limitations" upon the degree of assistance which the United States could supply to countries facing a Communist threat. The United States could not "furnish all the components" necessary to solve problems, but only the "missing component" in a situation which otherwise could not have been solved. In particular, he said, the United States could not supply "determination" and "the loyalty of a people to its government."[24]

Also, as pointed out in Chapter 3, Acheson made on this occasion a declaration concerning the limited U.S. defense perimeter which almost certainly contributed strongly to Stalin's assent to Kim Il Sung's persistent proposals to invade South Korea in June 1950. It almost certainly also contributed decisively to Moscow's and Beijing's recognitions of the DRV. Thus Acheson unwittingly created the diplomatic circumstances that led to U.S. intervention in both Korea and Vietnam..

The reader will recall that in my discussion of the U.S. response to the attack on South Korea, I described the myth which had developed in the Pentagon and was echoed elsewhere in Washington that the Soviets were hell-bent to expand their Communist empire by force or the threat of force. I wrote that the Pentagon was leading the way toward a policy of "militarized containment on a global scale" in response to its perception of the Soviet threat, and that this view was a distortion of the Kennan view and contrary to the substance of the estimates prepared by the CIA analysts up to that time. As a result, the military planners, whatever their own or the CIA analysts might have thought, accepted the proposition that the Soviets were aiming

23. Ibid., 673.
24. From Bernstein and Matusow, *Truman Administration*, 436.

at, and preparing for, a general war and that the United States had to do the same. I also quoted Henry Kissinger's view on the U.S. perceptions just described (see Chapter 3), namely, that "the belief that the Soviet leaders stood poised for general war reveals an extraordinary loss of touch with real power relationships."

So, having accepted the myth, only three days after the North Korean invasion began, President Truman issued the now famous and clearly misguided statement that led to the Korean War, the Vietnam War, and the economically destructive and dangerously Damoclean arms race which ensued: "The attack upon Korea makes plain beyond any doubt that Communism has passed beyond the use of subversion to conquer independent nations and will now use armed invasion and war." Then, in listing the military steps which the United States was taking immediately, he included the following regarding Indochina: "I have similarly directed acceleration in the furnishing of military assistance to France and the associated states of Indochina and the dispatch of a military mission to provide close working relations with those forces."[25]

Acheson did not wait for the North Korean attack before speaking out concerning Soviet and Chinese recognition of the Democratic Republic of Vietnam; he declared that Soviet recognition "should remove any illusions as to the 'nationalist' nature of Ho Chih Minh's aims, and reveal Ho in his true colors as a mortal enemy of native independence in Indo-China."[26] Dean Rusk, Acheson's Assistant Secretary for Far Eastern Affairs, was even more outspokenly pro-French and anti-Ho than Acheson. Rusk had served on the staff of Admiral Mountbatten, who commanded the China-Burma-India Theater during World War II and who had appointed the obviously pro-French General Douglas Gracey to command the Allied occupation force in South Vietnam. Rusk must have been aware of Ho's services to Allied forces in Southwest China, his guerrilla activities against the Japanese, and his repeated requests for American understanding and help. Rusk had also been Assistant Secretary of War in the early postwar period, and he must have absorbed the U.S. military's views on Soviet objectives. He had been, as noted by General Bradley, one of those who had taken a "hawkish stance" on the question of crossing the thirty-eighth parallel in Korea in September 1950. Hence, Rusk did not hesitate to add his voice to that of Acheson when he testified before the Senate Foreign Relations Committee in June 1950 on the situation in

25. Ibid., 438.
26. Quoted in Karnow, *Vietnam*, 75.

Vietnam: "This is a civil war that has been in effect captured by the [Soviet] Politburo and, besides, has been turned into a tool of the Politburo. So it isn't a civil war in the usual sense. It is part of an international war."[27]

It was therefore, Rusk stated, U.S. policy to support the former "Emperor" of Vietnam, Bao Dai, and the French in Indochina. The United States then made its first payment of military support funds directly to the Saigon government and established a full-fledged embassy there. The French government appointed General de Lattre de Tassigney as French commander and high commissioner for all of Indochina. In December 1950, Bao Dai was named chief of state for Vietnam and received a stipend of $4 million a year from U.S. funds. He appointed a new government and then spent most of his time at his lodge in the resort town of Dalat. One in the succession of cabinets which he appointed was described by the U.S. consul in Hanoi as composed of "opportunists, nonentities, extreme reactionaries, assassins, hirelings, and men of faded mental powers." The Saigon cabinet was in fact, the consul added, an indirect "propaganda tool" of the Vietminh and "a poor return for French blood and American money."[28]

As the guerrilla war went on in the North during 1951 and 1952, the Truman administration was too preoccupied with its military problems in Korea and its political problems in the United States to reexamine its policy and the situation in Southeast Asia. But a slightly new atmosphere in world politics began to emerge after General Eisenhower's inauguration in January 1953 and Joseph Stalin's death two months later. An armistice was signed in Korea, and the new political leaders in both France and the USSR were beginning to make noises about seeking a diplomatic solution in Indochina. That upset Ho Chih Minh in the North, who feared another betrayal by the French, and the anti-Communist nationalists in the South, who feared any compromise with Ho. It also upset John Foster Dulles, who feared that any deal with the Communists in Indochina would lead to further Communist gains in Asia. The Soviets and the Chinese were both urging Ho to show flexibility, and he finally complied with their wishes.[29]

President Eisenhower was not eager to get involved in another land war in Asia, having just ended one in Korea, and he was especially reluctant to commit the United States without the backing of America's allies. But the British steadfastly refused to join in any undertakings regarding Indochina.

27. See ibid., 192–93.
28. Quoted in ibid., 198.
29. Ibid., 192–93.

Then, in January 1954, the four occupying powers in Germany decided to call a meeting in Geneva in the spring among all the interested powers to try to resolve the Indochina problem. Eisenhower sent Secretary Dulles and Undersecretary Bedell Smith to the conference, which convened on May 8, 1954, one day after the fall of Dien Bien Phu to Ho's forces, which marked the destruction of the French military position in the North. By that time, even Eisenhower himself had turned his back on the rollback policy, having told a news conference on April 29: "You certainly cannot hope at the present state of our relations in the world for a completely satisfactory answer with the Communists. The most you can work out is a practical way of getting along."[30]

At the conference, Dulles—grumpy and unhappy—left after the first few days, but Bedell Smith stuck it out to the bitter end two and a half months later. Bedell Smith did not sign the accords, having been instructed to make no concessions, but pledged orally that the United States would abide by the agreements. The conference produced no solution, but it did produce some political changes. The dividing line between North and South was moved northward to the seventeenth parallel. The agreement called for nationwide elections in 1956 to lead to the formation of a single government for Vietnam. French forces would withdraw from the North and the Vietminh from the South. Bao Dai in Saigon denounced the agreements and appointed Ngo Dinh Diem prime minister. The Southeast Asia Treaty Organization (SEATO) was formed in September 1954 to provide a diplomatic cover for U.S. military intervention.

The Vietnam War thus entered a new phase in 1955. The United States came to play a much larger role in supplying financial aid to the South Vietnamese government and training the South Vietnamese army. Diem announced his refusal to participate in any nationwide elections, and the United States backed him up. There was a consensus in the U.S. intelligence community that the Ho regime would have won in an honest election. Diem also staged a referendum in the South that enabled him to get rid of Bao Dai and proclaim himself president. Ho Chih Minh accepted the Geneva agreements and went to both Moscow and Beijing to negotiate agreements for assistance. Ho's pilgrimages to Moscow and Beijing were a symbol of a self-fulfilling prophecy made by a variety of Democratic and Republican policymakers and military leaders during the preceding decade. After insisting for years that there was a worldwide Communist conspiracy run from Moscow

30. Quoted in ibid., 198.

of which Ho Chih Minh and his associates in Vietnam were devoted participants, the United States finally obliged him to play the part which U.S. policy-makers had assigned to him.

What was the actual relationship among the three governments—the North Vietnamese, the Chinese, and the Soviet—after the Chinese and the Soviets recognized the North Vietnamese government in 1949? As I mentioned earlier, the Chinese provided arms and military advice to North Vietnamese forces after the Chinese Communist troops arrived at the Vietnamese border in 1949. After the Geneva Accords of 1954, the Chinese Military Advisory Group in Vietnam brought General Giap and a Vietnamese delegation to Beijing in June 1955 to confer with the Chinese defense minister and the senior Soviet military adviser in China regarding the reconstruction of the DRV army and war plans for the future. According to the official history of the Chinese Military Advisory Group, they "reached agreement" on the "principal issues."[31] What happened after that is the subject of a study by Qiang Zhai, published in the Bulletin of the Cold War International History Project. The author points out that the official Chinese history does not explain why Giap made a second trip in October or why the Soviet participants had been changed. The report goes on:

> Perhaps disagreement emerged during the discussions of Giap's first trip, leaving some issues unresolved. In fact, according to the study by Guangxi Academy of Social Sciences, the Chinese and the Russians differed over strategies to reunify Vietnam. The Soviet advisors favored peaceful coexistence between North and South Vietnam, urging Hanoi to "reunify the country through peaceful means on the basis of independence and democracy." The Chinese Communists, conversely, contended that because of imperialist sabotage it was impossible to reunify Vietnam through a general election in accordance with the Geneva Accords, and that consequently North Vietnam should prepare for a protracted struggle.[32]

The North Vietnamese did not have an easy time of it during the next few years (after 1954) as their relationship with the Chinese Communists developed and their dependency on them deepened. In 1953, for example, the North Vietnamese had embarked upon a land reform program on the Chinese

31. See Qiang Zhai, "Beijing and the Vietnam Conflict," 33.
32. Ibid.

model. When it failed, it caused a dispute within the North Vietnamese party (then known as the Vietnamese Workers' Party) and some alienation from the Chinese. The party's new general secretary, Le Duan, removed the chief of the land reform program and accused him of applying the Chinese model "without considering the Vietnamese reality." Whether in response to that criticism or for other reasons is not clear, but in December 1955 the Chinese withdrew their military mission from North Vietnam, leaving behind only a small team of military experts. In April 1956, new advice from a Chinese economist—who was also a deputy premier—recommended that the North Vietnamese make agricultural development their first priority, and Chou En-lai on a visit to Hanoi a few months later recommended against collectivizing agriculture. That smoothed things over, and the North Vietnamese continued to consult with the Chinese on a variety of economic and political questions.[33]

During the next three years (from 1956 to 1959), the North Vietnamese concentrated upon economic development and implemented a new "Three-Year Plan" for transformation of the economy and society. Then, in the spring of 1959, the party adopted a policy of returning to revolutionary activity in the South. A year later, in 1960, Vietnamese leaders consulted with Chou En-lai and Deng Xiaoping and agreed that "political struggle [in the South] should be combined with armed conflict." It was then that the Vietnamese Workers' Party at its National Congress in September 1960 took note of "disintegration" which was "replacing stability in the South" and called for increased support from the North for the military struggle in the South.[34]

Outlook for Bloc Activism

The history of the principal points of contention between the United States and the Sino-Soviet bloc from 1958 through 1960 suggests that the bloc did not wage as vigorous a campaign against U.S. and allied positions as we had anticipated. Nor were those issues so fraught with danger as we had thought they would be.

The Taiwan "Crisis" turned out to have been a Chinese game designed to make U.S. leaders uncomfortable and mildly frightened, but—even if Mao had initially intended the bombardments as an opening ploy in a game of moving the Soviets toward a more aggressive line—it failed to do so. If any-

33. Ibid., 234.
34. Ibid.

thing, it strengthened Khrushchev's intention not to engage in a confrontation with the United States in Asia. While we in the intelligence business did not understand at the time the pivotal importance of the Taiwan affair in breaking down the Soviet-Chinese partnership in world politics, we did conclude in NIE 1-61 (January 1961) that the Chinese preferred "a policy of greater militancy even at considerable risk" to the comparatively low-risk policy of peaceful competition advocated by the Soviets.

Khrushchev apparently was more prepared to pursue an activist policy in Europe than to collude with Chinese activism in Asia. It was only a month after the Chinese bombardment of the offshore islands was cut back that he served up his ultimatum on Berlin. Even then he moved cautiously and accepted President Eisenhower's proposal for a four-power summit on the subject. When the conference blew up over the U-2 incident, Khrushchev was still prepared to withdraw the ultimatum and to wait for a new conference after the election of a new U.S. President.

According to Zubok and Pleshakov, what really excited Khrushchev was the Cuban revolution. Because it was spontaneous, he saw it as a sign that the forces of history were on the side of Communism. He saw the "Third World" as eventually joining the Communist camp. A groundswell of social transformation would demonstrate to the world and even to the United States that the "cause of Communism was the wave of the future."

In NIE 1-61, we also saw a lesson in the events happening in the emerging world, though not exactly the same lesson that Khrushchev saw. We wrote: "The world has entered into a new era. New leaders and new nations are arriving on the scene; there is a new relationship of military power; political and social instability have become epidemic in the southern two-thirds of the world; schisms and heresies have arisen within the Communist camp itself. There is no longer any question that radical change will occur in the world, but only a question of what direction it will take."

But the new estimate also pointed out that while many new revolutionary leaders were prepared to accept Communist advisers, economic aid, and diplomatic support, they were also "generally chary of embracing Communism." They did not want to accept "all that goes with Communist ideology"—including identification with the Soviet bloc and exclusion from Western economic aid and technical assistance. We in the Office of National Estimates thought, because of the enormous problems which many of the new states faced, that there would be a continuing tendency toward "some blend of authoritarianism and socialism." We did express concern that if the West did not "understand and help them," they would tend to "rely more and more heavily upon the Communists, until a point is reached when they can no longer extricate themselves from the Communist embrace."

That judgment proved to be the case with Vietnam. The United States government did not understand what had happened there after the Japanese surrender in 1945, nor did it understand the basic motivations of Soviet policy. By declaring mainland Asia outside the U.S. defense perimeter, it left it open to Communist bloc activism. But in 1945 to 1949, the Soviets were prevented from attending to Southeast Asia by their commitment to the Chinese Communists, and the Chinese Communists were preoccupied with their own civil war in China itself. When the Chinese were able to do so, they did provide some arms to Ho Chih Minh's struggling forces. Then, when Secretary Acheson and the Pentagon misread the North Korean attack on the South (which need not have occurred at all if attention had been paid to the CIA estimate on the subject), they classified Indochina as an immediate target of Soviet bloc military aggression.

The long history of the struggle in Vietnam up to 1959, which is briefly recounted in the preceding section of this chapter, indicates that, when reduced to its essentials, much has been obscured by U.S. policymakers, to wit:

1. Although Ho Chih Minh was a Communist, the Vietnamese revolution was not a Soviet-sponsored or Soviet-armed rebellion. It was a nationalist revolt against French colonialism. It was not supported by the French Communists; the Soviets did not endorse the revolution or even send an observer to Hanoi during its early years.

2. Despite repeated pleas from Ho, the United States never responded to his overtures or even his open promise in the spring of 1949 to guarantee Vietnam's neutrality in the Cold War then getting under way. (This was the time when, in Europe, the United States was trying to help Tito's Communist regime in Belgrade resist Soviet pressure and even a possible military attack.)

3. Ho was tricked into allowing French forces into North Vietnam in 1946 by a French promise to make Vietnam a "free state" in the French Union. Those forces then tried to destroy Ho's forces, which survived for three years by resorting to guerrilla tactics without any assistance from or endorsement by the USSR.

4. Early in 1950, after his promise of Cold War neutrality was ignored by the United States, Ho gave up and sought recognition from China and the USSR.

5. Three days after the North Korean invasion began in June 1950, Truman

directed accelerated military assistance to the French forces in Vietnam and establishment of a military mission. The United States recognized former emperor Bao Dai as "chief of state" and began giving him an annual stipend of $4,000,000. His so-called government proved both incompetent and corrupt.

6. The European NATO governments called a conference in Geneva to mediate the Vietnam question. It agreed upon nationwide elections in 1956 to form a single government. The U.S. delegate did not sign, but stated that the United States would honor the agreement.

7. When it was realized that Ho would win the elections, the United States directed the Vietnamese to denounce the agreement. It was then that Ho finally made a pilgrimage to Moscow and Beijing in seek of aid.

8. It was then that Chinese military aid began in earnest. But disagreements soon arose between the Chinese and the Soviets. The Soviets wanted to move toward peaceful co-existence of the two Vietnams, while the Chinese wanted to wage and win a protracted struggle if that was necessary.

9. From 1956 to 1959 the North Vietnamese were busy concentrating upon economic development, while the South was concentrating upon a military buildup with large-scale U.S. military assistance.

10. Finally, in 1959, with promised Chinese assistance, the Vietnamese Communist Party decided upon a political struggle in the South supported by armed conflict. A year later the Party decreed that the North would provide increased military support for the struggle in the South. That is where matters stood when John Kennedy took over the White House in January 1961.

Emerging Strains in the Communist World

Preceding sections of this narrative have described how the Soviets under Khrushchev's leadership were trying to exploit the trend toward nationalism and social revolution in the former colonial and underdeveloped areas of the world. They also recount how Khrushchev had experimented with using the USSR's growing capability to wage intercontinental warfare to gain credibility in the Arab world. But it was also becoming clear that Khrushchev was demonstrating considerable caution along with his political thrusts; he wanted to look like a peacemaker. A few months after his summit in Washington with President Eisenhower, he announced (in January 1960) that he was reducing the Soviet army by one-third, including the cashiering of 250,000 officers. We did not know whether that move was intended to divert more resources toward social and economic programs, or whether it was a signal that the Soviets were planning to use their newly acquired deterrent capability simply as a cover for more aggressive political and economic actions in emerging areas. As noted earlier in the chapter, Zubok and Pleshakov believe it was the former. Khrushchev hoped that revolutions such as that in Cuba, even more than Soviet successes in the nuclear arms race and missile technology, would demonstrate to the world that the "cause of Communism was the wave of the future."

That outlook was a long way from the hard-line view of a Soviet leadership determined to spread Communism by military aggression, as postulated by political leaders such as Dean Acheson and Paul Nitze and by most of the U.S. military establishment during the 1950s. When we in the Office of National Estimates began working on a new world estimate in the autumn of 1960, we were not of course privy to the material now available to scholars and historians. We had to rely upon our own methodology and experience, our interactive collegial self-criticism, and the judgment of outside consultants.

It had become clear nevertheless that Soviet-Chinese relations had seriously deteriorated and that the very future of what we called the Sino-Soviet bloc was at stake. As a consequence, we were obliged to admit that it was "impossible to predict with confidence the course of Communist policy in the decade ahead." We thought that the USSR would stick to its policy of seeking to win victories "without incurring serious risks," and we thought that China would persist in its policy of "pressing the USSR for a more militant bloc policy." We had noticed that the Chinese, despite their bellicose talk, had during recent years "refrained from actions which involved serious risk of large-scale military operations." While we did not mention Taiwan or the shelling of the offshore islands, we were indeed thinking of how the Chinese in late October 1958 had backed off from their daily shelling of the islands. But we did not know how deep a division between China and the USSR had developed over the Taiwan matter. Zubok and Pleshakov write that "the scar from [that] crisis was deep on both sides. Sino-Soviet relations continued to worsen, unbeknown to the outside world and even to many insiders."[35]

In 1959, ten months after the end of the Taiwan crisis, the Soviet Presidium sent a letter to the Chinese government stating the Soviets would not pro-

35. Zubok and Pleshakov, Inside the Kremlin's Cold War, 28.
36. Ibid., 233.

vide the Chinese with a prototype of the atomic bomb.[36] Two months after that, in October 1959, Khrushchev came to Beijing on the occasion of the tenth anniversary of the proclamation of the People's Republic. He came fresh from his détente-like summit meeting with President Eisenhower at Camp David. He promptly got into a heated exchange with Foreign Minister Chen Yi about the Sino-Indian war, during which Khrushchev yelled at Chen Yi, "Don't try to spit on us from up there. You haven't got enough spit!"[37] Then in April 1960 the newspaper *The People's Daily* opened a public campaign against Khrushchev's "revisionism" and "appeasement of imperialists."[38]

At that time, according to Zubok and Pleshakov, "most of the Kremlin leaders" were dismayed at the thought that "Khrushchev's peace overtures to the West might cause a schism," and they still "saw no alternative to friendly relations with Beijing."[39] But by July 1960 the Soviets finally gave up hope of restoring the relationship. All Soviet specialists were recalled from China, and by 1961 Khrushchev stopped paying even lip service to Sino-Soviet friendship.[40]

The inside information which Zubok and Pleshakov have revealed is supported by extensive detailed reporting in the *Bulletin of the Cold War International History Project*. Had we possessed such data in the autumn of 1960, we could have made more incisive judgments about the likelihood of a total break and its probable effects. We did say that the Soviet leaders would consider an open break "calamitous" for the world Communist movement, but that they would not go so far as to "surrender" to the Chinese position in order to avoid such a break. The Soviet leaders wanted not only to preserve Soviet leadership of the Communist movement but also to adhere to their "national interest in avoiding serious risk of general war." We thought that if the rift widened to the point of an open split, it would dim the image of the Communist bloc as "a great and growing power center." That in turn would reduce pressures on peripheral countries to accommodate to the Communist powers.

We came as close as we could, consistent with the available evidence, to saying that the Chinese could not cause the Soviets to change their policy, and we suggested that the Soviets would likely become increasingly disen-

37. Ibid., 202 and 232.
38. Ibid., 232.
39. Ibid.
40. Ibid., 234.

chanted with their Chinese allies. We wrote:

> Over the next decade at least, there appears to be a greater likelihood of flexibility in Soviet than in Chinese policy. The Soviet leadership's desire to prevent a general war, the wider range of Soviet contacts with the outside world, the continuing pressure at home for liberalization, and the growing capacity of the USSR to provide its citizens with a more comfortable life — these factors taken together may tend toward moderation in foreign policy and toward a recognition of some areas of common interest with the West. It is even possible that the Soviet leaders will come to feel that the USSR has little in common with China except an ideology which the Chinese interpret in their own way, and that by 1970 Communist China, with nuclear weapons and a population of almost 900 million, will be a dangerous neighbor and associate.

Even as time went by and the Sino-Soviet split became obvious to the world, its significance was not fully taken in by U.S. policymakers. It became clear that the Sino-Soviet alliance was at an end, and that Moscow's hold over Eastern Europe was weakening; taken together these made Communism look a lot less like a political avalanche ready to roll over the world. But U.S. policymakers clung to their established policies. And we in the intelligence community did not credit Khrushchev with so large a commitment to peace as he appears to have demonstrated in Communist councils up to the time of our writing. The U-2 incident and the failure of the Paris summit, along with fears generated in America by the Castro revolution and its reverberations, kept the U.S. and Soviet leaders mutually mistrustful. If, as it appears, Khrushchev was exploring the possibilities of moving toward a détente with the West, there were still strong obstacles in its way.

1960 The Strategic Situation and Its Dangers

NIE 1-61 (January 19, 1961) concluded that the decade ahead would be "an extremely dangerous one." We thought that the Soviets were "almost certain" to test the opportunity for gains provided by the changing situation in the underdeveloped areas of the world. Such tests, we thought, could give rise to "serious crises," and we mentioned Berlin and the Chinese offshore islands as examples of "situations in which retreat may become impossible."

Projected Soviet and Chinese Outlooks in 1961

Underlying that dire prediction was a recognition, as the estimate put it, that "the USSR is well on the road toward matching the U.S. in many of the indices of national power." We specified that Soviet progress in the field of rocketry "has probably had more effect upon world opinion than any development of the past two or three years." We went on:

> The Soviet leaders consider themselves to be in a position of great strength. They probably believe that they now possess, or will soon have, a powerful counter-deterrent to the existing U.S. deterrent force, and that this counter-deterrent will become more and more persuasive in the years ahead. They almost certainly feel that for these reasons they can frequently and vigorously challenge the U.S. on disputed

issues. They probably feel that the range of East-West actions which they can pursue with little fear of nuclear retaliation is growing, although they almost certainly recognize that they must act with caution lest they provoke the U.S. into precipitate action. The Soviet leaders evidently recognize that a general nuclear exchange could mean the destruction of modern society.

The "peaceful coexistence" policy of the Soviet leaders is partly the consequence of these cautionary judgments. It is also partly the consequence of the Soviet ideological outlook, which views history, not primarily as a contest of military power between states, but as a long-term social revolutionary struggle. The total power position of the Communist world—including but not focusing exclusively around its military ingredient—is viewed as an encouragement and a guarantee of success of revolutionary forces in the non-Communist states. In the Soviet view the situation, especially in the underdeveloped states, is now such that substantial gains can be won by vigorous pursuit of all forms of struggle short of war. The Soviets probably also feel that in carefully chosen circumstances they could wage limited war with Communist-supported, or even with bloc forces, without themselves incurring serious risk of general war. The comparative caution implied in this strategy has led to an open dispute between the USSR and Communist China.

We thought the Sino-Soviet dispute was partly a result of "growing self-confidence" within the Chinese leadership as an outgrowth of China's economic achievements. There had been, for example, especially dramatic increases in industrial production (33 percent in 1959 alone). Probably a more important factor underlying Chinese assertiveness we described in this way:

> The most striking characteristic of Communist China is not its economic progress but its great revolutionary élan. The Chinese Communist leaders are men of intense ardor who are deadly serious about transforming Chinese society completely and irrevocably. They are determined to create a "new Communist man," indeed even a "new Chinese Communist man," and to give the world the benefits of their "constructive contributions" to Communist dogma and social theory. Confident of their own righteousness and orthodoxy and reinforced in that confidence by what they regard as the great achievements of

the past decade, they are pushing, not only toward great power status in the world, but also toward at least co-equal status with the USSR in the world of international Communism. Indeed, it became clear during 1960 that Beijing was a major challenge to Moscow's position as the final authority in the Communist movement.

We thought the Chinese view of the world situation was uninformed and doctrinaire. They thought that imperialism was on its last legs, that the emerging peoples in Africa, Asia, and Latin America were ripe for revolution, and that they needed only the "active support" from the Communist powers to bring it off. While the possibility of some new Chinese adventure could create serious problems for the United States, as it did at the time of the Taiwan affair, the most serious danger in the times ahead seemed to us to lie with Soviet military power, not Chinese ambitions. That is why we stated that the "major problem" of the 1960s would be the accumulation of offensive weapons of mass destruction by the two great powers.

Nuclear Arsenals

We in the intelligence community were unable to agree upon an estimate of the likely size of the Soviet ICBM stockpile by mid-1963, which was two and a half years from the time of our writing. Estimates varied from 200 or fewer up to a figure of 700 advanced by some of the military intelligence people. In addition, there was the possibility of nuclear weapons being delivered by shorter-range missiles, by aircraft, and by submarines and surface ships. The question of numbers, however, was becoming increasingly meaningless because the Soviet capability at even the lowest figures would have posed "a grave threat to the U.S."

We did not think that there was very much we in the United States could do to prevent enormous damage to the United States. Even a preemptive attack by U.S. missile forces could do little because of such operational considerations as missile reliability, location of aiming points, geodetic and gravitational anomalies, and other problems. While anti-missile systems were under study and development, we thought that "early systems"—even if available by mid-decade—would "not be sufficiently developed or widely enough deployed to give assurance of destroying or neutralizing more than a small proportion of the missiles which the USSR will be capable of launching."

It was here that we received our first dissent. The Army chief of intelligence agreed with the general view expressed above, but he claimed that the intelligence community was "unable to adjudge the capability of the U.S. to develop an effective defense against ballistic missiles." The Army of course, was the Defense Department's agent for anti-missile development and did not want intelligence officers asserting that they were unlikely to succeed. We believed it was the mission of a national estimate on the world situation to make judgments about our own as well as our adversary's capabilities for resolving the very difficult problems which an anti-missile defense presented. Our adversary was, after all, bound by the same laws of physics and the same obstacles that we were. We were proven correct. No nation has yet, some thirty-five years later, developed an anti-missile system of sufficient effectiveness to ensure prevention of enormous damage either to the combatants or to the world at large.

We went on to estimate that even if the United States were attacked first by the USSR, the United States would "almost certainly" be able to wreak "enormous damage" in retaliation. We further estimated that it was "very unlikely" that the USSR would acquire during the next several years sufficient capabilities "to give it confidence that it can prevent an unacceptable level of U.S. retaliation." It was here that we got our second dissent, this time from the Air Force chief of intelligence.

The Air Force chief repeated a dissent which he had made a few months earlier to an NIE on "Soviet Capabilities and Policies." He thought that the United States was "entering a very critical twenty-four month period in which the USSR may well sense that it has the advantage" and that the Soviet leaders "may well press that advantage and offer the U.S. the choice of war or of backing down on an issue heretofore considered vital to our national interests." This Air Force position was not unlike that pressed by them back in 1953 and again in 1959, when I was working with the Net Evaluation Subcommittee. On the two visits which I paid to SAC Headquarters, the briefers had stressed that the critical date for a Soviet attack upon the United States was eighteen months hence. There apparently was a consistent Air Force tactic applied in strategic and budgetary discussions to keep high and comparatively imminent the perceived danger of a Soviet nuclear attack upon the United States.

Despite those reservations by the Army and the Air Force, we were able to get the agreement of all the members of the intelligence community to the following judgments:

Thus it appears likely that during most of the decade ahead the strategic situation will be one in which both the U.S. and the USSR will possess relatively invulnerable nuclear weapons systems capable of inflicting enormous destruction upon the other. The world must face the possibility that a general nuclear war—brought to pass through accident, design, or miscalculation—would kill many millions of people, destroy the capital accumulation of many decades, render large sections of the earth virtually uninhabitable for a time, and destroy the power of most of the modern nations of the world.

This strategic situation does not make general nuclear war impossible, but it does make it a highly irrational response to international disputes. As long as this situation continues, each side will be deterred by fear of the consequences (if by nothing else) from deliberately initiating general war. It is almost certain, moreover, that each side will be deterred from action or policies which involve serious risk of general war.

This evolving world strategic situation aroused a new level of fear throughout the world that somehow and at any moment the nuclear demon might again be released, with indescribable consequences. In the journalistic and academic worlds, as well as in the intelligence community, many people were wondering how to think about this new and dangerous world. Even among the politically and militarily sophisticated, it seemed to us, there was considerable puzzlement and disagreement about the deterrent effect of present and future nuclear capabilities, about the probable behavior of states in critical situations, and about the most suitable and effective strategic doctrines and weapons to develop.

The Soviet View of the USSR's Strategic Position

We thought that these problems troubled Soviet leaders as well as those of the West. We thought that the Soviets had not formed definite ideas about their force structure ten years hence, or about the precise role they would assign to military power in their campaigns to establish world communism. We explained what we thought their current views were:

They now see themselves as emerging from a period of strategic inferiority, and they surely consider it a prime objective not to let the U.S. draw ahead once more. As long as the weapons race persists, they will not be content with a strategic equilibrium, or with the progress they have hitherto made in weapons development. Beyond that, they will

continue to carry on scientific and weapons research and development programs with a high sense of urgency in order to find new
weapons and defenses against existing ones. They would do this even
without dreams of vast military conquests, simply in the interest of
defense.

We then added this conclusion about their current strategic doctrine:

> From what we know of Soviet ideas, however, we conclude that dur-
> ing the next five years—and perhaps longer—the Soviet leaders will
> conceive of their long-range striking capability in terms of deterrence
> and of employment in a heavy blow should they finally conclude that
> deterrence had failed, rather than in terms of their deliberate initia-
> tion of general war. In their view, a condition of mutual deterrence
> will provide an umbrella under which to wage a vigorous campaign,
> using a wide variety of methods, throughout the non-Communist world.

Here we got a second dissent from the Air Force. In a footnote to the paragraph in which the judgment above appeared, the chief of Air Force intelligence expressed his belief that "the evidence of offensive missile and bomber
production and deployment shows a definite intent by the Soviet rulers to
achieve a clear military superiority at the earliest practicable date." It had
long been evident to other members of the intelligence community that the
leadership of the Air Force itself was determined to establish and maintain
a clear military superiority over the USSR. That leadership did not accept
the principle of a general equivalency between the forces of the two powers.
It refused to face honestly and squarely the evidence from Soviet doctrine
and behavior which clearly indicated that the Soviets were striving to achieve
a Communist world by political means and without assuming any serious risk
of general war. Indeed, it was almost surely the U.S. effort, led by the Air
Force and its political allies, to promote the achievement of U.S. military
superiority which prompted the Soviet military programs which the Air Force
then claimed were demonstrative of a Soviet intent to achieve military superiority and to use it as nuclear blackmail to achieve a Communist world.

We did not entirely exclude the use of Soviet military forces over a comparatively minor matter if the Soviets thought the risks were comparatively
low. With the Korean War still in our minds, we also acknowledged that the
Soviet or other bloc forces might be used to assist armed local revolutionary
groups. We noted that it had become widely held that limited war capabili-

ties should be utilized to cope with minor threats, but that many of "the principles of their political and military use in the nuclear age remain to be developed and accepted." We also pointed out that even when the parties involved were proclaiming limited objectives, the rules of combat could still pose problems; the Soviets, for example, believed that limited wars "would carry particularly great risks of spreading into general war if nuclear weapons were introduced" in whatever form and for whatever purpose. We thought that "as a general rule and as a result of the experience in Korea, the Communist powers will probably try to avoid provocations which would permit the West to bring limited war capabilities to bear."

The Danger of Unintentional War

We were especially concerned about preventing miscalculations that might precipitate general war unintentionally. We wrote the following about this problem:

> Whenever international disputes arise there is a natural tendency for the parties concerned to place their forces on an alert status and progressively to strengthen the alert by various forms of deployment. In some cases these might be normal precautions and in some cases they might be intended to frighten the adversary, or both. In any case, there is likely to be considerable concern among neutrals and U.S. allies that the U.S. and the USSR will act in too bellicose a fashion, that both the U.S. and the USSR might become so committed that they would be unable to back down and thus would become involved in war, or that the state of alert on one side or both will become so advanced that, fearing a surprise attack, one would take pre-emptive action against the other.

The Arms Control Alternative

We felt that sometime during the decade of the 1960s, there would be movement toward arms limitation. This is what we wrote:

> In this situation of widespread fear of a general nuclear war, it is natural that the peoples of the world should look to arms control as a means of reducing the danger. Whatever the motivation, the USSR has carried on a many-sided campaign for general and complete

disarmament. The Soviet leaders probably are interested in achieving some degree of disarmament, to an extent which would at least slow down or stop developments which might harm their strategic position or increase the danger of accidental war. During the decade, it is possible that both sides will become sufficiently concerned with stabilizing the balance of terror that some limited agreements may be reached. In any case, it is possible that—in order both to achieve stabilization and to meet world pressures for reducing the danger of war— the two sides will undertake tacit agreements resulting in some degree of arms limitation.

Implications of the evolving strategic situation did indeed become clearer through events that occurred during the first two years of the Kennedy administration. Soon after he took office, the Bay of Pigs affair obliged President Kennedy to face the question of direct U.S. military intervention in the form of Air Force and Marine support for the Cuban revolutionary forces trying to establish themselves on Cuban soil. Soon afterward came Khrushchev's decision to erect the Berlin Wall and thus threaten four-power authority in Berlin. In both cases the United States refrained from military action. One year after that was the most severe crisis of the Cold War era, when there was a showdown between the United States and the USSR over the placement of Soviet missiles in Cuba, and the Soviets withdrew. Inherent in all three of these events was the possibility that one side or the other could have responded in a fashion leading to a U.S.-Soviet nuclear exchange.

President Kennedy's Crises

The Test at Vienna

Chapter 5 recounted the collapse of the Paris summit over the U-2 incident of May 1959, and Eisenhower's promise to Khrushchev that there would be no more overflights of the USSR as long as he was president. On January 24, 1961, just four days after his inauguration, President Kennedy sent a formal note to the USSR confirming that the no-overflight policy was being continued. Kennedy followed up early in March with a proposal to Khrushchev for a summit meeting. Accordingly, it was scheduled for July 3 and 4, 1961, in Vienna. The most important topic on the minds of both principals was the problem of Berlin.

Kennedy and Khrushchev made a lot of history together, indeed crucial history; what they did and did not do during the nearly three years they dealt with each other had a profound effect upon the years that followed. The Russian scholars Zubok and Pleshakov have provided a detailed account of that relationship. The talks in Vienna about Berlin, Cuba, and the possibility of war have been well chronicled by the two Russian writers as well as by Kennedy's associates Arthur Schlesinger and Theodore Sorensen. Zubok and Pleshakov described not only the Vienna talks but also the long journey which the two leaders took together, from the failed U.S.-led assault upon Cuba at the Bay of Pigs to the Soviet retreat on the high seas that ended the Cuban missile crisis.

The two Russian writers made quite a point of Khrushchev's early hopes for an improved Soviet-U.S. relationship to be built during the Kennedy presidency. They reported, for example, that during the presidential election campaign of 1960, Khrushchev "rooted for the young Democratic candidate and regarded him as a promising partner for future talks."[1] The Soviet KGB even directed its station in Washington to "inform the Center periodically about the development of the election campaign and to propose measures, diplomatic, propaganda, or other, to encourage Kennedy's victory."[2] After Kennedy's election, Khrushchev established and maintained a contact with the Kennedy brothers through a Soviet military intelligence officer who was posing as the chief of the Soviet press office in Washington. That contact, incidentally, was one of two confidential channels for the exchange of U.S.-Soviet communications outside of the regular diplomatic services. The second was through Ambassador Dobrynin himself, who has reported in his memoirs that these two channels remained open for many years.[3]

The Bay of Pigs affair was an important step in the evolution of Khrushchev's thinking. When Kennedy refused to intervene with U.S. forces, Khrushchev "had reason to believe that his [own] diplomacy of deterrence had worked again, as it had in the Suez crisis."[4] He also began to think of Kennedy as a "weak president not entirely in control of the state machinery."[5] Furthermore, he thought that at Vienna "he would be able to force the young and inexperienced American president to make concessions, in particular on Berlin."[6]

It did not work out quite that way. Rather than wring concessions from a weak Kennedy, Khrushchev stiffened Kennedy's resolve. Rather than increase the chances for an improved U.S.-Soviet relationship, the conference divided the two leaders even more sharply than before. Ted Sorensen, Special Counsel to the President, summed up the conference as "neither a victory or a defeat for either side."[7] Zubok and Pleshakov observed that for two days the two leaders were "engaged in an academic and misguided dialogue on the history of the Cold War."[8] Sorensen has reported that Kennedy later observed that "the Soviets and ourselves give wholly different meanings to the same words. We have wholly different views of right and wrong, of what is an inter-

1. Zubok and Pleshakov, *Inside the Kremlin's Cold War*, 236.
2. Ibid., 238.
3. Dobrynin, *In Confidence*, 52–54.
4. Zubok and Pleshakov, *Inside the Kremlin's Cold War*, 242.
5. Ibid., 236.
6. Ibid., 243.
7. Theodore C. Sorensen, *Kennedy* (New York: Harper & Row, 1965), 542.
8. Zubok and Pleshakov, *Inside the Kremlin's Cold War*, 245.

nal affair and what is aggression, and, above all, of where the world is and where it is going."[9]

Kennedy found out about the problem of meaning early on in the summit. I do not know whether he had read NIE 1-61 or whether one of his associates had done so. The reader will recall that we believed the Soviets would not initiate general nuclear war or assume any serious risk of provoking one, and that we considered the greatest danger of nuclear war lay in one side or the other "miscalculating" the risk involved in a particular policy or action. Kennedy's first concern at Vienna was precisely that problem, and it was one he returned to time and again during the two days of the conference. Kennedy's central thesis was that the two major powers should avoid situations where their vital interests could become committed, which could lead to a confrontation from which neither could back down.[10] Each time Kennedy brought up the subject, Khrushchev bridled and began to claim that U.S. concern was really prompted by its desire to confine Communism to the countries where it was already established.[11]

As the discussion proceeded it became clear that what the Soviets feared was U.S. military action to stop the spread of Communism, just as many in the U.S. military establishment feared that the USSR wished to use force to spread Communism. Kennedy responded by stating that he was only talking about "erroneous prediction of the other side's next move," and he admitted that he himself had made a misjudgment in the Bay of Pigs affair.[12] Khrushchev responded that revolution around the world was bound to occur and that "the Soviet leaders could not be responsible for every spontaneous uprising or Communist trend."[13] To buttress his point, Khrushchev stated that Castro was "not a Communist" but that through its actions the United States was "well on the way to making him a good one."[14] He went on to predict that the Shah of Iran would be "overthrown" also, but that the USSR "would have nothing to do with it." Kennedy and Khrushchev did agree on one thing — Laos was not worth a war.[15] Except for agreeing on Laos, a discussion that had begun on the dangers of miscalculation went nowhere. They were simply talking past each other.

9. Cited in Sorensen, *Kennedy*, 550.
10. Ibid., 585.
11. Ibid., 546.
12. Ibid.
13. Ibid.
14. Zubok and Pleshakov, *Inside the Kremlin's Cold War*, 244.
15. Sorensen, *Kennedy*, 546.

The "grimmest talk," Sorensen reported, was on Germany and Berlin: "Khrushchev was belligerent and Kennedy was unyielding."[16] According to Zubok and Pleshakov, Khrushchev "insisted that he had come to Vienna to reach some agreement with Kennedy similar to the interim agreement that he had discussed with Eisenhower."[17] Kennedy did not give any ground, insisting that the United States "could not accept the abrogation by one nation of the four-power agreement."[18] In Arthur Schlesinger's report on what followed, he quoted Khrushchev as saying that the "USSR intended to sign a treaty" with East Germany before the end of 1961, and that "if America wanted war over Berlin, there was nothing the Soviet Union could do about it."[19] That remark was followed by a further intemperate statement that he "might sign the treaty right away and get it over with," adding that "that was what the Pentagon wanted."[20] Schlesinger characterized the Khrushchev statement as "not quite a tirade"; it was "too controlled and hard and therefore the more menacing."[21] The exchange moved toward an end with a warning from Khrushchev which Schlesinger phrased as follows: "If the President insisted on occupation rights after a treaty, and if East Germany's borders were violated, whether by land, sea, or air, force would be met by force. The United States should prepare itself, and the Soviet Union would do likewise."[22]

Kennedy closed out the exchange by saying to the listeners on both sides that it would be "a cold winter." He was, Schlesinger reported, "deeply disturbed." But U.S. Ambassadors Llewellyn Thompson and Charles (Chip) Bohlen, who were part of the U.S. delegation, had been through such conferences before, and they thought that the President had "overreacted."[23]

Note how closely the discussions and especially the final dialogue of the Vienna conference resemble the warnings we at the O/NE issued in paragraph 74 of NIE 1-61. We had expressed concern in that paragraph that both the United States and the USSR would act in too bellicose a fashion and might become so committed on some issue that they would be unable to back down and thus could get into a war by miscalculation. When Kennedy opened the conference on the first day with a statement on the necessity of avoiding miscalculations that could lead to war, he almost certainly did not foresee

16. Ibid., 549.
17. Zubok and Pleshakov, *Inside the Kremlin's Cold War*, 247.
18. Arthur M. Schlesinger, Jr., *A Thousand Days* (Boston: Houghton Mifflin, 1965), 372.
19. Ibid.
20. Ibid.
21. Ibid.
22. Ibid., 374.
23. Ibid.

that he would soon be a party to a case study on precisely that subject. We now know that Khrushchev was quite certain in his own mind that the United States would not start a war over Berlin, but he apparently did not realize that playing his game of nuclear deterrence would not work unless he or Kennedy somehow backed down. The next sixteen months explored each's capacity to do so.

Berlin: Showdown Averted

Kennedy's reaction to the conference after he returned to Washington was described by Schlesinger as a determination not to give way. He wrote: "While Kennedy wanted to make this resolve absolutely clear to Moscow, he wanted to make it equally clear that he was not, as he put it, 'war-mad.' He did not want to drive the crisis beyond the point of no return; and therefore, while reiterating our refusal to retreat, he rejected [a] program of national mobilization and sought the beginnings of careful negotiation."[24] In a July 25, 1961, report to the American people on the conference, however, Kennedy indicated that he was asking additional funds for the defense budget and calling up some reserve units. These were, he said, defense measures to "prepare for any contingency."[25]

Khrushchev, on the other hand, told his Warsaw Pact allies at a secret conference in Moscow early in August that Kennedy, in his July 25 report, "had declared war on us and set down his conditions." Zubok and Pleshakov describe Khrushchev's report to his Communist allies (which has only recently surfaced in Party archives) as "rambling and incoherent":

> Khrushchev shared with the Communist leaders his confusion about the seemingly odd nature of U.S. politics. The American state, he said, is "barely governed." Kennedy himself "hardly influences the direction and development of policies." Power relationships in the United States were characterized by chaotic infighting among factions, where the "faction of war" was still greater than the "faction of peace." Therefore, "anything is possible in the United States," Khrushchev admitted. "War is possible. They can unleash it. The situation in England, France, Italy, and Germany is more stable." Khrushchev even had to admit, contrary to much of his previous

24. Ibid., 391.
25. Ibid.

rhetoric, that German militarism was much more under check than U.S. militarism!

The new U.S. president was no match for the huge military-indus-trial complex that his predecessors had nourished. Khrushchev expressed sympathy for the young inexperienced Kennedy who for all his best intentions was too much of a lightweight. "The U.S. state is too big, powerful, and poses certain dangers." At this moment, Khrushchev seriously questioned whether Kennedy would be able to keep "the dark forces" of his country at bay while he negotiated for a long truce.[26]

There were several noteworthy themes in that Khrushchev monologue. He does not sound like a bullying warmonger. There is a mild sadness about his rambling; he is afraid a war will come, and he is afraid the Americans will start it by an assault on East Germany. He is afraid of "dark forces" and American "militarists." He either knows about or senses the split between Pentagon intelligence officers and intelligence officers in the CIA and the State Department on the matter of the Soviet use of military force to expand the Soviet domain. He also seems to have sensed the increasingly powerful position which the military had won in American economic and political life. He sees the contrast between the U.S. and Soviet military establishments, the latter having been completely subjected to civilian political control. But most of all, the Khrushchev monologue shows him to have been a troubled man, already unsure of the consequences of his behavior in Vienna and of his use of the nuclear threat to achieve his goal for Berlin.

Khrushchev had other problems. One effect of the Berlin crisis was to cause large numbers of East Germans to fear for the future and flee to West Berlin. Over 30,000 fled in July alone. The East German leader Walter Ulbricht asked the Soviet ambassador in Potsdam early in July to tell the Kremlin that if the border to West Berlin remained open, "collapse would be inevitable."[27] Khrushchev finally agreed. On August 13, 1961, the gates to West Berlin were closed and barbed wire emplaced. A month later con-struction of a concrete wall began.

After the barbed wire had been laid down, Kennedy came to the conclu-sion that talks were better than war, and he directed Secretary of State Dean Rusk to begin secret talks with Foreign Minister Andrei Gromyko on the Berlin situation. Khrushchev responded by suggesting a renewal of the secret

---

26. Zubok and Pleshakov, *Inside the Kremlin's Cold War*, 252–53.
27. Ibid., 251.

correspondence between himself and Kennedy through the Soviet military intelligence channel in Washington. Meanwhile, General Clay, the U.S. commander in Berlin, was making plans to tear down the barbed wire. There was a tank standoff at Checkpoint Charlie which lasted for two days. The Soviets had allowed the tanks to cross the border, but then Soviet tanks blocked their further advance. The secret channel then apparently worked something out (the messages exchanged are still classified); the Soviet tanks pulled back, and the American tanks did the same thing twenty minutes later.[28]

Then, on October 17, 1961, Khrushchev told the Soviet Communist Party Congress, which was then in session, that "the Western powers are showing some understanding of the situation, and were inclined to seek a solution to the German problem and the issue of West Berlin." The Wall stayed up, but a military showdown was averted.[29] General Clay, who had frequently tried to force issues and who had created a war scare in Washington shortly after the Czech coup in February 1948, resigned in April 1962. After that, neither side pushed very hard to resolve the problem of Berlin, and life with the Wall went on in Berlin until 1989, when its destruction signaled the end of Communism in Eastern Europe.

But Khrushchev still worried about a new crisis arising from the pressure of the U.S. military on President Kennedy. According to Zubok and Pleshakov, "The more Khrushchev thought about it, the more he worried that the hardliners in America would take revenge by invading Cuba. And so he fixed his eyes on the island in the Caribbean sea that could drastically change the geopolitics of the Cold War."[30] It was mid-year 1962 when U.S. intelligence analysts noted an upsurge in the number of Soviet ships carrying military materials arriving in Cuban ports.

The Cuban Missile Crisis

The situation in Cuba had been a high-priority concern for both the Intelligence and Operations directorates of the CIA ever since the Castro regime came to power and especially after the Bay of Pigs disaster in April 1961. The Kennedy administration wanted to be rid of Castro, and of course Khrushchev knew that. But the Kennedy brothers at that point certainly preferred that Castro leave through an internal uprising without any overt help from the

28. Ibid., 257.
29. Schlesinger, *Thousand Days*, 400.
30. Zubok and Pleshakov, *Inside the Kremlin's Cold War*, 258.

United States. Twice in 1962 the national intelligence estimating process was geared up to produce papers about Cuba. The second of these, NIE 85-2-62 ("The Situation and Prospects in Cuba"), was approved on August 1, 1962, and was concerned primarily with Castro's relations with the "old" Communists in Cuba and with "potential" domestic resistance to the regime. The first two conclusions dealt with the Communist and Soviet questions:

> Fidel Castro has asserted his primacy in Cuban Communism; the "old" Communists have had to accommodate themselves to this fact, as has the USSR. Further strains may develop in these relationships, but they are unlikely to break the ties of mutual interest between Castro and the "old" Communists and between Cuba and the USSR.
>
> By force of circumstances, the USSR is becoming ever more deeply committed to preserve and strengthen the Castro regime. The USSR, however, has avoided any formal commitment to protect and defend the regime in all contingencies.

The remainder of the estimate did not offer much comfort to those in the U.S. government who were hoping to end the Castro revolution through an internal uprising. It concluded that the Cuban armed forces were loyal to the Castro brothers and would be able to suppress any popular insurrection and to repel any invasion short of direct U.S. intervention in strength. The economy was in "deep trouble," and only about 20 percent of the population were "positive" supporters of the regime. But few of those who were disaffected would accept the risk of "organized active resistance" for fear of surveillance and repression. It was unlikely that the regime could be overthrown "unless events had already shaken [it] and brought into doubt its capacity for survival and unless substantial outside support for the insurgents were forthcoming." As far as the prospects for a general Latin American revolution were concerned, the estimate held out little hope for the fulfillment of Castro's dream. There were militant pro-Castro groups in several countries, but there was also "widespread disillusionment" in Latin America regarding the Cuban revolution.

By the end of August, aerial photography of Cuba showed a continuing flow of Soviet military materiel as well as some ongoing military construction. These included materials for building surface-to-air missile sites, a few surface ships with a missile capability, some tanks and self-propelled guns, and at least sixty MIG fighter aircraft. By September 3, the number of Soviet military technicians on the island had risen to three thousand. All of this activity was then studied on an urgent basis by the intelligence community, and a Special National Intelligence Estimate, entitled "The Military Buildup in Cuba," was approved by the USIB on September 19, 1962. The first, third, and fourth of the five conclusions to the estimate are the most important in terms of what is said about what the Soviets hoped to accomplish through this military buildup:

a. We believe that the USSR values its position in Cuba primarily for the political advantages to be derived from it, and consequently that the main purpose of the present military buildup in Cuba is to strengthen the Communist regime there against what the Cubans and Soviets conceive to be a danger that the U.S. may attempt by one means or another to overthrow it. The Soviets evidently hope to deter any such attempt by enhancing Castro's defensive capabilities and by threatening Soviet military retaliation. At the same time, they evidently recognize that the development of an offensive military base in Cuba might provoke U.S. military intervention and thus defeat their present military purpose.

b. As the buildup continues, the USSR may be tempted to establish in Cuba other weapons represented to be defensive in purpose, but of a more "offensive" character; e.g., light bombers, submarines, and additional types of short-range surface-to-surface missiles (SSMs). A decision to provide such weapons will continue to depend heavily on the Soviet estimate as to whether they could be introduced without provoking a U.S. military reaction.

c. The USSR could derive considerable military advantage from the establishment of Soviet medium and intermediate range ballistic missiles in Cuba, or from the establishment of a Soviet submarine base there. As between these two, the establishment of a submarine base would be the more likely. Either development, however, would be incompatible with Soviet practice to date and with Soviet policy as we presently estimate it. It would indicate a far greater willingness to increase the level of risk in U.S.-Soviet relations than the USSR has displayed thus far and consequently would have important policy implications with respect to other areas and other problems in East-West relations.

We in the Office of National Estimates were sometimes taken to task, after the medium-range and intermediate-range missiles were discovered by U-2 flights over Cuba on October 19, for not specifically having predicted their emplacement in our estimate of a month earlier. What we did say, when the quotations above are carefully read, was based upon information then available, and we went beyond that to say that the military buildup was intended to deter, by enhancing Castro's defensive capabilities and by the "threat of Soviet military retaliation," any U.S. attempt to overthrow the Cuban regime. We then added that the Soviets would be tempted to increase the buildup by bringing in weapons of an "offensive" character but "represented" as being "defensive in purpose." Indeed, we went on to state that they would derive "considerable military advantage" from establishment of "short and intermediate range" missiles or a submarine base in Cuba. In short, we did issue a warning of a possible Soviet action which if it materialized, would threaten the United States.

How far the Soviets would go, we wrote, would depend heavily upon their estimate of whether such action could be accomplished "without provoking a U.S. military reaction." We then expressed our view that if the Soviets did in fact deploy such missiles or establish a submarine base in Cuba, it would have been "incompatible" with Soviet practice up to that time and would indicate a "far greater willingness to increase the level of risk in U.S.-Soviet relations." We thought it would, indeed, but did the Soviet leaders recognize it too?

Khrushchev himself discussed the Cuban missile affair in his memoirs published eight years later, in 1970. Strobe Talbott, in his introduction to the Khrushchev account, declared that it was the most open and coherent segment of Khrushchev's entire narrative (which Talbott had translated and edited). Khrushchev reported that he had frequently discussed the Cuban matter with other members of the Presidium and that they had all agreed that "America would not leave Cuba alone unless we did something" to protect its existence as a "socialist country" and as a "working example" to the rest of Latin America. One passage is especially illustrative of his thinking:

> We had to think up some way of confronting America with more than words. We had to establish a tangible and effective deterrent to American interference in the Caribbean. But what exactly? The logical answer was missiles. The United States had already surrounded the Soviet Union with its own bomber bases and missiles. We knew the American missiles were aimed at us in Turkey and Italy, to say nothing of West Germany. Our vital industrial centers were directly threatened by planes armed with atomic bombs and guided missiles tipped with nuclear warheads. As Chairman of the Council of Ministers, I found myself in the difficult position of having to decide on a course of action

which would answer the American threat but which would also avoid war. Any fool can start a war, and once he's done so, even the wisest of men are helpless to stop it—especially if it's a nuclear war.[31]

Khrushchev followed the above recital of his thinking by reporting that while on a visit to Bulgaria he had gotten the idea of "installing missiles with nuclear warheads" in Cuba "without letting the United States find out they were there until it was too late to do anything about them."[32]

Zubok and Pleshakov, in their analysis of the Cuban missile crisis, concluded that what "pushed" Khrushchev into the Cuban adventure was "his revolutionary commitment and his sense of rivalry with the United States." His "fear of losing Cuba" was similar to his "concern about the survival" of the East German regime. Khrushchev's assistant Troyanovsky told him that the Cuban enterprise was "far too risky" and later described Khrushchev as "a man driving out of control, gathering speed, and rushing to God knows where."[33] Zubok and Pleshakov also reported that Mikoyan and Gromyko "initially voiced their concern that the reaction of the United States would be fierce."[34] But Khrushchev succeeded in getting all the members of the Presidium and the Party Secretariat to go along with him at a meeting on May 24, 1962, and he made every one of them sign the directive that set the operation in motion. Some complained that they did not know enough about the problem to participate in the decision, but Khrushchev forced them to sign anyway.[35]

Was the decision to put missiles secretly in Cuba a new departure in Soviet policy indicative of a readiness to increase the level of risk in U.S.-Soviet relations? The evidence available to date strongly suggests that the answer is no. It was very much a Khrushchevian concept, not a conscious new Presidium policy on risk-taking. It was the same kind of boldness that had led to Khrushchev's denunciation of Stalin, to his missile-rattling during the Suez Crisis, and to his initiation of the Berlin Crisis. It was revolutionary romanticism—something quite different from Stalinist pragmatism.

During the last week of October, Kennedy and the executive committee he had appointed to assist him during this crisis were in almost continuous session at the White House, deciding what to do about the missiles and making

31. Khrushchev, *Khrushchev Remembers*, 493.
32. Ibid.
33. Zubok and Pleshakov, *Inside the Kremlin's Cold War*, 261.
34. Ibid.
35. Ibid., 262.

a series of moves designed to steer a course that would avoid nuclear war and still face down the Soviets. Meanwhile, Khrushchev and his associates were milling around Moscow in deep turmoil. The KGB was reporting from Washington that the U.S. military was pushing Kennedy toward a showdown. Khrushchev was becoming increasingly fearful that Kennedy "was too weak to stem the onslaught of the hard-liners." In Washington, Dobrynin was in touch with the Kennedy brothers and was advocating a trade of Soviet missiles in Cuba for U.S. missiles in Turkey. As Zubok and Pleshakov report it, one wave of panic after the other swept over Moscow as events unfolded. Finally on October 28, Khrushchev accepted Kennedy's terms for an immediate withdrawal of all "offensive arms."[36] So, the crisis itself ended, and the details of a Kennedy-Khrushchev secret agreement were soon worked out.

In sum, Khrushchev had finally come to realize that Kennedy was not going to accept Soviet missiles in Cuba even if he had to send in a U.S. invasion force, and that if this happened Castro would be wiped out and the only possible Soviet response would be to use the nuclear weapons stationed there. When he learned of the impact of his missile deployment upon the Washington scene and of U.S. military deployments, he realized that an invasion was imminent and that it could quickly lead to nuclear war. At that point, Khrushchev gave in. But he also won something. He avoided a nuclear war, and he still saved Castro. For his part, Kennedy agreed that the United States would not invade Cuba—a promise which has been kept to this day. Kennedy soon thereafter removed U.S. missiles from Turkey. But the most important consequence of the crisis was not the deal which ended it, but its effects upon future U.S.-Soviet relations. Those effects were profound although they were not fully understood in either Moscow or Washington at the time.

Our analysis of September 19, 1962, had quite accurately identified the Soviet policy contradictions that became evident as the crisis progressed. The Soviets did indeed put in "offensive" missiles as we said they would be tempted to do. Khrushchev thought of them as "defensive," since they were intended to deter a U.S. invasion. We pointed out that such a step would be incompatible with previous Soviet practice—and indeed it was. We thought that if it occurred, it would have "important policy implications" for future East-West relations. It did. But not exactly the implications which we had feared,

---

36. The information and quotations in this paragraph are drawn from Zubok and Pleshakov, *Inside the Kremlin's Cold War*, 266–67; the *Bulletin of the Cold War International History Project* has published most of the Soviet Foreign Ministry telegrams on the missile crisis in no. 5 (Spring 1995): 58–92.

namely, higher risk-taking. In fact, the crisis reduced the level of risk which the Soviets subsequently were willing to assume; having stared into the face of imminent nuclear war, they found that it was an experience they did not care to repeat.

One of the consequences of the crisis was that it contributed—though probably not decisively—to Khrushchev's ouster in 1964 in what Georgi Arbatov has described as a coup d'état. But Khrushchev had already learned his lesson. He had—according to Zubok and Pleshakov—"lost his faith in the nuclear deterrent: chaos and uncertainty overpowered the audacious ruler."[37] He also began to change his tune about Kennedy and wrote to him on October 30, 1962, "My role was simpler than yours, because there were no people around me who wanted to unleash war."[38] In his memoirs, Khrushchev praised Kennedy as "sober-minded and determined to avoid war," and as having demonstrated "real wisdom and statesmanship when he turned his back on right-wing forces in the United States who were trying to goad him into taking military action against Cuba."[39]

Khrushchev's successors seemed little interested in pursuing Khrushchev's doctrinal commitment to support further revolutions on the Cuban model. What they were primarily concerned about was not being humiliated again as they had been in the Cuban affair. They apparently established two new watchwords: "Don't stick our necks out" and "Oblige the Americans to respect Soviet military power." The Soviets wanted to be sure that the Americans did not think that because they had a preponderance of military power they could intimidate the USSR. The new relationship of military power which then emerged is discussed in a new world situation estimate I wrote in 1964. But there were other developments that needed to be taken into account in that yet-to-be-written estimate. One was Kennedy's reexamination of the U.S.-Soviet relationship in the wake of the missile crisis. The other was the growing vulnerability of the regime in South Vietnam to the threat of spreading Communist guerrilla activity.

Kennedy's Vietnam Decisions

Vietnam had not been at the top of Kennedy's foreign policy agenda during his first months in office. He had faced the Bay of Pigs affair, the Berlin

37. Zubok and Pleshakov, *Inside the Kremlin's Cold War*, 266.
38. Cited in ibid., 269.
39. Khrushchev, *Khrushchev Remembers*, 500.

crisis, and the Vienna Summit. Yet, soon after his inauguration he created a task force to prepare recommendations for him on Vietnam. The task force consisted of representatives from the CIA, the departments of State and of Defense, the USIA, and the White House. Almost simultaneously with that report, the Joint Chiefs of Staff submitted their own proposals on Laos. Both called for a commitment of U.S. combat troops in Vietnam. Kennedy approved more limited programs than those recommended and then sent his own fact-finding missions to Saigon—first Vice President Lyndon Johnson and then General Maxwell Taylor and Walt Rostow of the White House Staff. They all favored a U.S. troop commitment.

The advocates of a U.S. troop commitment argued that the American forces were needed, not so much for their numerical value—South Vietnamese troops already outnumbered those in the North ten to one—but for the morale and will which they would provide to Diem's forces and the warning they would provide to the Communists. In reporting that Kennedy was unconvinced by that argument, Ted Sorensen adds that Kennedy was "unwilling to commit American troops to fight Asians on the Asian mainland for speculative psychological reasons."[40] Kennedy did go along with the idea of a major counterinsurgency effort in Southeast Asia, with the United States supplying training, support, direction, better communications, transportation, intelligence, better weapons, equipment, and logistics.

In December 1961, Kennedy exchanged letters with Diem confirming the long-term U.S. commitment to Vietnam, but stressing that the primary responsibility lay with the Vietnamese. In a private message to Diem, he pressed for extensive political changes and social reforms. Sorensen reported that the only noticeable response to Kennedy's exhortations was "a series of anti-American stories in the controlled Vietnamese press."[41] While little or nothing was done on the political and social side to accede to U.S. wishes, the military side seemed to have been making a little progress during 1962, and Kennedy reported to Congress in January 1963 that "the spear point of aggression had been blunted in Vietnam."[42]

So, by the beginning of 1963, Kennedy had made the Vietnamese cause his own. Surrounded by warhawks from the Pentagon, the State Department, and the Operational Directorate of the CIA, he had gradually been drawn into the quagmire. Stanley Karnow describes Kennedy's state of mind as fol-

40. Sorensen, Kennedy, 653.
41. Ibid., 655.
42. Ibid., 656.

lows: "Kennedy rejected neutrality for South Vietnam, even though Hanoi was prepared to accept it, if only as a device to forestall American intervention. His decision was upheld by nearly every senior official in his inner circle. One exception was Chester Bowles, Undersecretary of State. . . . Kennedy dumped Bowles soon thereafter. He also rebuffed President de Gaulle, who warned him that Vietnam would trap him in a 'bottomless military and political swamp.'"[43]

Perhaps Khrushchev had been unusually perceptive when, in his rambling monologue to his Warsaw Pact allies in August 1961 after his Vienna meeting with Kennedy, he declared that "the new U.S. President was no match for the huge military-industrial complex that his predecessors had nourished." It was then, too, that Khrushchev wondered whether Kennedy could "keep the 'dark forces' of his country at bay while he negotiated for a long truce."

The year 1962 clearly was another turning point in the war. The United States proceeded to establish a new military command in Saigon—the Military Assistance Command, Vietnam (MAC, V)—and the number of U.S. "advisers" and the amount of military hardware were vastly increased. At about the same time, an important debate broke out in the Chinese Communist Party over the question of how actively China should assist national liberation movements. Chairman Mao chose the militant line, and his decision was followed by an increase in the supply of arms to the North Vietnamese forces. Although the Chinese were uncertain about how far the United States would go in its support of the Diem regime, they were readying themselves to support the North Vietnamese in their new struggle, however large the U.S. intervention turned out to be.[44]

The NIE on Prospects in Vietnam: Right the First Time

We in the Office of National Estimates initiated an estimate of the prospects in Vietnam in October 1962. The estimate was difficult to write and very difficult to coordinate with the intelligence agencies of the departments of State and Defense. Those departments, and our principal customer, the President and the National Security Staff, were all heavily engaged almost daily in making and carrying out decisions regarding Vietnam. At that stage in the history of the Vietnam War, a national intelligence estimate on Vietnam, we realized, could be superfluous or history-making, a nuisance or a directional

43. Karnow, *Vietnam*, 48.
44. Qiang Zhai, "Beijing and the Vietnam Conflict," 234–35.

signpost. The estimative process was long and tortuous; the estimate was finally approved by the USIB in April 1963, six months after it was initiated.

I was appointed board chairman for the review and coordination of the estimate. George Carver was assigned as the principal staff officer. George had recently returned from a tour in the CIA station in Saigon; he was a competent analyst and was bursting with up-to-date information on both the Viet /Cong (that is, the DRV-supported guerrillas in the South) and on the South Vietnamese Army. (During the latter days of the conflict, Carver became the Special Assistant to the Director of Central Intelligence for Vietnamese Affairs.) Carver had a first draft by the end of November. I have that draft before me as I write some thirty-five years later. What we in the Office of National Estimates had repeatedly laid out as Soviet policy regarding confrontations with the United States, Carver found to be consistent with Soviet policy in Vietnam. He pointed out that while the Soviets were "certainly sympathetic" with North Vietnam ambitions in the South, the USSR had no vital interests at stake in Southeast Asia and would not "countenance" any North Vietnamese action that escalated the level of conflict in Vietnam or risked a Soviet confrontation with the United States. He believed that most of the key figures in Hanoi, including Ho Chih Minh and General Giap, were pro-Soviet and not pro-Chinese, a stance that required the Soviets to provide North Vietnam with a modicum of support and encouragement.

Carver went on to say that the Chinese were likewise "sympathetic" with North Vietnamese ambitions in the South. Without benefit of the information cited above about Chinese–North Vietnamese relations, Carver was able to conclude that the Chinese wished to see those North Vietnamese ambitions realized under Chinese tutelage and direction in order to establish an effectively controlled satellite on China's southern border. He thought that the Chinese, "though not anxious for total war, would probably take a more sanguine view of the risks of escalation than the USSR or, in fact, the North Vietnamese." Carver expressed the likely North Vietnamese view this way: "We doubt that the DRV would wish to purchase victory at the price of becoming an outright vassal of the [Chinese], or indeed, if it would wish to see its territory traversed by Chinese troops easier to invite in than to invite out."[45] Thus, while the warhawks around Eisenhower and Kennedy were trumpeting the war in Vietnam as part of a world Communist conspiracy run by Moscow, the much better informed analysts in the Office of National Estimates

45. Quotations and comment drawn from the Carter (first) draft of NIE 53–62, dated November 19, 1962.

were spelling out the differing interests and doctrines of the three Communist governments involved.

For my part, while I completely agreed with Carver's challenge to the simplistic doctrine that underlay U.S. involvement in Vietnam, namely, the prevention at almost any cost of another Communist victory in Asia, I thought that this was not an appropriate time to fight that intellectual battle. I thought it better to deal with the immediate question before us, namely, the prospects for success in the venture upon which the U.S. government had embarked. I therefore chose to place the main thrust of the estimate upon the U.S. capacity to deal, not only with the ambitions of the regime in North Vietnam but equally with the defensive capability of the South Vietnamese regime. We needed to examine the political and cultural milieu in the South, and we needed to measure—insofar as possible—the capacity of the U.S. military, political, and economic programs to function effectively in that political and cultural milieu.

I worked closely with Carver in rewriting the draft and developing a set of conclusions. For the purpose of this history, it is not necessary to review all the problems in South Vietnam or to assign blame for any particular failure in Saigon or in the countryside. For this purpose the conclusions are explicit enough as well as indicative of our drafting difficulties. The principal ones were as follows:

a. There is no satisfactory objective means of determining how the war is going. The increased U.S. involvement has apparently enabled the South Vietnamese regime to check Communist progress and perhaps even to improve the situation in some areas; however, it is impossible to say whether the tide is turning one way or the other.

b. On the South Vietnamese side, new strategic concepts, such as the fortified hamlet, and shifts in military and security organization, training, and tactics have strengthened the counter-guerrilla effort. However, very great weaknesses remain and will be difficult to surmount. Among these are lack of aggressive and firm leadership at all levels of command, poor morale among the troops, lack of trust between peasant and soldier, poor tactical use of available forces, a very inadequate intelligence system, and obvious Communist penetration of the South Vietnamese military organization.

c. The struggle in South Vietnam at best will be protracted and costly. The Communists are determined to win control, and the South Vietnamese alone lack the present capacity to prevent their own

eventual destruction. Containment of the Communists and reestab-
lishment of a modicum of security in the countryside might be possible with great U.S. effort in the present political context of South
Vietnam, but substantial progress toward Vietnamese self-dependence
cannot occur unless there are radical changes in the methods and personnel of the South Vietnamese government. Even should these take
place without mishap, the Communists retain capabilities and support
which will require years of constructive effort to dissipate.

My colleagues on the Board of National Estimates undertook some dilu-
tion of the third conclusion by shifting its emphasis from the inherent difficulty of the problem—to which President Diem contributed—to an indictment
of the Diem regime itself. Its effect was to give the problem an apparent rem-
edy, namely, the removal of Diem. It read:

> With U.S. help, the South Vietnamese regime stands a good chance of
> at least containing the Communists militarily. However, the modus
> operandi of the Diem government, and particularly its measures to pre-
> vent the rise of contenders for political power, have reduced the govern-
> ment's effectiveness, both politically and militarily. We believe that unless
> radical changes are made in the methods of government, there is little
> hope that the U.S. involvement can be substantially curtailed or that
> there will be a material and lasting reduction in the Communist threat.

The coordination process on this estimate was an interesting case study of
the manner and extent to which a Department's bureaucratic interest can
influence its position on an intelligence estimate. Several representatives
from the Pentagon at the coordination meetings had served in South Vietnam
and had been appalled at the performance of the South Vietnamese military.
The emphasis in the paper on political weaknesses as a major cause of the
military failures quite naturally appealed to their professional instincts and
confirmed their own observations. The indictment of the Diem regime, however, no doubt because it called into question the existing U.S. policy of working with Diem, caused the State Department representative to reserve his
position on that aspect of the paper. He also thought the paper underestimated the prospects for gains through an improved military effort—a ploy
no doubt designed to put some of the responsibility for needed improvements
in South Vietnam upon the military services.

The DCI and the other members of the USIB were presented with a paper that, although the estimates board had eliminated reference to the gloomy long-term prospects, was still a fairly dolorous document. But it was encumbered with a State Department reservation, and this obliged the USIB to look at it carefully. The DCI, then John McCone, was particularly uneasy about it, since it seemed to contradict the more optimistic judgments reached by those in policy circles who had been sent to Vietnam to make on-the-spot appraisals and recommendations. He therefore decided to postpone USIB consideration and asked the Board of National Estimates to consult with some of those who had been sent on such missions.

The board then proceeded to meet with two senior military officers, Army Chief of Staff General Earle Wheeler and counterguerrilla expert General Victor Krulak. We also met with Roger Hilsman and Mike Forrestal, both senior civilian officials deeply involved with policy on Vietnam. None of these four consultations was particularly helpful. The witnesses seemed reluctant to make a frontal assault on the judgments of the paper but equally reluctant to endorse it. Instead, they showed a common tendency to take issue with a particular sentence purporting to state a fact rather than a judgment. All four held forth some degree of optimism, largely based upon the belief that things were better than they had been. That indeed might have been true, but it was not established how badly things had been going before or how this degree of improvement stood up to the task, namely, to deal with a determined and resourceful opponent who was immeasurably helped by the profound underlying political weaknesses in South Vietnam. None of them was attempting to mislead, but the simple fact was that each of them in some way and to some degree was committed to the existing policy, and none of them was intellectually free at that point or in those circumstances to stand back and look at the situation in its broadest aspects.

Carver and the other members of our Far East Staff, although weary of the controversy, were nevertheless much inclined to stick to their guns. I, however, had become inclined to shade the estimate in a more optimistic direction; perhaps we had been too gloomy. I also began to fear that if we did not compromise, the USIB members might themselves become engaged in the drafting process. If they then began to debate and amend the text at the USIB meeting, we might find ourselves with a piece of paper even more offensive to our judgment than we would have if we moved slightly toward a less pessimistic view. I chose to do that despite staff objections, the Board of National Estimates supported me, we reconvened the agency representatives, they and their chiefs agreed to our new wording, and the USIB quickly concurred. The new conclusions read:

a. We believe Communist progress has been blunted and that the situation is improving. Strengthened South Vietnamese capabilities and effectiveness, and particularly U.S. involvement, are causing the Viet Cong increased difficulty, although there are as yet no persuasive indications that the Communists have been grievously hurt.

b. Assuming no great increase in external support to the Viet Cong, changes and improvements which have occurred during the past year now indicate that the Viet Cong can be contained militarily. . . . However we do not believe that it is possible at this time to project the future of the war with any confidence. Decisive campaigns have yet to be fought and no quick and easy end to the war is in sight.

c. Developments during the last year or two also show some promise of resolving the political weaknesses, particularly that of insecurity in the countryside, upon which the insurgency has fed. However, the government's capacity to translate military success into lasting political stability is questionable.[46]

Thus the estimate rang no tocsin. But neither was it calculated to give anyone a sense of comfort. Frederick Nolting, who had served as ambassador in Saigon from 1961 to 1963 and whose assignment there had been to try to get along with Diem, volunteered to me one day when he was visiting the Office of National Estimates that he thought it was an excellent estimate and that it was too bad that the top policymakers had not paid more attention to it. I myself am not especially proud of my failure to make a fight of it. I was in good company in regretting a mistake; John McCone a year later expressed to Sherman Kent, then still chairman of the board, his regret for his part in weakening judgments which had been, as he put it, "right the first time."

Whether the estimate, as distributed in its final form, had any impact upon U.S. policy is highly doubtful. Perhaps the earlier versions might have had some impact, but by that time the U.S. military establishment was in a powerful position to advance its own views of what was going on in Vietnam and was also thoroughly committed to the cause of stopping Communism in Asia by military means. While Kennedy often rejected parts of their proposals, at no time did he or his major advisers develop proposals for reversing the policy established by the Truman administration in June 1950.

46. Quotations from and history of NIE 53-62 cited here are drawn from Willard C. Matthias, "How Three Estimates Went Wrong," in the CIA publication, *Studies in Intelligence*, vol. 12 (Winter 1968).

We know from Sorensen's biographical account that Kennedy had become concerned by mid-summer of 1963 (the NIE had been completed in April) over the "growing disunity and disorder within the non-Communist camp in Saigon." He sent Diem a long letter telling him there needed to be "important changes and improvements in the apparent relation between the government and the people in your country."[47] Diem did not listen. Then early in November 1963 a group of Vietnamese officers overthrew the Diem regime, assassinating him and his brother.

So, Kennedy's effort to save Vietnam had come to the verge of failure. There was no easy way out. For him the Vietnam conflict had always been a secondary concern; it was one he tried to leave to his staff and advisers while he pursued the more pressing matters of strategic military policy, relations with the USSR, and the crises over Berlin and Cuba. In any event, after the Cuban missile crisis, he had become more deeply reflective about avoiding nuclear war and getting along with the Soviets.

Kennedy's Move Toward a New National Strategy

Prime Minister Harold Macmillan told the British House of Commons after the Cuban crisis that its outcome represented "one of the great turning points in history." In his biography of Kennedy, Ted Sorensen (his principal speechwriter) has written that Kennedy himself thought that future historians looking back on 1962 might "well mark this year as the time when the tide began to turn." According to Sorensen, foreign affairs had been of "far more" interest to Kennedy than domestic affairs and had provoked "far greater changes in [the President's] own attitudes." He had "learned by experience" and grown in "wisdom." He had "mastered those complexities [which] he had previously oversimplified." Moreover, Kennedy took seriously the symbolism of the American eagle on the Great Seal, which is holding arrows in one talon and an olive branch in the other.[48]

Kennedy's commitment to the olive branch was sorely tried by his dealings with Khrushchev at Vienna and in the crises over Berlin and Cuba. Those trials also stimulated his thinking. He continued his contacts with Khrushchev, who himself was edging toward a proposal for joint "U.S.-Soviet management of the world."[49] Then, in May 1963, six months after the missile

47. Sorensen, *Kennedy*, 658.
48. Ibid., 509.
49. Zubok and Pleshakov, *Inside the Kremlin's Cold War*, 271.

crisis, Kennedy decided that the time had come for a "major address on peace." The speech was drafted by Sorensen and delivered on June 10, 1963, at the graduation exercises at American University in Washington.

In the speech, Kennedy declared that world peace was the "most important topic on earth." He was asking, he said, not for a "Pax Americana enforced on the world by American weapons of war," but a peace that would "enable men and nations to grow and to hope and to build a better life for their children." He went on:

> Some say that it is useless to speak of world peace . . . until the leaders of the Soviet Union adopt a more enlightened attitude. I hope they do. I believe we can help them do it. But I also believe that we must re-examine our own attitude—as individuals and as a nation—for our attitude is as essential as theirs. . . .
>
> If we cannot now end our differences, at least we can help make the world safe for diversity. For, in the final analysis our most basic common link is the fact that we all inhabit this planet. We all breathe the same air. We all cherish our children's futures. And we are all mortal.[50]

The reaction to the speech abroad and especially in USSR was even more favorable than the White House had hoped. Sorensen reported the following:

> England's *Manchester Guardian*—in contrast to the American press, which largely underplayed the speech, and then largely forgot it after the President's civil rights address the following evening—called it "one of the great state papers of American history." Various Congressional Republicans called it "a soft line that can accomplish nothing . . . a shot from the hip . . . a dreadful mistake." Khrushchev, in a later conversation with [Ambassador W. Averell] Harriman, would call it "the best speech of any President since Roosevelt."
>
> The "signal" the Soviet Chairman had awaited was loud and clear— and it was received by the Russian people as well as their leaders. The full text of the speech was published in the Soviet press. Still more striking was the fact that it was heard as well as read throughout the USSR. After fifteen years of almost uninterrupted jamming of Western broadcasts . . . [they] suddenly stopped jamming all Western broadcasts including even Russian-language newscasts on foreign affairs.

50. Cited in Sorensen, *Kennedy*, 721–22.

Equally suddenly they agreed in Vienna to the principle of inspection by the International Atomic Energy Agency to make certain that
the Agency's reactors were used for peaceful purposes. And equally
suddenly the outlook for some kind of test-ban agreement turned from
hopeless to hopeful.[51]

Three weeks after the Kennedy speech, on July 2, 1963, Khrushchev made
a speech of his own in East Berlin endorsing the atmospheric nuclear test-
ban treaty. Kennedy followed up quickly. He overruled the skeptics and nit-
pickers among his subordinates, and the negotiations with the Soviets concluded
with a treaty-signing on July 25.[52] Kennedy worked fast and hard to win early
ratification. Despite strong opposition from some Republican senators, some
nuclear scientists (e.g., Edward Teller), some former chiefs of staff (e.g.,
Admiral Radford and General Twining), and the Air Force Association, the
treaty was ratified on September 24 after three weeks of floor debate.[53]

According to Sorensen, Kennedy regarded the Test Ban Treaty as "more
of a beginning than as a culmination." It was in Kennedy's view a symbolic
"first step" and a forerunner of further agreements. It was an atmospheric
change that facilitated "a pause in the cold war" during which other, more
difficult problems could be stabilized.[54] The tragedy in Dallas on November
22 ended the beginning of a détente. It would be 1972 before a new era of
détente would begin.

Why Was Kennedy Assassinated?

At the present stage of American history, we still have no persuasive answer
to why Lee Harvey Oswald undertook to kill the President of the United
States. The Warren Commission's report admitted only the possibility that
some other hand might have been involved in encouraging or planning the
assassination attempt. There no doubt were many Americans who wanted
Kennedy out of the U.S. political scene and some of them were no doubt
relieved when the Dallas police apprehended a suspect who appeared to have
been acting alone or possibly in collaboration with a foreign government.
No such government or foreign citizen has been identified. There is no evidence in the public domain to suggest that Oswald was anything except what

51. Ibid., 733.
52. Ibid., 736.
53. Ibid., 739.
54. Ibid., 740.

a CIA psychological profile described as a confirmed loner with delusions of grandeur. Sorensen wrote that he accepted the "conclusion that no plot or political motive was involved," even though that judgment made the "deed all the more difficult to accept."[55]

What I have written about the Kennedy-Khrushchev relationship and about Khrushchev's thinking and actions make it difficult for me to entertain the idea that Khrushchev could have had any direct role in Kennedy's assassination. It is true that Khrushchev authorized the execution of Nagy in Hungary in 1956, and he did sanction the execution of Beria in 1953. But both were considered renegade Communists whose actions threatened the entire Communist cause. It was one of the principal characteristics of the post-Stalin era that political opponents were not executed but only excluded from power and exiled from Moscow. Both Khrushchev and Castro probably knew that the CIA had at one point targeted Castro for assassination, but both would almost certainly have realized that a botched or attributable attempt on the life of a U.S. president would have risked a nuclear counterblow by an angered American public. But the principal reasons for not attributing to Khrushchev any part in a plot against Kennedy were the facts that Khrushchev had achieved his basic objective in Cuba, namely, a promise not to invade the island and that he and Kennedy were beginning to work together to avoid a nuclear conflict.

Oswald could have had reasons of his own for wanting to assassinate the President—reasons which he might or might not have been prepared to explain to the world. He was an American Communist who had lived for a while in the Communist homeland and apparently found it wanting. He had absorbed the "materialist conception of history," but he saw the USSR failing or perhaps even abandoning the pursuit of the prescribed world revolution. He could have perceived himself to be a more correct instrument of history than the Soviet leaders themselves. Like Khrushchev, he had seen the Cuban revolution as a true example of a peoples' revolution; it therefore needed to be saved. Kennedy and American power were trying to destroy the Cuban revolution. And, worse yet, in the more relaxed state of U.S.-Soviet relations, Kennedy was leading Khrushchev astray. Kennedy, therefore, had to be eliminated. Then, perhaps, the Soviet Communist Party could find its way back to its proper historical role. The above, of course, is speculative, but at least it is an explanation in the light of evidence now available.

<hr />

55. Ibid., 750.

The Estimate That Changed the World

A World Trends Estimate: The Purpose and the Process

An estimate of the world situation is strategic intelligence in its purest form. The term "strategic intelligence" as used here was developed in the late 1940s by Sherman Kent, a Yale historian who later became the chairman of the Board of National Estimates.[1] Kent's definition was summed up by Donald Steury, a member of the CIA History Staff, as a "focus on long-term trends," with individual crises merely forming "blips" in "broader historical continuities." Steury described the Kent concept in practice as the emergence of "intelligence analysts [who] became encyclopedic in their knowledge of politics and economics, in the peoples and countries of the globe, but war or rather the potential for war, remained their bed-rock concern."[2]

Accordingly, it was my object in drafting "Trends in the World Situation" to direct the reader's attention away from current problems and toward developments that could have a long-term impact. My purpose was to discern trends and possibilities before they became threats or crises, to deflate any apparent threat that could not stand up under careful analysis, and to reduce

1. Sherman Kent, *Strategic Intelligence for American World Power*, rev. ed. (Princeton: Princeton University Press, 1966).
2. Donald P. Steury, ed., *Collected Essays on Sherman Kent and the Board of National Estimates* (Washington, D.C.: CIA History Staff, 1994), xv.

waning dangers to fading "blips" on the warning screen. Any trends paper should also identify, and if possible measure, changes in the structure of world power which our leaders would need to factor into both their day-to-day decisions and their long-term planning.

Such analyses should be made by agencies and analysts not responsible for past or present policy. The CIA—at least during my years there—took that responsibility seriously. While I was often given the drafting assignment, those papers which were intended to undergo the coordination process were passed through examination by the Board of National Estimates and then by the staffs of the other USIB members. That was the case with NIE 100-58 and NIE 1-61, which were discussed in earlier chapters. When I was directed at the end of 1963, in the wake of President Kennedy's assassination, to write a new world estimate, we decided to make it a board memorandum and to eliminate the interagency coordination process. That permitted a greater freedom of expression and a wider range of obiter dicta than a national estimate would have permitted. It also made the handling and dissemination of the estimate more flexible.

The Preparation and Release of the 1964 Memorandum

In this case we looked upon our director, John McCone, as our principal recipient. He had raised a number of questions about world politics and military affairs at a morning meeting with his deputies, and he glanced inquiringly at Kent as if to suggest that someone be assigned the task of responding to his concerns. Kent stopped by my desk on his way back from the meeting and dropped off a piece of paper with some scribbles on it. He told me to get to work on my favorite assignment.

I did not toss these things off in a few days. I read our latest estimates. I scanned the latest summaries of current intelligence. I looked over journals of research and opinion such as Foreign Affairs. I let a lot of information swirl around in my brain. When I began to see an outline of major themes emerge, I sat down and wrote—as everyone must—one paragraph at a time. Sometime in January 1964 I had a draft. My colleagues on the Board of National Estimates looked it over, and we talked about it. They were in general agreement and not disposed to argue small points. I made some revisions. I talked often with Abbott Smith, who was vice chairman of the board and with whom I had worked on previous world estimates. At one point, Abbott remarked, "You and I are the only ones around here smart enough to know how really good this paper is." He was partly wrong; he had not counted on John McCone.

McCone's executive assistant, Walter Elder, called me a day or two after the estimate was distributed within the Agency. He liked it and said that he was passing it on to McCone with the recommendation that he read every word. A few days later, Kent and I were at a pre-USIB meeting with McCone on another estimate over which I had presided. When that business was concluded, McCone turned to me and delivered what Kent later described as the "panegyrics." Apparently no one had heard McCone talk in such terms about any other analysis he had received. The paper immediately became a best seller within the Agency.

A few days later, the Director asked Elder to find out from me why I had classified the paper Secret. What data were there in it which required that classification? My response was that no such data were there, but that I was an officer of an Agency engaged in processing data which were secret and that the ideas and judgments which I had formulated were derived in part from such data. McCone wanted, he said, a clean unclassified copy which he could take to Gettysburg and show to General Eisenhower. Meanwhile, McCone thought the paper should be published so that the world could read it. He asked Kent to send a copy to Ham Armstrong and find out if he would run it in *Foreign Affairs*. In those circumstances I took another look in consultation with Abbott Smith. I made two or three minor changes, mostly for aesthetic reasons, and reclassified the paper to "For Official Use Only." Armstrong, who once had been "burned" for running an article by another CIA officer, decided not to run my paper in his magazine. We then gave the new edition a fairly wide circulation around town. It simply carried a note on the cover sheet above Kent's signature identifying me as the author and stating that the paper had general board approval without any attempt having been made to reach agreement on every point.

By the time all this had transpired it was early June 1964, and I was preparing to take leave from my duties on the Board of National Estimates to accept a diplomatic assignment at the U.S. embassy in Rome. About a month after my arrival in Rome, I received a telephone call on a Saturday evening from the duty communicator at the embassy, informing me that he had just decoded a message for me which he thought I ought to come in and read. The telegram reported that the *Chicago Tribune* had procured a copy of the Trends Memorandum and was about to publish a front-page story focusing upon a paragraph which expressed doubt that the United States could win a military victory in Vietnam. The State Department thereupon decided to make copies available in the press room, and the Secretary explained to certain press reporters that the paper was not administration policy; it was a think-piece and represented "only one man's opinion."

Because of the publicity I would be receiving the embassy decided to delay notifying the Italian foreign ministry of my arrival. The ambassador did not get excited about the matter, and I decided to stay away from reporters. Nevertheless, the *Tribune* story soon became a front-page item throughout the United States, Europe, Asia, and even Latin America. Since 1964 was an election year, Republican candidates and publicists used the memorandum to accuse the Johnson administration of following a "no-win" policy in Vietnam.

Aside from the furor over the Vietnam allusion, the Trends Memorandum received comparatively little press coverage. Yet it almost certainly was found to be an interesting and useful document in foreign ministries and intelligence services around the world. How much effect it had upon policy in the United States and elsewhere is a subject that, to the best of my knowledge, has not been researched.

In the history of U.S. intelligence, however, it was an important event. So far as I know, the Trends Memorandum was the first major CIA intelligence assessment to have been made public. McCone did want it published, but this was not exactly what he had in mind. Nevertheless, it probably had more impact upon world politics, through the *Tribune's* disclosure of the earlier "secret" version, than would have occurred if it had been published as a declassified report made available to a scholarly magazine.

What follows here are paraphrased excerpts from the sixty-two-paragraph memorandum covering those subjects most relevant to the broad thesis of this narrative.

Excerpts: Changes in the World of the Early 1960s

The first years of the 1960s have witnessed a further development of many of the trends in world affairs which appeared during the 1950s, as well as the emergence of several new ones. The world is less polarized politically, the turmoil in the underdeveloped areas has intensified, questions concerning the operation of military deterrents remain, and analyzing the risks involved in international initiatives still perplexes policymakers. Among the new tendencies are mounting economic difficulties in the Communist states, the increasing effort of the Soviet leaders to inject a new atmosphere into U.S.-Soviet relations, and the readiness of the current European leaders to explore new programs abroad. Moreover, the new style brought by President Kennedy to the conduct of foreign relations, the erection of the Berlin Wall, the Cuban crisis of October 1962, the death of President Kennedy, and the succession of Lyndon Johnson are all major international events that will have lasting effects upon international relationships.

Excerpts: The Evolving Role of Military Power

The military situation in the world today (1964) is one in which both the United States and the USSR can inflict enormous damage upon the other. The United States possesses greater striking power than the USSR and could wreak much greater damage in the USSR than the latter could in the United States. In this age of mobile striking power and hardened missile sites, it does not appear possible to build a military force capable of destroying an enemy's capabilities and simultaneously protecting oneself from unacceptable damage. Even large numbers of high-cost weapons can provide no assurance of victory or even survival. Thus, if there is any valid and rational concept today upon which to develop and measure a strategic military force, it is deterrence.

But there is no way to determine the level of forces needed to deter war. Deterrence is a mental state and depends to a preponderant degree not upon a precise level of forces but upon a variety of calculations peculiar to each situation of tension or confrontation. In such situations each side would need to estimate the chances of a confrontation leading to hostilities and the chances of hostilities leading to a general conflict. While it is most unlikely that the Soviet leaders would choose courses of action which they know to carry a high risk of general war, considerable uncertainty is likely to be present any time a serious U.S.-Soviet issue arises.

The Cuban missile crisis has helped to emphasize the consequences of taking action when there is uncertainty or misapprehension regarding its consequences. In this case, the rapidity and magnitude of U.S. mobilization and the firmness and sureness with which President Kennedy handled the crisis no doubt surprised Khrushchev and his colleagues in the Kremlin. Soviet misconceptions were dissolved, and the missiles were withdrawn. The effect of the lesson is likely to persist for some time.

Before the missile crisis erupted, the Soviets must have thought that their intercontinental striking force would have improved their bargaining position. That did not happen. The United States increased the tempo and size of its programs, thus forcing the USSR to choose between pursuing still more costly programs or falling further behind. Over the longer run, the acquisition of substantial strategic power by both the United States and the USSR will not only depreciate the value of such power in achieving particular objectives; it will also circumscribe the use of conventional military capabilities.

Any movement of military power into a new area—particularly one that is geographically proximate to the other—will tend to be regarded as threatening to upset the structure of world power or to alter political alignments in the area concerned.

These new inhibitions upon the freedom of action of the two great powers—either to brandish their strategic capabilities or to project their conventional capabilities into new areas—is causing some of the secondary and minor powers to view their own military capabilities in a more sanguine fashion. Some, believing that this new situation will permit them to acquire greater stature and influence in their own regions, have sought to acquire modern arms from the great powers, and some have built up their own arms industries. A nuclear capability in the hands of other than the two superpowers will be a nuisance and a potential source of trouble, but it will not become much of a factor in the world balance of military power or even in the respect accorded its possessors.

Over all, what is happening is that the great powers are becoming increasingly inhibited in the use of both their strategic and conventional power. Any policy undertaking involving the active use of military force could come to involve extremely high stakes. For the present at least, the military situation in the world, plus the problems which the Communist world is experiencing today, suggest that the likelihood of a military confrontation between the great powers has been somewhat reduced.

Excerpts: Problems of the Communist World

The manifest problems within the Communist world are also spectacular ones: the open quarrel and exchange of polemics between the two great Communist powers; the magnitude of the economic failure in China; the spectacle of the USSR coming to the West hat in hand to buy wheat and to ask for long-term credits. These phenomena are neither passing difficulties nor merely the consequences of misfortune. The source is deeper, and the problem will not soon go away. It lies fundamentally in the nature of Communism itself, how it should be defined, how its objectives should be translated into reality, whether it can be made to work.

The process of debate and redefinition going on today within the Communist movement is distinguishing one national Communist party from another and one regime from another. It is creating diverse currents of opinion within the various parties and regimes. Above all, it has openly split the Communist movement into two warring camps and created within each of these camps satellite groups which distinguish themselves from its leadership. The Sino-Soviet schism, the association of Albania with China, the ambivalence of North Vietnam, the independence of Yugoslavia, the growing divergence of the Eastern European states from the Soviet model, the tendency of the Western European Communist parties to criticize Moscow and to develop their own programs, the competing influence of Castroism in Latin America—all of those reflect national or regional interests. We can confidently expect that this situation will continue and that Communism in the future will come to possess still less doctrinal uniformity than it now has. Indeed, the national and doctrinal antagonisms that exist may occasionally lead to armed conflict; the Communist world may come to be as diverse and undisciplined as the non-Communist world.

An even more serious and certainly more immediate problem is that of making the Communist economic system work. A Communist system may be very effective for bringing a backward society up to date in infrastructure and basic industries, but it is evidently not very good for achieving adequate agricultural production; many aspects of food production require attention and devotion, which collective organization does not encourage. Moreover, as Communist societies become large and complex, the central planning methods which worked during the period of initial economic development tend to break down. Those two problems have survived all the expedients improvised to deal with them.

The Chinese economy is in bad shape. Economic experiments based upon ideological predilections have complicated what were already intractable difficulties. Industrial development is greatly handicapped by failures in agriculture and by the absence of large-scale outside aid. While the grave economic problems China faces may in time destroy the regime as we know it, those problems are not all to be attributed to the policies the Communist regime has adopted. Any regime would have staggered under the enormous problems of population and food supply that China faces.

By contrast, the economic problems of the USSR are tractable, but it is still uncertain that the Soviet leaders can solve them without fundamental changes in their ideological outlook. A fertilizer program will increase agricultural production, but it will not make the collective farmer a happy and constructive worker. Continued detailed central planning will keep the economy going, but it will not keep it going efficiently. There have been indications that the Communist leaders in the USSR may be gradually coming to realize that they must make some changes. Greater contact with the West may convince them that more flexible methods of planning and control will promote greater production and stimulate greater initiative. Meanwhile, Soviet economic problems have contributed to some greater prudence in Soviet policy and particularly in the current Soviet efforts to create a more friendly atmosphere in U.S.-Soviet relations.

Excerpts: Changing Attitudes in Europe

The Atlantic alliance has suffered a lessening of its unity of purpose, and U.S. influence in Europe has been reduced. Within the various Western European states, conservatives have become liberal and radicals less revolutionary. Along with a decline in the intensity of domestic politics there has developed a greater readiness to experiment with economic questions and to pursue foreign policies based upon national interest rather than upon those of the Atlantic community as a whole. Those changes derive in part from the growing strength of the European economies; they also reflect the personal characteristics of the new leaders who are arriving on the scene.

There also has appeared to be a new desire not to get bogged down in ideological debate, a recognition that revolution might destroy more than it could build, and a willingness to accept societal institutions as a basis for going ahead with progress and reform. One cause of this more cautious attitude toward revolutionary change has been a realization that it is not necessary to nationalize an economy in order to achieve the objectives of socialism; it is now realized that much the same ends can be achieved through welfare programs and use of the control mechanisms in modern fiscal and monetary systems. Perhaps more important is the fact that the economies of Western Europe have continued to expand at a rapid rate and that new economic structures are being forged and institutionalized—to the benefit of nearly all Western Europeans—through the Common Market.

Those changes in attitudes and accompanying changes in leadership have altered the role of the United States in European affairs. President de Gaulle's foreign policy is clearly designed to reduce the role of the United States and enhance that of France. He wants not only to restore France to what he regards as its rightful place in world councils but also to use its enhanced position to resolve some of the world's problems. But neither de Gaulle nor his neighbors wish to hazard their own security by destroying NATO or by weakening it so much that it has no more deterrent value.

Nevertheless, the differences between the U.S. view of the world situation and that of the Europeans have become even more striking than in the past. Most Europeans have always viewed the Communist threat somewhat differently; it has always seemed to them that the United States overestimates the danger of a Soviet military attack and underestimates the Soviet reluctance to become militarily engaged. They have always believed that it was the threat of force combined with domestic subversion and diplomatic maneuver which was the preferred Soviet strategy in Europe. Most of them look upon the alliance and the presence of U.S. troops less as a defensive arrangement and more as a deterrent to threats, coups, or collapse of will. They see the principal problem of the alliance as providing a greater degree of European control over NATO's forces and especially its nuclear arm.

Excerpts: Instabilities in the Underdeveloped World

Revolution and disorder in the southern two-thirds of the world has been intensifying. In all four major areas, Latin America, Africa, the Near East, and Southeast Asia, indigenous political forces are overthrowing governments, forming political alignments, and impinging to a degree hitherto unknown upon the concerns and even the vital interests of their more powerful northern neighbors. Despite similarities in the problems which most of them face, it has become increasingly apparent that each of the major areas of the underdeveloped world has tendencies and political forces peculiar to its particular problems, geographical location, and history.

Latin America: Nearly everywhere there is a high degree of political instability; the combination of strong pressure for change from growing numbers of dissatisfied people, revolutionary plotting, and the very difficult problems which most nations confront have kept the political pot boiling and will do so for many years to come. Most of the Communist parties are led by Moscow-oriented leaders who incapable of overthrowing or even exercising strong influence in any regime. Where Castroist groups have sprung up, they have more appeal than the Communists to the masses of workers in both rural and urban areas, because of their greater promises of quick success. While Castro-like movements have been aided and encouraged by the Cuban regime, for the most part their activities arise from their own passions and the example of Cuba. In some cases, military leaders of a traditionalist character will seek to head off leftist and Castroist groups by establishing military regimes; the consequence will be to drive moderate revolutionaries into the radical camp.

Africa: The situation in Africa is at least as unstable as that in Latin America, but revolutionary groups on the classic model are small or nonexistent, and there are few Communists. Plotting and violence occur, but usually by those who would like to replace those enjoying the privileges of office in order to enjoy those privileges themselves. Often the atmosphere of developments is that of comic opera rather than social crisis. Some of the new states in Africa might continue to be relatively stable and perhaps even grow in strength, but in most of Africa the picture is more clouded than it was a few years ago. There are likely to be more eruptions of violence and perhaps some major changes. By and large, the drift seems to be toward political and social chaos. The area is certainly becoming highly vulnerable to meddling from the outside.

The Near East: Arab nationalism is still seeking a form and definition acceptable to all. It is becoming increasingly apparent that not one of its competing doctrines or models is likely to earn an early or decisive victory. It will be a long time before political turmoil among the Arabs subsides. The various political currents and the various national interests are likely to remain in conflict for some years to come. The monarchies and sheikdoms, as long as they persist, are likely to remain fairly accommodating to Western interests, especially oil interests. They are not likely to hinder oil company operations; they know that they need oil company revenues and company facilities for marketing.

The Arabs, despite their unwillingness to make peace with Israel, recognize the danger of forceful action against the Jewish state. They respect Israeli military power, and some also realize that the West would prevent them from destroying Israel even if they could. Thus, while turmoil will continue as the Arabs quarrel among themselves, the chances are good that their turmoil will not spill over into conflicts likely to be critical for Western interests.

In two of the non-Arab states an interesting political experiment is under way. The royal regimes in Iran and Afghanistan have become, at their rulers' initiatives, instruments of revolution. The more dramatic case is Iran, where the Shah has turned against the upper and middle classes and begun a large-scale land and political reform. His effort seems to have flagged in recent months, but there is no sign of his turning back. If he fails or falters, his regime may go down with his program. In Afghanistan, the royal initiative had been less dramatic and more deliberate. Steps toward more rapid modernization and political reform are being taken cautiously. When the pace of change accelerates, it might run into serious trouble; it is too early to determine whether the king will have the courage to continue when the going gets tougher.

Southeast Asia: Of all the underdeveloped areas, the one in which major world powers are now most critically engaged is Southeast Asia, and it is the area which the major powers are having the greatest difficulty in handling. Local leaders and political movements have become more and more pow-

erful—in large part because they have received military materiel from foreign sources—and less and less disposed to follow the dictates or take the
advice of others. British influence in Malaysia is still strong, as is U.S. influence in Thailand and the former Indochina; together these put a brake upon
Indonesian aspirations in the south and Chinese designs in the north. The
USSR, while it has not given up its efforts to retain some influence in Laos
and North Vietnam, has evidently decided that its position is too weak to
enable it to strive for decisive influence on the mainland; in any event,
Indochina is not a good place for the Soviets to challenge Communist China.
They have sought instead to gain influence in Indonesia as a partial block to
Chinese scheming.

Regarding Vietnam, the memorandum contained the following, which is
recorded here as direct quotation rather than paraphrase:

> The guerrilla war in South Vietnam is in its fifth year and no end
> appears in sight. The Viet Cong in the South, dependent largely upon
> their own resources but under the direction and control of the
> Communist regime in the North, are pressing their offensive more
> vigorously than ever. The political mistakes of the Diem regime inhib-
> ited the effective prosecution of the war, which is really more of a
> political contest than a military operation, and led to the regime's
> destruction. The counter-guerrilla effort continues to flounder, partly
> because of the inherent difficulty of the problem and partly because
> Diem's successors have not yet demonstrated the leadership and the
> inspiration necessary. There remains serious doubt that victory can
> be won, and the situation remains very fragile. If large-scale U.S. sup-
> port continues and if further political deterioration within South
> Vietnam is prevented, at least a prolonged stalemate can be attained.
> There is also a chance that political evolution within the country and
> developments upon the world scene could lead to some kind of nego-
> tiated settlement based upon neutralization.

Excerpts: The New Structure of World Power

The preceding paragraphs clearly indicate that the structure of world power—
which had already undergone profound changes in the 1950s—is again undergoing major modification. The fact is that the two great powers have found
it difficult to bring their very substantial military power to bear in order to

achieve their objectives or to project this power into parts of the world where they have an interest. That has had important consequences. It has deterred the major powers from undertakings that might call their military capabilities into action. This in turn has enhanced the role of discussion, diplomacy, and negotiation at the great power level. At the same time, the natural centrifugal forces within the major power blocs have been released, and formerly suppressed national and cultural aspirations within Soviet satellite states have reemerged. These were bound to emerge in time, but the changing relation of military power has helped to free them.

Such phenomena as the gathering strength of India, the continuing vision of Arab nationalism, the increasing importance of African and Latin American developments in world affairs, the proclivity of emerging nations such as Indonesia to chart an independent course—all those represent strong secular trends that are probably irreversible and in turn have depreciated the role and influence of the great powers. As a consequence, a pluralistic world order is rapidly coming into being. World power is proliferating, divergences are emerging, and political dissimilarity is being encouraged.

Despite the greater importance which the world's leaders attach to diplomacy and negotiation as an alternative to confrontation, the danger of nuclear war with all its horrible consequences will continue to be the overriding problem of our time. This danger will continue to arise, as in the past, not from a deliberate attempt to destroy a competitor, but from undertakings and occurrences of a more limited character. Calculating risks will remain a major concern of policymakers. Indeed, the underdeveloped world is so disorderly that the great powers will no doubt have difficulty remaining aloof from the alarms and excursions which will arise. Once outside powers do become involved, whether by accident or design, their prestige might be engaged to a degree quite incommensurate to the intrinsic or strategic value of the trouble spot concerned.

The Future of the USSR

The final paragraph of the memorandum is quoted here in full because of its prophetic character:

> Over the longer run, the chances are good that the gradual changes taking place in the USSR will diminish its hostility to the West and the vigor of its revolutionary effort outside the Communist world. In particular, the climate of opinion within the USSR, the greater intel-

lectual freedom permitted, the sensitivity of the regime to intellectual opinion and [to] popular preoccupations with peace and a better life, the greater weight accorded to national interests and conventional modes of international conduct—all these have already contributed to the decline of Soviet aggressiveness and to a realistic appreciation of the modern world. This process of change may be slowed from time to time, or even halted, but it is probably irreversible. But whether it proceeds or halts, the evolution which has taken place, together with changes which have occurred within the Communist camp and in the world at large, suggest that for the next several years at least the world may be replete with strife and disorder but not on the verge of nuclear disaster.

The Furor over the Vietnam Paragraph

On December 25, 1964, the Paris daily *Figaro* published an end-of-the-year listing of the major news events of the year. For August 22, 1964, it listed two major events; one was a cyclone on the island of Guadeloupe which killed thirteen people; the other was a "Rapport retentissannte de services secrets US: Pas de victoire militaire en vue au Vietnam." The report was, of course, the Trends Memorandum. It did "resound" as *Figaro* had described it. The *National Progressive*, then a weekly newspaper in the United States, in its edition of August 31, 1964, called the report "The Memo Which Produced a Furor." It described the Trends paper as a "View of a World in Disorder," and it printed most of the text verbatim.[3]

Most of the U.S. media were not interested in the more thoughtful aspects of the paper. To them it was a Vietnam story, even though only one of its sixty-two paragraphs discusses the war in Vietnam. The *New York Times* published a major front-page story on August 23 in both its New York and International editions. In most cases the headline writers distorted the closing sentence of the Vietnam paragraph by treating its reference to negotiation as a CIA "recommendation." Even Jack Raymond's story in the international edition (from which I and many Europeans got our world news) had a distorted headline and sub-heading which read, "Pact on Vietnam Proposed in CIA. Intelligence Aide Suggests a Negotiated Settlement to Neutralize Area." In the body of his report, Raymond had carefully quoted my words that there was "serious doubt that victory can be won," and that at best "a prolonged

3. See *Le Figaro* and the *National Progressive* for the dates indicated in the text.

stalemate" could be attained; yet he treated as a "proposal" my statement in that paragraph that there was a "chance that political evolution within the country and developments on the world scene could lead to some kind of a negotiated settlement based upon neutralization."[4]

My raising the question of negotiation and neutralization was in response to President de Gaulle's advocacy of the idea, to Ho Chih Minh's stated willingness to accept it, and to my belief that the Soviets would welcome such a solution to head off eventual Chinese control of Southeast Asia. It was not advocacy; it was, rather, an oblique reference to a real possibility not worthy of further elaboration at that particular time.

From the standpoint of world history, however, Jack Raymond's treatment of the Vietnam paragraph—and that of many other journalists here and abroad—set in motion a new phase of the debate on Vietnam policy. Raymond had stated in his August 23, 1964, story that negotiating a way out of the Vietnam war was a view widely held in the government and the subject of recurrent official discussions. He went on to state that it was also "held that negotiations could be contemplated after military stabilization had been brought about by impressive victories against the Communist Viet Cong." On this latter matter, Raymond then quoted the paragraph's judgment that the guerrilla war was already in its fifth year and that "no end appears in sight." Indeed, the paragraph also noted that the Viet Cong were "pressing their offensive more vigorously than ever."

The next day, on August 24, 1964, the New York Times, citing the Raymond story, printed a lengthy editorial strongly urging that further disclosures on the Vietnam War needed to be made so that "the country can judge for itself whether the administration is right to reject" negotiation. The editorial showed no disposition to accept the arguments against negotiation by observing that it must be as clear to the Viet Cong as to the CIA that no end to the war was in sight. They could "maintain an atmosphere of insecurity" throughout the South. The time had come, the editorial concluded, to find out whether the "wasting confrontation" could be ended "by establishing a truly neutral Vietnam."[5]

I have not made a definitive study of editorial opinion on the Vietnam question in either the United States or abroad. But I have run through several hundred accounts of the Vietnam paragraph in the U.S. press. Opinion was divided between those who wanted to fight on and those who were puz-

4. New York Times, August 23, 1964, 1.
5. "Intelligence on Vietnam," New York Times, August 24, 1964, editorial page.

zled by U.S. policy in Vietnam in the light of the paper's gloomy assessment. The fact that a CIA officer and his colleagues on the Board of National Estimates, that is, persons with access to all available information and to analytic studies, doubted that the war was winnable opened the eyes of those who previously were unsure about how to assess the Vietnam policy. When it was no longer unpatriotic to express doubt openly and to ask for reconsideration of the U.S. position, many for the first time felt free to criticize it.

These criticisms did not, however, change the views of President Johnson and his immediate advisers—Secretary Rusk, Secretary McNamara, and Walt Rostow of the White House Staff. Rusk's position, as he explained it to his son Richard in his recollections, was quite simple. In the book which Richard encouraged his father to write, Richard quoted his father as having said, "There was the pledge [SEATO]. We had given our word."[6] I myself am amazed by that reasoning, as I was by the ideas and steps by which Secretary Dean Acheson took our nation into the Korean War. I am still surprised that two secretaries of state twice within a decade had so grossly failed to understand their adversaries, that they had so little appreciated that not all problems are soluble, and that they did not realize that the object of diplomacy was to explore all the alternatives before pledging the lives and fortunes of their countrymen.

SEATO, as we explained in NIE 1-61 (January 17, 1961), had always been a loose confederation with only one mainland member (Thailand) and basically incapable of serving as an effective instrument for stability in Southeast Asia, largely because its principal members (United States, United Kingdom, France) had no common view of the situation in the area and no common policy toward the states of Indochina. Moreover, Rusk seems not to have taken on board the rifts that had appeared in the Communist world and especially the Sino-Soviet split, which became open to the world in 1962, and the opportunities which that event provided for diplomatic maneuvering on Vietnam, and other issues in which the United States, the USSR, and China were involved.

Because I was in Rome when the furor began, I had to rely upon my associates in Washington to inform me about reactions there and around the world. Abbott Smith dropped me a line offering his congratulations on the wide play which the memorandum was receiving in the media. Sherman Kent reported that McCone was being "perfectly splendid," as had been some other "front offices" in town. Kent had examined a large batch of clippings

6. Dean Rusk, *As I Saw It, as Told to Richard Rusk* (New York: W. W. Norton, 1990), 420.

not only from newspapers in the United States but also from newspapers and radio broadcasts worldwide. He "doubted" that I had "any notion of how trends in the world situation have been altered" by publication of the paper.

McCone himself paid a visit to Rome in September, and he took Sally and me out to dinner, along with his new wife. He told me not to worry about the memo's leak or the problem it had created for Rusk. Unfortunately, several months later and while I was still in Rome, McCone resigned as director and returned to California. I have no inside information about his reasons, but I do know that, as the President's principal "intelligence adviser," he had tried to play a major role in the policymaking process. Clearly the Vietnam policies adopted by the Johnson administration had increasingly departed from the messages inherent in the CIA intelligence product, and I suspect that—whatever reasons he might have expressed—the underlying reason was differences with other policymakers on Vietnam questions.

The Trends paper was first disseminated in February 1964 and had been classified Secret. Any effect it may have had upon the administration's Vietnam policy took place earlier than the furor set off in August. The Pentagon Papers is replete with the texts of various studies and recommendations prepared from December 1963 to the end of 1964 about what should be done in Vietnam. Following upon our April 1963 estimate, which had indicated that the situation in Vietnam was far from comforting, administration policymakers were indeed studying political and military actions designed to turn the situation in a more favorable direction. For example, Maxwell Taylor, the chairman of the Joint Chiefs of Staff, reported to Secretary McNamara in January 1964 that the Joint Chiefs believed "victory" over North Vietnam required the United States "to put aside many of [its] self-imposed restrictions" upon U.S. military actions. This was required, the Joint Chiefs argued, because "our fortunes in South Vietnam are an accurate barometer of our fortunes in all of Southeast Asia." The domino myth was still alive and well at the Pentagon; a "loss of South Vietnam to the Communists," Taylor wrote, "will presage an early erosion of the remainder of our position in that subcontinent [sic]."[7]

All during 1964 there were dozens of reports and memoranda prepared by the Joint Chiefs, the Secretary of Defense, the U.S. mission in Saigon, Walt Rostow (then chairman of the State Department Policy Planning Council), and many others in high policy circles, all making proposals on what to do about Vietnam. Most contained suggestions for sending political signals to

7. "Excepts from the Pentagon Papers," New York Times, June 13, 1971, 35.

North Vietnam and for carrying out particular military actions. Nearly all proposed a reversal of the "cautiousness" hitherto apparent in U.S. policy, and—toward the end of the year—the introduction of U.S. ground combat forces.[8]

One clear step in the U.S. escalation of military action occurred in early August, shortly before the *Tribune* disclosure of the Trends paper's gloomy paragraph on Vietnam. This was the so-called Gulf of Tonkin incident and President Johnson's response to it. There was some kind of confrontation in the Gulf between North Vietnamese and U.S. naval forces, but what actually happened there between August 2 and August 4, 1964, is not entirely clear, although a good bit of research on the subject has since taken place. John Prados in his book, *The Hidden History of the Vietnam War* (1995) wrote this about the incident:

> To hear the Johnson Administration tell the story, American vessels innocently plying international waters were attacked without provocation, and when the North Vietnamese repeated the action against a renewed [U.S.] naval patrol, the United States had to respond. Incensed at Hanoi's apparent perfidy, Congress voted a joint resolution authorizing the President to take action, including the use of force. It was the legal authority Lyndon Johnson used to send American boys to fight an Asian war.
>
> Something happened in the Tonkin Gulf in August 1964, but not precisely what the Administration claimed. In later years, parts of the Administration's story came apart like layers of an onion. In time the Tonkin Gulf Resolution was repealed while the story of the incident itself became enmeshed in a whole series of controversies.[9]

The incident and the administration's exploitation of it to justify its intensified military effort helped to set the stage for the media's reaction to the *Tribune's* disclosure of the Trends Memorandum. Prados pointed out that "for many Americans, first notice of the Vietnam war came with the Tonkin Gulf incident of 1964. Before that, large though it might loom in White House councils, Vietnam barely registered in the American consciousness. Afterward, Vietnam mattered."[10]

---

8. Ibid., June 13, 1971, 35–40; June 14, 1971, 27–32; June 15, 1971, 19–24.
9. John Prados, *The Hidden History of the Vietnam War* (Chicago: Ivan R. Dee, 1995), 48.
10. Ibid.

The administration quite successfully suppressed the Trends Memorandum by asserting that it was only "one man's opinion." In fact, of course, the Board of National Estimates and many others in town agreed with the thrust of the Vietnam paragraph. The administration did succeed in reducing public doubts about the Vietnam policy through its campaign assertions that "Asian boys" should fight "Asian wars." But after the election, the Johnson administration from 1965 through 1968 proceeded to intensify the war. Then the Nixon administration, far from ending the war as it had promised, actually widened it. The Nixon administration did finally attempt negotiations, but by then it was impossible to negotiate an end to a war that was consistently being lost on the ground in Vietnam and even more rapidly being lost in American public opinion. In relation to the main thrust of the Trends paper, however, the Vietnam paragraph was like a blip on a radar screen. My principal concerns were trends in the U.S.-Soviet military relationship and what those trends implied for the likelihood of nuclear war. I was secondarily concerned with what was happening in the USSR and elsewhere in the Communist world. Those concerns were in my opinion much more important than the fate of South Vietnam, and history has borne that out. Indeed, when South Vietnam fell to the Communists a decade later, none of the consequences were as serious as the Joint Chiefs and the other hawks had been predicting. Some of the U.S. media—to their credit—did not limit themselves to the headline value of the Vietnam paragraph, but devoted some space and thought to other parts of the paper.

A comprehensive look at the Trends Memorandum did require some effort, since the State Department did not hand out copies but merely made them available in the Press Room. The Associated Press wire of August 22, 1964, while it stressed the Vietnam paragraph, did attach at its end two quotations from the section on problems of the Communist world: "We can confidently expect that this situation [i.e. turmoil in the Communist world] will continue and that Communism in the future will come to possess still less doctrinal uniformity than it now has. Indeed, the national and doctrinal antagonisms which exist may occasionally lead to armed conflict; the Communist world may come to be as diverse and undisciplined as the non-Communist world."

That was the kind of forecast of which any intelligence officer would be proud. The Soviets and Chinese fought two pitched battles five years later, on March 2 and 15 in 1969 over possession of an island in the Ussuri River on the Manchurian-Soviet border. China and the new Socialist Republic of Vietnam got into a hassle over the latter's military action against the murderous Pol Pot regime in Cambodia and over Vietnam's association with the Soviet-led CEMA of Eastern Europe. In February of 1979, the Chinese invaded northern Vietnam in an attempt to punish Vietnam, but they suffered serious losses and withdrew. The Chinese then kept the stew boiling by providing arms and support to Pol Pot.

The Associated Press also quoted a part of the final paragraph of the memorandum, which asserted that the changes taking place in the USSR, in the Communist camp, and in the world at large "suggest that for the next several years at least the world may be replete with strife and disorder but not on the verge of nuclear disaster."

United Press International stated in its wire of August 22, 1964, that "aside from the Vietnam neutralization reference, the document appeared to be a routine survey of the obvious changes brought about by the nuclear stalemate of terror between Russia and the United States, complicated by the Red Chinese–Russian ideological conflict." What may have been obvious to the UPI copy writer does not appear to have been obvious to either the Soviet or U.S. military planners; on each side the predominant doctrine was that the other side had achieved military superiority or was trying to achieve it. What was not, in my opinion, obvious to U.S. military planners and policymakers is what UPI digested from paragraph 10 of the memorandum:

> The fact that both the Soviet Union and the United States now have the nuclear capability to destroy each other has not only depreciated the value of strategic power in the achievement of particular objectives; it has also come to circumscribe the use of other instruments of military power," the CIA paper says. "It has become increasingly difficult for either of the great powers to project its military power in *conventional* form into other areas of the world or into disputes which may arise."

That particular passage in the memorandum in effect demonstrated the dilemma of the Johnson administration in 1964 and 1965, a dilemma that later troubled the Nixon administration as well. Despite pressure from some military and political leaders, Presidents Johnson and Nixon chose not to project full U.S. power into the Vietnam situation, lest it provoke one or the other major Communist power to retaliate—in the Far East or elsewhere— thus setting up a situation of provocation and response which could result in a nuclear exchange. As Lyndon Johnson told McGeorge Bundy in an agonized telephone conversation in May 1964, "It's damned easy to get in war.

But it's going to be awfully hard to ever extricate yourself if you get in."[11]

But President Johnson went in anyway and at the same time tried to prevent further escalation. The Trends Memorandum could possibly have been a restraining influence upon the President—had he read it—but in any event its implications ran counter to the doctrines of the Secretaries of State and Defense. By the end of August, when the memorandum came into the public domain, it was too late. The Gulf of Tonkin incident had just occurred; regardless of whether it was a Vietnamese or a U.S. provocation, the exploitation of it by the Johnson administration led almost inexorably to an intensified but unsuccessful effort to achieve "victory" and to a tragic denouement a decade later.

Soviet Reaction to the Memorandum

Some idea how the Soviets would have reacted had the United States attempted to project its full military power into South Vietnam was provided by a Radio Moscow domestic broadcast in Russian on August 31, 1964. The broadcast reported that the memorandum's Vietnam paragraph had forecast that at best "a continuous deadlock" could be attained by continued U.S. intervention, and that this deadlock would prevail only if the United States could prevent "a further worsening of the political situation" in South Vietnam. After noting that the United States had failed to recruit support from America's European allies, the broadcast concluded that if the United States sent in large troop units and transformed them into "a main striking force," there would be "no doubt that it would arouse such stormy indignation in the Asian and African countries that all positions of Washington in those countries would be seriously threatened." Finally, the commentary concluded that "many soberminded American politicians" were reaching the conclusion that it was time to search for a political settlement. The rather mild character and tone of the Russian broadcast suggests that the Soviet leadership, still dominated by Khrushchev, was not disposed to threaten the United States with a military response but only to give well-meaning advice.

A commentary more interesting to me than the Moscow broadcast was made by John Whitman, the chief of the Soviet Staff in the Office of National Estimates. On August 26, four days after publication of the memorandum, he sent a brief note to Sherman Kent saying that he himself had re-read the Trends paper and had tried to do so as if he were Nikita Khrushchev. He

11. *Washington Post*, February 18, 1997, A24.

thought it was "very much the sort of thing that Nikita would read himself." He thought also that Nikita would be very much interested in learning that "the notion of two great powers having common elements in their positions and interests had gotten quite far in the U.S.," and that the United States is "strongly inhibited from using force in non-European conflicts." Nikita, Whitman wrote, was himself "similarly deterred and encouraged to know that the U.S. was also."

Whitman thought that Khrushchev would "take the paper seriously." Khrushchev would be "inclined from the Soviet context to attribute greater importance to the CIA than it has in policy matters and disinclined to accept the Memorandum as the author's view alone." Finally, the Soviet leader would be pleased to have observed the memorandum's "moderate and rational tone and its low level of anti-Sovietism." Perhaps it was such a perception which accounted for the mild character and tone of the Moscow domestic service broadcast on August 31, 1964.

It is reasonable to conclude that release of the memorandum made at least a modest contribution to a reduction of anti-Americanism in Soviet ruling circles. In any event, it must have spurred doubt about the ubiquity of anti-Soviet hostility in the U.S. foreign policymaking community. If it did, this was almost certainly due to the fact that it was originally classified Secret. That lent it credibility, as did the furor which it engendered in the departments of State and Defense; the Soviets would have treated a document of lower classification as a piece of propaganda. In this country also, because of its original classification, the memorandum received wide press coverage, and that might have reduced some of the pervasive anxiety in America about an aggressive, threatening Soviet Union.

For example, an editorialist in the *Cheyenne State Tribune* found that the "U.S. show of determination in the Cuban missile crisis" had "convinced" the Soviet leaders that we "did mean business."[12] Another provincial newspaper, the *Jacksonville Times Union*, under the headline "Russia Bidding for U.S. Friendship?" reported the memorandum's assertion that the Soviets were seeking "better relations" with the West.[13] Even the *Chicago Tribune* quoted the Republican Party platform's assertion that "Communism" was still the "enemy of the nation," but under the headline "Amiable Kremlin and Unamiable Vietnam" also cited the memorandum's judgment that "the gradual changes taking place in the USSR will diminish its hostility to the West

---

12. *Cheyenne State Tribune*, October 7, 1964.
13. *Jacksonville Times-Union*, August 23, 1964.

and the vigor of its revolutionary effort outside the Communist world."[14]

In an earlier chapter, I described Khrushchev's troubles with his colleagues on the Presidium and attributed some of those troubles to his rashness in creating the Berlin and Cuban crises. In the memorandum, I referred to those troubles and indicated that he had apparently won his battle. But it proved only to have been a reprieve; he was ousted later in 1964. The last years of the decade presented Khrushchev's successors with some new problems but did not fundamentally change the trends discussed in my 1964 Trends Memorandum.

14. *Chicago Tribune*, August 25, 1964.

Prophecies and Events of the 1960s

Soviet Military Policy at Mid-Decade

With Khrushchev's departure from office in October 1964, CIA analysts realized the need to reconsider Soviet military and foreign policies. How much of a role had those policies played in his dismissal? According to Zubok and Pleshakov, Khrushchev was most sharply attacked in the Presidium on his foreign policy record, but at the Central Committee Plenum those who had plotted his ouster preferred to attack him on agriculture and other domestic matters, lest they "reopen fresh wounds to Soviet prestige inflicted by the Cuban missile crisis."[1] A few months later, my colleagues in the Office of National Estimates undertook a study of possible changes in the Soviet military under the new leadership. The results appeared in a new national intelligence estimate, NIE 11-4-65, "Main Trends in Soviet Military Policy," which was approved by the USIB on April 14, 1965.

The estimate reviewed the decade of Khrushchevian rule and pointed out that during those years there had been a virtual "revolution" in Soviet military affairs. When he came to power, Khrushchev inherited enormous land armies and masses of fighter planes and anti-aircraft guns for strategic defense, but very limited nuclear capabilities. When he departed office, the USSR had a formidable missile delivery capability, modernized strategic defense

---

1. Zubok and Pleshakov, *Inside the Kremlin's Cold War*, 272–73.

forces, and smaller but greatly modernized theater forces for land campaigns in a nuclear environment. Khrushchev had looked upon his missile forces "primarily as a barrier against war." His emphasis upon "deterrence of all wars through strategic rocket forces," however, "left scant basis" for the military to develop operational concepts and requirements for other components of the forces. Khrushchev's view was not one that Soviet marshals enthusiastically endorsed.

Prodded by Khrushchev, the marshals had begun to explore the implications of nuclear warfare. Unlike Khrushchev, however, who thought of a general war as something that would be decided in a very short time by an initial nuclear exchange, the marshals thought of nuclear warfare primarily in terms of the force requirements needed for fighting a new kind of war. Like U.S. military planners, they constantly warned their political chiefs that the USSR "should be prepared for the contingency in which deterrence had failed." After Khrushchev's fall, military writers began to advance the idea that military problems should be approached "comprehensively" and, like U.S. planners, called for "the further development of many types of forces against a variety of military contingencies."

NIE 11-4-65 summed up the new situation in its main conclusion:

> Soviet decisions since Khrushchev's fall do not indicate any general alteration in his military policies. During the next six years, we believe the main aim of the USSR's military policy and programs will remain that of strengthening the Soviet deterrent. In the strategic field, we expect the USSR to increase the numbers and effectiveness of a variety of weapon systems and, in particular, greatly to improve retaliatory capabilities. These programs may include the deployment of anti-missile defenses. But we think it highly unlikely that the Soviets could achieve a combination of offensive and defensive forces so strong as to persuade the leadership that it could launch a strategic attack upon the West and limit to acceptable proportions the subsequent damage to the USSR.

Winding up their analysis, the CIA writers and their intelligence community associates also concluded this about the future:

> Beyond the general mission of deterrence, we doubt that any single doctrinal design, meeting the tests of comprehensiveness and feasibility, will govern the development of Soviet military forces over the

next six years. Old debates which seem certain to outlive Khrushchev's departure, the momentum of deployment programs, the clash of vested interests, attempts to capitalize on some technological advance, an urge to match or counter various enemy capabilities—these are some of the factors which are likely to inhibit any far-reaching rationalization of military policy around a single doctrine.

The estimate's emphasis upon deterrence of a U.S. attack as the principal motivation of Soviet military policy and Soviet weapons research and development was contrary to the view of U.S. Air Force intelligence officers, as expressed in dissents to earlier estimates. In this case, the Air Force dissent was joined with that of the director of the NSA, who was also a senior air force officer. The dissent reads:

> The Director of the National Security Agency and the Assistant Chief of Staff, Intelligence, USAF, consider that the intensity with which the USSR is pursuing a massive military research and development program—the specific content and progress of which are not clearly known in the US—portends far more than an attempt merely to strengthen Soviet posture. They believe that attainment of strategic superiority continues to be the goal of Soviet political and military leadership and that the USSR is actively searching for ways and means of building toward parity and ultimate superiority.

The firmness and constancy with which the Air Force had held to its position that the Soviets were striving for strategic superiority over the United States has had an almost religious quality. One might presume that military personnel charged with the responsibility to order or to carry out attacks on another nation and people with the most horrible weapons in human history would have a tendency to demonize their opponents, thereby making their military mission morally acceptable to themselves. But the psychology of warfare ought not to dictate or color an intelligence judgment. One very troubling aspect of this dissent is that the NSA holds membership on the USIB because it is an information-producing agency, not an analytic one. No previous director of the NSA, to my knowledge, had ever intervened on an analytic matter. His intervention in this case clearly appears therefore to be an action based on Air Force policy and not on honest intelligence assessment.

The estimate did clearly recognize in its conclusions that the Soviets were pressing their "dynamic military and space" research and development programs, but then added that "Soviet security considerations demand vigorous efforts to prevent a Western military technological advantage which might threaten the credibility of their deterrent." The estimate's conclusions also stated that if the Soviets did achieve "a technological advance which offered the prospect of significant improvement in nuclear capabilities," they would seek to exploit it "for political and military advantage," but that decisions to deploy would involve weighing such an advantage "against economic considerations and the U.S. capabilities to counter."

Implicit in the estimate was a judgment that the Soviet civilian leaders, even in the post-Khrushchev era, had no desire to provoke the United States into a nuclear attack upon the USSR, only to strengthen their deterrent to the extent necessary to offset actual and planned U.S. capabilities to attack them. Meanwhile, in the United States, the Air Force was interpreting Soviet actions as implying an effort to achieve parity or superiority in the numbers, throw weights, and accuracy of their nuclear weaponry. That Air Force judgment in turn led U.S. planners into increasing the numbers, throw weights, and accuracy of U.S. weaponry. That in turn propelled the Soviets toward an increased effort, and the arms race thus progressed beyond reason. As the balance of terror became apparent to both U.S. and Soviet leaders, they began to exercise somewhat greater caution when dealing with political eruptions around the world. One such eruption occurred in the Near East in 1967.

The Six-Day War: How Intelligence Guided U.S. Policy

After the close of the Suez War of October 1956 and the establishment of the United Nations Emergency Force to secure the Egyptian territory that had been occupied by the Israelis, Israel withdrew its troops from Gaza and Sinai, and an uneasy armistice evolved into a modus vivendi between Israel and its Arab neighbors which permitted a modicum of order to prevail. In those neighboring Arab states, however, there ensued very considerable unrest, including a civil war in Lebanon and revolutions in Syria and Iraq. Jealousy and rivalry for leadership within the Arab world prevented any effective cooperation among the Arab states in dealing with Israel. One of the serious unresolved problems concerned division of the waters of the Jordan River and the Sea of Galilee. Because of a continuing inability of the various parties to agree on a solution, the Israelis set about in 1963 unilaterally to divert some of Galilee's waters to their agricultural projects. In response, the Arab leaders tried—but failed—to undertake common counteraction.

It was a Palestinian, Yasir Arafat, who then set out to play a Palestinian role in the water question. In 1965, he organized a guerrilla movement called al-Fatah, which began to carry out sabotage operations against the Israeli water-carrier system and to attack other civilian targets. Most of these commando raids were launched from Jordan, and late in 1966 the Israelis made a devastating retaliatory raid on the village of Samu in the Jordanian West Bank. It was that event which caused the O/NE to initiate "The Arab-Israeli Dispute: Current Phase." I was appointed to chair the estimate; our task was to discern whether the modus vivendi which had prevailed since 1957 was coming to an end and what the chances were for another Arab-Israeli war.

Writing an estimate in a situation already fraught with tension and instability is a difficult task. It took several months, and it was finally completed and published April 13, 1967, about two months before Israeli air strikes set off the Six-Day War on June 5, 1967. We did not and could not foresee the outbreak of a full-fledged conflict. What we could and did do was describe the policies and positions of the major players and judge what might happen if a conflict actually broke out. Our principal conclusions were as follows:

> Rivalries and disputes among the Arabs reduce their chances of doing anything significant about their quarrel with Israel; these rivalries also create some danger of precipitating crises from which large-scale Arab-Israeli hostilities could develop.
>
> The Israelis seem likely to continue existing policies, including occasional retaliatory action; they would resort to force on a large scale only if they felt their security seriously endangered.
>
> [The Israelis] could best any one of their neighbors and probably all of them collectively. Arab cooperation being what it is, Israel probably would not be obliged to take them on all at once.
>
> The Soviet leaders almost certainly view the Arab-Israeli dispute as promoting their interests. . . . But the Soviets do not want an outbreak of large-scale conflict in the area, since this would carry serious risk of a U.S.-Soviet confrontation and thus threaten the positions which the Soviets have already won in the area.
>
> Although periods of increased tension in Arab-Israeli dispute will occur from time to time, both sides appear to appreciate that large-scale military action involves considerable risk and no assurance of leading to a solution. In any event, the chances are good that the threat of great power intervention will prevent an attempt by either side to resolve the problem by military force.[2]

2. Matthias, "How Three Estimates Went Wrong."

We, of course, had overestimated the good sense of President Nasser. We thought that both he and the Israeli leaders would recognize, because of the threat of great power intervention, that it would be hopeless to try to resolve the Arab-Israeli dispute by military means. The war came about largely because of the factors mentioned in our first conclusion, namely, that "rivalries and disputes among the Arabs" would create "a danger of precipitating crises from which large-scale Arab-Israeli hostilities could develop." The crisis was stimulated by mischievous actions of the Soviet KGB, and it was intensified by ill-advised actions of UN Secretary-General U Thant.

As near as I have been able to reconstruct events, what happened was approximately the following. A new Syrian leadership, which had come to power through a military coup early in 1966, was trying to gain domestic support by stepping up anti-Israeli rhetoric and by carrying on such warlike activities as firing upon Israeli agricultural settlements from the Golan Heights. The Israeli prime minister Golda Meir warned that if the firing did not cease, her government would retaliate. There was even a dogfight between Syrian and Israeli aircraft in mid-April 1967. At about the same time, the Israelis began a military call-up and staged training exercises in northern Israel. The KGB told the Syrians and Egyptians that Israel was massing troops for a pre-emptive attack on Syria. That stirred up fears in Damascus and prompted Nasser to demonstrate his anti-Israeli posture by calling up reserves and moving tanks into the Sinai.

Up to that point, Nasser almost certainly was bluffing. His rivals in Syria and Jordan had been taunting him with hiding behind the skirts of the United Nations Emergency Force on the Egyptian side of the border, and they had been implying that he would not come to the rescue of the Syrians or any other Arab country attacked by the Israelis. To escape that charge, on the evening of May 16, 1967, Nasser called upon the UN commander to remove the UN forces from Egyptian territory. Nasser apparently thought that U Thant would refuse to do so and that such a refusal would absolve him of the insinuations against him, But U Thant did not understand Nasser's maneuver and did not reject the request outright. Instead, he tried to negotiate a way to keep the UN forces in the border area, but the effort proved futile. Three days later, on May 19, U Thant issued the order to withdraw.

Having gotten rid of the UN force and having obviously frightened the Israelis, Nasser again became a hero in the Arab world. Because he had also radically narrowed his options, he had no choice but to try to brazen the situation out. As he began to redeploy his forces, his confidence grew, and on May 22 he announced a blockade of the Gulf of Aqaba, thus closing Israel's access to the Red Sea. He then told his troops that Egypt was "fully prepared and confident" and that their objective was to "destroy Israel."[3]

All of this, of course, upset the Israelis a great deal. When the Egyptians closed the Gulf of Aqaba, some Israeli generals wanted to go to war at once, but were deterred by a request from President Johnson to defer action for forty-eight hours. Israeli foreign minister Abba Eban, not wanting to repeat the alienation from the United States that had occurred when Israel went to war in 1956 without consulting Washington, urged a delay and was dispatched to the United States to confer with American officials. Meanwhile, the American Jewish community was alerted to the new situation, and Jewish leaders began exerting pressure for a U.S. declaration of support for Israel. The U.S. ambassador to the UN, Arthur Goldberg, and the Rostow brothers, Eugene at State and Walt at the White House, were getting special attention.[4]

When Eban arrived in Washington on May 25, he was handed a top-secret cable from the Israeli prime minister directing him to seek from President Johnson an immediate declaration that "any attack upon Israel is equivalent to an attack upon the United States" and seeking specific orders to U.S. forces in the region to undertake "combined operations" with Israeli defense forces.[5] When the message was delivered to Secretary Rusk, it set off a scramble within the U.S. national security apparatus to review its assessments of the military situation. President Johnson had been out of the city all day and was informed when he returned to the White House that the Eban cable had been supplemented by a "hair-raising" account of Arab plans and capabilities that had been prepared by Israeli intelligence and handed earlier in the day to the CIA station chief in Tel Aviv.

Johnson called an immediate meeting of the NSC group with which he had been consulting as the crisis had progressed. CIA Director Richard Helms had already sent to the White House a CIA appraisal of the Israeli estimate based upon the U.S. NIE of a month earlier. The President directed, however, that before an NSC meeting scheduled for the next day, the CIA and the Joint Chiefs should "scrub down" the NIE. Helms passed the order on to us. I recall a small group of us gathered on the evening of May 25 in the office of the chief of the estimates staff, with the Israeli estimate and our own

---

3. The account of prewar maneuvering is taken in part from Arthur Goldschmidt's *Concise History of the Middle East* (Boulder, Colo.: Westview Press, 1988), 288–89, in part from Donald Neff's *Warriors in Jerusalem* (New York: Simon & Schuster, 19), 64–73 and 124–26, and in part from my own recollections.

4. Neff, *Warriors in Jerusalem*, 110–11.

5. Ibid., 132.

estimate of April before us. We reaffirmed our earlier position. Donald Neff, in his book on the Six-Day War, reported:

> [Both] had come to same conclusion. There was no immediate threat to the Israelis. The new Board of National Estimates report went even further this time. Israel could defeat any combination of Arab states or all of them at the same time and do it within a week.[6]

I do not remember our stating that the affair could be ended within a week's time. But I do remember that Helms reported upon his return from the NSC meeting that Secretary Rusk had turned to him after the meeting and said, "Dick, I hope you are right. But if this is a mistake, it will be a beaut." The United States made no declaration of the type demanded by the Israelis. As everyone knows, the Israelis did take the initiative with a brilliant attack upon the Egyptian air force and destroyed the entire fleet. They followed up by seizing the Sinai, the Golan Heights, and the West Bank of the Jordan.

Our April 13 NIE and our May 25 reassessment were crucial to the presidential decision. Already in trouble because of the deepening U.S. involvement in Vietnam, Johnson did not want to take on another military commitment, and he did not want to antagonize the oil-producing Arab states. Nor did he want to allow Israel to suffer the grave defeat which its leaders were predicting. He took the chance that we were right, even while he was under pressure from some Jewish-Americans fearing for the survival of the Jewish state. According to one reporter, Richard Helms has labeled the 1967 prophecy "one of his proudest achievements at the CIA."[7]

President Johnson's travail over how to deal with Israel's importuning was matched—and perhaps surpassed—by that of Soviet Premier Kosygin. We had said in the estimate that while the Soviets believed that the Arab-Israeli dispute favored their interests, they did not want an outbreak of large-scale conflict with its attendant risks of a U.S.-Soviet confrontation. When the war actually began, Kosygin got on the hot line to Johnson—the first time it was used—to say that the USSR would work for a quick cease-fire and hoped that the United States would try to restrain the Israelis. Johnson responded within the hour that he would take action to try to stop the fighting and that he appreciated that the USSR was doing the same thing.[8] A day later, Kosygin

6. Ibid., 140.
7. Cited by Rhodi Jeffreys-Jones, CIA and American Democracy (New Haven: Yale University Press, 1989), 165.
8. Neff, Warriors in Jerusalem, 212.

called again to urge that the two powers work harder for the cease-fire, adding that the USSR also wanted a return to the lines which existed before the fighting began.[9]

Meanwhile, the UN was working on a cease-fire resolution, and agreement was being held up over the Soviet proviso for a return to the original lines. Kosygin withdrew his request and the resolution was quickly approved. But Israel continued to press the attack. Thereupon, in the evening of the following day, the USSR sent a direct message to the Israeli government through its ambassador in Tel Aviv, stating that if Israel did not stop its fighting the USSR would reconsider its relations with Israel and take "other necessary steps which emanate from the aggressive policy of Israel."[10] Finally on June 10, the Soviets broke diplomatic relations with Israel and threatened "sanctions against Israel, with all the consequences flowing there from." The following morning, Kosygin told Johnson on the hot line that if Israel did not cease fighting within the next few hours, the Soviet Union would take "necessary actions, including military."[11]

Thus a U.S.-Soviet confrontation came close to reality. Johnson replied simply that the United States was pressing the Israelis to cease fire and had received assurances that the Israelis would do so. But Johnson also ordered the U.S. Sixth Fleet in the Mediterranean to reduce to fifty miles its restricted distance from the Soviet Mediterranean Squadron. A few hours later the Israelis gave in and ordered a cease-fire. The war ended.[12]

The war's outcome had no redeeming features for either Arabs or Israelis. Bitterness between them intensified, the Arabs set about rearming, and a new war began six years later. The world did gain something as the United States and the USSR moved their rivalry onto a higher plane. They communicated with each other on a hot line intended to cool crises. They did not rattle any missiles. They worked quickly and cooperatively to end the fighting. The respect they had acquired for each other in the Cuban missile crisis had carried over. Even the CIA gained in prestige and respect for the correctness of its analysis and steadfastness in adhering to its solidly based judgments.

9. Ibid., 223.
10. Ibid., 237.
11. Ibid., 278–79.
12. Ibid., 280.

1968 National Estimate on World Trends and Contingencies

The year that followed the end of the Six-Day War was one of accelerating change in the world and in the United States. The "Great Proletarian Cultural Revolution" in China, which had begun in 1965, was causing great turmoil there; a liberal revolution within the Communist Party of Czechoslovakia threatened to infect its neighboring Communist countries and was suppressed by a Soviet-Warsaw Pact invasion; in France, university students rose against the society and its educational system, occupying the Sorbonne in the process; terrorist action by young people against society spread to West Germany and Italy; the Viet Cong undertook a major offensive in Saigon against the U.S. embassy during the Tet holiday season in February 1968.

In the United States, agitation against the Vietnam War intensified, and President Johnson announced in March his decision not to seek a second elected term of office. Also in the spring of 1968, Martin Luther King was assassinated in Tennessee. That was followed by several days of rioting in Washington, as young unemployed and ill-educated black members of the city's underclass exploited the King murder, taking out their frustrations by looting shops and burning buildings in the districts where they lived. President Johnson was obliged to barricade the White House and order federal troops into the city to restore order. Shortly thereafter, Robert Kennedy was assassinated by a Palestinian émigré youth during his campaign for the Democratic presidential nomination. All of these events in the United States and in the Communist world reduced the stature and influence of both the United States and the USSR.

Early in 1968, a "Special State-Defense Study Group" was set up to carry out a high-level investigation of U.S. overseas base requirements. The study group was directed to project U.S. needs through 1978 in light of the world political environment. The O/NE was asked to do a world estimate on short-term trends and longer-term contingencies. I was appointed board chairman to carry the estimate through the process; in fact I wrote most of it myself. It became NIE 1-68, took about three months to complete, and was approved by the USIB on June 6, 1968. It was declassified and released to the public in April 1995.

As estimates go, it was a rather long, consisting of a two-page summary and sixty paragraphs of discussion. Because the study group was concerned with both short-term trends and longer-term contingencies—the latter being much more difficult to discern—we directed our attention toward both specific problem areas and the broader milieu in which policymaking would occur. On the latter subject we wrote this:

The political atmosphere of the world over the next decade seems likely to be dominated even more by uncertainty than in the recent past. There will be a growing tendency for various nations to defy the great powers which have been their protectors and sustainers. The world climate will be one in which host nations will less and less welcome foreign bases or the stationing of foreign troops, even when they find them advantageous for their economy and security.

At the same time, the national interests of the superpowers will become increasingly complex. Both will probably seek means to make the competition between them less overt, less expensive, and less binding than in the past. Terrorism, guerrilla warfare, and counterinsurgency as forms of conflict are likely to be more common than open military confrontations between national forces. In an atmosphere where confrontation between major powers becomes less direct, opportunities may develop to improve the formal and conventional relations between the superpowers, for example in the area of arms control. But it appears unlikely that any real detente can develop. . . .

Open antagonism between the U.S. and the USSR could abate, as it has from time to time, without any real reconciliation. Real change in U.S.-USSR relations, or any substantial and permanent reduction in the influence of the superpowers, would flow from the rise of other power centers—China, Western Europe, and Japan. These centers have already become so important to the future positions of both the U.S. and the USSR that each must divert some of its attention to courting, neutralizing, and countering them, thus diluting and broadening the competition for influence, power and world leadership. . . .

It might be possible in this kind of world for competing powers to unite in programs to attack hunger, narrow the dangers of nuclear warfare, explore space, exploit the high seas, or control the world's weather. This is not to say that the next decade will initiate an era of good feeling. Serious tensions and even threats of another world war will arise from time to time, but the chances appear good that a common interest for containing them will prevail.

Concerning specific problem areas, the estimate contained judgments about the USSR, the Arab-Israeli conflict, and Vietnam, which we can now recognize, in the light of subsequent events and of newly available data about Soviet policies and actions, as having been especially prophetic.

Notable Insights from the Trends Estimate

Regarding the USSR: The reader might recall that as early as 1958, we had listed (in NIE 100-58) some significant changes in Soviet society and concluded that in the long run those changes could "alter profoundly the content and structure of Soviet political life, possibly through a dissipation of the Communist Party's unchecked monopoly of power, more likely through a change in the political climate within the ruling party." Three years later (in NIE 1-61), looking ahead for a decade, we wrote that the Soviet leaders' desire to avoid general war, a wider range of contacts with the outside world, continuing pressure for liberalization, and a growing capacity to provide Soviet citizens with a more comfortable life—would all "tend toward a moderation in foreign policy and toward a recognition of some areas of common interest with the West."

Three years later, in the Trends Memorandum of 1964, I concluded the paper with a paragraph again dealing with "the longer run." I quote here a part of that paragraph:

> The chances are good that the changes taking place in the USSR will diminish its hostility to the West and the vigor of its revolutionary effort outside the Communist world. . . . This process of change may be slowed from time to time, or even halted, but it is probably irreversible. But whether it proceeds or halts, the evolution which has taken place, together with the changes which have occurred within the Communist camp and in the world at large, suggest that for the next several years at least the world may be replete with strife and disorder but not on the verge of nuclear disaster.

Four years later we returned again, in NIE 1-68, to the subject of changes in Soviet society and their effect upon possible changes in the character of the Soviet leadership. We expressed the thought that by that time the Soviet leadership had developed a "vested interest in the status quo" and that it wanted "to conserve and nurture" the political resources which it possessed in the outside world rather than "to use them in revolutionary ventures." But we had not seen any sign of significant change in the leadership's attitude; we had detected that the younger men prominent in the Party seemed to be less doctrinaire than their elders but equally hostile toward the West. We added, somewhat hopefully, that "if more flexible and potentially friendlier politicians" existed, they "have not revealed themselves to us, or, perhaps, even to each other."

When we came to the longer run, we wrote two paragraphs which tried to envision how a change in Soviet leadership might come about:

As in other states, Soviet political life is dynamic, and there will be changes in the leadership and in the influence of various sectors of society on the leadership. Our basic judgment is that such changes seem likely to produce gradual shifts in policy, rather than abrupt swings. But sudden and significant changes certainly cannot be ruled out. They could be provoked, for example, by the emergence of a single leader with the will to wrench Soviet society into new conformations. Rapid change could also come about as a consequence of a dispersion of political power among vested interest groups, the various regions, or even the people at large.

Dispersed authority might tend to divert energies to domestic concerns, stimulate discord, and obstruct clear courses of international action. Greater participation of the public in the political processes would almost certainly lead to more emphasis upon consumer welfare, partly at the expense of the military, and this in turn would probably in the long run make Soviet foreign policies less bellicose.

The 1968 estimate's projection of the effect upon Soviet politics of the social and economic changes that had occurred during the 1950s and 1960s was essentially correct—not for the 1970s, but for the 1980s. Khrushchev's Secret Speech in 1956 had set in motion profound changes in the Soviet body politic which we in the intelligence business had not fully apprehended. The most important of these was solidification of collective leadership, a change which in fact led to Khrushchev's own ouster in 1964. It is quite clear that the Presidium had become a genuine debating society in which all major decisions were discussed and even voted upon. The Brezhnev era was long, and it was also tedious in the sense that its benchmark was immobilism and the preservation of the status quo, both domestically and internationally.

It has also become quite clear, for example, that there was considerable debate about what sort of action the USSR should take to deal with the "Prague Spring" of 1968. It took a three-day session of the Presidium to decide upon military action. The decision they made was described by Brezhnev as "unanimous" although the Russian word he used implies a "unanimity of spirit" (*edinodushno*) rather than unanimity in an actual vote (*edinoglasno*).[13]

13. Analysis by Mark Kramer in "The Prague Spring and the Soviet Invasion of Czechoslovakia," *Bulletin of the Cold War International History Project*, no. 3 (Fall 1993): 11.

It is also now clear that Yuri Andropov (in 1968 still head of the KGB and not yet Party chairman) was very much interested in the opinions of younger people and students in the USSR. He sent to the Party's Central Committee a thirty-three-page report about the mood of Soviet college students; it was sent in November 1968, after the Czech invasion had occurred but written before that happened. According to Mark Kramer's analysis in the *Bulletin of the Cold War International History Project,* Andropov obviously attached high credibility to the report, whose source was a KGB informant and a recent graduate of the University in Odessa. Andropov wrote that his informant's account deserved "close attention" and that the views expressed coincided with "views from other sources." In his commentary upon the views of his fellow students, the agent said that "great interest" had been attracted by the "creation of opposition parties" in Prague.[14]

The KGB report is important, not merely for what it said about the attitudes of Soviet youth in the late 1960s, but primarily for what it said about Yuri Andropov. We pointed out in the 1958 World Estimate, as noted above, that the changes then taking place in the USSR were working to "alter" Soviet political life and that major change would likely occur "through a change in the political climate within the ruling party." Andropov obviously was becoming a symbol of change, even when still chief of the KGB. Hedrick Smith, in his book *The New Russians,* described in this way the situation in the USSR when Andropov took over from Brezhnev in November 1982: "Times were changing. . . . There was substantial sentiment for change within the Party as well as among the people. Widely regarded as the smartest member of the Politboro, Andropov seemed aware of the country's paralysis and bent on restoring a national sense of purpose."[15]

Andropov's realization that things had to change probably began in Budapest in 1956, when he had tried—and failed—to work out a new relationship between Hungary and the USSR. The growing crisis in Prague in 1968 and the reaction of youthful Russians and Ukrainians to the changes taking place in Czechoslovakia apparently strengthened his belief that changes in the USSR were really needed. It was fourteen years later that he finally became chairman and national leader. He launched a purge of corrupt officials and a campaign for better work discipline and greater economic efficiency. But he could not carry on; his health failed and he died after fifteen months. But he did select for advancement in the Party a number of younger, intelligent

14. Ibid., 68.
15. Hedrick Smith, *The New Russians* (New York: Random House, 1990), 30.

men, one of whom was Mikhail Gorbachev. It was Gorbachev who came to the chairmanship in 1985 and began to "wrench Soviet society into new conformations," as we had suggested some eighteen years earlier.

Regarding the Arab-Israeli Conflict: In NIE 1-68, we pointed out that the Six-Day War of a year earlier had not resolved the problem of how the two sides could live together in peaceful proximity. "Arab frustration" had risen, and "bitterness against Israel" had increased. We concluded that "the most likely thing the Arabs will do is to prepare for a new war against Israel. Israeli truculence being what it is, new fighting on a major scale will probably occur in the coming years and will result in new Israeli victories. The situation will be the source of pressures upon the great powers, who could promote an easing of tensions if they could agree among themselves, but this they probably cannot do." We added that the Soviets could not just shrug off all responsibility for their clients—Egypt and Syria—so that the USSR and United States would find it difficult to avoid confrontations even if they wished to.

Two years after the estimate was issued, Egypt came under the leadership of Anwar Sadat, Nasser having died in 1970. Egypt soon began having serious economic troubles, in part because the Suez Canal remained closed and was generating no revenues. President Sadat was also having political problems. His opponents and radical youths were complaining that the Israelis remained in occupation of Egyptian territory only 100 miles from Cairo.

At that time, I was writing the memorandum entitled "The World Situation in 1970," and I included the following paragraph on the Arab-Israeli situation:

> The most critical [ethnic conflict] during the next decade will be the Arab-Israeli conflict. There seems to be no way in which it can be resolved. The Israelis will not give up their high cards (the lands they hold and the nuclear technology they possess), and the Arabs refuse to recognize that the Israelis hold those cards. They believe that over time they can force the Israelis to yield, but that in any case they should continue the struggle. It does not seem likely that fighting on a large scale will break out again soon, but if it should the Israelis would not have such an easy time of it as in 1967—unless they resorted to nuclear weapons. While the Soviets wish to keep the level of tension low enough to head off a confrontation with the U.S., they are also publicly supporting the Arab cause. The Soviets seem to be aware that there are pitfalls and dilemmas implicit in their policy, but this is a delicate game and they could miscalculate—as they did in 1967. The

Arabs could easily go too far too fast, and the Israelis again become exasperated. Things could get beyond the capacities of the U.S. and USSR to control.

Pressures on Sadat, both domestically and in the Arab world, continued to mount, and the Israelis were hardening their position. By mid-1972, tensions were beginning to get out of hand, and they climaxed in the Yom Kippur War of October 1973.

Regarding Vietnam: Much history regarding Vietnam was made after NIE 53-62 was issued in April 1963 and after the publication of the famous Vietnam paragraph in the 1964 World Situation Memorandum. The Gulf of Tonkin incident occurred, the U.S. military commitment increased dramatically, and the first aerial bombardments of North Vietnam took place. By the end of 1965, the United States had 200,000 troops in the country. By the end of 1967, U.S. troop strength reached 500,000. At the end of January in 1968, the Tet offensive began. The U.S. Command in Saigon (MAC/V) thereupon asked for an additional 200,000 personnel. In February 1968, Robert McNamara left as Secretary of Defense and was succeeded by Clark Clifford. The U.S. political scene heated up with Senator Eugene McCarthy winning the Democratic presidential primary in New Hampshire, and Senator Robert Kennedy announcing his candidacy for the presidency. President Johnson announced on March 31, 1968, that he would not seek reelection. In May he sent Ambassador Harriman to Paris to open peace negotiations with the North Vietnamese. When we were preparing NIE 1-68 during May and June 1968, we tried to keep those developments in mind.

There were literally dozens of estimates and memoranda sent to the White House, State Department, and Defense Department from various CIA components concerning one aspect or another of the Vietnam problem during the years before and after the large-scale U.S. commitment. One of them of special interest in connection with NIE 1-68 was a memorandum from the Board of National Estimates to Director John McCone on June 6, 1964. It was prepared in response to a question from President Johnson about what dominos might fall in the East Asian area if South Vietnam and Laos fell under Communist control. It was cited by Robert McNamara in his (1995) apologia on Vietnam. He quoted the following portion of the memorandum: "The loss of South Vietnam and Laos to the Communists would be profoundly damaging to the U.S. position in the Far East, most especially because the U.S. has committed itself persistently, emphatically, and publicly to preventing Communist takeover of the two countries. Failure here would be damaging to U.S. prestige and would seriously debase the credibility of U.S. will and capability to contain Communism elsewhere in the area."[16]

The quotation from the board memorandum comes at the end of chapter 4 of his book *In Retrospect*. After the quotation, McNamara makes the following observation: "Their [i.e., the board's] analysis seemed again to confirm my and other's fear—misplaced in retrospect, but no less real at the time—that the West's containment policy lay at serious risk in Vietnam. And thus we continued our slide down the slippery slope."[17] That observation appears to be an attempt to lay upon the Board of National Estimates a part of the blame for the policies which he and the other high policymakers had advocated thereafter.

The reader might recall that in our 1963 estimate concerning Vietnam, we held out some hope that the Viet Cong could be contained "militarily," but added that "the government's capacity to translate military success into lasting political stability is questionable." Six months after that evaluation, the Diem regime was overthrown, with U.S. complicity. Several months later in the World Situation Memorandum of 1964, I included a paragraph which suggested that the struggle in Vietnam was more of a political contest than a military operation, that Diem's successors had not shown the leadership and inspiration necessary to defeat the Viet Cong, and that there remained "serious doubt that victory can be won." I am quite sure that McNamara knew about that paragraph; it was all over the newspapers, and I do know that McNamara had called John McCone on the telephone before the *Chicago Tribune* had published it reporting that there was a board memorandum floating around Republican National Committee headquarters. But McNamara, along with Secretary Rusk and the NSC staff, wished to bury the memorandum and discredit its significance.

Thus, in his memoir, Mr. McNamara preferred to rely upon the board's June 9 memorandum, which is quoted above. I did not participate in the drafting or discussion of the June 9 memorandum; I was preparing for my assignment in Rome. I perhaps would have phrased that memorandum somewhat differently. Nevertheless, a careful reading of it does not indicate that the domino effect was either certain or unavoidable. What it did say was that damage to the U.S. position in the Far East, if it did occur, would arise "especially, because the U.S. has committed itself persistently, emphatically, 'and publicly' to preventing" a Communist takeover. To put it more bluntly, U.S.

16. Robert McNamara, *In Retrospect* (New York: Random House, 1995), 124.
17. Ibid., 125.

political and military leaders had made such a big noise about stopping Communism in Vietnam that they had trapped themselves into putting American prestige and national strategy into a very questionable venture — a venture which by mid-1964 was already doomed because the South Vietnamese political and military leaders lacked the will and ability to win a war that was not supported by their own people.

What we were looking at concerning Vietnam in NIE 1-68 was the effect of the U.S. commitment in light of the conditions existing at that time. We were conscious of the situation in the rest of Asia as well as the effect of the Tet offensive upon the rest of Southeast Asia. We also took cognizance of the fact that a negotiated solution was being sought. We wrote in parts of paragraphs 29 and 30:

> Even if Vietnam fell fairly soon into the hands of a regime dominated by the Communists, the other regimes [in Southeast Asia] would probably not collapse, but their struggle for existence would become more intense and their survival more precarious. They have assets South Vietnam has never had, namely, relative peace, some sense of nationhood, and real successes against Communist subversion.
>
> U.S. intervention in Vietnam, Japanese alliance with the U.S., and U.S. presence in other areas of East Asia and the Western Pacific have probably accomplished much of what was intended. They have induced prudence in Peking and Moscow, encouraged a sense of security in the non-Communist countries, and provided some of the resources and skills for the development of more effective government and social and economic improvement.

Those words in NIE 1-68 represented a judgment that senior CIA analysts had arrived at in the autumn of 1967, nine months earlier. That earlier judgment was made in a highly confidential memorandum that CIA Director Richard Helms had sent to President Johnson on September 12, 1967. So far as I know it was not sent to any other high policymaking official, and I do not recall having participated in its preparation. McNamara obtained it and saw it for the first time when he was writing In Retrospect. He quoted Helms as stating in a summary conclusion what were "the broad and essential impressions which this paper has intended to convey." They were:

a. An unfavorable outcome in Vietnam would be a major setback to the reputation of U.S. power which would limit U.S. influence and prejudice our other interests in some degree which cannot be reliably foreseen.

b. Probably the net effects would not be permanently damaging to this country's capacity to play its part as a world power working for order and security in many areas.

c. The worst potential damage would be of the self-inflicted kind: internal dissension which would limit our future ability to use our power and resources wisely and to full effect, and lead to a loss of confidence by others in the American capacity for leadership.

d. The destabilizing effects would be greatest in the immediate area of Southeast Asia where some states would probably face internal turmoil and heightened external pressures, and where some realignments might occur, similar effects would be to unlikely elsewhere or could be easily contained.[18]

So that the President would get the full impact of the message in the memorandum, the final sentence of a final paragraph read: "If the analysis here advances the discussion [of whether the U.S. should accept failure in Vietnam] at all, it is in the direction of suggesting that the risks are probably more limited and controllable than most previous argument has indicated."[19]

As the year 1967 was drawing to a close, Secretary McNamara broke ranks with the Joint Chiefs over what to do about Vietnam. They wanted to expand the ground war and intensify the bombing. McNamara wanted to stabilize the military situation in the South and to stop the bombing in the North. He laid out his views in a memorandum to the President on November 1. He has stated that he never received a reply from the President or participated in any discussion on his proposals to reduce the level of U.S. military action. A month later he was chosen president of the World Bank—apparently to his surprise. He left the Pentagon on February 23, 1968, without knowing, as he put it, whether he "quit or was fired."[20]

I do not know whether Clark Clifford ever saw the Helms September memorandum. But he did see NIE 1-68. He came out to the CIA building a short time after the estimate was published and paid a call on the Board of National Estimates. He wanted to discuss the Asian and worldwide effects of a U.S. withdrawal from Vietnam. We reiterated our position. No longer tied down

18. Ibid., 293.
19. Ibid.
20. Ibid., 305–11, passim.

by the domino myth, Clifford then set to work to reduce the level of U.S. military action in Vietnam. He evidently felt that he was making progress when he told the country in September 1968 that Vietnam was no longer an unlimited drain on U.S. resources.[21] By then it was too little and too late. The country wanted peace. Democrats had led the country into two wars in Asia during the preceding twenty years. Richard Nixon promised peace, and he was elected president in November. The Vietnam War then became Nixon's war and went on for another six and a half years.

21. Karnow, Vietnam, 566.

The Nixon Era and the Beginning of Détente

The Beginning of the Nixon Era

Richard Nixon was one of the few presidents in this century well prepared for dealing with foreign and military policy questions. Like many of us born before 1920, he watched World War II come, served in the military, and entered government service after the war's end. His period of service in the Congress was distinguished primarily by his anti-Communism, a distinction that led Dwight Eisenhower to select him as a running mate. Eight years as Vice President during the 1950s gave him a close look at most of the international problems and movements of the decade. After losing the 1960 presidential election to Kennedy by a narrow margin, he won in 1968, also by a narrow margin. In seeking support from the moderate Rockefeller wing of the Republican Party, he selected Henry Kissinger, a Rockefeller protégé, as his national security adviser. Kissinger, a colleague of mine at the Center for International Affairs at Harvard University in the late 1950s, was a highly qualified scholar with an excellent knowledge of history and a penchant for decisive action.

Nixon did not resolve the Vietnam problem peaceably, as his campaign had led many voters to believe he would. Indeed, he reversed the Clifford course and accepted the Joint Chiefs' doctrine that the solution lay in expanding military action to the point where the North Vietnamese and their supporters in the South could not or would not continue the struggle. Both Nixon and Kissinger evidently realized that most Americans wanted peace, but they apparently also believed that the American public wished for some kind of "honorable" peace instead of an unceremonial withdrawal. That goal proved elusive, partly because the stubbornness of the Vietnamese proved greater than most American policymakers thought possible, and partly because they underestimated the readiness of Americans to accept any kind of U.S. withdrawal.

Kissinger has recounted in his book *The White House Years* that the new administration wanted to "draw the Kremlin into discussions on Vietnam." In a discussion before the inauguration with a Soviet embassy officer about future U.S.-Soviet negotiations, he told the officer that a general relaxation of tension would require that the real differences between them be "narrowed." The Soviet officer had indicated that the preeminent Soviet concern was disarmament, and Kissinger described his response this way: "We insisted that negotiations on all issues proceed simultaneously. The Soviet leaders were especially worried about the impact of a new arms race on the Soviet economy; they therefore gave top priority to arms limitation. This had the additional advantage to them that the mere facts of talks, regardless of their results, would complicate new defense appropriations in the United States and—though we did not perceive this—would disquiet the Chinese."[1]

The outside world indeed did not know much about the depth of the Sino-Soviet split, which had developed during the years from 1959 to 1961 and which I discussed in some detail in Chapter 5. We did write in NIE 1-61 (January 1961), just before the breakdown had become public, that there appeared to be—over the decade ahead—"a greater likelihood of flexibility in Soviet than in Chinese policy." Even after the split became obvious in the spring of 1962, its significance was not fully taken in either by U.S. policymakers or by such academic observers as Kissinger, who—in the citation above—acknowledged that he and his NSC associates "did not perceive" that a Soviet-U.S. rapprochement would "disquiet" the Chinese. Then, in the widely published 1964 memorandum, I wrote of the Sino-Soviet "schism" and of the Communist movement having been split "into two warring camps," each with its own satellite following. In the 1968 World Trends estimate, we referred to the "deepening hostility" between the USSR and China and to the new deployment of substantial Soviet military forces along the Chinese frontier.

1. Henry Kissinger, *White House Years* (Boston: Little, Brown, 1979), 128.

It took the Ussuri River War during the spring months of 1969 to cause Kissinger to take a genuine interest in the Sino-Soviet split. The war was a series of clashes involving major military units on the Ussuri River border beginning early in March 1969. In May there were also clashes along the Sinkiang-Kazakhstan border and along the Amur River border. Kissinger saw these clashes as an opportunity to open communications with China, and the United States undertook various steps toward the opening of talks with the Chinese government. Kissinger had been following the clashes carefully and concluded that the Soviets had been the aggressors. There was concern that the Soviets would carry out further military actions, and President Nixon told the NSC on August 14, 1969, that it would be contrary to U.S. interests for China to be "smashed" in a Soviet-Chinese war.[2] This was the first open recognition by a high U.S. official that the Soviet-Chinese split had fundamentally altered the structure of world power. No longer were "Communist" powers automatically enemies of the United States. So began the triangular diplomacy which characterized the Nixon era in world politics.

What Nixon and Kissinger were attempting was not only to bring the world's most populous nation into the international community but above all to use a U.S. rapprochement with China to pressure the Soviets into undertaking across-the-board negotiations of U.S.-Soviet differences, including Soviet help in ending the administration's Vietnam nightmare. A full-fledged détente was not then in their minds, and probably not in the minds of the Soviet leaders either. Nevertheless, the Soviets were putting out signals showing an interest in something more than a minimal concern with arms control. In so doing, they were responding to their own economic problems, to their nervousness about Chinese militancy, and to a widespread hope in Europe for a great-power détente to ease fears of a nuclear holocaust.

Positive movement toward resolving some of the West's differences with the Soviets began late in 1969, when Willy Brandt became the chancellor of the FRG. Brandt called his attempt to improve relations with East Germany and the USSR "Ostpolitik." It was not a policy embraced by the Nixon administration, but it quickly gained momentum, and the administration came to accept it "as necessary."[3] Ostpolitik succeeded in extracting concessions from East Germany, which in turn led to a Berlin access agreement in 1971—thus ending the thorny problem in East-West relations which had reached crisis proportions in 1958 and in 1961. That was followed by

2. Ibid., 10 182.
3. Kissinger, *Diplomacy*, 735.

friendship treaties with East Germany, Poland, and the USSR. Thus events in Europe during the first years of the Nixon administration were making it increasingly clear that the Soviets wanted peace in Europe, in addition to wanting arms limitations. SALT negotiations began in November 1969 and soon started to warm up.

So ended the year 1969, the first year of the Nixon administration. CIA analysts had, of course, been following the Soviet signals with great interest. One of my superiors (I think it was Helms) thought it would be a good idea to sum up what had happened in 1969 and what that portended for the 1970s. The result was a new memorandum, which I completed on January 9, 1970, entitled "The World Situation in 1970: Including an Examination of the U.S. and Soviet World Positions."

The Memorandum on the World Situation in 1970: The Communist World

Since the USSR and the international Communist movement were the declared adversaries of the United States and its allies, I devoted the first section of the memorandum to an analysis of the Communist world:.

> The Communist world as a whole has lost its capacity to act or even speak in a unified fashion. In short, the Communist world is replete with trouble. It is not necessary here to do more than list some of its problems: China and the USSR at odds on everything, and China fearing a Soviet military attack; North Korea run by a self-anointing intractable dictator scornful of Soviet tutelage; Tito still defiant and experimenting with new forms of socialist polity; Eastern Europe a hotbed of nationalism with emerging tough leaders who care less about Communism than about power and independence and who do not intend to make Dubcek's mistake and give the USSR cause to intervene; the East Germans the kind of friends the Soviets would happily exchange for less difficult enemies; the Italian (and to a lesser degree, the French) Communist party openly disagreeing with Soviet policy and openly divided over doctrine and tactics; Castro a costly, recalcitrant, and inefficient satrap whose dreams of Cuban economic success at home and revolutionary success abroad are turning to dust; the many Communist parties around the world which have found either that they must remain small, ineffective, and ridiculous, or become bourgeois in method—and almost in doctrine—if they hope to gain a place in their nation's political life.

As a consequence, the Soviet leaders have had to devote an increasing proportion of their time, energy, and resources to trying to maintain a semblance of order in their own camp, and they are not having a great deal of success at it. For example, the military build-up against China has absorbed resources which otherwise would have been devoted to the improvement of their out-of-date and inadequately supplied forces in the western USSR. International Communist conferences designed to show that the Communist world is not falling apart suffer delays, postponements, and then dissenting opinions and abstentions on final resolutions anyway.

In many areas outside the Communist world, the USSR has not done very well either, and seems to be narrowing both its activities and its hopes. Its foreign aid and subversive activities have converted no nations to Communism; some, such as Ghana and Indonesia, have even become anti-Communist; some, such as Syria, have become problem children. In two major nations, India and Indonesia, Soviet arms shipments have even made our problems easier; they strengthened India against China, and they better enabled the Indonesian armed forces to liquidate the Indonesian Communist party. The USSR has expanded its diplomatic and commercial contacts around the world, but it has found its efforts in some countries (Tanzania and Yemen, for example) challenged by Chinese Communists. And in some places, such as Congo Kinshasa and the Ivory Coast, its diplomatic and cultural missions have been severely restricted or asked to leave. There has been a surge of nationalism in nearly every part of the world, and ardent nationalists don't make the kind of Communists the Soviets like.

Indeed, it is far from clear that leaders of the Soviet Union are actually trying to build up a Communist empire, whatever Soviet rhetoric may proclaim. Competition and movement under Khrushchev have given way to preservation and safety under his successors. Many of their activities have been defensive: to restore position among the Arabs after failing to come to their aid in 1967, to preserve influence in India after the antics of the Chinese Communists in 1962, to stop the hemorrhage in Berlin (in 1961) and to preserve the Communist system in Eastern Europe (in 1968), to prevent the liberal infection among intellectuals from threatening the Soviet system at home, to continue the great effort to pull closer to the United States in total strategic power. This is not to say that they have retreated from any attained positions or refused to exploit opportunities. But they have not seized every opportunity to make mischief (as for example in Africa) or rushed to pursue aggressively every opening they have had (as for example in Syria). They have tempered their doctrinal commitment to world revolution by a heavy dose of realism. They act as if they do not want to take on additional clients that will cause more trouble than they are worth or expose the Soviets to countermeasures which might not only lose them the game but expose the USSR itself to danger.

It would not be correct to say that the Soviets are simply trying to maintain the status quo. They are a thrusting and ambitious power, concerned to enlarge their world position. They are seeking to gain influence and position in places denied to them. They want to become a major factor in the affairs of nations, and they are pursuing the age-old formula that the object of international politics is to increase the number of one's friends and decrease the number of one's enemies. But they are tempering their ambitions with estimates of feasibility and are controlling their hostility with measurements of power and risk. In Europe and in relations with the United States, for example, they are showing a keen interest in legitimizing the positions they have attained. They are upset over the situation in Eastern Europe, and—whether they are aware of it or not—they may have an insoluble problem; economic and political liberalization threatens Communist control, but a refusal to liberalize risks economic stagnation and fails to engage popular cooperation and constructive managerial effort.

It is probably in relation to the United States that the USSR is behaving with the keenest eye for a realistic view. The U.S. is clearly the USSR's strongest and most effective adversary today, but China in some sense is viewed as potentially even more dangerous. It is more bitter toward the USSR, less rational about the risks and horrors of nuclear war, both more populous and a closer neighbor, and also a possible collaborator with the U.S. against the USSR. Partly because of these dangers from the Chinese side, there has been a shift in Soviet thinking toward the view that perhaps with the more rational Americans it might be possible to arrange some sort of stabilization in Europe, in the Middle East, in the arms race, or even possibly in Asia. This can, partially at least, explain the pressure for a European security conference, the two-power and four-power talks on the Middle East, the encouraging opening of the strategic arms talks, and the suggestion of a need for some form of collective security in Asia.

The Soviets have other reasons, of course. In the field of strategic armaments itself, they are confronted with unpalatable alternatives. To actually surpass the U.S. would require high expenditures and place a heavy squeeze on resources; it might not work anyway, since the U.S. could, if it wished, easily out-build the Soviets. To allow the U.S. to press on and make the USSR sadly inferior is not acceptable either. The Soviet leaders are also coming to realize that their economy is not what it ought to be in terms of modernization and efficiency. The economy has such a high degree of centralized control and has so many built-in obstacles to the application of new technology, to the most efficient forms of investment, and to the most creative endeavors of workers and management, that it is failing to grow nearly as rapidly as desired, and—worse—it is failing to narrow the gap between the USSR and the industrial nations of the West.

The Soviet leaders cannot do very much about this unless they adopt measures which would reduce the control of the political apparatus over the economic establishment. This they are afraid to do for fear of the ultimate political consequences, and they certainly do not want to do so when their enemies abroad might be able to take advantage of it. But until or unless they do so, the armaments race will prove very costly, and the USSR will hardly appeal to the leaders of the developing states as the best model for economic advancement.

Excerpts: The U.S. World Position

The unique position the United States enjoyed after World War II—military invulnerability, enormous financial resources, and the will and respect of most of the world's peoples—was bound to disappear. It was one of those moments in world history that occur by happenstance. And it was our policy not to try to perpetuate it. We recognized that we could not rule the world, even if we had wished it. We recognized that the use of our economic resources to help others in reconstruction and development was preferable to letting them slip into despair and chaos. We recognized that other people had different cultures and social systems and that they would not wish to follow, and might even challenge, our own.

The policies we adopted, most of them in response to particular situations and contemporary judgments, were not—in hindsight—always the right ones, and we have modified many of them as the situation has changed. We have lost influence in some respects, gained it in others, and sometimes found a substantial loss followed by a substantial gain, or vice versa. If one judges influence by the pliancy of foreign offices, there is no doubt that the loss — on a worldwide basis — has been substantial. But if one judges by the popularity of American jazz and its variants, the prevalence of Coca-Cola, or the demand for American products — from tractors to toothpaste — the gain has been substantial. Indeed, the American lifestyle is being copied throughout a world which recognizes and seeks to acquire the superior American technology upon which that lifestyle is based. In terms of world economic activity (investment and development of resources, expansion of trade, transfer of technology, and operations of multinational corporations), the United States and its Western European allies have become the managerial and financial center of an economic community embracing all the non-Communist world and greatly affecting the prosperity of the Communist world itself.

There can be no doubt that U.S. credibility as a guarantor of security to some nations is under hazard, and there are areas of the world where U.S. commitments and interests are endangered. The point need not be labored that a precipitate abandonment of commitments, or a sudden denial of a previously affirmed interest, would upset people and make them suspect they were dealing with a fickle nation. The real question is the effect of measured withdrawal, and this is largely a question of atmosphere. The Western Europeans are already psychologically adjusting themselves to a reduction of the U.S. military presence in Europe, and they certainly support our phased withdrawal from Vietnam. No one in Europe — and few in Asia — seriously doubts that we have done at least what our commitments called for, and perhaps more. As long as our actions do not give the impression of a pell-mell retreat from world responsibility, they may be regretted in some quarters, but not widely regarded as a default of obligation. Indeed, in many quarters our withdrawal from Vietnam is regarded as a wise decision and a sensible reordering of external responsibilities and national priorities.

The Soviets and Chinese can have no doubt about our military capabilities, either against them or in areas of possible conflict. What they and our allies could come to doubt is our willingness to use them. The management problem of U.S. policy is to find the best ways of combining the restraint dictated by both domestic politics and good diplomacy with the firmness required by national security.

Excerpts: Problems in the Exercise of Power

It will be increasingly difficult to formulate national policy in the world of the 1970s. It is already harder to separate the "good guys" from the "bad guys."

It is already harder to draw lines defining areas of vital national interest; politics, economics, and technology have a way of making these obsolete.

There seems to be a growing tendency for smaller nations to defy the great powers. A willingness to fight as guerrillas—even against great odds, as in Vietnam—makes it difficult to apply conventional military power effectively. There are strong inhibitions against resort to nuclear weapons, and also against indiscriminate killing from aerial bombardment and artillery fire. Even conventional ground force operations are inhibited by fears of escalation to nuclear warfare. Thus, the use of military power in combat by the great powers seems likely to become more and more discriminate and likely to discourage both the United States and the USSR from military interventions in local situations.

The great powers will also be discouraged from openly taking on responsibility for nations—in addition to those they already support—by such concerns as economic costs, a fear of getting inextricably involved, the difficulty of controlling local leaders, the often intractable problems some of these nations face, and the political costs in world politics which such actions risk.

This is not to say that we are entering an era of everyone minding his own business; it is merely to say that there are strong rational reasons why the great powers will be more prudent about—and less prone to—open, expensive, and binding commitments.

Indeed, much progress has been made toward improved U.S.-Soviet relations through efforts to establish a common database and to understand each other's objectives. The Soviets have a good idea, as we do, what a nuclear war would be like. Neither of us can say the same about the Chinese. One cannot be certain that the United States and USSR over the decade ahead will always keep their options open and seek to avoid confrontations, but most likely they will.

Reactions to the 1970 Memorandum

The memorandum "The World Situation in 1970" met with a favorable reception in high quarters. Helms liked it and promptly passed copies to the President and to Henry Kissinger with personal notes. Kissinger responded a few days later with a note which said: "Your excellent report describing the world situation as we begin a new decade is most thought-provoking. I know the President will find it very interesting, and we will make use of your paper in developing the President's annual review of foreign policy." Soon thereafter, on a Monday morning, Helms called Abbott Smith and asked him to stop by and to bring me along. Helms, obviously elated, reported that on the previous afternoon the President had called him at home—the first time during the year in which he had served Nixon as DCI that Nixon had called him at home. The President had been highly complimentary of the paper and had asked him to pass on to the writer his personal thanks.

I was pleased that the president did not seem to have been disturbed by the memorandum's implicit criticism of some U.S. policies of previous years, its challenge to some of the doctrines upon which U.S. postwar policies had been based, and its implicit implications for future U.S. policy decisions. We normally did not receive enough feedback to know how much of a contribution our estimates and memoranda had made to the formulation of major policy decisions. Unless our reportage reached the public prints—as had been the case with the 1964 Trends Memorandum—the impact has been largely unseen even if it had been reflected in actual policy decisions or the thinking of policymakers.

The following year, 1970, was not a very good one for Nixon and Kissinger. Demonstrations against the war had already begun in the autumn of 1969, soon after Senator Charles Goodell of New York announced his intention of introducing a resolution requiring the withdrawal of all U.S. forces by the end of 1970. The "Peace Movement," as Kissinger called it, increased its activity in May 1970 in the wake of a large-scale U.S. incursion into Cambodia. The largest peace demonstration ever took place in Washington, four students were killed by Ohio National Guardsmen at a demonstration at Kent State University, and Nixon created a White House "plumbers group" to carry on surveillance of his critics in the media and government.

The Beginning of Détente

Despite these domestic problems, Nixon and Kissinger nevertheless went on with their higher-priority effort to bring about better U.S.-Soviet and U.S.-Chinese relations. The SALT negotiations, which had begun in November 1969, warmed up as 1970 progressed. They realized that the Berlin access agreement, signed in 1971, was also a sign that the Soviets wanted stability in Europe. Then, in October 1971 the U.S. and Soviet governments announced that a Soviet-U.S. summit meeting would take place in Moscow in May 1972. Before the summit, both Kissinger and Nixon visited Beijing to seal the opening of U.S.-Chinese relations and to indicate to both the Soviets and the Chinese that the United States was genuinely interested in negotiating to resolve world problems.

The summit itself was primarily concerned with the Anti-Ballistic Missile

Treaty. But there were two associated seminal documents, both more political and atmospheric in tone than the hard legal language which dealt with military weaponry. One was "Basic Principles of Relations" between the United States and the USSR. The signatories agreed to "do their utmost to avoid military confrontations and to avoid the outbreak of nuclear war." They were "prepared to negotiate and settle differences by peaceful means." They would continue the practice of "exchanging views on problems of mutual interest" and would try to do this at the highest level. They would "continue their efforts to limit armaments—with the objective of general and complete disarmament." They would strengthen their commercial and economic relations and develop cooperation in science and technology.

The other declaration in the communiqué was a reference to a "European Security Conference" similar to declarations contained in Soviet treaties with America's European allies. This declaration led to the Helsinki Accords signed in 1975, which have proved more important than was believed at the time. They recognized the national independence and the existing borders of the countries of Europe. They were honored by the Soviets fifteen years later when popular revolts unseated pro-Soviet regimes in Eastern Europe and resulted in the withdrawal of Soviet military forces.

Soviet Military Policy in Transition

U.S. and Soviet military doctrines and capabilities were the principal reasons for the détente movement. Each side was hiding under its nuclear umbrella to improve its geopolitical position, and each in turn feared triggering the other's nuclear attack capability during a critical confrontation. That is why it became incumbent upon both parties to promise to negotiate differences and to exchange views on matters of mutual interest. While the pre-summit maneuvering was going on, we in the Office of National Estimates were involved in preparing our annual round of military estimates on the Soviet bloc. My responsibly was the chairmanship of NIE 11-14-71, "Warsaw Pact Forces for Operations in Eurasia," which was completed early in 1972. It was followed soon thereafter by NIE 11-4-72, "Issues and Options in Soviet Military Policy." If, as it appeared, the Soviet government was moving toward détente, we believed it useful to examine how the Soviet leaders and their military commanders were viewing their capabilities and doctrines.

The U.S.-Soviet military relationship by 1971 had obviously changed from that of the early postwar years, when the United States had a clear numerical superiority in nuclear weaponry and when the Soviets had a clear superiority in conventional forces in Europe. Each had a capability with a strong deterrent effect upon any propensity of the other to initiate military action. By 1970, when the USSR acquired a rough strategic parity with the United States, the Soviet need for large, well-equipped conventional forces in Europe had substantially declined. At the same time, however, the rise in Soviet-Chinese enmity, as exemplified by the border clashes of 1969, was seen in Moscow as endangering the Soviet position in East Asia and creating the need for stronger Soviet forces there.

In 1971 there were some twenty-seven Soviet and thirty-one East European divisions opposite the Central Region of NATO. Another thirty or so Soviet divisions could be brought forward within a few weeks. This high level of Warsaw Pact strength facing west raised the question of the presumed mission of such large forces in the light of the new strategic and geopolitical situation in Eurasia. We expressed doubt that the Soviets seriously believed that NATO posed an imminent threat to Eastern Europe and the USSR. Yet a few years earlier, when Warsaw Pact forces invaded Czechoslovakia, they used only a few of the Soviet forces stationed in East Germany and instead mobilized reserve divisions. Information now available indicates that they were afraid of the defection of the Czech army and a subsequent incursion of NATO forces from the West to assist the Czechs.

The Soviet leaders' decision not to draw down their strength in East Germany in order to carry out the Czech operation strongly suggests that—despite their own improving nuclear deterrent—Soviet anxiety over Eastern Europe and distrust of the West were still so great that they believed it necessary to maintain an overwhelming level of conventional power in Central Europe. As of our writing in 1971, the Soviet détente policy was still in its initial stages; the German accords had not been signed and sealed, and U.S. military policy for Europe was still unclear. There was at that time, for example, strong pressure in the U.S. Congress to draw down U.S. troop strength in Europe, and the Soviets might have feared that if the United States departed Europe and left the field to the Germans, the USSR might have been in graver danger than with a continued U.S. presence.

We pointed out also that the structure, training, and armament of Warsaw Pact forces continued to be directed toward the conduct of offensive operations. We went on to say, however, that this offensive strategy and posture was in fact a drawback from the Soviet point of view. For example, in the typical Warsaw Pact exercise, NATO attacks eastward, the Soviets launch a counteroffensive and rapidly penetrate NATO's forward defenses, and then NATO resorts to tactical nuclear weapons. In response, the Soviets engage in a massive use of tactical nuclear weapons, and the Soviet Strategic Rocket Forces and Long-Range Air Force attack strategic targets in Europe with nuclear weapons. Since it would be imprudent for the Soviets to engage in strategic attacks in Europe without at the same time unleashing a first strike against the continental United States, the Soviet offensive strategy had a built-in thrust toward general nuclear war.

We thought the Soviets were aware of their problem and might be reviewing their options. Their interest in détente and their response to Ostpolitik suggested to us that they might conclude that their security would be better served by legitimizing the status quo in Europe than by perpetuating a high level of military force in Central Europe. On the whole, however, we thought that their concern to keep a firm brake upon political and economic experimentation in Eastern Europe, plus their distrust of the West, would exert a strong pressure toward keeping a substantial military force in place.

NIE 11-4-72, which was approved on March 2, 1972, engaged in a more extensive study of Soviet thinking on military doctrine and strategy. In their discussion of Soviet policy in Europe, the authors of this estimate thought that Moscow was coming to accept the view that it could reduce its forces in Central Europe, particularly in East Germany, and still have sufficient force to intimidate the East Europeans and retain a strong posture against NATO. They also judged that concern about China was an additional factor in the Soviet calculations on force requirements in the West. From 1965 to the time of writing the estimate (1972), Soviet ground force divisional strength in the Far East had risen from 15 divisions to 40, tactical aircraft from 200 to over 1,000, and tactical missile launchers from 50 to over 300. The estimators thought that some further expansion was likely, probably to have a more credible deterrent to any Chinese incursions. They also thought that the Soviets might choose to meet that objective by undertaking some reductions in the West.

Concerning the thrust toward general nuclear war in the Soviet offensive posture in the West, the authors of NIE 11-4-72 considered whether the Soviets might see some advantage in moving toward a strategy of graduated response, that is, one with less emphasis upon offensive and more on defensive weaponry, and one counseling the application of only such force—conventional or nuclear—necessary to maintain or restore the status quo ante. But they also recognized that most Soviet authorities believed it would be difficult, if not impossible, to limit the use of nuclear weapons to the immediate battlefield. They thought, therefore, that the Soviets would be unlikely to move in that direction. Hence, Soviet strategy seemed likely, for the immediate future, to remain caught in the dilemma of having deployed forces in Europe which could not be used without high risk of setting off a general nuclear war.

The most important issue in Soviet military policy was not, however, Eurasian strategy and deployment. It was to determine the most appropriate means to ensure continuance of the newly won parity with the United States in strategic nuclear power. There were, no doubt, those in the USSR—as there were in the United States—who wanted to charge ahead with building more and better strategic nuclear weapons. Likewise, there no doubt were those who argued against programs and deployments that would upset the strategic balance. The estimate concluded that for the immediate future the Soviets would try to stabilize that relationship through negotiations.

Much would depend upon the SALT (strategic arms limitation talks) and ABM (anti-ballistic missile) negotiations then going on. But the authors of NIE 11-4-72 concluded that whatever the outcome of the talks, military research and development (R&D) would go on; the Soviets were highly respectful of U.S. R&D and would not want to fall behind in any aspect of strategic power again.

The estimate covered another aspect of Soviet military policy which deserves exposition here, namely, whether the Soviets would carry out in a "consistent manner" programs that would enable them to project military power into distant areas. The situation as of March 1972 was described in the estimate this way: "The Soviets now have substantial ground, air, and naval forces which can be used to establish their *presence* in distance areas. This capability enables them to support political forces friendly to their policies and influence. It may make it possible in some situations to preempt the actions of others or to deter their intervention. But Soviet capabilities *to use force* at long range against opposition are limited."

The question the writers of NIE 11-4-72 were asking themselves was whether, having attained nuclear parity, the Soviets would be able to exercise wider political and military options in distant areas in the years ahead. They did not think that the Soviet deficiencies for operations in distant areas could be easily overcome, and they further noted that up to 1972 the Soviets had acted with great caution in establishing facilities for their naval and air power in foreign countries. The estimate went on: "Of the countries which could offer both the location and the kind of facilities the Soviets might want, few would be politically willing to grant bases."

A few months after that estimate was completed, a new problem for the Soviets arose in the one place where they had established a substantial presence, namely Egypt. President Sadat, during the year or two preceding the U.S.-Soviet summit, had been trying to get the Soviets to help him modernize his forces in order to put him in a better position to negotiate Israeli territorial withdrawals. Finally, in July 1972, in an apparent fit of anger, Sadat ordered all Soviet military personnel and their dependents (some 40,000 in all) to leave the country forthwith. Had he expected some friendly gesture from the United States for this anti-Soviet action, he was mistaken. He got none. And the Israelis simply began to harden their position. Early in 1973, with the détente documents in place, the Soviets changed their minds. They evidently decided that Sadat's troubles provided an opportunity to recoup their position in Egypt and also to warn the Israelis that it might profit them to be a little more agreeable to the Arabs. The Soviets began a major resupply of modern weapons to both Egypt and Syria.

Then, in July 1973, the UN Security Council helped Sadat by passing a resolution deploring Israel's continued occupation of Arab territories. The vote was thirteen to one with one abstention (China). The U.S. vote against, however, constituted a veto. Israel continued its occupation of Arab territories, and the arms deliveries to Egypt and Syria continued to mount. Arab military leaders started to draw up battle plans, By September, signs of impending conflict became obvious. The Yom Kippur War began on October 6, 1973, on both the Egyptian and the Syrian fronts.[4]

The Yom Kippur War: A Test for Détente

It is still not entirely clear which side actually began the hostilities. Certainly the major ground action was initiated by the Egyptians and Syrians. The Israelis were not adequately prepared for a major assault, and the Arabs made impressive gains both in the Sinai and on the Golan Heights. Within a few days, however, the Israelis were fighting back effectively. They found a weak spot in the Egyptian line in the Sinai, poured tanks through it, and even crossed the Canal. By October 17, eleven days after the fighting began, it looked as if the Israelis were on their way to another stunning victory. But both the Egyptians and the Israelis were in trouble. The Israelis had suffered heavy losses of men and materiel, and the Egyptians looked to be on the verge of disaster.[5]

---

4. Most of the historical data in this and the preceding paragraph is drawn from William R. Polk, *The Arab World Today* (Cambridge: Harvard University Press, 1991).
  5. Ibid., 262.

All parties at that point, including the United States and the USSR, were faced with critical decisions. A year earlier, in May 1972, Presidents Nixon and Brezhnev had signed "détente" agreements in Moscow pledging, among other things, to do "their utmost to avoid military confrontations and to prevent the outbreak of nuclear war." They also promised to exchange views on problems of mutual interest, and each now had a client state crying for help. The situation which confronted them in October 1973 was not exactly what the two powers had in mind in May 1972. A team of journalists from the *Sunday Times* (London) made an extensive and objective study of the interests of the parties involved. It outlined those interests as follows:

> Kissinger wanted a limited Israeli defeat. The nicety lay in calculating the optimum scale of defeat: big enough to satisfy the Arabs; modest enough to preclude a propaganda triumph for the Russians; sobering enough to bring Israel to the conference table; bearable enough to avoid the collapse of Mrs. Meir's government and its replacement by rightwing intransigents.[6]

I wrote in my 1970 world situation memorandum that "things could get beyond the capacities" of the USSR and the United States to control them. They did. The Israeli breakthrough on the Egyptian front certainly spoiled the Kissinger dream. It also foreshadowed one of the "new Israeli victories" which we wrote in 1968 would happen if there were a new Arab-Israeli war. What then ensued has been fully and carefully reported in Walter Isaacson's biography of Kissinger. Here I am selectively recounting the events relating to U.S. and Soviet actions in the crisis which followed.

On October 19, two days after Israeli forces broke through the Egyptian line, Brezhnev cabled the Soviet embassy in Washington with a request that Kissinger come to Moscow to negotiate an immediate cease-fire. Kissinger went. President Nixon sent him cabled instructions to work out with the Soviets a comprehensive peace plan to be imposed upon the Arabs and the Israelis by the United States and the USSR. Kissinger ignored Nixon's instructions and negotiated a cease-fire. The UN Security Council approved a cease-fire resolution on October 22, and Kissinger flew to Israel to explain what he had done. The Israelis did not want to stop fighting when they were so far ahead, and they didn't. The Soviets and the Egyptians felt deceived. Sadat on October 24 asked that U.S. and Soviet troops be sent in to enforce the

6. Cited in ibid., 261.

cease-fire. On the same day, the Soviets notified Kissinger that the USSR would support a UN resolution calling for U.S. and Soviet troops to be introduced to support the cease-fire. Kissinger told Ambassador Dobrynin that the United States would oppose any Soviet attempt to send troops to the area. Brezhnev responded that if the United States did not agree to acting cooperatively, the USSR would take "appropriate steps unilaterally." The crisis sharpened.

In Washington, the Watergate scandal, the Saturday Night Massacre, and rising cries for impeachment had so distracted President Nixon that Kissinger and General Haig (White House Chief of Staff) decided not to consult with him. They convened a rump NSC group in Kissinger's office at the State Department on October 25. The group decided to ask Sadat to withdraw his request for troops to enforce a cease-fire. They sent a message to Brezhnev rejecting the idea of injecting either U.S. or Soviet troops into the region. They then capped their consultation by placing all U.S. nuclear forces and troops on a worldwide nuclear alert. The alert soon became public knowledge here and abroad and frightened a lot of people.[7]

Sadat came to the rescue by withdrawing his request for U.S. and Soviet troops and proposed instead the creation of a UN peacekeeping force. On the following day, Brezhnev also responded. Isaacson characterized the Brezhnev response as follows: "It simply ignored all of the overnight hullabaloo and politely accepted an American suggestion that nonmilitary observers rather than soldiers should be sent in. The Soviets, Brezhnev added, were happy to do this in conjunction with the United States. He ended by expressing hope that such cooperation would continue."[8] So once again a U.S.-Soviet crisis ended with a Soviet concession and a demonstration that the Soviet leaders did not want any conflict of interest to lead to a military confrontation. The outcome showed that the U.S.-Soviet détente agreements were still alive and well.

"Cooperation" is hardly the word to describe U.S. relations with the Arabs during the crisis. On October 17, the day the Israelis broke through the Egyptian line, the Persian Gulf members of OPEC (the Organization of Oil Exporting Countries) were meeting in Kuwait, and—without the Iranian delegate present—voted an embargo on oil shipments to the United States and Europe until UN Resolution 242 was implemented. (Resolution 242 called

---

7. This and the preceding paragraph are based on Walter Isaacson, *Kissinger: A Biography* (New York: Simon & Schuster, 1992), 524–31.
8. Ibid., 532.

upon the Israelis to return the Arab lands they had seized in the 1967 war.) King Faisal of Saudi Arabia argued for moderation and sent to his ambassador in Washington which instructions to call upon President Nixon and urge him to work for a settlement in the Near East. But the day after the interview, Nixon asked Congress to appropriate $2.2 billion to supply arms to Israel. (The U.S. Air Force airlifted 22,300 tons in thirty-three days during the 1973 war. The highest previous annual provision of arms to Israel was in 1971 and amounted to $600 million, and that was seven times as much as ever given in the Johnson administration.) King Faisal regarded the Nixon request to Congress as a personal insult and an outright rejection of his overture. On October 20 Saudi Arabia suspended oil shipments to the United States.[9] Within days, long lines appeared outside U.S. gasoline stations, and the American public quickly became angry at the Arabs. It took a year of intense diplomatic effort to bring a modicum of order into Israel's relations with its neighbors and to restore a working relationship between the United States and the Arab states of the Near East.

It was not an especially remarkable feat of forecasting to have suggested in 1968 and 1970 that a new Arab-Israeli war was likely to occur. Still, we did forecast such a war, and we also predicted that the Israelis would have a more difficult time of it than they had had in 1967. One would expect that American policymakers would have made sincere and resourceful efforts to forestall a new war and to develop some kind of long-term program to resolve the problem. Secretary of State William Rogers did just that. But economic, demographic, and cultural problems, plus historical claims and anomalies, and the intensity of feeling on both sides, all militated against his success.

Yet U.S. policymakers did not, during the five years after the 1968 estimate was issued, utilize the opportunities available to try to surmount those difficulties. They did not, for example, try to capitalize on the strains between Egypt and the USSR which had materialized after the 1967 war. They did not try hard enough to reestablish a working relationship with Egypt and with President Sadat after the Soviet military advisers were expelled. They consistently overestimated Soviet influence in Egypt and Syria, and they dismissed the intelligence community view that the Soviets were anxious to avoid confrontations with the United States. They were oversuspicious of the leaders and policies of the revolutionary regimes, and they failed to explore opportunities to improve relations with those regimes and to influence their policies. They extended—especially during the Nixon years—so much mil-

9. Polk, *Arab World Today*, 262–63, 413n.

itary and economic aid to Israel as to encourage the Arabs to believe that the United States was supporting an Israeli plan to seize additional Arab lands. U.S. policymakers appeared to have selected the Shah's regime in Iran as their chosen instrument for maintaining U.S. access to the oil of the Persian Gulf region. They failed to exert pressure on the Israelis to the extent necessary to encourage them to be less truculent and more compassionate in dealing with the Palestinian Arabs.

The Early 1970s   A New World Environment

Changes and Challenges Ahead

Following upon the political and military analysis in the memorandum "The World Situation in 1970," I wrote some reflections upon the broader social, political, and economic problems that world leaders would face in the decade or two that lay ahead. The quarter-century since the end of World War II had witnessed numerous wars, threats of war, and rumors of war. Yet during those years the world had not only escaped another world conflict, but it was moving toward a structure of world power and a U.S.-Soviet relationship that boded well for the future. Détente had kept the two great powers from a nuclear conflict, but would this encouraging outlook persist? Was the world changing so fast that it was basically unstable? Could its statesmen cope? The paragraphs that follow are selections from my reflections on those questions.

The various international contests going on will be affected by many things that are unpredictable. Events often have a way of turning apparent victories into defeats and vice versa. The apparently insoluble may suddenly become soluble. Leaders die or are assassinated; new leaders and movements suddenly emerge from latent or unidentified political forces.

But the world is also being changed by forces more fundamental than those which happen by chance or by the calendar. Ideologies articulated a hundred years ago have less appeal, and material comforts are more widely sought and cherished. Advances in technology, especially in communications, have caused individuals to believe that they have rights as persons they did not know they possessed or had reason to believe could be realized; many sanctions of the old order are being challenged. The conduct of war and the well-practiced ways of enforcing compliance with governmental edict are being exposed, debated, and contested.

The rapid urbanization in world population which is occurring in the last half of this century will be important largely because of what it is doing to cities, rather than because of the increase in total numbers. Cities will grow enormously, partly because less labor will be needed in rural areas. Hopes for some improvement in personal status—as against hopelessness in many rural areas—and the illusory attractions of the city will draw large populations even where there is no visible employment opportunity. This will create grave problems in housing, sanitation, medical care, education, transport, crime, etc. Most of these needs will not be met.

As a result of this rapid urbanization of the world's population, and the failure or inability to cope with it, there will be an increasing complaint about "the system" and a rather considerable revolutionary potential. This seems likely to be non-ideological in character, though ideologues will try to make something of it. And it seems likely to be world-wide rather than confined to the underdeveloped or poverty-stricken economies.

Related to the complaints of the urban poor is the growing dissidence of students, intellectuals, many workers, and even middle classes. This arises from the inability or unwillingness of governments to cope with problems affecting them—outmoded educational systems, antiquated laws, unresponsive bureaucracies, inadequate urban transportation, fossilized wage structures and business management, unfair taxes, and the like. Most of these people do not want revolution, they just want things done so that they can live better, and they tend to think that much of what politicians and government leaders talk about and devote their energies to is simply irrelevant and self-serving. It is not possible to state just what this kind of attitude will do to the political system, but it does possess a potential for social conflict, particularly if these non-poor dissenters and the urban poor should be driven to work together.

Anti-establishmentarianism has already taken violent form in the U.S., UK, France, Italy, Germany, India, Pakistan, Mexico, Brazil, Argentina, Japan, China, to name only the larger nations. Even when it embraces only middle and upper class elements, it throws a fright into political leaders—of both the incumbents and the opposition. And it particularly upsets those who have some stake in society, but not enough to feel secure.

Some of this violence will take the form of ethnic (socio-religious) and racial violence of the type now going on [i.e., in 1969 and 1970] in Palestine, Nigeria, Southeast Asia, the white-dominated areas of South Africa, and the United States. In some cases ethnic or racial violence proceeds, not from ethnic or racial difference in themselves, but from resentments and fears based upon the political predomi-nance, economic privileges, foreign occupation, and group cultural or commercial achievement.

Rapid technological change also creates problems in foreign and military policy. Fears of falling behind, efforts to steal or copy some one else's technological know-how, embargoes and security controls and efforts to circumvent them have all become commonplace in the life of nations. One of the main problems of the next decade will be to ensure that one is not living in a false and complacent para-dise nor wasting one's resources in a vain effort to do the hopeless or unnecessary.

The abundance of economic, social, and political problems which the large nations of the world have come to face raises the question of whether modern life may not have become too complicated to cope with in large political units. The nations with the most advanced tech-nology or the largest populations seem to be having the greatest prob-lems—China, the USSR, the U.S., India, Indonesia. The small modern countries—the Scandinavian and the Low Countries—seem better able to treat with youth, technological change, poverty, inflation, and the like. Since the problem of coping seems to apply to democrat and dictator, capitalist and socialist alike, it is not a simple question of political or economic philosophy. Handling some problems requires managing people in ways that require their cooperation—and a coop-eration which they are not always prepared to give. So, the years ahead could see both failures to cope and a search for new ways to govern states and manage their economies.

A Revolutionary Age

The "Changes and Challenges" described above were not explicitly limited to particular countries or regions; the language used was designed to imply that while changes and challenges would not be universal, they were nevertheless prone to occur worldwide. There had been political violence in many countries, great and small, and—while the causes might vary—political violence seemed likely occur again and again. We in the United States saw a revolutionary spirit arise within many student communities during the years of the Vietnam War, and we saw many American students also protest against a social and political system that had led the country into the war and then used conscripted troops to fight it. Student and intellectual protest, for one cause or another, indeed became widespread in the world during the 1960s and 1970s.

During the 1960s and 1970s it was in Eastern Europe where intellectual and student groups instigated the most significant revolutionary changes. The most active political ferment took place in Czechoslovakia. Alienation of students and the intellectual elite from the Communist political structure is now well documented. Many Czechs had joined the Communist Party in the wake of World War II because of disillusionment over the Western sacrifice of their country to Nazi Germany in 1938 and 1939. But in the decade after 1955, intellectuals increasingly began to criticize the Communist regime. At the Fourth Congress of the Writers Union in June 1967, members openly attacked the Communist Party leadership and demanded changes in government policies and practices. In November 1967, university students staged a march through Prague complaining about the lack of light and heat in their rooms. Many were arrested and beaten. The brutality of the police was widely criticized, and the government actually admitted that it had made a mistake.[1]

The hard-liners in the Czechoslovak Communist Party had more and more trouble controlling the situation in the Party in the spring of 1968, and they began to appeal to the Soviets to intervene. As I mentioned earlier, there was considerable debate within the Soviet Presidium about what to do. It now seems quite clear that a decisive role in that debate was played by the Soviet secret police (KGB). Mark Kramer, in his study "The Prague Spring and the Soviet Invasion of Czechoslovakia," has written that the ferment in Czechoslovakia was causing problems for "every department and branch" of

1. Jan F. Triska, "Czechoslovakia: A Case Study in Social and Political Development," in *The Changing Face of Communism in Eastern Europe*, ed. Peter A Toma (Tucson: Arizona University Press, 1970), 175–76.

the KGB. Its most subservient agents in the Czech secret police, for example, had been removed from their positions. There was fear of a "spillover" into the USSR itself and especially into the Ukraine. Reformist influence had even spread into the Czech armed forces, and that added to KGB concerns. It was, wrote Kramer, "the perception within the KGB that the Prague Spring was a threat to the external and internal security of the Soviet Union." In its quest for arguments in favor of military intervention, the KGB even carried out covert operations designed to create the illusion of a threat of an impending CIA-sponsored coup. KGB agents posing as tourists planted caches of American arms in the German border area, so that they could be discovered and played up in the Soviet press as evidence of CIA plans. Despite such provocations, there was still opposition to the invasion by some of those ordered to carry it out. A few soldiers committed suicide, and others were sentenced to death for refusing to go along with the invasion armies.[2]

Czech intellectuals, students, and party reformists were, of course, crushed by the invasion and by the oppressive puppet government then imposed by the Soviets. But the message of the Czech reformist movement, like that of the Hungarian explosion of a dozen years earlier, did not go unheard in the USSR. As I noted earlier, Yuri Andropov—himself the chief of the KGB— took note of the impact of the Prague Spring upon the attitudes of Soviet students and passed on to the Party's Central Committee members a report about the great interest Soviet students were taking in the creation of opposition parties. Moreover, Andrei Sakharov has said that he and other dissidents had taken "inspiration" from the Czech reforms.[3]

Beyond the spread of dissent among students and intellectuals, something else started to happen in the USSR. There began an ongoing debate among party intellectuals about how to deal with "the scientific-technological revolution"—or STR, as it came to be called. The basic premise of the STR theorists in the USSR was that in the twentieth century the application of advanced science and technology to production—in the form of nuclear power, automation, and computers—could transform the human condition.

As explained by Cyril Black, onetime professor of history and director of the Center for International Studies at Princeton University, the Soviet STR theorists saw the ultimate "socialist" victory as dependent not upon class conflict or military victory, but rather on the question of who had the superior

2. Drawn from Kramer, "The Prague Spring and the Soviet Invasion of Czechoslovakia," 2–10, passim.
3. Ibid., 7.

society to develop and apply advanced science and technology. They pushed not only for innovation in production but also for a decentralized economic structure and greater institutional pluralism across the board. They established numerous "science-production associations" in the USSR to bypass the slow clearance procedures of the central bureaucracy and to bring technology, design, and production into closer association. Although STR theorists did not openly challenge Marxist-Leninist doctrine, in effect they challenged the primacy of party controls and the overlapping of party controls with governmental structure and industrial experimentation.[4]

The STR movement did not start in the USSR but in Eastern Europe, primarily in Czechoslovakia, East Germany, Poland, and Hungary. The Soviet system was a tough nut to crack with any new idea which threatened the old guard's political control. But the ideas generated within the scientific and technological communities during the 1960s and 1970s no doubt eased acceptance of Mikhail Gorbachev's perestroika during the late 1980s. Finally, of course, in the 1990s there were general political and economic revolutions throughout Eastern Europe which wiped out political oppression and intellectual stagnation.

While Czech students were being suppressed in Prague in the spring of 1968, a student revolt in France came close to toppling the Gaullist regime. It began in Paris in March and spread to universities and secondary schools all over the country. It involved street fighting, the use of fire bombs, and clashes with police. Police brutality then created widespread sympathy for the students, and in mid-May there was a march of 800,000 students in Paris. There was no single political allegiance guiding the protesters; some raised the red flag of Communism, and some raised the black flag of Anarchism. The student protests were primarily against the educational system, but some of them also demanded a "revolutionary transformation" of "bourgeois society." The Communist establishment had little sympathy for the students, but many industrial workers got caught up in the movement and staged sit-down strikes demanding reduced hours, better wages, better retirement, and a voice in management. President de Gaulle appeared genuinely frightened, and there were calls for his resignation. He ran off to West Germany to secure the backing of the commander of the French occupation forces there for his plan to dissolve parliament and call new elections.

---

4. Drawn from Cyril E. Black, "The Impact of U.S.-Soviet Trade on Soviet Society," in *Common Sense in U.S.-Soviet Trade*, ed. Willard C. Matthias (Washington, D.C.: American Committee on East-West Accord, 1979), 108–11, passim.

In the campaign for the June parliamentary elections which followed, de Gaulle appealed to students and workers by promoting "participation," a political-socioeconomic scheme designed to replace both communism and capitalism. Workers and students supported his party; conservatives were not enamored of his plan to replace capitalism with "participation," but voted for his party anyway in fear of a student-worker revolution. The Gaullist party did win an increased majority, and with it the crisis ended. De Gaulle's political reforms, however, ran into strong opposition in the new parliament. He then appealed to the public in a referendum, but he failed to get a solid endorsement and resigned.[5]

In the United States, student protests were essentially protests against the war in Vietnam. They began in earnest after a violent police response to student demonstrations at the Democratic National Convention in Chicago in the summer of 1968, and they reached a peak with a huge demonstration in Washington in the spring of 1970.

Most of the protests had a strong anti-military coloration. The military were distrusted because they viewed all wars—as they had World War II—as something to be "won" and viewed "winning" as the unconditional surrender or utter destruction of the declared enemy. Moreover, the protesters believed that the war needed to be terminated lest, to use Henry Kissinger's words, it "whet the government's appetite for further foreign adventures."[6] The high draft calls and the casualties among conscripts, the disdain of the political and military leadership for the arguments of the protesters, and the callousness of the U.S. military leaders in determining strategy and measuring their military successes in terms of body count—all those raised questions about the morality of U.S. political and military leaders. Young people in particular felt powerless when called upon to support and fight a war into which the United States had stumbled without clear reasons and without consulting the people's representatives. All such thoughts and emotions, and especially the outrage at sending American youths into battle for a questionable cause, prompted many youths to question the whole fabric of a society that had taught them that American causes had always been noble. A large sector of American youth came to believe that their country had departed from its moral roots. And so they turned against the U.S. political, military, and educational systems and shook them to their foundations.

---

5. This paragraph and the preceding one were drawn from Joel Coulton, "The Fifth Republic," in the *Encyclopedia Americana*, 11:803–4.

6. Quotation taken from Henry Kissinger's description of the Peace Movement in his *Diplomacy*, 688.

Like France, where student protests led to President de Gaulle's resignation, so their protests contributed to President Johnson's decision not to seek another term of office in 1968. When students saw President Nixon resort to unlawful means to combat antiwar sentiment, their protests spread to other groups and ultimately led to his resignation.

In our 1968 World Situation estimate, we took note of the traumatic events of that spring in France and the antiwar protests in the United States, and we thought those events signified something new in the Western world's political history. We wrote:

> There appears to have arisen a nagging and sometimes widespread annoyance with the whole business of parties and politicians, of priests and parliaments. Antagonism to present ideologies and political processes appears most stark in the discontent and even alienation of growing numbers of younger people and students. This discontent has broader causes than student grievances against university regulations or opposition to the Vietnam war, and it is not confined to those young people who participate in demonstrations or who have ostentatiously dropped out. It is an attitude held by many of the brightest and most capable among college and university students. We think this will not prove to be a transient phenomenon. Certainly some students will abandon their present attitudes as they leave the university and enter upon working and family responsibilities. But a large proportion will, we believe, hold to the conviction that sweeping changes must be undertaken quickly in their societies.

But there has been no major political or social revolution in the United States or France since the late sixties and early seventies. But there have been important changes. In France, reforms of the educational system were adopted, and an agreement was reached with labor which provided for substantial wage increases and concessions on working hours and retirement. De Gaulle was succeeded by a Conservative president, Georges Pompidou, but the Socialist Party began to acquire increased political support. In 1981 France elected a Socialist president, François Mitterrand, and reelected him seven years later. In the United States, one president, Lyndon Johnson, left office rather than face defeat in the 1968 presidential election, and his successor, Richard Nixon, resigned in 1974 to avoid removal from office for illegal actions designed to discredit critics of his Vietnam policy. He had in fact reduced U.S. troop strength, and the Viet Cong and the invading DRV forces had won battle after battle against the faltering South Vietnamese army and finally seized Saigon in 1975.

Those political changes in the United States and France took place more or less concurrently with social changes that reflected an altered outlook on the part of both the "baby boomers" and their maturing parents. Women moved into a much more important role in the business, intellectual, and government communities. A sexual revolution occurred that gave women greater freedom to leave unhappy marriages and to contract temporary liaisons or permanent marriages on the basis of equality with men. The advance of technology led to the greater use of computers and communications equipment; this widened the social and intellectual horizons of millions of people in the advanced countries. Technological progress and its impact upon the social and economic structures of the advanced nations is still multiplying, with political consequences still not clear.

With the fading of the Communist empire and a reduced fear of Communism at home and abroad, Western power establishments have reasserted their predominance. The former protesters and revolutionaries are still out there, but they are hardly a majority force. Whether they can combat the rampant cupidity of the post-Communist era by moral suasion alone, or whether there must be a return to government enforcement of more rigid rules of conduct for Western society and commerce, will be one of the main concerns of the new millennium.

A Glimpse at the Year 2000

In the spring of 1969, with the beginning of a new decade approaching, the world seemed considerably less dangerous than it had even in 1964, when I concluded that year's World Trends memorandum with the encouraging words that while the world was still "replete with strife and disorder" it was "not on the verge of nuclear disaster." I wondered whether it might be possible to write something useful about the state of the world in the year 2000— some thirty years hence. I decided to put a few ideas on the subject to the Office's Panel of Consultants, which was about to have its semiannual meeting. It had been enlarged and consisted of academics and retired foreign service officers with a variety of regional specialties, along with a number of generalists. I included in their packet of papers a memorandum asking some questions on how we might go about drafting an estimate on the year 2000.

It seemed to me that one should, along with looking at the great powers, give major attention to factors that would be the mainspring of national policies and politics wherever those factors would matter. I thought a listing of mainsprings ought to include the size and age distribution of populations, the pace and impact of the continuing revolution in communications, likely technological advances, the revolt of youth, the decline in religious values, urbanization, and likely changes in the size and character of elites. I then appended "a tentative set of hypotheses" about some of the major factors; I am quoting them here:

a. The size of populations and their growth rate are not so important as the age distribution within those populations, and the relation of that size and age distribution to the natural and human resources confined within a nation's boundaries.

b. Growth of GNP or even of investment is not so important as the kind of investment or the character of the elite or the numbers of people being educated and what they are being taught.

c. Technological growth — except in the area of mass media communication — is not so important as the social and political capacity of a people to absorb it and use it.

d. The most important factor in determining the future will be the progress of the knowledge explosion. I mean this not in the sense of an explosion of information for decision-making, but in the sense of an explosion in an individual's *awareness* of events, history, conflicts of ideas, living standards, etc.

e. The rate of urbanization and of the knowledge explosion is breaking down established social, political, moral, and religious systems everywhere, and there is little distinction among states except in timing and degree. These exceptions may prove critical.

f. The next twenty-five years will witness an appalling paradox: more people than ever in history will deplore the use of force, and more — even among those who deplore it — will be disposed to use it. This will lead to highly polarized and therefore inherently unstable societies and governments everywhere, with an increasing use of force — more often against individuals and groups than against other nations. There will be a kind of international civil war reminiscent of the 1930s.

g. From this melee the opponents of the existing order will likely emerge victorious, though not everywhere at the same time. It might be a Pyrrhic Victory; the most constructive fighters could be lost. Generally speaking, the changes will be achieved by gradualism. The powers and operations of governments will be circumscribed, and both the national and international systems will become more pluralist. There will be a sort of anarchism in which affairs will be managed increasingly by non-sovereign and non-political organizations transcending national boundaries; the state will be their enemy and gradually lose its power to control.

h. In terms of traditional international politics, foreign offices and military forces will become increasingly irrelevant, though they will remain as a kind of public welfare system gradually deprived of intelligent and capable leadership. The essential problem for the non-political men of action (by 2000 most of the educated will be these) will be how to deprive these people of their weapons and of the chance that they will use them.

I concluded the memorandum with a confession that I felt uncertain whether judgments such as those I advanced would be useful to policymakers. I added, however, that "if we could say with conviction that we are talking about the USSR as well as the West, and that indeed the Communist system as we have known it would break down into something quite different, then we would be saying something useful." I also stated that we might be saying something useful if we could conclude that "the mess" in Africa, Latin America, and the Near East would get worse.

Since I wrote those words, the Communist system of course did break down and a good deal earlier than the year 2000. Even China has become a society with aggressive state capitalist behavior. Things have improved in Latin America, but have become worse in Africa and the Near East. Western governments have lost much of their power to control cross-border finance, commerce, crime, and terror. Almost everywhere, governments are coming under attack as part of the problem rather than the solution. Ethnic and religious violence has increased in Europe and in the Near and Middle East. Military organizations are busy trying to think of useful missions, and they are so afraid of casualties that they no longer advocate foreign intervention or even peace-keeping missions. They search for *possible* foreign threats as justification for keeping their weaponry up to date, their military personnel in good morale, and their appropriated funds flowing.

In 1969, however, it was difficult for a responsible governmental organization to engage in what would have seemed to be fanciful speculation. Most policymakers and even longer-term policy planners have always had plenty of short-term problems with which to deal. We did not go ahead with the effort; almost certainly if we had done so and predicted the end of Communism "as we have known it," we would have been laughed down. Yet, it happened only twenty-two years, not thirty years, later.

The New Diplomacy

Although we strategic analysts were not prepared to indulge in speculative predictions about the year 2000, we were provided ample food for thought in events that occurred during the two years following delivery of the January 1970 memorandum to President Nixon and Henry Kissinger. Between then and the summer of 1972, considerable history was made. The culminating event was the signing of the détente agreements in Moscow on May 26, 1972. Two weeks later, on June 7, CIA Director Richard Helms delivered the opening address to the annual National Strategy Seminar describing the "new diplomacy"—in which the Moscow agreements were playing a major role. Held at the Army War College and attended by invited high military officials, academics, and journalists, it was an opportunity for Helms to report on Agency thinking about what the seminar planners called the "International Environment." He asked me, as he had in previous years, to draft his speech, and I welcomed the chance to take a fresh look at the developing world scene. Here are some excerpts from that speech:

> One of the trends of the past decade which has struck me as especially meaningful is the care which the great powers have taken to avoid dangerous confrontations with each other. In the perspective of a decade, the Cuban missile crisis of 1962 appears to have been a watershed. Then, faced with the moment of truth, the Soviet leaders chose peace. Their behavior since 1962 strongly suggests that the Cuban missile crisis was not an experience they would like to repeat. In the years since then they have shown a strong reluctance to engage in military action and a healthy appreciation of the advantages of non-confrontation. We have seen this, for example, in the Arab-Israeli conflict in 1967, the Jordan crisis of 1970, and the India-Pakistan War of 1971.
>
> The nuclear powers simply cannot afford to confront each other in particular conflict situations unless they are prepared for total nuclear struggle. This is not to say that the nuclear powers cannot and do not pursue their national interests. Indeed, the fact of mutual deterrence encourages limited and gradual pursuit of national interest. But it also imposes caution on blatant expansionism, and it discourages challenges to positions which have already been staked out. All those conditions encourage a certain stability.
>
> How should we characterize the principles of statecraft which are emerging and guiding the relations of the great powers? I would describe

them as Communication and Adjustment. In today's environment there are things that a responsible nation cannot do. And if there is something you cannot do anything about, you have to adjust to it. One must recognize what national power cannot do. One must know the range of the possible, and one must make calculations of risk. To do this, we as a nation must understand both the relations of power and the meaning of political events taking place throughout the world. The basic purpose of the intelligence community is to help with this understanding.

What is important about the kind of diplomacy which has developed over the past year or two is that chiefs of government have never talked to each other so much. Heath and Pompidou have met, as have Pompidou and Brandt, Brandt and Brezhnev, Brezhnev and Pompidou, and President Nixon with a wide range of interlocutors, including the Communist leaders in Peking and Moscow. What is happening is that cards are being laid on the table. Leaders are telling each other what their problems and interests are.

Military power plays an important role in the process of Communication and Adjustment. The size, structure, doctrine, and tactical concepts upon which a national military force operates are part of the data which an adversary examines when he tries to judge intentions. The character and magnitude of strategic offensive systems, and the balance between offensive and defensive systems, provide clues about a nation's readiness to accept mutual deterrence or to go for something more decisive. The balance between nuclear and non-nuclear components, and the balance between land-bound and far-reaching forces tell something about the degree of flexibility which a nation had provided for itself. And the extent and character of the arms control programs to which a nation is willing to commit itself tell us something about its willingness to make adjustments.

What the present international environment does is to set limits upon tensions and hostility, while communication provides a framework within which adjustments can be worked out. If communication is kept up, if the data base is shared, if power is regarded as a form of communication and not merely as a means of imposing one's will, then global non-confrontation politics will avoid nuclear disaster.

In Europe, no Western nation is about to give up the American alliance and cast itself upon the mercy of the Soviets. And the Soviets are not about to retract their power from Eastern Europe. But if adjustment proceeds in a manner not threatening to the security of established positions, perhaps a more open and relaxed Europe will arise. In East Asia, the world admitted China to the comity of nations even before President Nixon's visit, and the trip itself marked the opening of a Chinese-U.S. dialogue. The Japanese and the Soviets have begun to consider ways of resolving their differences and ways for cooperating in the exploitation of Siberia's resources. Japanese and Chinese contacts will no doubt increase. Thus, a new quadrilateral relationship—among China, Japan, the USSR, and the United States— is beginning to evolve.

There are many smaller nations which are trying to find themselves, to establish their own national identities, and to mold their own economic and social systems in a rapidly changing world. There is a strong eclecticism in their approach, and that is one of the hopeful signs of the times. This world of the developing countries no doubt will be messy at times and sometimes chaotic. Events in those areas will impinge upon relations among the great powers and create or exacerbate tensions among them.

Another factor in world relationships which is becoming increasingly decisive is economics. Modern economies, even in the Communist countries, must be finely tuned to function properly. Almost inexorably, the world is becoming a single economic unit. World trade is rapidly expanding, technology is exported, and the raw material market is now a world market. Inflation and high interest rates in one major trading nation affect employment and prices in another. Imprudent economic policy in one can cause economic stress in another. Economic relationships are becoming a curb upon national sovereignty. Even the Communist nations appear eager to broaden their economic contacts and to tap the technology and financial resources of the capitalist world, and this trend is one of the imperatives encouraging them to engage in communication and adjustment.

Looking at the world environment today, I sometimes wonder whether those of us who are concerned with national security and world politics have achieved the proper balance among the various targets of our concern. We must, of course, continue to be concerned with the military threat posed by the Communist powers, despite their increasing appreciation of the virtues of non-confrontational politics. And the widening impact of international economic relationships must also be recognized.

Perhaps more important yet, the world system as a whole seems to be encountering new pressures. Some scholars now suggest that the world system is facing rising forces which cannot be resolved by the historical solutions of migration, territorial expansion, and economic growth. Through its population growth, its rising living standards, and its technological achievements, the world is creating a load on its natural resources that may be too great. The earth, its atmosphere, its land, its fresh waters, and its minerals are finite. It would be ironic if we frittered away our time, our intellectual energy, and our capacity for commitment on assorted matters of world politics while our natural eco-systems were degenerating at a fatal pace.

Perhaps we ought to widen our definition of national security, perhaps we ought to widen it a good deal. If there is now hope that we can avoid nuclear catastrophe, the question is still open whether we are courting ecological catastrophe. If some of the warnings being addressed to us are valid, that is reason enough for the great powers to adjust their relationship with each other and move on to a new era of international cooperation.

One of the seminar guests was Stanley Karnow, author of an authoritative account of the Vietnam War and a columnist for the *Washington Post*. Karnow discussed the Helms talk in a column published on June 10. He referred to one of the principal themes in the speech, namely, increasing communication among the world's leaders, and their recognition that reaching accommodations on their differences was the only reasonable course in a world in the shadow of nuclear weapons. Karnow was also interested in the closing paragraphs of the Helms speech, which pointed out that at some time in the future the world would have to confront its ecological problems. Karnow concluded, "It may be that the cold war will be observed in retrospect as a minor interlude compared to the coming struggle for environmental salvation."

Several months later, early in August, I was telephoned by an instructor at the National War College in Washington. He reported that Henry Kissinger, still tidying up loose ends after the Moscow summit, had backed off from his commitment to deliver the opening address to the new class at the War College scheduled for August 9. He asked if I would fill in for Henry. I protested that I had written a speech which Helms had delivered in June at the Army War College, and that it had contained what new ideas I had. I put him off until I could talk with Helms. The Director said it was my speech anyway, so I should go ahead and deliver it at the National War College.

The audiences at both War Colleges appeared receptive to the overall optimistic tenor of our presentations. Indeed, during the following eighteen months, there were positive developments in U.S.-Soviet relations which justified that optimism. But détente had also, almost from the start, encountered criticism from ideologues in both Washington and Moscow. Criticisms later turned into assaults from Communist-haters in the United States and from Communist activists in Moscow and other parts of the Communist world.

Renewal of the Cold War

Détente Under Attack

The upbeat tone of the War College speeches was based upon a judgment that world politics was moving from a period of grave danger to one in which the great powers were prepared to negotiate and adjust their differences. Henry Kissinger, who had been a principal architect of that change, remarked in his book *Diplomacy* that détente had introduced a "new fluidity" to European diplomacy—"a theatre that had been virtually petrified since the final consolidation of East-West spheres of influence in 1961."[1] The détente agreements, as we have seen, had not only brought stability to the German question and cleared the road toward stabilization in strategic arms, they had also brought to a peaceful end a threatened U.S.-Soviet confrontation during the Yom Kippur War in the autumn of 1973.

Nevertheless, soon after their signing the détente, agreements ran into serious political trouble in the United States. A large part of the trouble came from conservatives who simply hated Communism. This is how Kissinger described their attitude: "Conservatives were uneasy with the number of agreements being signed with a declared enemy. They did not believe America could remain vigilant while seeming 'progress' was being made under the aegis of détente. They were convinced that American preparedness could be

---

1. Kissinger, *Diplomacy*, 733–34.

honed only by ideological militance. They wanted uncompromising verbal hostility; they sometimes seemed to prize rhetorical intransigence more than toughness in substance."[2]

In his analysis of the domestic opposition to détente, Kissinger also pointed to liberals who were complaining because détente was not being used to "change the Soviet domestic structure."[3] Their leader was Senator Henry "Scoop" Jackson, a Democrat from the state of Washington who worked closely with trade union leaders. Most U.S. trade unionists preferred to utilize unionism to improve working conditions and gain higher wages rather than trying to use it to alter the economic system. They were, therefore, largely antisocialist in political orientation. In particular, most U.S. trade union leaders were strongly antagonized by Soviet suppression of free unions in the USSR and Eastern Europe and by the behavior of Communist-dominated unions in parts of Western Europe. The Nixon administration had welcomed Jackson's support on the Vietnam War and was surprised to discover how deeply and fiercely he opposed détente. As Kissinger described it, Jackson implemented his views by "erecting a series of legislative hurdles that gradually paralyzed our East-West policy." In doing so, Kissinger added, Jackson was aided by "one of the ablest—and most ruthless—staffs I encountered in Washington." Besides trouble from the Jackson Democrats, Kissinger and Nixon were annoyed to hear from liberals who had demanded peace at any price in Vietnam but who were then clamoring "for a course whose practical consequence was to elevate confrontation into a principle of policy."[4]

The trouble from Senator Jackson arose when the U.S.-Soviet trade agreement containing a Most Favored Nation (MFN) proviso was being readied for congressional approval. Jackson had sponsored an amendment to the enabling trade bill which would deny MFN treatment to any nation that did not permit freedom of emigration. Representative Vanik of Ohio sponsored a similar amendment to the trade bill in the House of Representatives. These amendments were clearly anti-Soviet measures designed to pick up support for Jackson's anti-détente sentiments from Jewish-American politicians and the Jewish-controlled portion of the media. Jackson wanted, Kissinger has reported, a guaranteed annual minimum number of exit visas and eased emigration not only for Jews but for all nationalities;[5] he was obviously trying to craft a trade agreement that the Soviets would reject. As the issue wore on

2. Henry Kissinger, *Years of Upheaval* (Boston: Little, Brown, 1982), 983.
3. Ibid., 984.
4. Ibid., 985.
5. Ibid., 253–54.

through 1972, 1973, and 1974, Jackson picked up support in the United States and abroad from everyone who wanted to utilize détente to punish the Soviets or to oblige them to change their domestic political system. Even Andrei Sakharov sent a public letter to Senator Jackson supporting the amendment.

The trade bill was finally passed late in 1974 with the Jackson-Vanik amendment, and the Soviets rejected the trade agreement. Concerning this unhappy affair, Kissinger wrote some eight years later:

> The opponents of detente had achieved one part of their objective. They had turned what we had conceived as a safety valve into a contentious issue both domestically and vis-à-vis the Soviets. Our policy toward the Soviets was based on a balance between the carrot and the stick. But we had failed to produce MFN; we seemed to be unable to organize the financial mechanisms for even such a trade as there was — and all this despite Soviet concessions on Jewish emigration that would have been considered inconceivable a few years earlier. By the summer of 1974 the carrot had for all practical purposes ceased to exist.[6]

The constant chipping away at détente by a variety of U.S. politicians and interest groups, and particularly the prolonged efforts to find a way out of the Jewish emigration problem, tried everyone's patience, while the emerging Watergate scandal weakened Nixon's support among even his own long-standing anti-Communist constituency. By the end of 1974 the only visible sign of hope in the détente process was recollection of the role it had played in October 1973 in ending the Yom Kippur War.

There was, nevertheless, one unspectacular part of the détente process going on — even though the Nixon administration did not place much faith in it. This was the Conference on European Security and Cooperation, a Soviet-sponsored part of the summit communiqué. The conference was large; it contained thirty-five nations of Europe and America. The Soviets were anxious to have all of the participating nations agree on existing borders, even though most of them had been previously agreed to in other treaties and agreements. The negotiations seemed endless, but agreement was finally reached early in 1975. In addition to agreeing on borders, the signatories agreed to a section on human rights, which the Western negotiators had urged and which they hoped would curb Soviet repression. President Ford went to Helsinki to sign the Final Act, a deed for which he was roundly criticized. Just before

6. Ibid., 997–98.

the signing, the *New York Times* wrote that "the 35-nation Conference on Security and Cooperation in Europe, now nearing its climax after 32 months of semantic quibbling, should not have happened. Never have so many struggled for so long over so little."[7] Kissinger himself finally had to admit the value of the Helsinki Accords when he concluded in 1994 that they had "moderated Soviet conduct" while in the planning stages and that afterward "they had accelerated the collapse of the Soviet Empire."[8]

The ideologues on each side proved more resilient than détente's supporters had believed. The world had been longing for peace after the tensions of the postwar era, the threatening intentions which both the United States and the USSR ascribed to the other, and the obvious piling up of nuclear weapons. So it was a great relief to have witnessed the Moscow summit of May 1972 and to have read the détente agreements and communiqués. The ensuing process did indeed ease tensions as a practical matter, but it did little to bring on board the ideologues on both sides who continued to stand ready—at least rhetorically—to continue the conflict. Nikolai V. Podgorny, then president of the Soviet Union, put the Soviet position this way:

> As the Soviet people see it, a just and democratic world cannot be achieved without the national and social liberation of peoples. The struggle by the Soviet Union for the relaxation of international tensions, for peaceful coexistence among states and different systems does not represent, and cannot represent, a departure from the class principles of our foreign policy.[9]

Kissinger himself had always been impatient with the questions of Soviet "intentions" and "ultimate aims" which were so important to ideologues and military intelligence officers. Wondering whether each new move was "a prelude to a global showdown"—as Truman, Acheson, and their military advisers had done during the early postwar years—was in his view "irrelevant." Instead one should look at Soviet practice. "Nothing could be more mistaken than to fall in with the myth of an inexorable Soviet advance carefully orchestrated by some super-planners," he wrote.[10] At the same time, however, Kissinger also affirmed:

7. Cited in Kissinger, *Diplomacy*, 760.
8. Ibid.
9. Kissinger, *White House Years*, 117.
10. Ibid., 120.

Efforts to reduce the danger of nuclear war had to be linked to an end of the constant Soviet pressure against the global balance of power. We were dedicated to peaceful coexistence. We were equally determined to defend the balance of power and the values of freedom. If we fulfilled *our* responsibility to block Soviet encroachments, coexistence could be reliable and the principles of détente could be seen to have marked the path to a more peaceful future.[11]

There lay the rub. One side wanted to expand the Communist world, peacefully, and the other side wanted to confine it—peacefully. A kind of "cool" war was therefore bound to continue, but it needed to be kept cool and localized; it could not be allowed to get "hot" and lead to a U.S.-Soviet confrontation. In any event, military power needed to be balanced and diplomatic exchanges kept open, so that neither side would come to believe that its existence was threatened.

The Angolan Affair

Soviet ambassador Anatoly Dobrynin opened one chapter of his memoir on the Nixon-Ford period in U.S. foreign policy with this sentence: "If any one point of controversy over regional conflicts soured Americans on détente, it was Angola, a country on the Atlantic coast just under the bulge of Africa which few Americans and probably fewer Russians had ever heard of before."[12] In December 1975, a little over a year after he had assumed the presidency, President Gerald Ford called in Dobrynin to discuss Angola. According to the ambassador's report, Ford said he was not interested in Angola from a strategic point of view, but that events there were "being perceived by Americans and played up by the media as a test for the policy of detente."[13] Ford mentioned Soviet arms shipments to Angola and the transport of Cuban troops to support one faction in a struggle to control the country. The United States was supporting another faction, and Ford asked, "Was it really necessary for both our countries to challenge each other in such a faraway place which was of no particular value to either of them?"[14]

Dobrynin reported the conversation to Brezhnev, who replied a week later. Dobrynin described the reply as follows:

11. Ibid., 125.
12. Dobrynin, *In Confidence*, 360.
13. Ibid., 361.
14. Ibid.

What was happening in Angola was not a civil war, but direct foreign intervention, and on the part of South Africa in particular. . . . Peacemaking had to be focused on jointly stopping foreign intervention, and the Soviet Union was not interested in viewing the events in Angola through the prism of "confrontation between Moscow and Washington" or "as a test of detente policy."[15]

A few days later, Kissinger discussed the matter with Dobrynin again and proposed referring it to the Organization of African States as a "face-saving" way out. Kissinger, Dobrynin wrote, did not care "who won"; he just wanted the winner to do so without the "outside help of a superpower."[16]

Then, in January 1976, Kissinger was in Moscow for several days of negotiations and "pleaded for a Soviet gesture to ease the superpower confrontation in Angola." According to a report by Jim Hershberg in the 1996/1997 winter issue of the *Bulletin of the Cold War International History Project*, recently declassified transcripts of those talks indicate that Brezhnev and Gromyko rebuffed Kissinger's "entreaties" with the response that "any complaints should be taken up with Havana, since Cuban intervention was the result of decisions made between two sovereign states, Angola and Cuba, and the USSR could not speak for them."[17] The same *Bulletin* issue contains two extensive reports on what happened before 1976 which shed some light upon the Soviet claims.

A study of Cuban involvement in Africa from 1959 to 1976 by Piero Gleijeses, which appeared in the issue of the *Bulletin* cited above, indicates that Cuban interest in Africa long pre-dated the Angolan affair. The Cubans saw similarities between their own revolution and that of the Algerians against French rule during the late 1950s and early 1960s. In December 1961, for example, they unloaded a cargo of weapons for the Algerians at a Moroccan port and brought back to Cuba wounded fighters and Algerian children from refugee camps. Later, in 1963 when Algeria was threatened by Morocco, Cuba sent to Algeria a military force of 686 men with heavy weapons. By 1964, the Cubans came to believe that "revolution beckoned" in Africa; there were guerrillas fighting against the Portuguese in Angola, Portuguese-Guinea (now Guinea-Bissau), and Mozambique. There was also a revolutionary regime in Congo-Brazzaville, and "above all, there was Congo-Leopoldville

15. Ibid.
16. Ibid.
17. See "The Cold War in the Third World and the Collapse of Détente in the 1970's," *Bulletin of the Cold War International History Project*, no. 8-9 (Winter 1996–97): 1.

(later called Zaire) where armed revolt had been spreading with alarming speed since the spring of 1964, threatening the survival of the corrupt pro-American regime that Presidents Eisenhower and Kennedy had laboriously put in place."[18] In order to save the Congo regime of Mobuto Sese Seko, the following took place, as recorded by Gleijeses:

> The Johnson Administration raised an army of more than 1,000 white mercenaries in a major covert operation that was obvious to all but the U.S. press and provoked a wave of revulsion even among African leaders friendly to the United States. The Cubans saw the conflict as more than an African problem: "Our view was that the situation in the Congo was a problem that concerned all mankind," Guevara wrote.
>
> In December 1964, Guevara went to Africa on a three month trip that signaled Cuba's growing interest in the region. In February 1965, he was in Dar-es-Salaam, Tanzania, which was then, as the Central Intelligence Agency pointed out, a "haven for exiles from the rest of Africa plotting the overthrow of African governments, black and white." After a general meeting with the liberation movements, he met separately with each, and three times with Laurent Kabila and Gaston Soumialot.
>
> "[Kabila] impressed me," wrote Che. "I offered him, on behalf of our government, about thirty instructors and all the weapons we could spare, and he accepted with delight.". . . Che left Dar-es-Salaam with the joy of having found people ready to fight to the finish. Our next task was to select a group of black Cubans—all volunteers—and send them to help in the struggle for the Congo.[19]

And so it went; the Cubans wanted to help the revolutionists. But they succeeded only in Guinea-Bissau. By the time the Cubans arrived in the Congo, the CIA covert operation had succeeded, and rebel strength had been broken. U.S. intelligence apparently knew a good deal about what the Cubans were up to, but did not worry very much about them. Gleijeses referred to a CIA national intelligence estimate of November 1967 on Communist subversion in Africa, which, as he put it, "barely mentioned Cuba."[20] Over the next several years, indeed up to the end of 1974, Cuban relations with the

---

18. The quotation and other materials in this paragraph are drawn from Piero Gleijeses, "Havana's Policy in Africa 1959–76: New Evidence from Cuban Archives," *Bulletin of the Cold War International History Project*, no. 8-9 (Winter 1996–97), 5–13.

19. Ibid.

20. Ibid., 7.

Angolan revolutionists whom Guevara had dealt with at Dar-es-Salaam were friendly but not close.[21] The Popular Movement for the Liberation of Angola (MPLA), led by Agostino Neto, had shown interest in Cuban military instructors, and a few were sent to Cuba for training. But it was not until a group of radical Portuguese military officers overthrew the Lisbon regime in April 1974 that things in Africa and especially in Angola took on an entirely new appearance.

Almost everybody got in on the act. In December 1974, two senior Cuban officials went to Dar-es-Salaam and met with Neto and other MPLA leaders; they then went on to Angola for a two-week inspection trip.[22] Arne Westad, in another study reported in the issue of the *Bulletin* cited above, has written:

> In 1975, Fidel Castro initiated Cuban armed support for the MPLA without Moscow's agreement or knowledge, and thereby reducing the Soviet leaders' role for several crucial months to that of spectators to a war in which the Cubans and their Angolan allies gambled on prospective Soviet support to win. Although it certainly was the direction of Soviet foreign policy itself which poised Moscow for the Angolan adventure, it was Castro and MPLA President Agostino Neto who conditioned and shaped the intervention.[23]

The CIA a decade earlier had, of course, fought a covert war against Congolese rebels trying to oust Mobuto, and later it supported the National Front for the Liberation of Angola (FNLA), headed by Holden Roberto, in order to offset the more radical MPLA. In January 1975, the NSC's "Forty Committee" authorized an increase in covert support for the FNLA. It was then that the Soviet embassy in Brazzaville sent a report to Moscow which Westad has paraphrased as follows: "The Soviet Embassy . . . concluded that the American assistance would lead Holden Roberto to make an all-out bid for power very soon. The embassy experts realized that there was little the Soviet Union could do to assist the MPLA to resist the initial attacks by Roberto's forces."[24]

Roberto's forces did initiate an offensive in the early summer of 1975 along

---

21. Ibid., 7–8.
22. Ibid., 8.
23. See Odd Arne Westad, "Moscow and the Angola Crisis: A New Pattern of Intervention," *Bulletin of the Cold War International History Project*, no. 8-9 (Winter 1996–97): 21–29.
24. Ibid., 24.

the coast and in the northern part of Angola. Local MPLA forces fought back with considerable success after receiving Soviet arms. According to Westad, the Soviets reacted as follows to the new situation: "The Soviet experts did not believe that the United States would stage a massive intervention, nor did they give much credence to MPLA reports of South African or Zairean involvement. Their main worry was the Chinese, who had stepped up their FNLA assistance program from bases in Zaire. Moscow found particularly disturbing the fact that the Chinese were joined as instructors in these camps by military personnel from Rumania and North Korea."[25]

At about the same time that Roberto undertook the FNLA offensive, the NSC staff evidently believed that through covert action the United States could win a major victory in Angola before the MPLA could get the upper hand in advance of the final Portuguese withdrawal in November 1975. So, the Ford administration in mid-July authorized a large-scale covert operation to support the FNLA and UNITA (a guerrilla group led by Jonas Savimbi which had been receiving Chinese training assistance). Westad has reported: "Over three months the CIA was allocated almost $50 million to train, equip, and transport anti-MPLA troops. In early August South African forces, at first in limited numbers, crossed the border into southern Angola, while regular Zairean troops joined FNLA forces fighting in the north. By mid-August, the MPLA offensive in the north had been turned back and Neto's forces were retreating toward Luanda."[26]

That foreshadowed real trouble for the MPLA. It had a Congo-Brazzaville "connection" through which it had been receiving Soviet supplies, but that had ended after its leader quarreled with Neto. Moscow then asked Castro to intercede with the Congolese, with whom he had close relations. Castro responded with a proposal that Moscow increase its aid to the MPLA, help with the introduction of Cuban troops, and send Soviet staff officers to help in planning military operations. That upset the Soviets. Westad has reported:

> The Soviets were not pleased with the content of the Cuban plan. First of all they objected to the use of Soviet officers and even Soviet transport planes prior to independence. The Soviet leaders worried that such a move would damage the policy of detente with regard to the United States. . . . The Cubans were, in the Soviet view, not sufficiently aware of how even a Cuban intervention could upset great

25. Ibid., 25.
26. Ibid.

power relations, since the Ford administration would see Cuban forces as proxies for Soviet interests. . . .

Brezhnev flatly refused to send Soviet officers to serve with the Cubans in Angola. The Soviet General Staff opposed the Cuban operation, and even the KGB . . . warned against the effects of a direct Soviet intervention on U.S.-Soviet relations.[27]

By September, the MPLA was still in retreat, Westad reported, "hard pressed by Zairean and mercenary-led FNLA troops in the north, and UNITA forces supported by advisers and material from South Africa in the south."[28] The MPLA position and the Cuban policy were saved by one of their enemies— the South African government, which decided in October to mount a full-scale invasion of Angola.[29] When the Soviets heard of that, they decided to "infuse enough Cuban troops and Soviet advisers to defeat the South Africans." Westad also wrote, in connection with the Soviet decision: "The Soviet perception of the widening role of the CIA in assisting FNLA forces from bases in Zaire also played a role in Moscow's re-evaluation of its Angolan policy."[30]

The result was that by the end of November in 1975, the Cubans had stopped the South African advance on Luanda. The South African government then decided to withdraw because of its military failure and because the U.S. Senate voted to block all U.S. funding for operations in Angola.[31] That was when Ford and Kissinger realized that they were losing on the ground in Angola and made the approaches to Dobrynin and to Brezhnev described above.

From the accounts of the Angolan affair which appeared in the *Bulletin*, it now appears that the United States had been playing a much more activist role in West African affairs than had the USSR. It also now appears that the United States played a leading role in suppressing a leftist revolt in northern Congo-Leopoldville in 1964 and in the 1965 selection of Mobuto Sese Seko as president of the new nation, which he renamed Zaire. It also appears that Mobutu and Zaire were selected by the Americans as their chosen instrument to prevent the emergence of any revolutionary regime in West Africa which might associate itself with the USSR. And there can be no doubt that the United States had constructed and supported the FNLA as its army to

27. Ibid., 25–26.
28. Ibid., 26.
29. Ibid.
30. Ibid.
31. Ibid., 27.

capture control of Angola. Moreover, there seems to have been, at a minimum, coordination of the CIA-ordained offensive in the north with the South African incursion into southern Angola.

The role of the Soviets was muted and tardy. It is clear that the Cubans were aggressive in their support of leftist revolutions in Africa. Their romantic view of a peoples' revolt against colonialism and capitalist imperialism had appealed to Khrushchev in the late 1950s and early 1960s, and it continued to receive support among those in the Soviet leadership who regarded revolution as the road to the ultimate Communist world. The Soviets were not, as Kissinger has alleged, engaged in "constant . . . pressure against the balance of power." They were, in this case at least, responding to U.S. machinations designed to block any revolutionary movement which might have had the effect of reducing U.S. power and influence. It was a part of Kissinger's definition of détente that the Soviets would forswear fomenting or helping revolutionary movements. Because the Cubans were involved, it was assumed in the United States that the African revolts were Soviet-inspired and, if successful, would be additions to the Soviet empire.

The Angolan affair became, then, a pivotal event in U.S.-Soviet relations. Subsequent events in eastern Africa and southern Asia were seen in the same light, whatever may have been the precipitating causes or aspirations of the participants. Kissinger wrote about this in 1982 in his conclusion to the *Years of Upheaval*:

> Nations do not have the right to send proxy forces around the world because they have been denied MFN [Most Favored Nation treatment]. There is no excuse for the Soviet-Cuban expeditionary forces in Angola and Ethiopia, the Soviet encroachment in South Yemen and invasion of Afghanistan, the Kremlin's encouragement of North Vietnam's takeover of first South Vietnam and Laos and then Cambodia, and the brutal pressures on Poland. Other nations have suffered disappointments without assaulting the international order in response. Though we made our share of mistakes, the fundamental assault on detente came from Moscow, not Washington.[32]

To blame the collapse of détente upon Soviet pique over the denial of MFN treatment gives too much credit to Senator Jackson and his Communist-hating political allies. It also fails to take account of developments in Africa

32. Kissinger, *Years of Upheaval*, 1030.

and Asia over which neither the United States nor the USSR had control. Not all the disorder, disaffection, and revolutionary activity in the Third World was, as the intelligence estimates repeatedly pointed out, the consequence of Soviet subversion. The far-likelier causes in these countries were overpopulation, mismanagement, capital shortages, and exploitation by their rulers. If anything, the Soviets were slow to engage in Angola and anxious not to offend the United States, but at the end they were not prepared to allow the United States and its proxy armies to rule West Africa. Some of the other claims made by Kissinger in the passage quoted above can also be debated; China's role in Southeast Asia greatly exceeded that of the USSR, and Vietnam's later invasion of Cambodia served more a humanitarian purpose than a Soviet one.

Angola was an important event in the decline of détente largely because of the importance attached to it by both Kissinger and the opponents of détente in the United States. Despite the determined assault on détente mounted by those opponents, the Soviets continued to pursue it, most probably because of its arms control aspects. They stuck with it during the Yom Kippur War, and they showed reluctance to enter the fray in Angola. But the Watergate scandal and the collapse of the Nixon policy in Vietnam not only destroyed the President's leadership but also convinced the American public to look skeptically at foreign adventures elsewhere. Congressional action banning funding for operations in Angola also was also a serious blow to Kissinger's doctrine that the Soviets should show restraint in the Third World—even though the United States itself was already engaging in expensive covert military operations in the same area.

The Soviets won only a partial victory in Angola. At this writing, even with the collapse of Mobuto's Zaire, fighting and maneuvering was still going on in northern Angola, where Mobuto's erstwhile legionnaires were seeking refuge from Kabila by joining up with remnants of the CIA-sponsored FNLA-UNITA forces. But Brezhnev considered his actions regarding Angola as "benchmark" evidence that the USSR "could advance socialism in the Third World during a period of détente with the United States," reported Odd Westad in his summary of the Angolan affair.[33] In one manner or another during the next several years, the Soviets provided arms and other military assistance to a number of countries in Africa and Asia, a policy which Brezhnev considered quite compatible with détente but which some Americans considered a breach of faith. And Kissinger himself, as we have seen, was embit-

33. Westad, "Moscow and the Angola Crisis," 27.

tered by Brezhnev's failure to help him when his own policy was under severe attack at home.

But even without the damage done to détente by Kissinger's fellow countrymen, his decision to link agreements on arms control, trade, and other matters to Soviet behavior in the Third World was fatally flawed; there was too much else going on in the world. In my memorandum on the World Situation in 1970, I pointed out that the world was no longer simply divided between Communist world and free. I explained:

> There are many conflicts, but they exist on intersecting planes—the U.S.-Soviet contest, the Chinese-Soviet contest, the Arab-Israeli contest, the Soviet–Eastern European contest, the contest between the industrialized and richer nations (the U.S., the USSR, Japan, and Europe) and the poorer and primarily agricultural nations (China, India, the Near East, Africa, and Latin America), the contest between home-grown nationalists (in the Near East, Africa, and Latin America) and the corporations and governments which exercise economic and political influence in their lands, the contests within various countries between political forces which are supported by outside powers. . . .
>
> Thus it is impossible to devise any simple formula for measuring where we stand. A loss of U.S. influence or position in one arena is not necessarily a gain for the USSR, China, or whoever our competitor may be. Our loss may be his loss too. It is not a two-sided poker game; it is multilateral.

Those intersecting contests undermined Kissinger's hopes for containing the USSR. Unlike his predecessors in Democratic administrations, Kissinger had recognized the possibilities in the widening Sino-Soviet split and exploited them to bring détente into being. But disorder in the United States—the Watergate scandal, the ignominious exit from Vietnam, and continued sniping at détente from the Congress and within the Nixon-Ford administrations—plus troubles abroad were more than Kissinger could cope with. Indeed, the 1970s became increasingly disorderly abroad, more disillusioning at home, and more threatening to the structure of peace.

An Era of Disorder

It was in Africa that much of the disorder occurred, which tempted Soviet intervention and stirred up much of the American distrust of Soviet behavior. Ermias Ababe, an Ethiopian-born scholar who was educated in Russia and the United States, reported in a *Bulletin* study of Soviet activities in the Horn of Africa that Brezhnev had once described Africa as "a main field of battle for Communism."[34] As late as 1977, Fidel Castro—who after Angola had continued his campaign for revolution in Africa—told East German leader Erich Honecker that "in Africa, we can inflict a severe defeat on the entire reactionary imperialist policy. We can free Africa of the influence of the USA and the Chinese. . . . Ethiopia has a great revolutionary potential. . . . So there is a great counterweight to Sadat's betrayal of Egypt. . . . We must have an integrated strategy for the whole African continent."[35] It did not happen quite that way. Castro was obviously thinking in much more revolutionary terms than were the Soviet leaders in Moscow.

In the Horn of Africa: The USSR had negotiated, in 1974, a mutual assistance pact called the Treaty of Friendship and Cooperation with the military regime of Mohammed Siad Barre in Somalia, who had seized power there in 1969. He had sought and received Soviet military assistance in return for granting the Soviets access to the port of Berbera on the Gulf of Aden. The Western countries, including the United States, did not approve of the USSR gaining a military foothold in East Africa but did nothing about it. Things changed after the revolution against the Haile Selassie regime in Addis Ababa in 1974, just before things started to heat up in Angola.

It was not a Soviet-inspired revolt. One Ethiopian military officer, who had been part of the revolutionary group but who had later defected, has reported that the new Ethiopian military leaders were so "ignorant of ideology" that they sent delegations to Tanzania, Yugoslavia, China, and India—but not to the USSR—in order to "shop" for one.[36] After Haile Mengistu Mariam emerged victorious in February 1977 from a series of bloody feuds within the revolutionary group, he actually sought Soviet support and even "played the China card" to do so.[37] The Soviets were apparently wary of the Mengistu regime because of the many executions it had carried out. They wanted Mengistu to establish a Marxist-Leninist party to institutionalize the revolution and to transform the society. Mengistu, however, resisted that proposal because he wanted to prevent "Soviet infiltration into his power structure" until he had "weeded out" potential contenders and adversaries.[38]

34. Cited in Ermias Abebe, "The Horn, the Cold War, and Documents from the Former East BLOC: An Ethiopian View," *Bulletin of the Cold War International History Project*, no. 8-9 (Winter 1996–97): 40.
35. Ibid.
36. Ibid.
37. Ibid., 42.
38. Ibid., 43.

Seeing what was happening in Ethiopia, Barre decided to seize the Ogaden, an area of longtime contention between tribes in Somalia and Ethiopia. He initiated an invasion in 1977 and at the same time abrogated the Soviet-Somali Treaty of Friendship. The USSR then carried out a massive sea- and air-lift of 12,000 Cuban combat troops and 1500 Soviet military advisers to Ethiopia. The speed and size of the Soviet show of force was apparently designed to terminate the Somali attack and to avert internationalization of the conflict.[39] Guerrilla warfare went on until 1988, when a peace agreement was finally reached. Barre was thrown out in Somalia in 1991, and Mengistu was ousted in Ethiopia at about the same time.

The Horn of Africa affair is significant in a number of ways: the United States steered clear of political and military involvement, even though some in the U.S. military thought the United States should intervene; the Soviets stalled around, disliking having to choose between two ambitious and unscrupulous leaders; and the Soviets failed to establish the kind of government in Addis Ababa which they thought necessary to convert Ethiopia into a reliable ally. This was one case, at least, when the Soviets learned that supplicants for Soviet aid were not very good candidates for genuine membership in a worldwide Communist revolutionary movement.

In West Africa: Aside from the Zaire-FNLA tie, U.S. policy in Africa before Angola had been one of "benign neglect." The United States enjoyed economic and political advantages through its ties with the "Western" culture of the former colonial powers. Except for the confrontation over Angola, there were no serious differences between the United States and the USSR in Africa during the Cold War period. Neither government had made the continent an arena of active competition. Both powers provided arms to their clients in Angola, but the principal action on the Communist side was instigated and carried on by the Cubans. The Soviets were being very practical and unrevolutionary. The United States had an established and corrupt client in West Africa (Mobuto Sese Seko), while the Soviets were searching, quite unsuccessfully, for one in East Africa.

The troubles started when the United States, having been driven ignominiously out of Saigon and having tried to regain "face" through the ridiculous Mayaguez caper, made a play to "win one" in Angola—and failed. By treating the Angola affair as a test of détente and losing, Kissinger weakened his position at home and in effect signaled to Americans the collapse of détente. Angola thus became a much more important signpost in post–World War II history than it was worth.

39. Ibid., 43–44.

The Soviets, unable to match the Western political legacy in Africa, made a play for leftist politicians who had learned social and economic eclecticism from their European tutors; they provided technical and economic assistance and political support to some of the new nations. They accepted clients in East Africa, but neither Mengistu nor Siad Barre permitted the kind of political entree the Soviets desired, and each had his own political agenda. In North Africa and West Africa—for example, in Egypt, Libya, the Sudan, Guinea, and Ghana—the Soviets did gain limited political positions, but by 1978 they had lost most of the ground they had ploughed in the 1950s and 1960s. In short, Africa never became the battleground which the American cold warriors had predicted.

In Asia: It was a different story in Asia. In the southwest, the Yom Kippur War of October 1973 did nothing to resolve the Arab-Israeli problem; it actually intensified bitterness between the two sides. Egypt under Sadat and Mubarak moved closer to the United States, but most of the Arabs kept the United States at arm's length. At the southeastern corner of Asia, the victorious Vietnam regime settled in, and then moved against the fiendish Pol Pot regime (the Khmer Rouge) in Cambodia, which was being subsidized and encouraged by the Chinese. As CIA analysts had predicted, the other mainland and island nations of the southeast Asian area did not fall to Communism after the fall of South Vietnam. The Vietnamese even cooperated with the United Nations in the effort to end the slaughter in Cambodia and to restore a modicum of decency and order there.

The most onerous unrest, from the standpoint of U.S. interests, occurred in Afghanistan and Iran in the later years of the decade. The Shah of Iran was a willing collaborator in the U.S. plan to make his country America's chosen instrument for maintaining order in the Persian Gulf and to ensure a regular supply of oil to Western Europe and the United States from the Gulf region. To accomplish that, he had to be seen as the strongest military power in the area and secure at home. Security at home was the mission of SAVAK, an internal police organization associated with the CIA. Things did not work out quite as planned.

The Shah's corruption, his blatant adoption of a Western lifestyle, and the alienation of many people in the business and intellectual community undermined his position. Disorder broke out in the summer of 1978; shorn of support across a wide sector of Persian society, and ill with cancer, he fled the country in January 1979. After much maneuvering among political factions and new elections, failed to bring a consensus, power was seized by supporters of the Ayatollah Khomeni, an exiled Muslim cleric who returned among great fanfare. There is no evidence that the USSR or Tudeh (the Iranian Communist Party) played any significant role in the Shah's overthrow. The anti-Western character of the new radical religious regime and the identification of the United States with the hated Shah led to a wave of anti-Americanism that culminated in November 1979 in the seizure of the U.S. embassy compound and the imprisonment of its entire staff.

Shortly before the disorders broke out in Iran which led to the Shah's departure, a Communist coup took place in neighboring Afghanistan. What appears to have happened is that the government of Mohammed Daoud, which had been trying to carry out reforms and economic development, ran into trouble from landowners and conservatives on his right and aggressive reformers and modernizers on his left. The latter group included the Communist-led Peoples' Democratic Party of Afghanistan. Daoud decided to arrest the party's leaders, and when the roundup began, the party's leaders (who included a sizable faction in the army) staged a successful coup. It was April 1978.

Soviet documents made available to Odd Arne Westad for his study of the Afghan affair, published in the issue of the *Bulletin* cited above, include minutes of Soviet Presidium (Politburo) meetings, reports to the Central Committee of the Soviet Communist Party, texts of telegrams sent and received at the highest level, and records of conversations and telephone calls. After studying these documents, Westad concluded: "The Soviet leaders gradually increased their commitment to the Afghan Communist Party (the Peoples' Democratic Party of Afghanistan) after the coup of April 1978. In spite of their misgivings about the lapses and limitations of the Afghan Communist leaders, the members of the Soviet Politburo could not bring themselves to give up on the building of socialism in a neighboring country."[40]

As the years went by, the Afghan affair became a Soviet tragedy as well as one for the people of Afghanistan. Westad summed up its impact on the USSR this way:

The [Soviet] intervention in Afghanistan was the start of a war of almost unlimited destruction leaving more than one million Afghans dead or wounded and almost four million driven into exile. For the Soviets it became a death knell, signalling Moscow's international isolation,

---

40. Odd Arne Westad, "Concerning the Situation in 'A': New Russian Evidence on the Soviet Intervention in Afghanistan," *Bulletin of the Cold War International History Project*, no. 8-9 (Winter 1996–97): 129.

its leadership's inconstancy and fragmentation, and its public's growing disbelief in its purpose and direction of Soviet rule. By the time its forces left in early 1989, the Soviet regime was crumbling; two years later it was gone.[41]

Soviet intervention did not come quickly or without thought and debate in the Kremlin. When a rebellion broke out in West Afghanistan in March 1979, almost a year after the coup, the Presidium discussed intervention and decided, "In no case will we go forward with a deployment of troops in Afghanistan." Prime Minister Kosygin and Central Committee Secretary Kirilenko argued that "the Afghan Communists themselves were to blame for the rebellion." Kirilenko said: "We gave [them] everything, and what has come of it? Nothing of any value. After all, it was they who executed innocent people for no reason and told us that we also executed people in Lenin's time. You see what kind of Marxists we have found."[42]

Then, in October 1979, the coup government's number-two man, Hafizullah Amin, murdered the regime's president, Nur Mohammed Tariki. Brezhnev considered Amin a "dirty fellow," and the KGB suspected him of planning an alignment with the United States which would allow the Americans to place "their control and intelligence centers close to [the Soviet's] most sensitive borders." Amin went so far as to demand the recall of the Soviet ambassador in Kabul in late November 1979, and that convinced some members of the Presidium that they had to eliminate Amin and engage in some form of military intervention. Kosygin and Kirilenko continued to resist, as did the chief of the Soviet general staff and his deputies, but KGB chief Andropov, Defense Minister Ustinov, and Foreign Minister Gromyko persisted. The détente factor in the Presidium's thinking is described by Westad as follows:

> The increasing strains in East-West relations—including in the essential field of arms control—over the last months of 1979 may also have influenced Andropov and Ustinov's decision, and certainly made it easier for them to convince some of their colleagues. The long-awaited Carter-Brezhnev summit in Vienna in June 1979 had, despite the signing of the SALT II treaty, failed to generate much momentum toward an improvement in ties between Washington and Moscow. Moreover, the NATO decision that Fall to deploy a new class of medium-range

41. Ibid., 131.
42. Ibid., 129–30.

nuclear missiles in Europe and the increasing reluctance of the U.S. Senate to ratify the SALT II pact removed the concerns of some members over the effects a Soviet intervention might have on detente. . . . The bleak outlooks on the diplomatic front helped carry the day with Foreign Minister Gromyko, who at the best of times was a somewhat pusillanimous participant in Soviet high policies.[43]

Finally Andropov, Ustinov, and Gromyko won Brezhnev to the cause. The Presidium on December 12 agreed to go ahead—with Kosygin absent and Kirilenko reluctantly going along. The operation began on Christmas Day. Paratroopers and KGB forces stormed the presidential palace on December 27 and executed Amin.

The Impact of Afghanistan

The invasion of Afghanistan was greeted by quite an uproar in the United States. President Carter called it "the greatest threat to peace since World War II." Ambassador Dobrynin in his memoirs described the intervention and the U.S. response as "a final turning point in Soviet-American relations." It was the hinge that turned a decade of détente under Nixon and Ford to the years of confrontation under Reagan. In his view, some of the responsibility for the "new cold war" flowed from "intransigence on both sides over the Afghan question." In any case, wrote the ambassador: "Carter's entourage in the White House was handed a rare opportunity to convince the president of the thesis that the Soviet Union posed a global threat to the United States."[44] Dobrynin went on to say that the "deeply erroneous" Soviet action had provided "the American right" with a "pretext for another spiral in the arms race and renewed attacks on detente."[45]

I have referred frequently in this history, back as far as the early years after World War II, to the differences of view on Soviet policies and objectives held by the CIA and State Department analysts on the one hand and those held by representatives of the military services on the other hand. The range of different perceptions of the Soviet Union held by opposing groups in the United States was addressed by George Kennan in the Outlook section of the *Washington Post* in December 1977, at the end of President Carter's first

43. Ibid., 131, passim.
44. Dobrynin, *In Confidence*, 444.
45. Ibid.

year in office and two years before the Soviet invasion of Afghanistan. One side, he wrote, saw the Soviet leaders as "a terrible and forbidding group of men — monsters of sorts really, because lacking in all the elements of common humanity — men dedicated to the destruction or to the political undoing or enslavement of this country and its allies." The other view, he went on, looked at the Soviets as men "seldom easy to deal with . . . who have a fixation about secrecy, but who despite all these handicaps, have good and sound reasons, rooted in their own interests, for desiring a peaceful and constructive relationship with the United States within the area where that is theoretically possible."

The former view, expressed originally and forcefully by Paul Nitze in NSC-68 back in 1950, has been widely held in military circles and among many of the Cold Warriors in the operational directorate of the CIA. It was part of the political theology of those who hated Communism and opposed détente, and it was strengthened by each Soviet mistake — from Korea to Cuba to Afghanistan. Hence, after the fall of Saigon and the apparent deterioration of the U.S. world position in the wake of events in Southwest Asia, increasing criticism was directed at the Board of National Estimates for not having taken a sufficiently harsh view of Soviet objectives and policies.

The intelligence estimators of the O/NE tried not to adopt a fixed position about the Soviets, but to keep Soviet actions under continuing review and to watch for changes, not only in Soviet policies, but also in Soviet society, in the Soviet Communist Party, and in the Communist world generally. The process we used obliged us to coordinate our estimates with representatives of the action departments of the government, namely, the departments of State and Defense. They often had policy interests and pressures that colored the attitudes and positions of the representatives with whom we dealt, and that accounted for some of the dissents which were attached to crucial national intelligence estimates.

Major changes in the CIA's direction, authority, and procedures took place beginning in 1973, partly as a result of Watergate and partly as a result of the mounting political and bureaucratic power of those who opposed our analytical approach. Their continuing assault upon the Board of National Estimates and the national intelligence estimative process degraded the intellectual integrity of the estimates, eventually destroying their value as guides to Soviet intentions and military policy.

An Assault upon the National Intelligence Process

The Board of National Estimates in the Dock

Richard Nixon had won the presidential election of 1968 with only 43 percent of the vote. Moreover, his Vietnam policies had gotten him into serious political trouble with those who wanted an end to the war. He realized that he would need a wider base of popular support to carry out the foreign policies he and Secretary Kissinger were developing. In other words, he needed to "win big" in 1972. In an effort to acquire information to use against his Democratic opponents, a group working for his reelection broke into the Democratic National Committee headquarters in the Watergate Hotel in order to plant listening devices. They were caught red-handed and arrested. To head off a scandal over the break-in, Nixon's White House concocted a scheme to have the CIA inform the police and the FBI that the break-in was part of a CIA operation and have the CIA ask them to knock it off. Richard Helms refused to comply with the request. The culprits were indicted in September of 1972 and their trial was put off until January of 1973. The break-in affair quieted down, and Nixon was reelected with 61 percent of the vote. He punished Helms by removing him as Director of Central Intelligence and appointing him ambassador to Iran. He then appointed James Schlesinger the new Director of Central Intelligence.

Schlesinger took over as director in February of 1973 and left a few months later to become Secretary of Defense. He quickly became an unpopular figure at the CIA. He was arrogant and threw his weight around. Morale sank, and many officers resigned or retired in disgust. Even before Schlesinger arrived, however, the Board of National Estimates had come under attack from both within and without the Agency. Its prestige had suffered because of the failure of Agency directors to retire some of its aging members and to recruit distinguished replacements from the academic and governmental communities. We were particularly unpopular at the Pentagon because we did not produce estimates that supported certain Pentagon procurement programs and positions in arms control negotiations. We were also unpopular with Henry Kissinger at the White House, who believed that he was better qualified than we were to analyze what was going on in the world—particularly if our estimates in any way complicated the execution of his policy plans or current negotiations. There was also a flap when Kissinger heard that some senior CIA officials were pushing Robert Bowie, director of the Harvard Center for International Affairs, to succeed the retiring Abbott Smith as chairman of the Board of National Estimates. (Kissinger had served Bowie as deputy director at the Center, and the relationship had proved unhappy for both.)

When Schlesinger arrived at the Agency, he quickly zeroed in on the Board of National Estimates. Some of us on the board saw the handwriting on the wall and applied for retirement. John Huizenga, a fine professional who had been named chairman to succeed Abbott Smith, made a valiant effort to save the board, but he too left in mid-1973. William Colby, a former station chief in Saigon and later the Agency's executive director, was appointed by Nixon to succeed Schlesinger, and he shortly thereafter abolished the board. In its place he established a system of national intelligence officers, each in charge of estimates on a particular region of the world or on a functional subject related to world affairs. Without staffs of their own, each was dependent upon analysts in other offices of the Intelligence Directorate or in other agencies of the intelligence community for preparation of the initial draft of national estimates. Collegiality went out the window, and the CIA's primacy was diluted.

I do not know whether it was Schlesinger's or Colby's idea to abolish the board and to alter the system for preparing estimates. Both defended the changes at hearings of the Senate Select Committee (Church Committee) on Foreign and Military Intelligence in 1975 and 1976. Here is what Colby told the committee:

> A board? You say why don't you have a board also? I have some reservation at the ivory tower kind of problem that you get out of a board which is too separated from the rough and tumble of the real world.

I think there is a tendency for it to intellectualize and then write sermons and appreciations. . . .

I think there is a tendency to become institutionally committed to an approach and to an appraisal of a situation and to begin to interpret new events against the light of a predetermined approach to those events.[1]

To suggest that the members of the Board of National Estimates were inhabitants of an ivory tower separated from the real world can only indicate that Colby had not taken the trouble to learn about its membership. Most of us had served in uniform during World War II; during my time in the Office of National Estimates we had the former chief of plans at SHAEF and a corps commander in Europe. Two members were career ambassadors, one a former assistant secretary for European affairs and the other a former ambassador to Moscow. Three had been CIA chiefs of station, and others had served in embassies abroad. Only a few of us were career intelligence officers, and nearly all of us had attended a war college or been seconded to other agencies or academic institutions in order to refresh our minds and broaden our knowledge and experience.

Colby also implied that we had become "institutionally committed" to a particular "approach" which led us to see new events in the light of that "predetermined approach." The same claim was made by Schlesinger in his testimony before the Select Committee:

The Intelligence Directorate tends to make a particular type of error systematically in that the Intelligence Directorate tends to be in close harmony with the prevailing biases in the intellectual community, in the university community, and as the prevailing view changes in that community, it affects the output, of the Intelligence Directorate. . . .

So we must be careful to balance what I call the academic biases amongst the analysts with the operational biases amongst other elements of the intelligence community.[2]

Whether there were indeed "biases" and where they might lie is, of course, a crucial question. John Huizenga in his testimony said the following:

---

1. Select Committee to Study Governmental Operations with Respect to Intelligence Activities, United States Senate, *Final Report*, book 1, April 26, 1976, 75 n. 17.
2. Ibid., 76.

In the Defense Department, intelligence is often seen as the servant of desired policies and programs. At a minimum there is a strong organizational interest in seeing to it that the intelligence provides a vigorous appraisal of potential threats. It is not unfair to say that because of the military leadership's understandable desire to hedge against the unexpected, to provide capabilities for all conceivable contingencies there is a natural thrust in military intelligence to maximize threats and to oversimplify the intentions of potential adversaries. It is also quite naturally true that the military professional tends to see military power as the prime determinant of the behavior of states and of the movement of events in international politics.[3]

Huizenga's argument strongly prevailed in the Select Committee's findings:

In the area of providing finished intelligence, the Committee discovered that the DCI (Director of Central Intelligence), in his role as intelligence adviser, has faced obstacles in ensuring that his national intelligence judgments are objective and independent of department and agency biases. The Committee has been particularly concerned with pressures from both the White House and Defense Department on the DCI to alter his intelligence judgments. . . .

The Committee believes that over the past five years the DCI's ability to produce objective national intelligence and resist outside pressure has been reduced with the dissolution of the Board of National Estimates and the subsequent delegation of its staff to the departments with responsibility for drafting the DCI's national intelligence judgments.[4]

The Committee had looked into one specific occasion when pressure was put upon the board by the White House to alter a judgment regarding Soviet missile capabilities, and it was aware of another occasion when a board judgment was withheld from circulation because it would have undermined a policy decision that had already been made. In another case Director Helms himself deleted a paragraph from an estimate after the office of the Secretary of Defense pointed out to Helms that the position taken in the estimate contradicted the public position of the Secretary. The critical part of that para-

3. Ibid., 76 n. 19.
4. Ibid., 432–33.

graph dealt with a very important judgment related to U.S. strategic policy and procurement, to wit: "We believe that the Soviets recognize the enormous difficulties of an attempt to achieve strategic superiority of such order as to significantly alter the strategic balance. Consequently, we consider it highly unlikely that they will attempt within the period of this estimate to achieve a first-strike capability, i.e., a capability to launch a surprise attack against the U.S. with assurance that the USSR would not receive damage it would regard as unacceptable."[5]

The estimate was titled "Soviet Strategic Attack Forces" (NIE 11-8-69) and had been approved by the board just prior to a USIB meeting of August 28, 1969. To his credit, the State Department member of the USIB inserted the deleted material as a dissenting footnote to the relevant portion of the estimate. Had Helms not deleted the paragraph at issue, there would have been an Air Force dissent.

In connection with those and similar events, Huizenga made the cogent observation in his testimony that "in times of political stress on intelligence," it was more a question of "invisible pressure" than of "being leaned upon" to make particular changes in judgment. He went on to say: "When intelligence producers have a general feeling that they are working in a hostile climate, what really happens is not so much that they tailor their product to please, although that is not unknown, but more likely, they avoid the treatment of difficult issues."[6]

The more serious charge against the board than Colby's "ivory tower" description was his charge that the board was guilty of "a predetermined approach" to "new events." This was echoed by Schlesinger's assertion quoted above that the board had a "bias" and that this "bias" was due to its close association with the "academic community." He thought that the board should have given more weight to the "Air Force bias."[7] It is indeed true that the Office of National Estimates had a panel of consultants. The panel's membership and venue changed over the years. It was originally chaired by Board Chairman William Langer of Harvard. Raymond Sontag, a board member on leave from the University of California at Berkeley, took over the panel when Langer returned to Harvard, and Board Vice Chairman Abbott Smith served as panel chairman when Sontag returned to California. The first meeting of the panel, which I attended, was at Princeton in 1952; the consultants

5. Ibid., 78.
6. Ibid., 82.
7. Ibid., 77.

then were George Kennan of the Institute for Advanced Study, Samuel Flagg Bemis of Yale, and the former ambassador to Japan Joseph Grew.

I assumed the chairmanship of the panel in 1967 when Abbott became chairman of the Board of National Estimates. We gradually expanded the size of the panel to about twenty, and we met regularly twice a year for a three-day session outside the Washington area. The membership roster over the years reads like a who's who of diplomatic historians and directors of international studies programs throughout the United States. All were cleared for top secret, and we brought to the sessions copies of all major estimates produced since the preceding meeting and certain other estimates in process upon which we wanted the panel's advice. Not all were academics; Hamilton Fish Armstrong, editor of *Foreign Affairs*, was one nonacademic; former ambassador Ray Hare was another, as was Harold Linder, onetime president of the Import-Export Bank. We always had the head of the history department at the U.S. Military Academy. Several others had been in and out of government, including Robert Bowie of Harvard, Robert Byrnes of Indiana University, Joseph Strayer of Princeton, Marshal Shulman and Philip Moseley of Columbia, and Max Milliken of MIT. Other academics included John Lindbeck of Columbia, William Griffith and Lucian Pye of MIT, Sam Huntington and George Lodge of Harvard, Klaus Knorr and Cyril Black of Princeton, and Gordon Craig and John Lewis of Stanford. They were not all of one mind and certainly not denizens of ivory towers.

They were important to us because they brought much experience and learning to our deliberations. The exchange functioned two ways; they found out how we were responding to changes in the world, and we assured ourselves that we were tapping into their thinking about subjects which we had under review.

Schlesinger did point to an important problem in estimating, even though he no doubt raised it because judgments of the Board of National Estimates were different from his own and therefore "biased." The real question, however, is not with "bias," but with the intellectual framework into which historical data and new information are placed when encountered by the individual analyst or group of analysts involved.

The Estimator's Problem

The intelligence estimator almost never has all the facts he would like to have in order to project the behavior of other nations. Some "facts" come easily; they are simply events: a riot has occurred, a government is voted out of or into office, political leaders have made public statements, a new weapons system has been tested, military movements have been announced or discovered, a secret intelligence report has been received purporting to give the "inside story" on some apparent event or to disclose another government's plan to carry out certain policies.

Sometimes the available "facts" are really "estimated" or "calculated" facts, as for example the accuracy and reliability of a missile system; such "facts" could actually be judgments based upon a series of assumptions that in turn were derived from a few events observed electronically and compared with U.S. experience on similar types of weapons. Some "facts" are judgments based upon limited anecdotal evidence, as for example judgments about the fighting spirit or lack of it in another country's military forces. For many of these so-called facts the estimator must question how the report was acquired or the judgment derived.

In the case of judgments about China today and the USSR in the past, the estimator has been working on regimes with a passion for secrecy, leaders of uncertain staying power, a penchant for conspiratorial methods, and a decision-making process often laborious and uninformed. Those factors make the estimator's problem much more complicated than it is for nations more open and less centralized. But whatever the source of his information, the estimator tries to judge its trustworthiness and to fit it into an intellectual construct of his own making. That construct, framework, or model is something he has developed from his training, profession, experience, personal beliefs, and habits of thought.

As John Huizenga has pointed out, the U.S. military professionals have tended to "see military power as the prime determinant of the behavior of states and of the movement of events in international politics." This has led to their attempts "to hedge against the unexpected" and "to provide capabilities for all conceivable contingencies." That was the fundamental reason for most of the differences between the Board of National Estimates and the Pentagon over the years after the board's creation in 1950. To the degree that we yielded to Pentagon pressure to move to a higher level of Soviet military capability than we thought was justified by the evidence and Soviet behavior, or to the degree that we permitted the Pentagon representatives to insert in the estimates a range of figures, the highest of which were derived from their calculations, to that degree there were overestimations of the Soviet military threat.

Once engrossed in an estimate, and sometimes even without being openly included in it, the U.S. Air Force, Army, or Navy used these overestimates to justify new procurement programs and to develop new weapons systems. Such new programs in turn frightened the Soviet military planners and Party Presidium members into initiating new programs in response. As this process went on, and as these new Soviet programs were discovered by sophisticated U.S. collection systems, *U.S. overestimates became in effect self-fulfilling prophecies.* Critics of the CIA and especially of the Board of National Estimates then looked at the enhanced Soviet capabilities which had been prompted by the U.S. overestimates and asserted that the Pentagon had been correct all along and that the board had consistently underestimated Soviet strategic intentions. It was the adoption of those criticisms by Schlesinger and Colby which was largely responsible for the dissolution of the board in 1973. The Pentagon won at least a temporary victory.

What we in the Office of National Estimates had been striving to do was not to become engaged in any institutional approach to the estimating of Soviet intentions and capabilities. An institutional approach with a built-in predisposition to a particular set of judgments — such as that of the U.S. Air Force — does make estimating easier. When one does not have at hand the minutes of the Soviet Presidium or when one is trying to figure out what the Soviets are trying to accomplish with a new weapons program, then it is much simpler to fall back upon a threat doctrine calling for protection against all conceivable contingencies than it is to probe into their thinking or try to see the world as they see it.

If one believed that the Soviet leaders were determined to dominate the world and to do so by force if necessary, many problems became simpler, to wit: the Soviets were aiming at military superiority, they would engage in nuclear blackmail, they would slice away at the non-Communist world by seizing weakly defended territory either by force of arms or by subversion and revolution; the only way to deal with the Soviets was to prepare to fight a general nuclear war and to demonstrate a readiness to fight it. The information we now have and the disclosures from Soviet archives strongly suggests that those beliefs were wrong.

There were other approaches to estimating Soviet intentions. Historians tended to put heavy emphasis upon Russian historic desires for warm water ports and access to the Mediterranean Sea or Indian Ocean. Geopolitical thinkers tended toward economic determinism and looked at Soviet intentions in terms of needed resources for economic development or autonomy. Another approach was to pay special attention, not to national and doctrinal objectives, but to the character of the leaders, their personal ambitions and psychological drives.

In the Office of National Estimates, most of us adopted what I like to call a rational approach to estimating about the Soviets. We recognized that they had an ideology to which they paid their respects from time to time. We recognized that they had historic interests which they had inherited from the tsars. We also recognized, as Kennan has pointed out, that they were not easy to deal with and that they would make mistakes and need to be brought up short from time to time. But we also recognized that when we stood firm against their pressure, their behavior had been dominated by a strong tendency to act in accordance with the most rational course for them to have followed in view of the options open to them at the time. The reporting in this book shows that they made some mistakes, but that even in Stalin's time they were often unsure of what to do and often frightened of Western intentions or of the effect of their actions upon possible Western and especially U.S. responses. And as I have indicated at several points in this narrative, the Soviets did make some serious errors in calculating their risks and prospects (e.g., in Korea, Cuba, and Afghanistan). But when they recognized their miscalculations, they were careful not to intensify the ensuing crises.

The Schlesinger Approach in Action

The rational approach to estimating did not disappear with the dissolution of the Board of National Estimates, but there was a slow movement away from it. One of the last general estimates of Soviet strategic policies undertaken by the board was "Issues and Options in Soviet Military Policy," approved in March 1972. In my review of that estimate in Chapter 10, I record the estimators' conclusion that the most important issue facing Soviet military planners was to select "the most appropriate means to assure continuance of the newly won parity with the U.S. in strategic nuclear power." The estimate predicted that "for the immediate future" the Soviets would try to stabilize the U.S.-Soviet strategic relationship "through negotiations," and that they would in any case continue their research and development in order to avoid falling behind the United States again "in any aspect of strategic power."

With Helms's dismissal after Nixon's reelection in November and his replacement by James Schlesinger in the first weeks of 1973, the political climate within the CIA began to change. At that time, Robert Gates was still a middle-level analyst in the Agency (he was appointed DCI by President Bush in May 1991), but in his recent memoir, he describes how Schlesinger's brief tenure as director began to affect estimates of Soviet objectives. As Gates put it, Schlesinger was "intent on making our analysis of Soviet strategic developments more tough-minded and realistic." Schlesinger scheduled a new NIE titled "Soviet Strategic Programs and Detente: What Are They Up To?" This was in the spring of 1973, a few weeks before Huizenga and I retired. Gates was directed to write the first draft, and it was then handed over to a Schlesinger protégé brought in from the Rand Corporation for a rewrite. Published in September 1973, Gates described it as having told U.S. policymakers "less ambiguously than usual" that the Soviets were trying "to have it both ways," getting "the advantage of detente" and "an unconstrained strategic build-up."[8]

Gates concluded that with the publication of that estimate (SNIE 11-4-73), which he described as a reflection of "Schlesinger's intellectual legacy," the CIA and the intelligence community "fell to the back of the detente parade."[9] Gates's comments about the estimate were made some twenty years after it appeared, but they demonstrate a tendency to distort intelligence reporting to fit his own thinking. The estimate did not go so far as he claimed; it did not state that the Soviets were aiming to engage in "an unconstrained strategic build-up." It did state, and in my view quite correctly, what was going on; it took note of certain Soviet strategic force modernization programs which had been under way when the détente agreements were signed in May 1972 and which had not been altered thereafter. SNIE 11-4-73 concluded:

> We believe the Soviet leadership is currently pursuing a strategic pol-
> icy it regards as simultaneously prudent and opportunistic, aimed at
> assuring no less than the continued maintenance of comprehensive
> equality with the U.S. while at the same time seeking the attainment
> of some degree of strategic advantage if U.S. behavior permits. The
> Soviets probably believe that the unilateral restraints imposed on the
> U.S. by its internal problems and skillful Soviet diplomacy offer some
> prospect that a military advantage can be acquired. To this end, they
> can be expected to exploit opportunities permitted them under the
> terms of SALT. At the same time, since they cannot be fully confident
> of such an outcome even as they probe its possibilities, they are prob-
> ably also disposed to explore in SALT the terms on which stabiliza-
> tion of the strategic competition could be achieved.

8. Robert M. Gates, *From the Shadows* (New York: Simon & Schuster, 1996), 43.
9. Ibid.

It is quite likely that the Soviet leaders see no basic contradiction between their detente and arms policies. Indeed they have publicly said as much on numerous occasions. Even if they do not recognize a potential for conflict, they are probably uncertain about how far the U.S. is prepared to insist on linking the two, and hence are probably inclined to test what the traffic will bear.

The Air Force did not get its alternate view written into the body of the estimate. It was obliged to dissent in a footnote. The Air Force intelligence chief was obviously unprepared to accept the idea stated in the conclusion above that the Soviets were "disposed to explore in SALT the terms on which stabilization of the strategic competition could be achieved." His view was the following:

The available evidence suggests a strong Soviet commitment to achieving both numerical and qualitative strategic superiority over the U.S. They probably view detente as a tactic to that end. Whatever its other advantages, the Soviets need detente to bring about a slowdown in U.S. technology. They need to gain access to U.S. guidance and computer technology, to buy time to redress their current technology imbalance and to exploit what they consider to be a favorable opportunity to attain a technological lead during the next 10 to 15 years. The Soviets are no doubt aware of the impact detente is already having on NATO and U.S. defense outlays and gaining easier access to U.S. technology. Accordingly they must view detente as a principal means of forestalling U.S. advances in technology while enhancing their own relative power position.

That Air Force dissent describes quite well the model into which its department fits the history of Soviet military policy and the U.S.-Soviet military relationship. It was in essence a confession of faith buttressed by selected facts set into a mold drawn from Communist doctrine and historical pretensions. What the dissent says is a new form of the old story: the Soviets intend to take over the world by force; everything they do, including détente agreements and arms treaties, is designed to advance that goal. That is much more than an analytic "bias"; it is an affirmation dismissing the analytic process and diplomatic activity through which the CIA, the Department of State, and the White House National Security Staff had been working to avoid mutual annihilation or American surrender.

In July 1974, nine months after SNIE 11-4-73 was published, Robert Gates left the Agency to join the White House National Security Staff. It was a month before President Nixon's resignation. Kissinger was Secretary of State and General Scowcroft was running the NSC staff. However much Gates might have considered himself a professional, dispassionate intelligence analyst, he was very much a policy-oriented staff officer. In his memoir, he issued the following blast at CIA estimates and at U.S. policy before he himself became engaged: "From 1969 to the end of 1974, American policy toward the Soviet Union and U.S.-Soviet relations generally were characterized by smoke and mirrors—obscuring the reality of continued competition and enmity, as well as détente's limits and failures, magnifying its modest successes, a time of secret deals and public obfuscation (and deception), all reflecting more accurately than they imagined the personalities of its principal architects."[10]

George Bush's Team A–Team B "Experiment"

The issue of what Soviet objectives really were was joined openly and forcefully in 1976 in NIE 11-3/8-76 ("Soviet Forces for Intercontinental Conflict Through the Mid-1980s"). The years 1975 and 1976 were the time of the congressional investigations of the intelligence activities of the U.S. government, including the CIA, and it was during those investigations that the national estimates process came under criticism for allegedly underestimating the Soviet "threat." One of the most active critics of the positions taken in the estimates was a group that called itself the "Committee on the Present Danger." It was founded in 1976, three years after the abolition of the Board of National Estimates. Its membership of about 150 had three co-chairmen, Henry Fowler, Lane Kirkland, and David Packard; an executive committee chairman, Eugene Rostow; a chairman of policy studies, Paul Nitze; and an executive committee of a dozen members, most of them conservative Republicans and Democrats known for their strong anti-Soviet beliefs and policy advocacy. The group was organized shortly after George Bush was recalled from China, where he was head of the U.S. Liaison Mission to the Communist Government, and appointed DCI.

The chairman of President Gerald Ford's Foreign Intelligence Advisory Board, Admiral George Anderson, suggested to Bush that as an "experiment," he appoint a team of outside experts (Team B) to review the Soviet strategic

10. Ibid., 49.

estimate prepared by the CIA experts (Team A). The outside experts were to concentrate on Soviet objectives, that is, on the principal subject upon which CIA and the Pentagon had so often disagreed. Team A was headed by Howard Stoertz, the longtime chief draftsman and staff officer for Soviet military estimates in the Office of National Estimates. Team B was headed by Richard Pipes, a historian from the Harvard Russian Research Center and a member of the Executive Committee of the "Committee on the Present Danger." His team included two retired generals, one Army and one Air Force, both well known around town as Russia-hating political generals. Team B also had an advisory panel which included in its membership Paul Nitze and former ambassador to the Soviet Union Foy Kohler.

The estimate was approved by the USIB on December 21, 1976, a month before the new Carter administration assumed office. In a letter to the estimate's recipients, Director George Bush declared that "the assembling of a panel of outside experts, and the consideration of their views, was agreed upon by me and the President's Foreign Intelligence Advisory Board as an experiment, the purpose of which was to determine whether those known for their more somber views of Soviet capabilities and objectives could present the evidence in a sufficiently convincing way to alter the analytical judgments which otherwise would have been presented."

It did not work out exactly as planned. Donald Steury of the CIA History Staff, who wrote a brief history of the "experiment," has reported that the two teams chose quite different methodologies. Team A followed the pattern pursued in previous NIEs, but gave "prominence" to the dissenting opinions within the intelligence community. Team B, according to Steury, "abandoned the formula agreed upon for the experiment, in favor of a detailed critique of the assumptions and methodologies that underlay strategic forces NIEs produced over the previous decade or so. Discussion focused on the role played by ideology, strategic doctrine, and national character in determining Soviet nuclear policy."[11]

When the draft estimate was nearing completion, leaks to the press about the "experiment" prompted sharp criticism of the whole affair. Ray Cline, hardly a dove on Soviet matters and at the time a director of studies at the Center for Strategic Studies (who had previously served in the Office of National Estimates, as CIA Deputy Director for Intelligence, and as Director

11. Donald P. Steury, ed., *Intentions and Estimates on Soviet Strategic Forces, 1950–1983* (Washington, D.C.: Center for the Study of Intelligence, Central Intelligence Agency, 1984), 335. A complete account of the Team A–Team B exercise appears in Anne Hessing Cohn, *Killing Détente* (University Park: Pennsylvania State University Press, 1998), 100–184.

of Intelligence at the Department of State) declared that the exercise was a "subversion" of the estimative process by the employment of a "kangaroo court of outside critics all picked from one point of view." Pete Scoville, who had been CIA's Deputy Director for Science and Technology, said that it was difficult for Agency analysts to "stand up to the pressure of a biased point of view when the people at the top" want "to prove something."

Bush was obviously stung by those and similar criticisms. In his letter to the estimate's recipients, Bush nevertheless made the following statement: "The views of these experts did have some effect. But to the extent that this estimate presents a starker appreciation of Soviet strategic capabilities and objectives, it is but the latest in a series of estimates that have done so as evidence has accumulated on the continuing persistence and vigor of Soviet programs in the strategic and defensive fields." Thus, according to Bush, the dissolution of the Board of National Estimates in 1973 had produced the effect desired by its enemies, with Team B having provided the final punch.

It was a long and indeed a controversial estimate. The estimate proper ran to seventy-five printed pages, and Team B's contribution ran to an additional fifty-five pages. Following are the estimate's "Key Judgments" on the topic "Soviet Objectives and Expectations":

> The growth of Soviet capabilities for intercontinental conflict over the past decade has provided the USSR with a powerful deterrent and has contributed to its recognition as a superpower equal to the U.S. An assessment of the perceptions and objectives underlying present Soviet programs is a matter of interpretation and considerable uncertainty. Much that we observe can be attributed to a combination of defensive prudence, superpower competitiveness, worst-case assumptions about U.S. capabilities, a military doctrine which stresses warfighting capabilities, and a variety of internal political and institutional factors. But the continuing persistence and vigor of Soviet programs give rise to the question of whether the Soviet leaders now hold as an operative, practical objective the achievement of clear strategic superiority over the U.S. during the period of this estimate.
>
> The Soviet belief in the eventual supremacy of their system is strong. They see their forces for intercontinental conflict as contributing to their ultimate goal of achieving a dominant position over the West, particularly the United States, in terms of political, economic, social, and military strength. Having come this far in strategic arms compe-

tition with the United States, the Soviets may be optimistic about their long-term prospects in this competition. But they cannot be certain about future U.S. behavior or about their own future strategic capabilities relative to those of the U.S. They have seen U.S. technology mobilized to great effect in the past and are concerned about current U.S. force modernization programs. Thus, they probably cannot today set practical policy objectives in terms of some specific relationship between their intercontinental capabilities and those of the United States, to be achieved in a specific period of time.

We do not believe that the Soviet leaders presently count on a combination of actions by the USSR and lack of action by the U.S. which would give them, in the next ten years, a capability for intercontinental conflict so effective that the USSR could devastate the U.S. while preventing the U.S. from devastating the USSR. Soviet expectations, however, reach well beyond a capability that merely continues to be sufficient to deter an all-out attack.

In our view, the Soviets are trying to achieve war-fighting and war-surviving capabilities which would leave the USSR in a better position than the U.S. if war occurred. The Soviets also aim for intercontinental forces which have visible and therefore politically useful advantages over the U.S. They hope that their capabilities for intercontinental conflict will give them more latitude than they have had in the past for the vigorous pursuit of foreign policy objectives, and that these capabilities will discourage the U.S. and others from using force or the threat of force to influence Soviet actions.

The Key Judgments recorded above from the CIA estimate do show, as Director Bush indicated in his letter of transmittal, that the "views of the [outside] experts did have some effect." The Key Judgments describe a Soviet leadership more aggressive and self-confident than previous national estimates had presented, and indeed much more aggressive and self-confident than recent documentation shows the Soviet leaders to have been.

The State Department, to its credit, held to the more rational interpretation of Soviet military programs and expectations, to wit:

The Director, Bureau of Intelligence and Research, Department of State, agrees with the statement above on the ultimate Soviet goal but believes that the Soviet leaders have more modest expectations for their strategic programs. He would emphasize that the Soviet leaders:

— know that the U.S. need not concede the USSR any meaningful strategic advantage and do not expect the U.S. to do so, whatever their assessment of present U.S. resolve might be; and

— do not entertain, as a practical objective in the foreseeable future, the achievement of what could reasonably be characterized as a "war-winning" or "war-survival" posture.

Rather, in his view, Soviet strategic weapon programs are pragmatic in nature and are guided by more proximate foreign policy goals. He sees the Soviets undertaking vigorous strategic force improvements with a view to achieving incremental advantages where possible but, above all, to avoid falling behind the U.S. in a strategic environment increasingly characterized by qualitative competition—and thus losing the position of rough equivalence with the U.S. which they have achieved in recent years through great effort.

The State Department's intelligence director also thought it unlikely that the Soviet leaders anticipated any improvement in their strategic situation relative to that of the United States which would substantially alter their behavior or—inclinations to take risk—during periods of crisis or confrontation with the West.

The Department of Defense; the Energy Research and Development Administration; the Assistant Chief of Staff for Intelligence, Department of the Army; the Director of Naval Intelligence, Department of the Navy; and the Assistant Chief of Staff for intelligence, Department of the Air Force, all joined together in another dissent. They believed that the Soviets did see as an attainable goal a capability to wage an intercontinental nuclear war and "survive it with sufficient resources to dominate the postwar period." The Air Force added a separate and extensive dissent asserting that the Soviets were staging a drive for "general strategic superiority over all perceived constellations of enemies and for attaining a war-winning capability at all levels of conflict." The views of the military brethren on Soviet Objectives and Expectations were, of course, based upon pre-judgments consistent with the assumptions and mythology to which they had so often subscribed in previous estimates.

In this case, those views were also consistent with the views of Director Bush's so-called outside experts of Team B, many of whom were in fact former defense community insiders. As indicated earlier, Donald Steury reported that Team B had abandoned its commitment to advance evidence to support a starker view than that of the CIA "experts" about Soviet objectives. Consequently, the Team B report dealt not with intelligence evidence on Soviet actions and plans, but with their own undocumented opinions about the thinking of the Soviet leadership and about the nature of Communism. Here follow some excerpts from their summary which indicate the tenor of their contribution:

> Team B found that the NIE 11-3/8 series through 1975 has substantially misperceived the motivations behind Soviet strategic programs, and thereby tended consistently to underestimate their intensity, scope, and implicit threat.
>
> This misperception has been due in considerable measure to concentration on the so-called hard data collected by technical means, and the resultant tendency to interpret these data in a manner reflecting basic U.S. concepts while slighting or misinterpreting the large body of "soft" data concerning Soviet strategic concepts. The failure to take into account or accurately to assess such soft data sources has resulted in the NIEs not addressing themselves systematically to the broader political purposes which underlie and explain Soviet strategic objectives. . . .
>
> Analysis of Soviet past and present behavior, combined with what is known of Soviet political and military doctrines, indicates that judgments [in the NIEs] are seriously flawed. The evidence suggests that the Soviet leaders are first and foremost offensively rather than defensively minded. They think not in terms of nuclear stability, mutual assured destruction, or strategic sufficiency, but of an effective nuclear warfighting capability. They believe that the probability of a general war can be reduced by building up one's own strategic forces, but that it cannot be altogether eliminated, and that therefore one has to be prepared for such a war as if it were unavoidable and be ready to strike first if it appears imminent. . . .
>
> Team B feels that the USSR strives *for effective strategic superiority in all the branches of the military, nuclear forces included.* For historic reasons, as well as for reasons inherent in the Soviet system, the Soviet leadership places unusual reliance on coercion as a regular instrument of policy at home as well as abroad. It likes to have a great deal of coercive capability at its disposal at all times, and it likes for it to come in a rich mix so that it can be optimally structured for any contingency that may arise. After some apparent division of opinion intermittently during 1960s, the Soviet leadership seems to have

concluded that nuclear war could be fought and won. The scope and vigor of Soviet strategic programs leave little reasonable doubt that Soviet leaders are indeed determined to achieve the maximum possible measure of strategic superiority over the U.S. Their military doctrine is measured not in terms of assured destruction but in those of a *war-fighting and war-winning capability.*

The NIE and the B team reports were declassified and released into the public domain in October 1992. When they did become available, Don Oberdorfer of the *Washington Post* wrote a news story describing the estimate as "the most controversial intelligence estimate of the Cold War era." Oberdorfer devoted a large portion of his article to the Team B report; he noted with peculiar interest those passages which contended that CIA had relied too much on "hard data" which it had acquired through sophisticated collections systems and had paid insufficient attention to "soft data" such as public and private statements of Soviet intentions. Oberdorfer quoted italicized statements from the Team B report including one which stated that while the Soviets hoped to "crush the capitalist realm by other than military means, the *Soviet Union is nevertheless preparing for a Third World War as if it were unavoidable.*"[12]

Oberdorfer asked William Hyland (a former senior staff officer in the Office of National Estimates and a former deputy national security adviser to President Ford) about what had been the effect of the Team B report. Hyland doubted that it had had much effect, especially since the incoming Carter administration had ignored it. Hyland added that soon after the Team B report was written, Soviet policy had begun to shift in the direction opposite from that alleged by Team B; in a January 1977 public speech, for example, Brezhnev "refuted many of [the Team B] premises." Hyland further added that "in hindsight," the Brezhnev speech had "signaled the beginnings of a process that led to the last Soviet leader, Mikhail Gorbachev."[13]

Paul Nitze, of course, took a rather different view. He told Oberdorfer that "within a few years most of the substantive recommendations and many of the organizational and procedural changes we had urged were implemented." He added that he thought the Team B report was "first class," and that after just having read it again, he did not "find anything wrong with it at all."[14]

12. Don Oberdorfer, "Report Says Soviet Buildup for War," *Washington Post*, October 12, 1992.
13. Ibid.
14. Ibid.

Indeed, Nitze continued his campaign for increased U.S. military programs to counter the Soviet buildup. In October 1978 his Committee on the Present Danger published the pamphlet "Is America Becoming Number 2?" It painted a very dolorous picture for America's future if existing trends continued. It alleged that the debate—which his group and the U.S. Air Force were carrying on—had "already produced a consensus judgment that if present trends continue, the U.S. will soon be in a position of military inferiority." Soviet "strategic superiority," the argument went on, "would confer on the Soviet Union the ability to intimidate and coerce the West into accepting unfavorable bargains." The United States would then have to recognize that if a crisis were to escalate to a strategic nuclear war, the Soviet Union would expect, at a high but perhaps not intolerable cost, to prevail while maintaining a post-war preponderance of global military power."[15]

The Paralysis of the National Intelligence Machinery

Despite the fact that Hyland thought the Team B report had had little effect upon the Carter administration, the exercise itself and the controversy it stirred up at the time appear to have had a very serious effect upon the intelligence community. Admiral Stansfield Turner, Carter's DCI, told Oberdorfer that the Team B report could "have caused intelligence analysts to lean over backwards not to underestimate the Soviet Union."[16] While the immediate policy impact upon the Carter administration might not have been especially memorable, the history of Soviet strategic estimating after 1976 strongly suggests that the "experiment" led in effect to a virtually complete breakdown in the community's capacity to produce authoritative judgments on Soviet plans and objectives.

The first major Soviet estimate initiated and completed during the period of Admiral Turner's directorship was NIE 11-4-78, "Soviet Goals and Expectations in the Global Power Arena." Don Stuery, in his brief history of the Soviet estimates after the "experiment," described its message this way:

> NIE 11-4-78 noted that if the Soviets' military position had improved, they still lacked confidence in their superiority over NATO while Soviet military policy continued to be influenced by "a deeply ingrained

15. Committee on the Present Danger, "Is America Becoming Number 2?" (Washington, D.C.: Committee Pamphlet, 1978), 44.
16. Oberdorfer, "Report Says Soviet Buildup for War."

tendency to overinsure against perceived foreign threats and to over-compensate for technological deficiencies." The estimate concluded with a description of a Soviet leadership preoccupied with domestic problems and—with the aging Soviet Premier, Leonid Brezhnev, in ill health—working under the shadow of a succession crisis.[17]

The estimate had moved too close to the Pentagon's position to be accepted by the State Department's Director of Intelligence. In his dissent he said that he agreed with the general thrust of the paper, but stated:

> The Soviets have a less positive, even a more ambivalent view of the military balance in Europe and would be less confident of the supe-riority of the Warsaw Pact's forces over those of NATO than the net judgments of the Estimate suggest. . . .
> The Soviets are very conservative in their calculations and make a number of assumptions which highlight their own weaknesses and Western strengths; the Soviets have greater fear of Western attack than the Estimate suggests.

In March 1980, a new strategic forces estimate was completed, NIE 11-3/8-79. What happened to that estimate and the one that followed it, NIE 11-3/8-80, issued in December 1980, is described by Steury:

> The 1979 strategic forces estimate was the first to be prepared fol-lowing the failure of the Senate to ratify SALT II. Although the limi-tations imposed by the temporary protocol remained in effect through 1985, this Estimate had to consider the possibility that the Soviets would abandon the arms control process as a whole and resume the unrestrained expansion of at least their strategic offensive forces—and possibly their strategic defensive forces as well, despite the still-valid ABM Treaty.
> In this situation, the controversy over Soviet strategic objectives once again came to the fore. The continued inability to resolve this issue brought a total disaffection of the military intelligence services from the summary judgments presented in NIE 11-3/8-79. The DCI, Admiral Stansfield Turner, played a major role in drafting this por-tion of the NIE.

17. Steury, *Intentions and Estimates*, 336.

To prevent a repetition of the military's disassociation from 11-3/8-79, the following year's NIE 11-3/8-80 contained two sets of Key Judgments. The first, ascribed to the Director of Central Intelligence, was an expansion of the summary judgments contained in the previous year's NIE. The second, which differed substantially in style and presentation, was coordinated among the member agencies of the intelligence community.[18]

Admiral Turner's term as DCI was clearly a time of tribulation. As the Steury account indicates, the intelligence community simply failed to perform its major task—the assessment of Soviet objectives and capabilities. Turner had other problems as well. He was not a popular figure in the Agency. At the same time, he and President Carter's national security adviser, Zbigniew Brzezinski, were rivals for the President's ear, and Turner found himself increasingly excluded from White House councils. Brzezinski and his deputy, David Aaron, were not much interested in intelligence estimates; indeed, within my hearing, Aaron once described estimates as a "nuisance." According to Robert Gates, Brzezinski and Aaron were primarily interested in the CIA as a covert action agency and were disturbed at the CIA's "lack of enthusiasm" for covert action.[19] To add to Turner's isolation from White House councils, Gates, who had served on the NSC staff under Ford and Scowcroft, was asked to return to the staff in May 1977. He thus became readily available to call upon the CIA's resources without the direct involvement of the director.

A dozen years after Turner was replaced by William Casey as President Reagan's DCI, the CIA's Center for the Study of Intelligence and History Staff staged a two-day conference at the Kennedy School of Government in Cambridge, Massachusetts, titled "Estimating Soviet Military Power, 1950 to 1984." One of the sixty conferees was Stansfield Turner, along with some of us who had also participated in the preparation of estimates during the period under discussion. At one point, Turner stunned the group by stating that during his directorship the CIA had failed the President by not foreseeing the collapse of the Soviet Union and especially by mishandling the estimates on Soviet strategic power and objectives. According to the *Washington Post* reporter present (and his report is consistent with my own recollection), Turner said the estimates were not inaccurate, but "irrelevant."[20]

18. Ibid., 335–36.
19. Gates, *From the Shadows*, 441–42.
20. Christopher Daly, *Washington Post*, December 3, 1994.

Turner was referring to what had been under discussion in 1979 and 1980 as a possible "window of opportunity" for the Soviets around 1983. That was the time set by U.S. military planners when the Soviet leaders might have thought they could attack the United States with nuclear weapons and survive to win world dominance. Turner recalled that if such an attack had occurred, the United States could have absorbed it and delivered "a counterpunch that would have destroyed 70 percent of the Soviet economy." In those circumstances, the CIA should simply have stated that both sides already had "too much firepower to need any more." He assumed part of the blame himself, adding that the Agency should have told President Carter that there was no need to build more weapons "except for purely political reasons."[21]

I think one must recognize, as a result of the A-B exercise and the course that events took after 1976, that the estimative process had lost its intellectual integrity. It was no longer a rational research and analytic process, but a political-bureaucratic arena dominated by the military services and anti-Communist ideologists, collaborating under the aegis of the Committee on the Present Danger, in order to corrupt and harness the intelligence system. When President Reagan appointed William Casey, an active member of the Committee, to be the DCI in 1981, victory was complete. Steury sums up William Casey's doctrine and impact as follows:

> Casey saw his task to be a reform and reorientation of the intelligence community. In his tenure, the debate over Soviet objectives was to be subsumed by a new analytical paradigm that understood the strategic arms race in connection with "the main threat," defined by Casey as "the Soviet ability and will to project its power worldwide through subversion and insurgency." It was important, Casey felt, not to become fixated on "the surface questions and manifestations of [the] competition with the Soviet Union" but to remember the nature of the contest—the lineal descendent of the conflict Western civilization had struggled with for millennia—state despotism versus . . . individual freedom and creativity.[22]

21. Ibid.
22. Steury, *Intentions and Estimates*, 457.

f o u r t e e n

The Early 1980s Years of Danger

Divided U.S. Perceptions of the USSR

With Casey's arrival at the CIA, the campaign to shift control of national estimates to the hard-line anti-Communist faction of the intelligence community was over. The rational approach, with its commitment to keeping Soviet
behavior under continuing review, was replaced by one that simply identified the USSR as an implacable and changeless enemy determined to enslave
the world. The only questions were when and how the Soviets would attempt
to do so. The issue was "slavery" versus "freedom." All other questions were
superficial. Even if one sets aside Mr. Casey's extravagant language, the fact
is, as this narrative has shown, that the history of intelligence estimating on
the USSR from 1946 through 1980 has been a history of the contest between
those two points of view.

One reason why the U.S. military services have played such an important
role in the evolution of U.S. attitudes toward the USSR is that military leaders of the pre–World War II era had failed to foresee and to forewarn either
their political chiefs or their subordinate commanders about the deeds and
plans of the German Nazis and the Japanese militarists. Their successors
wanted to be sure that the military establishment did not fail again. It was
that frame of mind, plus the military's proclivity to judge "threats" by the size
and composition of the military forces of other powers, rather than by judgments about the intentions of potential adversaries, that led them to press for

rearmament programs. At the same time, the rhetoric of Soviet leaders, and their seizure of opportunities provided by political instability in many parts of the world, contributed to an impression of the USSR as a thrusting, ambitious power against which it was necessary to achieve and maintain military superiority in order to protect the interests of the United States and even its survival.

It was that perception which prompted NSC-68, the inauguration of the CIA's covert operational activities, and the creation of a network of alliances encircling the Soviet Union. Those American policies, loose talk about "preventive war" by some high military officers, and an across-the-board orientation of U.S. military doctrine and exercises toward a war with the USSR prompted the Soviets to take a variety of defensive actions. The result was creation of the Warsaw Pact, the Communist coup in Czechoslovakia, a sizable enlargement of the Soviet air defense system, a strengthening of Soviet ground force capabilities in Europe, and a high-pressure effort to build a nuclear stockpile and missile system that would constitute a counter-deterrent to the growing U.S. stockpile of nuclear weaponry.

There were, then, two contrasting perceptions of Soviet objectives: one of the USSR as an expansionist power aiming to create overwhelming force with which to intimidate and dominate the world; the other of a Soviet Union suspicious of the West, feeling increasingly encircled, and fearful of America's growing strategic power and its crusading anti-Communist spirit. The former perception was held by many American observers and, as I noted in Chapter 13, led to the formation of the "Committee on the Present Danger" under the leadership of Paul Nitze. That committee's study of the Soviet buildup during the 1960s and 1970s, published in 1978 under the title "Is America Becoming Number 2?" concluded that the Soviet buildup, in its "size, sophistication, and rate of growth far exceeded Soviet requirements for defense."[1]

That conclusion is not supported by the military history of the years after 1945. The Soviets undertook, as reported in earlier chapters, a number of defensive actions during the late 1940s and early 1950s in response to the inauguration of large U.S. nuclear weapons development programs, the creation of NATO, and the decision to rearm West Germany. The substantial ground force capability they maintained in the occupied areas of Eastern Europe was obviously designed to intimidate the local populations and to protect the puppet Communist regimes. But the size of those forces, and the training and weaponry associated with them, make it quite clear that they

---

1. Committee on the Present Danger, "Is America Becoming Number 2?" 46.

were viewed by the Soviets as the only counterdeterrent they possessed to off-set the growing U.S. nuclear-delivery capability. Indeed, as soon as their missile capability against Western Europe materialized, the Soviets reduced their military manpower and pushed ahead with the development of large weapons that could pose a threat to North America. There can be little doubt, then, that the Soviets were pressing their armament programs as if there might be a future military confrontation with the United States. But to what degree— if at all—did those programs "exceed" Soviet requirements for defense?

There were three events that apparently set off a substantial increase in Soviet arms programs in the 1960s. The first of these was John Kennedy's election campaign in the autumn of 1960. The intelligence community had recognized as early as 1958 that the USSR was developing missiles capable of threatening North America. Leaks to the press from Pentagon sources in 1960 led some journalists to allege that the Soviets were well ahead of the United States in missile production and deployment. Kennedy excoriated the Eisenhower-Nixon administration for allowing a "missile gap" to arise. So, when Kennedy assumed office, a large missile production program was initiated and carried through—even though later and better intelligence demonstrated that no such gap had ever existed.

The Soviets realized that they were about to fall far behind the United States in strategic power, and they then decided to establish a minimal threat to the United States by placing short-range missiles in Cuba. The U.S. response—a limited naval blockade and a threat to invade—did more than bring the Soviet scheme to an end; it demonstrated to the USSR and to the world that the USSR was a second-rate power and could be forced to accede to U.S. wishes. The USSR was weak at sea, it could not project military power beyond its immediate periphery, and it still had no substantial capability to bring the United States under attack.

The USSR's humiliating withdrawal of its missiles from Cuba, on top of the Kennedy missile-building program, prompted the Soviets to further increase the scale of their own nuclear-weapons delivery programs, to enlarge their naval ship-building facilities to enable them to challenge the virtual American monopoly of the high seas, and to strengthen further the forces arrayed against NATO in order to maintain the European leg of their counter-deterrent against the United States. Nevertheless, even with the moderniza-tion of the Soviet forces facing the West, the relative balance of forces in Europe in 1978 was about what it had been in 1970. The Soviets, for exam-ple, had more tanks, but the United States had more antitank weapons. Moreover, the Polish, Czech, and Hungarian divisions in the Warsaw Pact complement could hardly be described as reliable; and to bring many of their own divisions up to strength, the Soviets would have been obliged to call up their reserves and retrain them before sending them into combat.

The third matter pushing the USSR's military programs was the problem of protecting its eastern and central Asian borders. By 1978, Soviet military strength in Asia had been increased five-fold over its strength in 1973 to the point where about one-quarter of Soviet ground and tactical air capabilities were deployed against China. Even so, that level of strength was insufficient for anything more than cross-border raids or strikes against strategic targets: it was not sufficient for extended combat. While China could not have carried on a war of movement against the USSR, the four-thousand-mile Soviet-Chinese border could not everywhere be protected against Chinese actions to disrupt or destroy communications between Soviet Asia and Soviet Europe. The Soviet maritime provinces were indeed vulnerable to Chinese attack and harassment, especially if the Soviets wished to maintain substantial alert forces in the West.

If all of the above history was known by Paul Nitze and his associates, it is difficult to understand how they could blithely conclude that the "size, sophistication, and rate of growth" of Soviet programs "far [exceeded] Soviet requirements for defense." The fact is that Nitze and his associates did not make, and could not have made, a "net estimate" that played out the USSR's military capabilities against those of its potential adversaries—especially if those enemies acted in concert. They confined themselves largely to "bean counting," that is, measuring tank inventories, missile silos, warheads, throw weights, small warships, etc., as if the United States and the USSR were the only two nations in the world. They did not take into account the military capabilities of the other NATO powers or of China and Japan. Above all, they could not have taken into account the enormous complexities involved in modern military operations on a global scale, e.g., the effect of equipment failures, the complications for targeting and missile-flight planning from geodetic anomalies, hazards to electronic communications, human failures, and political unknowns.

The history of the U.S.-Soviet military relationship, as outlined above and as explored in the various estimates of the years from 1951 to 1973, strongly suggests that the principal impetus driving Soviet armament programs was U.S. policy and behavior. Soviet military policy was essentially reactive and defensive. Indeed, the estimates consistently concluded that the Soviet leaders would not undertake any action which they believed carried a serious risk of general war with the United States, and that they would not deliberately initiate general war against the United States unless they believed that they were about to suffer a preemptive nuclear attack by the United States

That is not to say that the Soviet leaders did not hope to derive some political benefits from a stronger military position. They wanted not to be humiliated again, and they wanted the world to recognize their might and their political message. There can be little doubt that they did indeed gain world respect for their scientific achievements and for their role as an alternative source of political and economic support to weaker nations who were resisting U.S. diplomatic and economic pressures.

But the Soviets clearly did not want to take on the United States. In all the years of U.S.-Soviet enmity, there had never been a direct military encounter; at the Bering Strait, for example, where U.S. and Soviet territories abut, there has always been a careful and prudent relationship. And during crises such as that at Berlin in 1962, in the Mediterranean in 1973, and during the Iran affair in 1979, the Soviets were careful not to let things get out of hand. The history of Soviet deliberations during crisis situations, which is presented in this narrative, clearly demonstrates that those assessments are correct. Even when the Soviets supported satellite aggression, as in Korea, they did so in the expectation that the United States would not engage militarily.

The Triumph of the Hard-Liners

Even though evidence supportive of the views which I have expressed above was available in the public domain, it was by 1980 of little interest to the intelligence community or to journalists and commentators. At the time, there were comparatively few American political leaders in either party willing to step forward and espouse the rational view of keeping Soviet objectives under continuing review. America had just suffered a trauma over the seizure of the U.S. embassy in Teheran and the imprisonment of its personnel. After the ignominious failure of the military effort to free and rescue the U.S. hostages in Teheran, the United States began to look like a clumsy giant, and public dismay multiplied over what appeared to be a deterioration of the U.S. world position. Revolutions in the Third World, the U.S. defeat in Vietnam, and the increasing military power of the USSR were frequently cited as signs that the United States was losing stature in the world, while the USSR was gaining world respect.

Within the Carter administration, the policy struggle between Secretary of State Cyrus Vance and White House Security Adviser Zbigniew Brzezinski resulted in Vance's resignation. Thereafter, President Carter increasingly associated himself with the hard-liners in the White House and at the Pentagon. Robert Gates, known around the CIA for his strong anti-Communist views, had returned to the NSC staff in May 1977 (after a short stay at the Agency following a previous tour at the NSC). He quickly supported Brzezinski's plans to carry out a variety of anti-Soviet policies and activities around the world. He summed up his views on the U.S.-Soviet relationship at the time in this way in his memoirs:

> Both the intelligence community and policymakers in the Carter Administration believed by the end of the 1970s that, while the Soviet Union had not acquired strategic superiority, maintaining the balance required continuation of the U.S. modernization programs—and additional measures. The geopolitical consequences of the extraordinary Soviet build-up beginning in the mid-1960s were equally obvious: the loss of U.S. military superiority [sic] and growth of Soviet military power had given the Kremlin new confidence to pursue its ambitions internationally more aggressively and without much concern for U.S. sensibilities.[2]

Gates might have believed that, but it is quite clear—from the Soviet documents utilized by the scholars working with them at the Cold War International History Project and cited in this narrative—that the Soviets did not.

In their efforts to demonstrate the need for new U.S. armament programs, both President Carter and Secretary of Defense Harold Brown played fast and loose with CIA estimates of Soviet military expenditures. The CIA economists had warned, when publishing their estimates, that it was difficult to compare the U.S. and Soviet military establishments because they differed so widely "in missions, structures, and characteristics." The CIA analysts also warned that their calculations, when translated into dollar-cost terms, tended to "overestimate Soviet activities relative to those of the U.S." The CIA figures showed—even in the form which "overestimated" the Soviet effort—that U.S. military expenditures during the 1960s exceeded those of the Soviet Union by 40 percent. It was when the Soviets were attempting to catch up that the CIA calculations showed Soviet expenditures exceeding those of the United States. Those were the Soviet military expenditures that President Carter found "excessive" and that Secretary Brown found "disquieting as an index of both Soviet capability and intentions."

2. Gates, *From the Shadows*, 172.

The Defense Department responded to the increases in Soviet capabilities by drafting a new strategic doctrine known as Presidential Directive Number 59. It was leaked to the *New York Times* in August 1980, and after the leak occurred, Secretary Brown sought to explain it in an address at the Naval War College. He asserted that "deterrence" remained the fundamental U.S. "strategic objective," but what he actually did was to redefine deterrence. Under the directive, he said, U.S. nuclear-capable forces would become "a wall against nuclear coercion or attack upon our friends and allies." U.S. strategic forces, he explained, "must contribute to deterrence of conventional aggression" as well as to deterrence of a Soviet nuclear attack upon the United States itself. Brown acknowledged that the new strategy was designed "to deter any adversary from any course of action [including conventional aggression] that could lead to a general nuclear war."

In short, the U.S. government was arrogating to itself the right to decide which Soviet actions or threats of action it might object to, and which ones therefore would prompt the United States to respond with a nuclear attack upon the USSR, not necessarily with massive retaliation, but perhaps upon the Soviet forces involved or upon Soviet centers of command and control. It was not "a new doctrine," Brown said, but only a "refinement, a codification" of previous statements. Brown claimed that it was not "a first-strike strategy," but the United States appeared to be announcing that it would massively retaliate or respond at some lower level of military action to any Soviet action or threat of action of which the U.S. government disapproved. We might, for example, drop a few nuclear weapons upon selected targets, either the offending Soviet forces or their bosses back in Moscow. Brown and his associates showed no sign of having heard of a Brezhnev remark of two years earlier that "the first time one of these things is fired in anger, everything is lost. The warring nations would never be able to put things back together." PD 59, as Brown explained it, was not really deterrence; it was in effect compellence.

Two weeks earlier, the Soviet leadership had taken note of the leaked report in the *New York Times*. *Pravda*, the official Communist Party organ, called the reported strategy an "ominous" sign of the "loss of common sense" in Washington. The *Pravda* commentator noted that the State Department and the Arms Control Agency had been excluded from the preparation of the strategy, and he attributed it to Brzezinski and Brown. Instead of being a prescription for preventing a major conflict, as claimed by the authors, the new strategy—said *Pravda*—was a prescription for stimulating the arms race.[3]

3. Anthony Austin, *New York Times*, August 8, 1980.

The strategy was also sharply attacked in the United States. The *New York Times* stated editorially on August 21, immediately after Brown spoke at the War College, that it raised more questions than it answered. Brown had defended the strategy as a response to the big Soviet missile buildup and had said that the USSR might already have the potential to destroy U.S. missiles in silo. But the editorialist responded that it "strained credulity" to think the Soviets "would be foolhardy enough to try" to attack the United States in view of the virtual invulnerability of the U.S. strength in long-range bombers and missile-capable submarines. The *Times* writer was also "alarmed" at the extension of nuclear deterrence to a variety of lesser aggressions, "even including conventional military aggression." The editorial concluded with the observation that while the new strategy might deter some conflicts, if one did break out it would "increase the likelihood that nuclear weapons would be used."[4]

Secretary of State Edmund Muskie (who had succeeded Vance when the latter resigned over the Iranian rescue affair) was asked by the Senate Foreign Relations Committee to discuss the new doctrine. He made clear to the committee that he had not been consulted about the formulation and issuance of the directive, that a matter of such importance had a "significant foreign dimension," and that he had been assured by President Carter that the State Department in the future would be consulted on "such major national security policy decisions" as PD 59. He nevertheless came to the defense of the new "countervailing doctrine," as it was called by the Defense Department. He did put a somewhat softer face on it by clearly implying that the United States would retaliate with nuclear weapons only if the Soviets initiated a "nuclear attack," whether it was a massive attack against the United States or a "more limited one against the U.S. or its allies." What Muskie did not explain was why the Soviets, in view of the massive numbers and great variety of U.S. nuclear weaponry, would be so foolish as to initiate a nuclear attack under any circumstances. Muskie said it strengthened deterrence and provided a firmer basis for "our diplomacy with the Soviets." Moreover, it underlined our determination to respond to "any challenge to our vital interests."[5]

The new doctrine left open a number of very important questions. What are U.S. vital interests? Who decides what they are? Are there any standards that our adversaries ought to understand? Did the doctrine really apply only

4. "The New Nuclear Strategy and Its Perils," *New York Times*, August 21, 1980, editorial page.
5. "U.S. Nuclear Strategy," Department of State, Current Policy Number 219, September 16, 1980.

to nuclear aggression? Does it apply only to aggression against U.S. allies? Or to U.S. "friends" as well? Do we give warning when we take on a new "friend"? Was the United States committing itself only to "responsive" action? If so, why was the United States developing a "first-strike" capability? What message were the Soviets actually receiving? Most of those questions became the problem of the next administration. The Carter administration came to an end in January 1981.

The Perilous Years

One of the major factors in the victory of Ronald Reagan in the November 1980 general election was public disillusionment with the evolving world situation. The unique position of power and respect the United States had won through its victories in World War II had faded over the years as other nations recovered their strength and began to pursue their own national goals. Indeed, the paramount postwar U.S. position was soon challenged by the new power centers in Moscow and Beijing, which were posing an alternative to the West's world leadership. Many revolutionary leaders in the Near East, South Asia, and Africa appeared drawn to the example posed by the USSR and China and by the support they offered in their struggles against imperialism.

After the events of the 1970s in Vietnam, Iran, and Afghanistan, there seemed to be no way to explain to the American public that some setbacks to American ideals and to the American world position were inevitable. Nor was there any way to convince the U.S. media and public that American security interests could still be protected by combining patient diplomacy with firmness of principle. It was widely believed that something had gone wrong, America was being pushed around, and a new direction was needed. The Reagan campaign captured popular disillusionment and won an easy victory at the polls.

The first years of the Reagan administration featured a good deal of rhetoric about the "evil empire" and the need for increased armament to meet the Soviet threat. Yet for the most part, the new administration continued the armament programs and doctrines of the Carter years. Except for the ill-advised Strategic Defense Initiative aimed at creating an anti-missile defense, there was no new coherent military strategy articulated to deal with the presumed forthcoming Soviet acts of aggression.

It was not for want of free advice. Within weeks after the election, *Foreign Affairs* published a long article by Paul Nitze entitled "Strategy for the Decade of the 1980s." European critics, Nitze wrote, had found American policy "erratic" because it lacked "a sound strategic concept." It was his purpose in the article to propose such a concept. He proceeded with his usual cant about Soviet objectives and strategies, including the myth that the Soviets had "demonstrated by the surprise attack by North Korea upon South Korea that they were prepared actually to use military power under their control in support of their political aims." He went on to state that it was in response to that action—the origins of which were quite different from how they are portrayed in the myth—that U.S. armament programs of the 1950s and onward were undertaken.[6]

Nitze believed that during the late 1970s, the Soviets would have calculated that the "correlation of forces," to use their theoretical terminology, had shifted in their favor. But what he considered as evidence of successful Soviet expansionism was very thin indeed. I took issue with his so-called evidence in a letter to the editor of *Foreign Affairs* in which I wrote:

> There are a number of assertions in his account which are either devoid of substantial evidence or based upon events which, given his underlying thesis, are treated as evidence. The public record contains no clear or persuasive evidence, for example, that the Soviets played a "major role in encouraging" the October 1973 attack upon Israel and the subsequent OPEC oil squeeze, that the hostage seizure in Teheran in November 1979 involved members of the Moscow-controlled Tudeh party, or that the assault on the Grand Mosque in Mecca and the activities of the Red Brigades in Italy were "supported and perhaps instigated" by Soviet agents. And almost everything that occurred in the world during the 1970s which might be regarded as unfavorable to U.S. interests is attributed to Soviet action. Mr. Nitze even believes that events since 1973 in Cambodia, Laos, Somalia, Ethiopia, Angola, South Yemen, and Zaire have given evidence of Soviet determination to expand the sway of Soviet influence across Africa and the routes of access to the Persian Gulf. Exactly what Cambodia and Laos have to do with Africa and the Persian Gulf, Mr. Nitze does not say.[7]

I added a few facts about the Soviet world position of which Nitze seemed unaware. I pointed out that in 1980 there were a lot fewer Communists in

6. Paul Nitze, "Strategy in the Decade of the 1980's," *Foreign Affairs* 59 (Fall 1980): 82–101.
7. Willard C. Matthias, "Confronting the Soviets," *Foreign Affairs* 59 (Winter 1980/81): 422–23.

the world allied with Moscow, or under its influence, than there had been in 1950, because "the Soviets have lost their influence, or most of it, in the Communist states of China, Yugoslavia, and Albania. They have been faced with strong recalcitrance in Rumania, Poland, Hungary, Czechoslovakia, and the Communist parties of Italy and Spain. They have had favorable positions slip away from them in Indonesia, Egypt, Ghana, Mali and the Sudan."[8]

I also added a few facts about the Soviet domestic situation, namely, that they have had to worry about failures to meet economic goals, about technological backwardness, about a growing imbalance between Russian and non-Russian peoples, and about a general lack of creativity and enthusiasm in Soviet society. I then concluded that "when the Soviet leaders look at their situation today and consider their courses of action, it is highly unlikely that they view the correlation of forces in quite so favorable a light as Soviet propagandists suggest or as Mr. Nitze thinks they should."[9]

Mr. Nitze also seemed to have been unaware of the changes that had taken place in Soviet society and in the Soviet Communist Party itself since the death of Stalin. I attempted to apprise him of these changes and their significance in my letter as well:

> More than ever before, Soviet policy has become the result of competition among individuals, bureaucratic entities, interest groups, nationalities, professions, and generations. There are debates about arms control versus arms expansion, forward strategy versus quietism in the Third World, economic autarky versus trade and interdependence. One of the liveliest debates has been over how to apply modern science and technology to the Soviet economy and how to deal with its consequences. Indeed, Professor Cyril Black of Princeton University sees the 1970s debate over the scientific-technological revolution [STR] as resulting in sweeping changes, which have transformed Marxism-Leninism in the direction of a more pluralistic society. The party hacks who have dominated Soviet policy are already giving way to a new generation of managers and professionals with a more pragmatic orientation.[10]

8. Ibid., 423.
9. Ibid.
10. Ibid.

As of 1980, however, Nitze believed that the "central concern" of the Soviets was how to deal with "the contingency of a direct confrontation of Soviet military forces with Western military forces." This is a subject upon which *Foreign Affairs* had opened its pages to Nitze's views twice previously. On this occasion he wrote that the Soviet leaders believed it "unlikely" that "the West" would let them "have the world without a fight." The Soviets, in pushing out the perimeter of their area of control, would try to deploy their forces in such a way as "to achieve local military superiority," thereby minimizing the prospect for a direct U.S.-Soviet military confrontation. If there were such a confrontation, according to the Nitze theory, the Soviets would expect "the West" to "escalate to the use of nuclear weapons." Hence, what the Soviets were trying to do was to put themselves into the position to win such a war and to survive with enough of "their power base" to recover.[11]

To deal with that contingency, according to Nitze, the United States would have had to increase its defense spending by some 35 percent above current levels. "What is clear beyond doubt," Nitze concluded, "is that if the United States does not act along the lines proposed here, the kind of threats to world peace that have arisen in the last five years will multiply inexorably and perhaps, in the end, irretrievably."[12]

I discuss this very contingency in my letter to the editor of *Foreign Affairs*. I quote a part of my response to Nitze's article here:

> There is indeed a danger of general nuclear war, though there is at least a reasonable case to be made that it lies as much in U.S. doctrine and capabilities as in Soviet doctrine and capabilities. The MX missile was established as an Air Force requirement, for example, in 1971, and an advanced development program was begun in 1973. This missile, together with the Trident II system and the current deployment of the Mark 12A warhead on the Minuteman III, will give the United States a substantial first-strike capability against the largest and most vulnerable sector of the Soviet strategic force—the Soviet missile forces in silo.
>
> With these U.S. capabilities in the process of becoming reality, and with the extended deterrence openly declared in Secretary of Defense Brown's exposition of Presidential Directive 59 at the Naval War College, what are the Soviets to do? Unless they are ready to sit tight

11. Nitze, "Strategy," 87.
12. Ibid., 91.

and allow themselves to be incinerated, they must also prepare for a first strike. Thus, the stage is being set for one side or the other to take preemptive action and in a situation of tension, plunge the world into unmitigated disaster. . . . The problem now is to get out of that predicament. . . .

The problem of U.S. policy is not to inject more military power into the evolution of world politics, but to try to surmount the need to dispose and brandish it. This involves encouragement of pluralism and experimentation—and reassessment—in the Communist world, encouragement of economic interdependence and cosmopolitanism, and a recognition that we, the Communist nations, and the aspiring populations of the southern two-thirds of the world have a common problem in making this planet in the twenty first century a place fit for human habitation.[13]

The views of Mr. Nitze and of the Committee on the Present Danger, of course, prevailed in Washington. The U.S. government went ahead with new large military programs; it paid for them by increasing the deficit and the public debt. The mathematics of destruction became a growth industry. The NIEs became almost incomprehensible except to the aficionados of military planning, equipment, and operations. The estimates continued to be dominated by the military agencies, with the CIA joining them on most judgments, and with the State Department standing alone in dissent on major issues. The final paragraph of NIE 11-3/8-83, "Soviet Capabilities for Strategic Nuclear Conflict, 1983–93," summarizes both positions:

The evidence shows clearly that Soviet leaders are attempting to prepare their military forces for the possibility of having to fight a nuclear war and are training to be able to maintain control over increasingly complex conflict situations. They have seriously addressed many of the problems of conducting military operations in a nuclear war, thereby improving their ability to deal with the many contingencies of such a conflict, and raising the probability of outcomes favorable to the USSR. There is an alternative view (*held by the Director, Bureau of Intelligence and Research, Department of State*) that wishes to emphasize that the Soviets have not resolved many of the critical problems bearing on the conduct of nuclear war, such as the nature of the

13. Matthias, "Confronting the Soviets," 424–25.

initiation of the conflict, escalation within the theater, and protracted nuclear operations. According to this view, the Soviets recognize that nuclear war is so destructive, and its course so uncertain, that they could not expect an outcome that was "favorable" in any meaningful sense.

While the hard-liners at the Pentagon, the CIA, and the Committee on the Present Danger were beating the drum for new armament programs, CIA economists were pointing to Soviet economic problems as posing a threat to Soviet political stability. We in the Office of National Estimates had frequently reported that the Communist world was encountering problems in deciding what Communism was all about and in figuring out how to make their economies work better. Back in 1964, for example, the World Trends memorandum noted the "spectacle of the USSR, after the boastful claims and plans of a few years ago, coming to the West hat in hand to buy wheat and to ask for long-term credits." The memorandum had gone on to say:

> These phenomena are not passing difficulties, nor are they merely the consequences of misfortune. The source is deeper, and the problem will not soon go away. It lies fundamentally in the nature of Communism itself, how it should be defined, how its objectives should be translated into reality, whether it can be made to work. . . .
> Soviet economic problems have contributed to some greater prudence in Soviet policy and particularly to the current Soviet efforts to create a more friendly atmosphere in U.S.-Soviet relations.

In the years that followed, the CIA economists kept Soviet economic problems under close scrutiny. According to Gates: "In the late 1970s, the Agency began to chronicle not only deepening economic difficulty, but also social problems—popular disaffection, ideological erosion, material frustration, and ethnic unrest. In August 1979, CIA published the assessment that 'Soviet consumer discontent is growing and will cause the regime of the 1980s serious economic and political problems.'"[14]

Gates returned to the CIA in January 1980 after nearly three years as executive assistant to Brzezinski at the NSC. When Director Turner appointed him CIA National Intelligence Officer for Soviet Affairs, direct responsibility and wider contact with intelligence information on the USSR caused him to reflect upon the message the Agency had been sending to policymakers

14. Gates, *From the Shadows*, 173.

about the Soviets. It was, he wrote, "mixed, and therefore confusing," because CIA military and strategic analysis was published "independently" of political and economic assessments. (There was, of course, no longer a Board of National Estimates to assume corporate responsibility and to see that the intelligence product represented careful group thinking.) Having then identified the problem, Gates wrote a memorandum to the Director at the end of October 1980 trying to make a course correction. Here is Gates's account of the memorandum:

> I said that the Soviets had a different perception of the strategic environment in the 1980s than CIA had been publishing. I believed the Soviets saw themselves as an isolated superpower, facing the combined hostility of the United States, Western Europe, Japan, and China even as they confronted serious problems in Eastern Europe, instability on their southern border, and deep economic problems. Meanwhile, they saw the United States pursuing a number of weapons programs intended to reverse the strategic trend of the mid-1960s and a strategy (again in their view) aimed at acquiring a U.S. first-strike capability, strategic superiority, or provoking a conflict that would be fought exclusively in Europe and the USSR. Further, they confronted a changing internal situation, including long-range industrial, energy, agricultural, social, and demographic problems, as well as a leadership transition just begun by the death of Kosygin. I wrote, in October 1980, that Soviet aggressiveness internationally and their vigorous military programs masked what they saw then as very real vulnerabilities.[15]

That analysis—made inside the Agency—was almost identical to that which I had included in my letter to the editor of *Foreign Affairs*, which was written shortly thereafter and a full three years after my last contact with the Agency. Neither Gates's analysis nor mine had any effect.

The new crowd around Reagan was determined to change everything. Most of all, they wanted to frighten the Soviet leaders. Indicative of the "frighten them" school of thought was the statement of Defense Secretary-designate Caspar Weinberger at his confirmation hearing in January 1981: "We should never enter a war we do not intend to win, or in which we do not expend every single effort of every single weapon and every facility that we have to win. If troops are committed, if we are in an active engagement,

15. Ibid., 176.

we have every obligation and every duty then to go all the way forward and win. I do not want to be misunderstood about that."[16]

Weinberger probably did frighten the Soviets, but he also frightened a lot of U.S. policymakers. For years we had been building a powerful and expensive military establishment which, according to his doctrine, we could no longer use in support of our diplomacy without running the risk of a nuclear exchange. We had become caught in a paralysis of power of our own making. We could no longer pose any credible threat of major military action without running the risk of escalation into a nuclear conflict.

A year later that point was brought home to our military and diplomatic establishments when we deployed a contingent of U.S. Marines into Lebanon. They were part of a UN plan to stabilize the situation there and were assigned the mission of guarding the international airport. The U.S. contingent was subjected to repeated sniping and finally to a terrorist attack which caused some 240 deaths of U.S. military personnel. In those circumstances, we either had to withdraw or to expand our military commitment greatly beyond the area of the airport if we were to protect the airport and the forces guarding it. The Lebanese army had collapsed, and the U.S. contingent was surrounded by hostile militias. The U.S. army attaché said, "We either had to get serious about defending ourselves or we had to get out."[17] Expansion could have led to large-scale combat in the region, a prolonged military presence, and the possibility of Soviet intervention. We withdrew.

U.S. political leaders nevertheless still felt the need to demonstrate their manhood. Without regard for international law and the principles of national sovereignty, the administration invaded the small island country of Grenada, bombed Libya in an effort to kill Qaddafi, and mined Nicaraguan waters. The NSC staff at the White House violated U.S. law by selling U.S. military equipment to Iran and using the proceeds to pay and equip a guerrilla force that was attempting to overthrow the government of Nicaragua. These actions angered U.S. allies in Europe, even those of the most conservative stripe.

But the central priority of Ronald Reagan was not the sideshows in Lebanon, Libya, Grenada, or Nicaragua. He wanted to make the United States impregnable. Reagan accepted the views of those around him who believed it possible to do so, and he went before the American public in March 1983 with a "vision" of discarding deterrence in favor of a program to intercept and

---

16. Senate Committee on Armed Services, *Hearings on the Nomination of Caspar Weinberger to Be Secretary of Defense*, 97th Cong., 1st sess., 1981, 38–39.

17. Quoted in Lou Cannon, *Reagan, Role of a Lifetime* (New York: Simon & Schuster, 1991), 455.

destroy incoming missiles. This became known as the "Strategic Defense Initiative," or SDI. Those who were advising the president to adopt an anti-missile program evidently did not choose to tell him that there would still be a threat from the Soviet long-range air force and from nuclear-missile-equipped submarines and surface ships. Nor did they apparently make clear to him that scientists were far from agreement about the feasibility of the proposed anti-missile system. But Reagan wanted it, and the program began.

According to Robert Gates, the year 1983, when Reagan launched the SDI, was the "most dangerous" of the late Cold War era. He wrote in his memoirs that it was the time when the "risk of miscalculation" and "level of tension" were at their highest. He also wrote what looks like a "mea culpa" with Gates taking upon himself and other hard-liners some of the blame for this state of affairs. He wrote:

> While we in the American intelligence community saw the tension in the U.S.-USSR relationship firsthand, we did not really grasp just how much the Soviet leadership felt increasingly threatened by the United States and by the course of events.
>
> Why did we fail to understand that? The answer, I think, lies in the fact that we did not then grasp the growing desperation of the men in the Kremlin, a state of mind that established the frame for how they would look at events that year. By the beginning of 1983, there were no more illusions in Moscow that, relative to the West, Soviet problems were transitory and manageable by modest adjustments to the system. The Western economies had begun their strong expansion, and the boom in technological developments had started. The Soviets' great fear in the 1970s that the U.S. industrial and technological prowess might be unleashed in a new military build up, had been realized, and they saw the U.S. defense budget growing at a staggering pace, seemingly without any economic strain. By the early 1980s, they saw strategic weapons being deployed and new programs undertaken that they believed would provide the United States a first-strike capability. The Kremlin saw renewed confidence in the West, and a willingness to use military force.[18]

18. Gates, *From the Shadows*, 258–59.

The Approach of Apocalypse

What Gates saw as the Kremlin's belief in 1983 was really only a worst case of what they had seen for years, almost from the beginning of the postwar period. They had always perceived the United States as the principal obstacle to fulfillment of their historic myth—the goal of a Communist world attained through their example and efforts, and "they saw American military power as the continuing threat to the achievement of that goal." But science and technology had brought the American military threat to them in a new and dangerous form. It was indeed a new predicament for the Soviets, *as well as for the United States.*

In the spring of 1982, I delivered a lecture at the George Mason University seminar "Conflict and Conflict Management"; my title was "Surviving in the Post-Detente World." I reviewed the strategic situation existing at the time and pointed out that the United States had achieved a very high probability of destroying a very large proportion of the Soviet forces in a first strike, while the Soviets would have a much smaller chance of doing the same thing to us. I went on:

> Thus, if the Soviet leaders come to believe that we were planning to attack them, they would have no alternative but to attack us in order to reduce the weight of attack upon them.
>
> We have, then, arrived at the ironic condition that the nuclear forces designed to deter an attack by the other side have in fact become forces that tend to provoke an attack by the other side. Forces designed to deter have reduced their capacity to deter. . . .
>
> The simple fact is that whatever we may think of Communism or the Soviet leaders or the people of the Soviet Union, whatever further development of military armament we might spend our energies upon, . . . our lives and fortunes in the final analysis are dependent upon Soviet restraint and rationality as well as our own.[19]

The same thoughts were clearly in the minds of many people in America and Europe. There were demonstrations in Western Europe against the NATO-ordained deployment of U.S.-manufactured intermediate-range missiles. During that same summer of 1982, there were arms control negotiations going on with the Soviets, led on the U.S. side by Paul Nitze, who had

19. Willard C. Matthias, "Surviving in the Post-Detente World," in *Conflict Management and Problem Solving,* ed. Dennis Sandole and Ingrid Sandole (London: Francis Printers, 1987), 240.

been appointed by Reagan as his principal arms control negotiator. On the intermediate-range missile issue, Nitze and the leader of the Soviet team arrived at a compromise that the administration rejected outright. Gates has written that "while many experts liked the compromise, the Secretary of Defense [Weinberger] was apoplectic, and his cohorts derided the compromise and called for Nitze's scalp." (Even Nitze was too moderate for Weinberger and his fellow warriors!) Also during 1982 and into 1983, there was considerable agitation in the United States against the proliferation of nuclear arms. There was a demonstration of several hundred thousand people in New York City. There was a "nuclear freeze" movement pushing for both sides to stop manufacturing nuclear weapons. A "nuclear winter" alarm was set off by a group of nuclear scientists. One of the television networks broadcast a movie, *The Day After*, which depicted what it might be like after a nuclear attack. The film frightened a lot of people and led to prayer services in the churches.

Gates reported much of the above in the context of the deployment in Europe of the intermediate-range missile system, a deployment designed, of course, to frighten the Soviets. But Gates showed no interest in the implications for the world of the multiplication of nuclear weapons systems—including high-megatonnage first-strike weapons—on both sides. He did acknowledge, writing in 1996, that the year 1983 might have been a frightening one:

> The Soviets truly may have thought that the danger of war was high. While the U.S. government did not share that apprehension, the American people did.
>
> By 1983, many in the United States were worried, even scared. . . . The political dialogue between Moscow and Washington had collapsed even as both sides were building and deploying new generations of strategic nuclear weapons.[20]

Gates himself, however, showed no concern about the dangerous situation which he had recognized. His view was really quite simple. By the end of 1983 the United States was getting stronger and the USSR weaker, the correlation of forces had shifted "irreversibly in favor of the United States," and it was time for the West "to begin gathering the harvest."[21] It apparently never occurred to Gates, by then Casey's Deputy Director for Intelligence, that this

20. Gates, *From the Shadows*, 276.
21. Ibid., 277.

was precisely the situation when—in desperation—the Soviets might have felt obliged to attack the United States. Instead of thinking about whether the Soviets would continue to show restraint and act rationally, Gates was exulting in Soviet fear and discomfort.

That harshness and thoughtlessness within the Reagan administration is difficult to fathom. There apparently was a group, both military and civilian in composition, determined to beat down the Soviets, to humble them, to force them to back down, even if it meant Armageddon. They were indifferent to the possibility that the Soviets, in fear and despair, might let loose their nuclear forces upon the United States. That disregard is especially difficult to understand because many of those hard-liners also had been insisting, in order to frighten the American public and Congress into approving large defense budgets, that the Soviets were planning to fight and win a nuclear war. If so, why gratuitously frighten them into starting it?

Ambassador Dobrynin, in his memoirs of the early 1980s, took up the question of whether the USSR feared a U.S. nuclear strike. He reported that the leaders whom he knew—Khrushchev, Brezhnev, Andropov, and Chernenko—all proceeded on the assumption that the United States posed "a real military threat to our country's security in the long run." Soviet military planning was therefore "keyed to an overwhelming strategy of defense based on the possibility of retaliating by inflicting unacceptable damage." They believed, except for Andropov, that an attack would not take place "unexpectedly at any moment," but was more likely in a time of crisis. The "political and social structure of the United States was the best guarantee against an unprovoked strike."[22] Dobrynin went on to write, however:

> Considering the continuous political and military rivalry and tension between the two superpowers, and an adventurous president such as Reagan, there was no lack of concern in Moscow that American bellicosity and simple human miscalculation could combine with fatal results. Andropov once said to me in a very private conversation "Reagan is unpredictable. You should expect anything from him." All in all, the Kremlin leaders took Reagan seriously—perhaps more so than he took his own antics—and they therefore watched him with increasing vigilance. Our intelligence services were also more on alert than during other presidencies to pick up any advance signals of U.S. military action.[23]

22. Dobrynin, *In Confidence*, 522–23.
23. Ibid., 523.

The Soviet military and political leadership, Dobrynin went on to write, "felt they had no choice but to reckon with the possibility of a nuclear war," and they "did not really believe that a nuclear war might be winnable." Moreover: "They profoundly hoped that the supreme military leadership in Washington believed as they did. But they were by no means confident that their potential opponents really felt the same way, and the incessant American attempts to attain strategic superiority made them fear otherwise. Hence our determination to make irreversible the nuclear parity we had achieved."[24]

Dobrynin also cited remarks made to him by Marshal Sergei Akhromeyev, chief of the Soviet General Staff, during the 1980s. The marshal's words bear a strong resemblance to those of the U.S. Air Force in its dissent to NIE 11-3/8-76, where it ascribed to the Soviets an intention to attain "general strategic superiority." He quotes Akhromeyev:

> Suffice it to remember the Arab-Israeli conflict of 1973, when the United States put its armed forces on high combat alert against us. Incidentally, that happened in a period of detente under Nixon. Now, does President Reagan inspire more confidence? That is why my motto as Chief of General Staff is "National military security along all azimuths." We proceed from the worst conceivable scenario of having to fight the United States, its West European allies, and probably Japan. We must be prepared for any kind of war with any kind of weapon. Soviet military doctrine can be summed up as follows: 1941 shall never be repeated.[25]

The apocalypse did not arrive. Dobrynin went on to report that "Reagan's policy began to turn" in 1984 and that as a result Moscow's attitude became less "paranoid." That was when Secretary of State George Shultz began to win a few battles against the hard-liners in the Reagan administration.

24. Ibid., 524.
25. Ibid., 525.

fifteen

The Road to Peace   1983–1991

Emerging Policy Splits in the Reagan Administration

It has now become clear from recent biographical material that the Reagan administration was gravely divided in 1982 and 1983 on the question of how to deal with the Soviets. There were the hard-liners (Weinberger at Defense, William Clark at the NSC, and Casey at the CIA, with Gates as a willing and admiring collaborator) on one side, and on the other side Secretary of State George Shultz, who had succeeded General Haig in 1982. Shultz, according to Gates, was "virtually alone" in Reagan's senior foreign policy team in perceiving that the President saw America's resurgent military power as a "means to an end," as a way to reduce nuclear weapons and to promote a more peaceful world through a more constructive relationship with the USSR.[1]

One of the things that Shultz tried to do after he succeeded Haig was to bring Ambassador Dobrynin into a dialogue with President Reagan, in the hope of beginning a process of reconciliation with the Soviets. The first meeting between the two took place on February 15, 1983. A few days before the session with Dobrynin, Reagan and Shultz had talked about China and the USSR at a private dinner at the White House. Shultz wrote this about Reagan's attitude at the dinner:

1. Gates, *From the Shadows*, 281.

[Reagan] realized, I thought, that he was in a sense blocked by his own White House Staff, by the Defense Department, by Bill Casey at CIA, and by his own past rhetoric. Now that we were talking in the family setting, I could see that Ronald Reagan was much more willing to move forward in relations with these two Communist nations — even travel to them — than I had earlier believed. Reagan saw himself as an experienced negotiator going back to his days as president of the Screen Actors Guild. He was self-confident about his views and positions. He had never had a lengthy session with an important leader of a Communist country, and I could sense he would relish such an opportunity.[2]

The meeting took place in the President's private apartment on the second floor of the White House. Dobrynin has given a dramatic and detailed report on the meeting in his memoirs. He had arrived at Secretary Shultz's office at 5 P.M. for what he presumed was a routine call. Shultz told him that the President wanted to see them both at the White House right away. They were whisked from the State Department's basement garage to the White House grounds through the private East Entrance. The President had been well prepared for the session, which lasted almost two hours. Shultz told Dobrynin later that the President's "entire entourage," except for Nancy Reagan, Shultz himself, and Michael Deaver of the President's personal staff, had opposed the meeting but that the President had gone ahead with it anyway. This showed, Dobrynin concluded, that — having come at the beginning of the third year of his presidency — Reagan had a "personal desire to examine Soviet-American relations more closely."[3] For his part, Shultz reported that Reagan had "impressively engaged Dobrynin" on a range of issues and that the President had spoken with "genuine feeling and eloquence" on the subject of human rights and related matters.[4]

Although the Dobrynin-Reagan dialogue in February 1983 opened the way toward improved U.S.-Soviet relations, there was still much tension and rhetorical warfare ahead. The Soviet downing of Korean airliner KAL 007 in September was blown all out of proportion on the U.S. side, although in fact it almost certainly was a misidentification rather than an act of brutal aggression. By the following summer, however, when — according to Dobrynin —

---

2. Dobrynin, In Confidence, 517–20.
3. George P. Shultz, Turmoil and Triumph (New York: Charles Scribner's Sons, 1993), 164.
4. Ibid.

Mikhail Gorbachev began to dominate the Presidium, the Presidium had made two important decisions. The first was to renew disarmament talks with the United States, and the second was to move toward a summit with President Reagan. Dobrynin himself continued to worry about the sharp Shultz-Weinberger differences, but felt that Reagan had "undergone an evolution" toward acquiring a favorable image as a "strong president and a peacemaker."[5]

During the 1984 presidential election campaign, Reagan's associates even began to intimate that because his policies were succeeding, he could become more agreeable to the USSR. The White House even issued an invitation to Foreign Minister Gromyko to visit Washington in September for a conversation with the President. That invitation was followed in Moscow by a shift from confronting Reagan to trying "to reach agreements with him."[6] Then, after Reagan's reelection in November 1984 and Gorbachev's ascension to General Secretary in March 1985, movement toward a summit took on speed. On July 23, 1985, it was announced in Moscow and Washington that President Reagan and General Secretary Gorbachev would meet in Geneva on November 19 and 20, 1985.

Early in November Shultz went to Moscow to meet Gorbachev and the new Soviet foreign minister, Eduard Shevardnadze. As he was leaving Washington, Shultz recorded his thoughts as having been these:

> Word from the intelligence community and other Soviet specialists around the government was that the Soviet Union would never, indeed could never, change, no matter how bad their internal economic and social problems were. I didn't see it that way. The generational shift in the Soviet leadership, I thought, was significant. The old guard Communists had either ignored internal problems, as did Gromyko, or covered them up, as did Brezhnev. Gorbachev and Shevardnadze came from a different mold.[7]

Shultz's judgment was perhaps a bit overstated, but it clearly shows the degree to which respect for the CIA's views had deteriorated following the departure of Richard Helms, the dissolution of the Board of National Estimates, the creation of a new system for the preparation of NIEs, and the new leadership of the Agency's Intelligence Directorate. The quality of the product began

5. Dobrynin, *In Confidence*, 478–79.
6. Ibid., 555.
7. Shultz, *Turmoil and Triumph*, 586.

to decline with the Schlesinger and Colby directorships beginning in 1973, and by 1985 most of the remaining intellectual authority had disappeared.

Before that decline had set in, however, the Office of National Estimates had repeatedly cited changes that were occurring in the USSR. In the World Situation estimate of 1958, for example, we said that the changes then taking place could in the longer run "alter profoundly the context and structure of Soviet political life, possibly through dissipation of the Communist Party's unchecked monopoly of power, more likely through a change in the political climate within the ruling party."

Ten years after that, in the World Trends and Contingencies estimate of 1968, we said that there would be changes in the leadership of the country and in the influence of various sectors of the society. We thought that "such changes seem likely to produce gradual shifts in policy, rather than abrupt swings. But sudden and significant changes certainly cannot be ruled out. They could be provoked, for example, by the emergence of a single leader with the will to wrench Soviet society into new conformations."

Another forward-looking statement about change in the USSR was made by Richard Helms in the spring of 1971 to the National Strategy Seminar at the Army War College:

> There are already prominent people in the USSR who believe that too much power resides in the Communist Party bureaucracy and who advocate, in the interest of socialism, a greater range of personal freedom. One such voice is that of Andrei Sakharov, one of the USSR's leading nuclear physicists. Another is Alexander Solzhenitsyn. Yet another voice is that of the *Chronicle of Human Events*, a clandestine journal published every two months, circulated in typescript, and recounting events in the struggle for political rights in the USSR. This has been going on for three years. The network has not been rolled up by the Soviet political police, and we do not know why it has not been.
>
> Today, of course, these dissenters are voices crying in the wilderness, but this may not always be so. We must allow for the unexpected. We must recognize that the neo-Stalinists as well as the reformers are trying to assert themselves. While these forces contend, we must be patient. Our problems with the USSR cannot be settled in a hurry in any case.

Those views were, of course, anathema to the hard-liners who had come to dominate the Agency and the community in 1981. Indeed, Casey became the leader of the pack. Gates, in his memoirs (1996), made an effort to explain his role and that of the Agency's professional analysts during the years when Shultz was contending, as Gates put it, "against the field." After Casey's arrival at the Agency, Gates moved from his job as National Intelligence Officer for the USSR to the director's office as chief of his executive staff. Gates has reported that he and Casey had "hit it off at the beginning." They had, averred Gates, "similar views about the Soviet Union."[8] Gates described Casey's role in the councils of state this way:

> Without parallel in the history of postwar American intelligence, Bill Casey as DCI had his own foreign policy agenda, and as a Cabinet member, pursued that agenda vigorously and often in opposition to the Secretary of State. Indeed, Casey was boastfully blunt about his use of intelligence. He told intelligence community leaders at an out-of-town conference on December 11, 1983, "Our estimating program has become a powerful instrument in forcing the pace in the policy area." In meetings, he would sometimes offer his own views of a situation overseas without being explicit that they were his personal views and not necessarily shared by CIA's experts or others in the intelligence community.[9]

CIA Muffs the Call on Gorbachev

Obviously, one of the most important questions facing Soviet analysts at the CIA during the early 1980s was how to think and write about Mikhail Gorbachev. A protégé of Andropov, he had moved to Moscow in 1978 when he became secretary of the Communist Party Central Committee. Two years later, in 1980, he became a member of the Party Presidium (Politburo). Then in 1985, upon the death of Party chairman Konstantin Chernenko, Gorbachev became General Secretary of the Communist Party of the Soviet Union and chairman of the Presidium. He clearly had a different style from that of the other Soviet leaders, and the hard-liners at the CIA did not quite know what to make of him.

At the CIA, Casey continued to move Gates upward and appointed him Deputy Director for Intelligence in January 1982. In that position, Gates commanded the entire Intelligence Directorate and, in effect, controlled the

8. Gates, *From the Shadows*, 222.
9. Ibid., 286.

flow of intelligence reporting and analysis to Casey, the NSC staff, and the President. When John McMahon, a CIA professional, resigned as Deputy Director of Central Intelligence in 1986, Casey arranged for Gates to succeed him. When Casey died in January 1987, Gates became acting director, and—following Casey's expressed wish just before his death—President Reagan nominated Gates to be DCI.

Gates obviously did not like Gorbachev. Writing in a cynical tone, he said in his memoirs that "CIA had been enthusiastic about Gorbachev since he emerged as Andropov's protégé early in 1983," and Gates went on to complain that "CIA's enthusiasm about Gorbachev was, needless to say, a curious phenomenon."[10] Finally, in February 1985, about a month before Gorbachev succeeded to the chairmanship, Gates began to take a serious interest in Gorbachev and wrote to one of the Soviet experts, "I don't much care for the way we are writing about Gorbachev. We are losing the thread of what toughness and skill brought him to where he is. This is not some Soviet Gary Hart or even Lee Iococca. We have to give the policymakers a clearer view of the kind of person they may be facing."[11]

The Agency's first "comprehensive look" at Gorbachev was produced in June 1985, just before the announcement was issued about the upcoming Reagan-Gorbachev summit in November. The Agency memorandum said that Gorbachev's first priority was domestic economic reform and that in foreign policy his "impact" had been largely "stylistic." Gates further reported that "a variety of sources" had told the CIA that "Gorbachev was not disposed to [make] concessions on arms control, and intended to expand previous efforts to drive wedges between the United States and its allies." Moreover, "Gorbachev's early actions had suggested support for key Third World allies."[12]

Those judgments were not tough enough on Gorbachev to satisfy Casey, who put a cover note on the memorandum, which Gates described as follows:

> He wrote that Gorbachev and those around him "are not reformers or liberalizers either in Soviet domestic or foreign policy." He told Reagan that the Soviets had to be convinced that the "original Reagan agenda is here to stay: revived U.S. military power, revived alliance leadership, revived engagement in regional security matters, and a revived ideological challenge to the inhuman features of the Soviet

---

10. Ibid., 327.
11. Ibid., 329.
12. Ibid., 332.

system." Casey concluded with a policy prescription that went far beyond the intelligence analysis he was forwarding and beyond what was appropriate for a DCI. He said: "Achieving this Soviet conviction against the doubts that are accumulating in Moscow will require political victories for your policy agenda in the Congress, the U.S. public, and the Alliance."[13]

And so it went on like that during the summer and fall of 1985, with each faction in the struggle for Reagan's ear pushing its own view of the Soviet leader and of the political and economic milieu in which he was operating.

In mid-November, shortly before the summit, Casey convinced Reagan to meet with CIA analysts to talk about Gorbachev and his problems and plans. It was Gates's show, but several of his colleagues joined him in the hour-long session. Writing about it later, Gates said that the briefing had "captured both the strengths and weaknesses of CIA's analysis" of the Soviet leader. Gates went on to admit that in the years which followed, "We more often than not failed to anticipate how far he would go."[14]

Gorbachev and Reagan at the Summit

The Geneva conference did see Gorbachev go a lot farther than Gates and his associates had anticipated. An "agreed statement," issued by the two leaders just before their departures for home, endorsed the idea of a 50 percent reduction in nuclear weapons and called for an interim agreement on intermediate-range nuclear weapons; it also called for talks on conventional arms reduction and on confidence-building measures. Most important of all, both sides "agreed that a nuclear war cannot be won and must never be fought."[15]

Both Reagan and Shultz were elated over the results. Shultz wrote: "The fresh start that the President wanted had become a reality in Geneva, not least because the two leaders had come to like and respect each other."[16] Upon his return to Washington, Reagan went straight to a joint session of Congress, where he concluded a report with these words about his relations with Gorbachev: "We understand each other better, and that's a key to peace. . . . We are ready and eager for step-by-step progress."[17] Even Gates

13. Ibid.
14. Ibid., 344.
15. Shultz, *Turmoil and Triumph*, 605.
16. Ibid., 606.
17. Ibid., 607.

acknowledged that the dialogue in Geneva had led to "a change in attitude and approach that would eventually change the world." He wrote: "Nearly everyone knew that, with the new Soviet leader, something fundamental had changed between the two powers. Even those of us in CIA."[18]

The next conference was at Reykjavik in October 1986, some eleven months later. That conference, like the one in Geneva, is extensively reported in the memoirs of its participants. It is clear from them that the two leaders were close to agreement on the elimination of offensive nuclear weapons, but that they were hung up on Reagan's unwillingness to give up the Strategic Defense Initiative. The conference broke down with visible disappointment among participants on both sides. Yet, Reagan said to Gorbachev as he left, "I still feel we can find a deal."[19]

Shultz believed that despite the appearance of collapse, the achievements of the conference had been very substantial, certainly "greater than any U.S.-Soviet meeting before." He summed up his views this way:

> What happened at Reykjavik seemed almost too much for people to absorb, precisely because it was outside the bounds of the conventional wisdom. Ronald Reagan was attacking that accepted wisdom across the board. Reagan's presidency was turning out to be the most radical since FDR's. That simply was not commonly perceived or appreciated. Reagan had stood up to totalitarianism, and its weaknesses were now exposed; he had stood up for freedom fighters, and their cause was gaining strength; and he was turning back the tide of the arms race. We were on the verge of eliminating intermediate-range nuclear weapons in Europe—perhaps everywhere—and we were contemplating the notion of a world without nuclear weapons.[20]

Shultz and Gorbachev Move Ahead

Defense Secretary Weinberger, Admiral Poindexter of the NSC staff, and the military establishment generally did their best to undermine the Reagan-Shultz policy; they simply did not want nuclear weapons eliminated. They had based their military doctrines and military planning on the concept of either deterring, or fighting, a war with nuclear weapons. Nevertheless, Shultz

18. Gates, *From the Shadows*, 345.
19. Shultz, *Turmoil and Triumph*, 793.
20. Ibid., 777.

moved doggedly on, despite the active opposition of the Defense Department and the misperceptions of the general public. He was assisted in his efforts by Paul Nitze, who by this time had parted company with Weinberger and the Pentagon warriors. Shultz's task was a difficult one, since the President himself had become weakened by the Iran-Contra scandal and was keeping quiet while nursing his wounds.

At the same time, the CIA's reputation was approaching a new low because of its suspected role in the Iran-Contra affair and in Central American policy generally. As the year 1987 began, with Gates as Acting Director of Central Intelligence, Shultz launched an offensive against the role which the Agency had been playing in the policymaking process, not only with respect to Gorbachev and the USSR, but also regarding Central America, Southern Africa, Iran, and Afghanistan. In a sharp exchange with Gates, Shultz accused the Agency of a "lack of objectivity" and of trying to "manipulate" him. He accused the NIOs of trying to make policy and going "beyond a legitimate intelligence role."[21] By February, Gates's nomination had run into serious trouble in the Senate, and Gates asked that it be withdrawn and that he remain in the position of deputy director. FBI Director William Webster then was named DCI, and things settled down, at least temporarily.

Gorbachev was not prepared to allow the peace process to halt, whatever happened in Washington. He set about to strengthen his political position in the Soviet Union and to launch further reforms. He also undertook to reopen the arms negotiations which had been so suddenly halted at Reykjavik; he announced in February 1987 that he would like to resume talks on the intermediate-range nuclear-missile issue. Shultz responded promptly, and formal negotiations took place during the summer. In October 1987, Gorbachev proposed a treaty-signing summit in December. He came to Washington for the big event, and he became the hero of the hour as many thousands of Washingtonians lined the streets to catch a glimpse of him.

Gorbachev became a hero in the USSR as well. He undertook new reforms that fundamentally changed the Soviet political system, and he thereby started a chain reaction that changed the world. The chain of events he set off was symbolically dramatized on November 9, 1989, when the world watched as Berliners knocked down the Wall that had divided them since 1961. The Cold War had ended, but a Russian revolution still lay ahead.

21. Ibid., 864–67, passim.

The Last Russian Revolution

When George Kennan explained his containment doctrine in his memoirs, he suggested that while doing what we could to support and inspire resistance to the expansion of Soviet political influence, we should "wait for the internal weakness of Soviet power, combined with frustration in the external field, to moderate Soviet ambitions and behavior." His advice to U.S. policymakers was to stand up to the Soviet leaders "manfully but not aggressively, and give the hand of time a chance to work."

One of the principal messages of this narrative has been the view expressed in national intelligence estimates that the political complexion of the USSR was indeed changing. We noted in the 1958 world estimate, for example, that the most likely movement toward political change would occur through a modification of the "political climate within the ruling Party." And in 1968 we suggested that "sudden and significant" change could be provoked by "the emergence of a single leader with the will to wrench Soviet society into new conformations." As noted earlier also, it was Yuri Andropov, the KGB chief, who brought Mikhail Gorbachev to the fore in the Party because he—like Andropov—wanted to bring new life and reform to the Party and the country. Reformers in the Communist Party, of whom Helms spoke in 1971, were actually gaining ascendancy during the 1980s, and when Chernenko died in March 1985, Gorbachev was their choice to succeed him. When he came home late in the evening after his selection, he told Raisa what he had also told his confidants, "We can't go on like this."

With Gorbachev's ascension to the Party leadership, reformists seem to have come out of the woodwork. Many were advocates of the scientific-technological revolution (STR) who had been trying to raise productivity and living standards through the application of advanced science, and through decentralization of decision-making authority. The STR movement was noted by Professor Black of Princeton during the 1970s, and some of its proposed reforms had been carried out by Eduard Shevardnadze in the Soviet Republic of Georgia, when he was Party chief there (before he joined Gorbachev in Moscow as Soviet foreign minister).

I took note of the putative reformists in the Soviet Union when I wrote a piece for *Newsday*, which was published in September 1978 (the same year Gorbachev moved to Moscow) under the title "Don't Shut the Door on the Soviet Liberals." I wrote then:

> There are in Soviet society millions of bureaucrats, technocrats, and professionals who feel the dead hand of Party control and who would like to have Soviet society move in the direction of liberalization, a

liberalization that would permit greater personal initiative, more free-dom of artistic expression, less centralization, a freer flow of infor-mation to and from the Soviet Union—and the more interesting and pleasant and efficient lifestyle that such a movement would produce. It is these quiet dissidents—a truly silent majority—who will eventu-ally direct the evolution of Soviet society.

It is a source of amazement to me that the Agency's Soviet analysts dur-ing the 1980s failed to see what the Agency's Soviet analysts had discerned as early as 1958. Indeed, by 1968, the Agency's Soviet analysts had begun looking for reformist leadership to emerge, and by 1971 had taken notice of the reformists as genuine contenders for power.

Actually, Gorbachev's reformist career had its ups and downs even after he became Party leader. Those of whom I had spoken as "quiet reformers" and "a silent majority" became quite articulate and even noisy. They pressed hard for fast, comprehensive reforms. Gorbachev talked a lot about "glas-nost" and "perestroika" and did institute many reforms, but he held back on rapid and revolutionary change in an apparent fear of the political and eco-nomic consequences of recklessness.

He was correct to be cautious. What glasnost and perestroika soon pro-duced were strikes, ethnic violence, and further declines in economic per-formance. A public opinion poll taken in 1989 showed that about half of those polled thought that daily life had deteriorated under Gorbachev. Moreover, during 1989 his popularity actually plunged from 94 percent to 44 percent. Even a substantial majority of Communist Party members parted company with Gorbachev's desire to preserve socialism and thought that movement toward a market economy would be a good idea.

Nevertheless, he scored a big success at a Party Congress in 1990 and strengthened his position by transferring political power from the Party to the government and getting himself elected president of the government. He then received wide powers to rule by decree. But he soon found himself caught between those who wanted revolutionary change and those in the old guard who had witnessed the collapse of the Communist-dominated regimes in Eastern Europe and wanted to restore order in the Soviet Union. As he maneuvered between these two factions, he satisfied no one. Some of his reformist associates, Yeltsin and Shevardnadze for example, deserted him. Finally, in August 1991, the old guard itself staged a revolt. But the coup attempt was badly organized and soon collapsed. Boris Yeltsin became the man of the hour as the world watched him stand atop a tank and defy the military forces sent to arrest him.

What happened in the USSR was that Gorbachev the Reformer set in motion forces which destroyed the Soviet Union and the Soviet empire in Eastern Europe. As Hedrick Smith had put it in his book, *The New Russians*, published a year before the actual denouement occurred, Gorbachev "uncorked the process and set the yeast of change to work." The reform which he began took on "a life and dynamism of its own."[22]

There is a another view, however, expressed by many Americans associated with the military-industrial complex, that it was the tough policies of the United States and the massive Reagan-era defense spending which caused the collapse of Soviet Communism. All the money we had spent on U.S. arms had been worthwhile. Soviet Communism had been destroyed without a single missile having been fired. Hedrick Smith stated his reaction to that belief this way:

> But the evidence is overwhelming that Gorbachev's reforms blossomed forth from forces germinating within Russia itself. The impulse for change was homegrown. It took a generation for the forces favoring reform to gather and for a broad base of support to develop. Because of the secretive way in which Soviet society moved in the past, this process was almost entirely hidden from view. . . . In fact, by the time Gorbachev became the top man in the Kremlin, reform had hidden constituencies at every level of Soviet society. Still these forces were dormant, inchoate, until Gorbachev set them free, galvanized them and gave them direction and form. They were the tinder, and he set the match.[23]

Gorbachev's reforms by 1991 became a popular revolution that swept away the USSR itself. One after another, the constituent republics in both Europe and Asia proclaimed their independence. The symbols of Soviet Communism — the Hammer and Sickle and the statues of its heroes — disappeared into the trash cans of history. The president of the USSR, Mikhail Gorbachev, became unemployed, and the government of Russia took over the Kremlin. Russia and the other former Soviet republics entered upon a new way of life, the Western World emerged from a long nightmare, and everyone hoped for better times ahead.

The United States of America did not "win" the Cold War. America's Cold War simply died for want of an enemy.

22. Smith, *The New Russians*, xxx.
23. Ibid., 6.

References

**CIA Intelligence Estimates and Intelligence Memoranda Cited in Text
(In order of appearance)**

Chapter 2
> ORE-1 "Soviet Foreign and Military Policy" July 1946
> Memorandum: "Vandenberg to the President" August 1946
> ORE 1/1 "Revised Soviet Tactics in International Affairs" January
> 1947
> CIA 1 "Review of the World Situation as It Related to the Security of
> the United States" September 1947
> ORE 41-49 "Effects of a U.S. Foreign Military Aid Program"
> February 1949
> ORE 29-49 "Prospects for Soviet Control Communist China" April
> 1949
> ORE 32-50 "The Effect of Soviet Possession of Atomic Bombs on the
> Security of the United States" June 1950

Chapter 3
> ORE 3-49 "Consequences of a US Troop Withdrawal from Korea in
> Spring 1949" February 1949
> Memorandum: "Smith to the President" October 1950

Chapter 4
> NIE 25 "Probable Soviet Courses of Action to Mid-1952" August 1951
> NIE 48 "Likelihood of the Deliberate Initiation of Full-Scale War by
> the USSR Against the US and Its Western Allies Prior to the End
> of 1952" January 1952

NIE 11-5-54 "Soviet Capabilities and Main Lines of Policy Through Mid-1959" June 1954
NIE 100-58 "Estimate of the World Situation" February 1958

Chapter 5
NIE 1-61 "Estimate of the Word Situation" January 1961

Chapter 7
NIE 85-2-62 "The Situation and Prospects in Cuba" August 1962
SNIE 85-3-62 "The Military Buildup in Cuba" September 1962
NIE 53-62 "Prospects in Vietnam" April 1963

Chapter 8
Memorandum: "Trends in the World Situation" June 1964

Chapter 9
NIE 11-4-65 "Main Trends in Soviet Military Policy" April 1965
NIE (number classified) "The Arab-Israeli Dispute: Current Phase" April 1967
NIE 1-68 "World Trends and Contingencies Affecting US Interests" June 1968

Chapter 10
Memorandum: "The World Situation in 1970" January 1970
NIE 11-4-72 "Issues and Options in Soviet Military Policy" March 1972
NIE 11-14-71 "Warsaw Pact Forces for Operations in Eurasia" February 1972 (not released)

Chapter 13
NIE 11-8-69 "Soviet Strategic Attack Forces" August 1969
SNIE 11-4-73 "Soviet Strategic Arms Programs and Detente: What Are They Up To?" September 1973
NIE 11-3/8-76 "Soviet Forces for Intercontinental Conflict Through the Mid-1980's" December 1976
NIE 11-4-78 "Soviet Goals and Expectations in the Global Power Arena" May 1978
NIE 11-3/8-79 "Soviet Capabilities for Strategic Nuclear Conflict Through the Late 1980's" March 1980

NIE 11-3/8 80 "Soviet Capabilities for Strategic Nuclear Conflict Through 1990" December 1980

Chapter 14
NIE 11-3/8-83 "Soviet Capabilities for Strategic Nuclear Conflict 1983–1993" March 1984.

Index